Journey to the Frontier

Two Roads to the Spanish Civil War

Journey to the Frontier

Two Roads to the Spanish Civil War

Peter Stansky &
William Abrahams

Stanford University Press
Stanford, California

Stanford University Press
Stanford, California

First published in 1966 by Little Brown
Reissued in 1983 by the University of Chicago Press
Reprinted by Stanford University Press, 1994
Printed in the United States of America
ISBN 0-8047-2341-9
LC 94-65010

To Polly, Thomas and Willem

Acknowledgements

In the course of writing this book, we have been the recipients of extraordinary kindnesses and acts of generosity from the families, friends, and acquaintances of Julian Bell and John Cornford.

We would single out first Quentin Bell and Christopher Cornford, each of whom has patiently answered innumerable questions, has listened with equal patience to a host of theories and speculations, and has made available to us without restrictions his brother's letters and papers. Although *Journey to the Frontier* is in no sense authorized biography—and the authors take full responsibility for errors of fact and questions of interpretation—it could hardly have been written without their unfailing co-operation.

We are greatly indebted, too, to Margot Heinemann, John Lehmann, Sir Edward Playfair and Lettice Ramsey, who have given unstintingly of their time, as well as letters and photographs in their possession.

Many others have helped us in various ways. A mere listing cannot do them justice, but we would like to record our profound gratitude to the following:

Harold Acton
Lord Annan
Mrs Quentin Bell
Sir Isaiah Berlin
A. C. Cochrane
Mrs Christopher Cornford
D. Crichton-Miller
Richard Eberhart
T. C. Elliott
E. M. Forster

Mr & Mrs David Garnett
Mrs Grace Huggins
James Joll
G. F. Jones
Victor Kiernan
James Klugman
Lord Llewelyn Davies
Juan Marichal
Mr & Mrs Christopher Morris
Charles Mauron
Andrew Mylett
Bishop Newbigin
John Ounsted
Ralph Payne
Sir Richard Rees
Samuel Russell
G. W. H. Rylands
Mr & Mrs I. A. Richards
Stuart Samuels
Mrs Edward N. Slade
Reginald Snell
John Sommerfield
Stephen Spender
Michael Straight
J. Duncan Wood
Leonard Woolf

For their generosity in allowing us to quote unpublished works in which they retain full copyright, we are deeply grateful to W. H. Auden for his letter to John Cornford; to Mrs T. S. Eliot for an excerpt from a letter from T. S. Eliot to Sidney Schiff; and to Leonard Woolf for excerpts from reminiscences of Julian Bell by Virginia Woolf.

We should also like to thank the following authors and publishers for permission to quote from the works cited:

Edward Arnold Ltd for E. M. Forster, *Goldsworthy Lowes Dickinson;* Cambridge University Press for G. E. Moore, *Principia Ethica;* Jonathan Cape Ltd for *John Cornford: A Memoir* (ed. Pat Sloan); Chatto and Windus Ltd and the Hogarth Press for Julian Bell, *Winter Movement* and *Work for the Winter, Julian Bell: Essays, Poems and Letters* (ed. Quentin Bell), David Garnett, *The Flowers of the Forest, New Signatures* (ed. Michael Roberts), Virginia Woolf and Lytton Strachey, *Letters,* Virginia Woolf, *Orlando* and *A Writer's Diary;* the Cresset Press for lines from the poems 'To a Fat Lady Seen from a Train', 'Ode', 'Youth', 'Tapestry Song' and 'The Madman and the Child' from Frances Cornford, *Collected Poems;* Faber and Faber Ltd for Franz Borkenau, *The Spanish Cockpit,* Gwen Raverat, *Period Piece,* and Tom Wintringham, *English Captain;* Hamish Hamilton Ltd and A. D. Peters & Co. for Stephen Spender, *World Within World;* Harper & Row for Hugh Thomas, *The Spanish Civil War,* copyright 1961 by Hugh Thomas; Rupert Hart-Davis for J. M. Keynes, *Two Memoirs;* Alfred A. Knopf, Inc. for E. M. Forster, *Howards End;* Lawrence & Wishart Ltd for John Sommerfield, *Volunteer in Spain;* Macmillan &

Co. Ltd and St Martin's Press, Inc. for Roy Harrod, *Life of John Maynard Keynes;* Martin Secker & Warburg for Richard Rees, *A Theory of My Time,* copyright Sir Richard Rees, 1963; Sidgwick & Jackson Ltd for *The Collected Poems of Rupert Brooke;* A. Watkins, Inc. for John Lehmann, *The Whispering Gallery,* copyright 1954-1955, John Lehmann.

Copyright in the unpublished works of Julian Bell is retained by Quentin Bell. Copyright in the unpublished works of John Cornford is retained by Christopher Cornford. The photographs, 'Tea at Charleston' and 'The Islanders', are by Lettice Ramsey and copyright by her. The photograph of the bust of Vanessa Bell by Marcel Gimond is used by courtesy of the National Portrait Gallery.

Contents

Illustrations (between pages 222–3)

Journey to the Frontier

Prologue

For our title, *Journey to the Frontier*, we have fused the titles of two characteristic works of the 1930s, *On the Frontier*, a play by W. H. Auden and Christopher Isherwood, and *Journey to the Border*, a novel by Edward Upward. Our point of view is close to that expressed by Donald Davie in 1955 in his poem 'Remembering the Thirties':

> A neutral tone is nowadays preferred.
> And yet it may be better, if we must,
> To find the stance impressive and absurd
> Than not to see the hero for the dust.

Heroism, in all its impressiveness and absurdity, does not lend itself to generalizations. Although our book was begun as a general consideration of the art and behaviour of English intellectuals in that far-off decade, it became, by a process of particularization, a study of two of its representative and most remarkable young men: Julian Bell and John Cornford.

Julian Bell, the son of the art critic and historian Clive Bell and the painter Vanessa Bell, nephew of Virginia Woolf, grandson of Sir Leslie Stephen, was born in Bloomsbury, on February 4, 1908. He was killed on July 18, 1937, at Villanueva de la Canada, in the battle of Brunete, driving an ambulance with the Loyalist Forces in the Spanish Civil War.

John Cornford, the son of the classicist F. M. Cornford and the poet Frances Cornford, great-grandson of Charles Darwin, was born in Cambridge, on December 27, 1915. He was killed on the day of his twenty-first birthday, December 27, 1936, or the next day, at Lopera, on the Cordoba Front, fighting with the Loyalist Forces in the Spanish Civil War.

It is generally agreed that the Spanish Civil War was a crucial event, indeed *the* crucial event, in the history of the young men of the Left in England in the 1930s. At its beginning, in 1936, they were raised to a pitch of highest enthusiasm. At its end, with the fall of the Republic in 1939, their disillusionment was complete: they resigned themselves to the coming of the Second World War, which the defeat of Fascism in Spain, they believed, would have made unnecessary.

One of our first considerations was to ask why it was, and how it was, that young men like John Cornford and Julian Bell, both of them poets and sons of the intellectual aristocracy of England, went out to Spain to fight for the Republic. But we had no sooner begun our researches than it became evident that in our phrasing of the question we had been misled by legend, which has tended ever since 1939 to overpopulate the Spanish conflict with poets, especially young English poets, "exploding like bombs". In fact, some eighty per cent of the English volunteers for the International Brigades came from the working class, and they were simply and precisely that: workers, many of them out of jobs, not worker poets. Yet John Cornford and Julian Bell, and a handful of others—Ralph Fox, Christopher Caudwell, George Orwell—were more or less what the legend claimed. Accordingly we rephrased our question: Why, and How, had John Cornford and Julian Bell gone out to Spain? We were launched upon biographical as well as historical investigation.

Our answers do not begin in July 1936. They go back into the early 1930s, and the 1920s, and the years of the First World War, and the plush Edwardian era, and even the final decades of the nineteenth century: and they make up the study that follows.

Part One

Julian Bell

1 A Bloomsbury Childhood

Bloomsbury has its international fame. Studious visitors from abroad know it as the area of the British Museum and the University of London. Readers of fiction, from *Vanity Fair* to *Mrs Dalloway*, feel an immediate familiarity with its Georgian streets and squares, each with a fenced-in handkerchief of green park at its centre, and lined with those well-proportioned, tall-windowed, large but not ostentatious houses that served as homes for professional and merchant families throughout the nineteenth century. For the past three decades Bloomsbury has been increasingly vandalized, in part by the destructions of war, in part by the constructions of the University of London. As early as 1940, Max Beerbohm was complaining that there seemed to be no limits to the University's "desire for expansion of that bleak, blank, hideous, and already vast whited sepulchre, which bears its name". But in 1904 the changes of Bloomsbury that war and the University were to effect had not yet occurred: past and present were still harmoniously conjoined.

Early in that year, nine years after the death of his second wife, Julia Duckworth, Sir Leslie Stephen had died of cancer. He was seventy-two years old. In his time he had been the first editor of the *Dictionary of National Biography*, editor of the *Cornhill Magazine*, essayist, literary critic and historian, biographer, religious doubter, and a celebrated mountaineer and Alpinist—he was the first man to climb the Schreckhorn. Soon after his death, the four children of his second marriage, Vanessa, Thoby, Virginia and Adrian Stephen, sufficiently grown up and with sufficient money settled upon them to do as they pleased, moved from the family house in Hyde Park Gate, Kensington, across London to Bloomsbury, where they took a house together in Gordon Square: No. 46. It was an agreeable arrangement, but it had never been thought of as other than provisional, and it was soon altered: first, in the summer of 1906, by the sudden death of Thoby Stephen—of typhoid, contracted while travelling in Greece; and second, a year later, by the marriage of Vanessa Stephen to Clive Bell. In the new arrangement of things Virginia and Adrian Stephen moved to a house of their own near by in Fitzroy Square, and the Bells kept No. 46. It was there, on February 4, 1908, that Julian Heward Bell, their first child, was born.

Bloomsbury, however, is not merely a place. It has a figurative as well as a physical existence. It stands for an idea, a philosophy, a style. It serves as a word of praise or deprecation. It provides an occasion for disagreement, for nostalgia, for condescension or approval. In all these aspects it would play an important part in Julian Bell's life, from his earliest childhood even to the circumstances leading up to his death—that he went out to Spain as an ambulance-driver rather than as a member of the International Brigade.

Julian was always conscious of Bloomsbury, of its values and standards, from which he knew he was not to be exempted, conscious also of its high expectations for him: that he was to be not less than its son. Of course, something of this sort would never be said; it would simply be taken for granted. But the pressure was there: the possibility of tension and opposition. There is no question that Julian loved and admired Bloomsbury, and respected it, and even believed in it; yet at the same time, although only rarely explicitly and openly, he was in rebellion against it.

But how is this Bloomsbury, which figures now in literary histories as The Bloomsbury Group, to be described? There is something rather daunting, or at least cautionary, about a statement by Clive Bell, one of its founding members, that Bloomsbury never really existed, that it was an invention of outsiders.[1] Of course, he does not expect (perhaps does not even want) to be believed; still, one does well to go cautiously. To speak of 'members' where Bloomsbury is concerned is more than a little misleading, for it was never a *formal* Group, never issued a manifesto or declaration of principles, was never a movement (*Bloomsburyisme*) in the style of the Continent, not even, as its detractors darkly imagined, a conspiracy for self-advancement or a mutual admiration society. On the whole one does best to conform to Bloomsbury's own usage and describe it simply as a group (lower-case) of friends, many of them living in the same district of London (Bloomsbury), who saw a great deal of one another, either there or in the country (usually Sussex), and who gained imposing reputations in the various arts they practised during the period 1910-1940: painting (Vanessa Bell, Duncan Grant); the novel (Virginia Woolf, E. M. Forster); criticism (Clive Bell, Roger Fry); political theory (Leonard Woolf); biography (Lytton Strachey); and economics (John Maynard Keynes).

Let us make a first approach to Bloomsbury—and to Julian—by way of an exchange of letters. It is April 1908. On Wednesday the 22nd, Virginia Stephen, who is on holiday in Cornwall, writes to Lytton Strachey in London. She has taken rooms at Trevose House, Draycot Terrace, St Ives, and she has been attempting to write a review for the *Cornhill Magazine* of a life of Delane, the editor of *The Times*. But the conditions are not favourable:

> My landlady, though a woman of 50, has nine children, and once had 11; and the youngest is able to cry all day long. When you consider that the family sitting room is next mine, and we are parted by folding doors only—what kind of sentence do you call this?—you will understand that I find it hard to write of Delane "the *Man*" . . .
>
> I spend most of my time, however, alone with my God, on the moors. I sat for an hour (perhaps it was 10 minutes) on a rock this afternoon, and considered how I should describe the colour of the Atlantic.

On Thursday the 23rd, Strachey replies:

> I went away last Friday, partly to get rid of my cold, to the

> Green Dragon, on Salisbury Plain, where James and Keynes and others were for Easter. Of course it finally destroyed me—the coldest winds you can imagine sweeping over the plain, and inferior food, and not enough comfortable chairs. But on the whole I was amused. The others were Bob Trevy . . . Moore, Hawtrey, and a young undergraduate called Rupert Brooke—isn't it a romantic name?—with pink cheeks and bright yellow hair—it sounds horrible, but it wasn't. Moore is a colossal being, and he also sings and plays in a wonderful way, so that the evenings passed pleasantly.

This letter leads us to the beginnings of Bloomsbury, but before we follow it there, let us attend to Virginia's reply, written five days later. It is Tuesday, April 28, and she is still at Trevose House in St Ives.

> Your letter was a great solace to me. I had begun to doubt my own identity—and imagined I was part of a seagull, and dreamt at night of deep pools of blue water, full of eels. However, Adrian came suddenly that very day . . . Then Nessa and Clive and the Baby [Julian, aged three months] and the Nurse all came, and we have been so domestic that I have not read, or wrote. My article upon Delane is left in the middle of a page thus—"But what of the Man?"— . . . A child is the very devil—calling out, as I believe, all the worst and least explicable passions of the parents—and the Aunts. When we talk of marriage, friendship or prose, we are suddenly held up by Nessa, who has heard a cry, and then we must all distinguish whether it is Julian's cry, or the cry of the 2 year old—the landlady's youngest—who has an abcess, and uses therefore a different scale . . .
>
> We are going to a place called the Gurnard's Head this afternoon—and now I look up and behold it pours! So we shall sit over the fire instead, and I shall say some very sharp things, and Clive and Nessa will treat me like a spoilt monkey, and the Baby will cry. However, I daresay Hampstead is under snow. How is your cold? I got a stiff neck on the rocks—but it went.[2]

A certain acerbity in this need not be taken seriously—in fact, Virginia would prove to be the most affectionate of aunts, devoted to her sister's three children, Julian, Quentin and Angelica, and they, as we shall see, were devoted to her. But that is the future, to be looked at as it happens. Now we must go back, a few years at least, to the past, to where Bloomsbury begins: to Cambridge.

In the autumn of 1899, Lytton Strachey, next to youngest son amongst the ten children of Lieutenant-General Sir Richard and Lady Strachey—a family long associated with the administration of India—went up to Trinity College. Very soon there formed about him a circle of young men almost as brilliant as himself. There was Leonard Woolf, from St Paul's School, the son of a London barrister. There was Clive Bell, from Marlborough, of a Wiltshire 'huntin-shootin' county family who had got their money a generation back as owners of Welsh coal-mines. There was Julian Thoby Prinsep Stephen.

Thoby Stephen died too early to fulfil the promise that his family and friends had recognized in him, but he would be remembered glowingly—especially by his sisters, who had worshipped him, and who looked for him, as it were, in the next generation, in Julian. He was truly a founder of Bloomsbury, for he introduced Clive Bell to his sister Vanessa, and Leonard Woolf to his sister Virginia, and the marriages that grew out of these introductions—the Bells were married in 1907; the Woolfs in 1912—would give the group a centre, a coherence, and a strength that came with family interconnection that it would not otherwise have had. (In all this there is a curious resemblance between Bloomsbury and the Clapham Sect, that evangelical group or movement of a hundred years earlier, among whose members had been the great-grandfather of Vanessa and Virginia Stephen, the great-great-grandfather of E. M. Forster, and the great-grandmother of Lytton Strachey.)

Strachey and his friends at Trinity—Bell, Woolf, Thoby Stephen, A. J. Robertson and Saxon Sydney Turner—caught up in the prevailing Cambridge passion for 'little groups', formed an informal one of their own, The Midnight Society, which met on Saturdays at midnight in the rooms of Clive Bell. It was dedicated to the reading aloud of plays of a rather formidable character—*The Cenci*, *Prometheus Unbound*, *Bartholomew Fair*—but the meetings were not as austere as this may suggest. The members fortified themselves with whisky or punch and meat pies, and when the last speech was spoken—usually at about 5 a.m.—they would sally forth, still exhilarated, to listen to the nightingales and sometimes to chant passages from Swinburne as they perambulated through the cloisters of Neville's Court in Trinity.

There was another 'little group', distinguished in lineage, and ostensibly secret, to which Strachey, Woolf and Thoby Stephen—but not Clive Bell—also belonged, and which also met on Saturday evenings, but a good deal earlier. (Indeed The Midnight Society chose the midnight hour not for any esoteric reason but simply to allow the three to attend both meetings.) Founded in about 1820 by a future Bishop of Gibraltar, this was The Conversazione Society, or *The* Society, or—to use the name by which it is best known—The Apostles. Throughout its history The Apostles had had as members many of the most brilliant Cambridge undergraduates, from Tennyson and Hallam on, and most of them, as it happened, were at Trinity College. In 1899 the form was much as it had been since the beginning of the society: weekly meetings, at which a paper was delivered by one of the members and discussed (dissected) by the others. Tradition provided that there should be a full and frank response to any question, objection, or speculation that might be raised, even at the risk of hurt feelings. On the whole, Apostolic papers were dedicated to abstract, or metaphysical, or political, or poetical, or ethical problems; and the Apostolic aim was to pursue the truth with absolute devotion and personal candour. (On occasion, however, the aim seems to have been simply to amuse, as when Lytton Strachey addressed himself to the question 'Ought the Father to Grow a Beard?' Since Victorian fathers were usually bearded, one presumes that the correct, Stracheyan answer would have been No! Strachey himself, in the later years of his life, grew a luxuriant beard, but never married.) The concerns of the society had always been more philosophical than literary; now, at the turn of the century, the inclination and professional interests of certain of its older members strengthened the claims of philosophy. At this time the number of undergraduate members was comparatively small: only about six. (Here a late-comer must be mentioned: John Maynard Keynes, who did not arrive in Cambridge as an undergraduate until the autumn of 1902, and who so impressed Strachey and Woolf when they went to call that he was brought into the Society in the winter of his first year.) But the membership as a whole had never been limited to the number of biblical Apostles, and there were still many active members who had already received their degrees. These included men not only still at Cambridge—usually as dons—but others who came up often from London—future literary figures in the very early stages of their careers, like Desmond MacCarthy and E. M. Forster—to attend meetings. In Cambridge the most eminent of these older members—who of course were still young men at the time—were Alfred North Whitehead, Bertrand Russell, G. E. Moore (the Moore mentioned in Strachey's letter to Virginia Woolf) and Goldsworthy Lowes Dickinson, so that it is hardly surprising that the bent of the society should have been philosophical.

The young Apostles of 1900 felt quite consciously the need for a new philosophy for the new century. Strachey had already persuaded his friends to question the Utilitarian pieties of the past, and to hold in high disdain what appeared to be the hypocrisies, deceits, catchwords, cant and uncertainties of their immediate ancestors, those Eminent Victorians. One recognizes a familiar pattern: the opposition of fathers and sons, the war of the generations. Sir Leslie Stephen had been an agnostic, and he had resigned his fellowship at Trinity Hall because of doubts. But he doubted the existence of God with all the passion and soul-searching that his Claphamite ancestors had devoted to affirming God's existence. With equal passion his descendants and their friends would claim the problem was not even worth considering. In 1906, after reading a memoir of Henry Sidgwick, an earlier Apostle who had suffered like Sir Leslie from doubts, Keynes commented: "He never did anything but wonder whether Christianity was true and prove that it wasn't and hope that it was . . . And then his conscience—incredible. There is no doubt about his moral goodness. And yet it is all so dreadfully depressing—no intimacy, no clear-cut boldness. Oh, I suppose he was intimate but he didn't seem to have anything to be intimate about except his religious doubts. And he really ought to have got over that a little sooner; because he knew that the thing wasn't true perfectly well from the beginning."[3]

The publication of G. E. Moore's *Principia Ethica* in 1903 struck the Midnighters and Apostles with the force of revelation. A half century later, looking back, Clive Bell testified to Moore as "the dominant influence in all our lives".[4] Lytton Strachey, we are told by E. M. Forster (in his biography of Lowes Dickinson), welcomed *Principia Ethica* with the words, "the age of reason has come!"[5] And Keynes summed up its effect upon himself and his friends as "the beginning of a renaissance, the opening of a new heaven on a new earth".[6] Clearly, the future Bloomsburyans (or Bloomsberries, as they were called by Molly MacCarthy) had found their Bible.

It should be said at the outset that Moore's was very much a private philosophy—in itself, and as interpreted by his disciples, who were not above picking and choosing amongst its elements those they found most congenial. As such, it provided a dramatic contrast, and contradiction, to the public philosophy of the nineteenth century, the Utilitarianism of Bentham, Mill, Spencer and other thinkers in the Victorian galaxy. The Utilitarian notions of 'good' as something fixed, already defined, and as publicly in the world as the memorial to Albert the Good in Hyde Park, were firmly rejected. 'Good' is an indefinable attribute, Moore explained; the sense of it is instinctive in oneself; one's discriminations, based upon it, lead to evaluations of one's own. One asks questions, one questions the questions: "What *exactly* do you mean?" That famous, often parodied Bloomsbury remark originates here, in Moore's own conversation—which his younger friends could find intimidating—and in the very first sentence of his Preface to *Principia Ethica*: "It appears to me that in Ethics, as in all other philosophical studies, the difficulties and disagreements, of which its history is full, are mainly due to a very simple cause: namely to the attempt to answer questions, without first discovering precisely *what* question it is which you desire to answer."

But Moore contributed more to Bloomsbury than a conversational gambit. The crucial aspect of his doctrine, as it helped bring about a Bloomsbury 'attitude', was his assertion that "By far the most valuable things, which we know or can imagine, are certain states of consciousness, which may be roughly described as the pleasures of human intercourse and the enjoyment of beautiful objects. No one, probably, who has asked himself the question, has ever doubted that personal affection and the appreciation of what is beautiful in Art or Nature, are good in themselves; nor, if we consider strictly what things are worth having *purely for their own sakes*, does it appear probable that any one will think that anything else has *nearly* so great a value as the things which are included under these two heads . . . [This] is the ultimate and fundamental truth of Moral Philosophy. That it is only for the sake of these things—in order that as much of them as possible may at some time exist—that anyone can be justified in performing any public or private duty; that they are the *raison d'être* of virtue; that it is they . . . that form the rational ultimate end of human action and the sole criterion of social progress: these appear to be truths which have been generally overlooked."[7]

Here then was the new Gospel, but, unlike the old, arrived at, so its believers thought, with complete rationality. In fact, there was considerably more in *Principia Ethica* than this exaltation of "certain states of consciousness", but Moore's disciples chose not to notice those aspects of it that dealt with the relation of ethics to conduct. "We accepted Moore's religion, so to speak, and discarded his morals," Keynes wrote in 1938. "Indeed, in our opinion, one of the great advantages of his religion, was that it made morals unnecessary—meaning by 'religion' one's attitude towards oneself and the ultimate, and by 'morals' one's attitude towards the outside world and the intermediate." What Keynes and his friends took from Moore's "religion, so to speak" was the belief that "one's prime objects in life were love, the creation and enjoyment of aesthetic experience and the pursuit of knowledge".[8]

Obviously, if one is to practise a religion that gives primacy to "certain states of consciousness", one must be capable of discriminations and subtlety and deep feeling. But there are two preconditions outside oneself that must also be fulfilled: first, a stable society; and second, a measure of financial security. A chaotic or threatened society involves the individual in its concerns; anxieties about money, the mere business of survival, pre-empt the major areas of consciousness. But at the time of which we are writing, both preconditions obtained. In 1903 the world was at peace: no 'shadow of a war', such as darkened the 1930s, haunted the imagination of the sensitive. Indeed, as Leonard Woolf has recalled, there were events like the vindication of Captain Dreyfus that seemed to justify one's taking an optimistic view of the future: the day of reason was almost at hand. As for financial security, that too, in varying degree, Moore's young disciples had. None was rich—Strachey and Woolf could count on very little money—but all had the assurance, the poise of identity, that was inherent in belonging to a certain class in a certain place at a certain moment in history. None was in the position of poor Leonard Bast in E. M. Forster's *Howards End.* A clerk, living on the very fringes of the middle class, Leonard has been educated (at the expense of the state) up to a level of cultural aspiration: he yearns, shall we say, for 'certain states of consciousness'. But for him they are unattainable; and Forster makes it clear that it is because Leonard lacks money. "Give people cash, for it is the warp of civilization, whatever the woof may be. The imagination ought to play upon money and realize it vividly, for it's the—the second most important thing in the world. It is so slurred over and hushed up, there is so little clear thinking—oh, political economy of course; but so few of us think clearly about our own private incomes, and admit that independent thoughts are in nine cases out of ten the result of independent means. Money: give Mr Bast money, and don't bother about his ideals. He'll pick up those for himself."[9]

The period in which Forster was writing, in which Bloomsbury was coming into being, was the Edwardian hey-day: a time when money was having a golden age. Rarely has it been regarded with such adulation. After all, it was England's main product—money making money—and most of the coupon-clippers, the *rentier* class, had little sense, and cared less, of what was actually happening in some vague place in the Empire in order to keep them in pounds. Money was to be collected and spent. It was the era of the last great splurge—the fantastic country house week-ends devoted to killing as many birds as possible, changing into as many clothes as possible, and eating as much food as possible. In all this, Edward VII, in his liking for bankers and financiers, set the tone of his age. England, as Beatrice Webb had noticed thirty years before, was much more egalitarian than the Continent, and would permit the plutocrat "to get ahead in society". But it had never happened at quite the pace that was set in the first fourteen years of the twentieth century.

Ironically, the money making money that made possible the endless extravagance of the *echt* Edwardians also made possible the life of Bloomsbury with its emphasis upon personal relations and aesthetic experience. The money of their Victorian forebears had been wisely invested. Certainly in the Cambridge period, the members of Bloomsbury did not concern themselves with the sources of their income. As Apostles they had made it a point, in the rather austere tradition of the society, to turn away from worldly values. (Here, perhaps, it should be noticed that Clive Bell, who was not an Apostle, was the one among the group who chose to have a foot, as Desmond MacCarthy observed, in two very different communities within the University. "He seemed to live, half with the rich sporting set, and half with the intellectuals." And MacCarthy recalled that at their first meeting Bell was "dressed with careless opulence" in a dark fur coat with a deep astrakhan collar.[10] Not, one ventures to think, the ideal of Apostolic costume.) Unconcerned with wealth and power, indifferent to fame and success, they tended to regard the world where such things mattered with contempt—although with some pity also for its being so unenlightened. As late as 1906 Keynes was writing to Strachey, not humorously, "How amazing to think that we and only we know the rudiments of a true theory of ethic."[11] This was an abiding characteristic of the Apostles—a certain élitist point of view towards the world—and it was reinforced by Moore's philosophy with its emphasis upon the importance of individual judgments and discriminations. At the same time, and this too was Apostolic, there was a willingness to enter the world, if one were summoned, and help it along its way. (It seems not unreasonable to suggest that Keynes's attitude towards economics, and one basis for his economic theory, derive from this cast of mind.)

In fact, when their period at Cambridge ended, Moore's disciples did not, as one might have expected, withdraw into contemplation and a further refining of sensibility. Instead, at their own pace and in their own fashion, they began careers—as writers, artists, editors, publishers, civil servants—they went into the world. There was remarkably little dispersion. Except for Leonard Woolf, who went out to Ceylon for five years as a junior colonial officer, carrying in his luggage a set of Voltaire in ninety volumes, they remained a group in London as they had been in Cambridge. Only the setting of the conversation changed: from Neville's Court to Gordon Square. From time to time they added to their number: most importantly, in the pre-war years, Roger Fry, David Garnett ('Bunny'), Desmond MacCarthy and the young painter Duncan Grant, who was a cousin of Lytton Strachey. And they proceeded with their work.

Moore's text speaks of "the enjoyment of beautiful objects". Keynes, in his paraphrase, makes a significant addition: "the creation and enjoyment of aesthetic experience". Indeed, the creation proved formidable in quality, and in quantity. It is worth remembering that Virginia Woolf, for example, despite long periods of illness when she could do no writing at all, had produced twenty-four books before her suicide, at the age of fifty-nine, in 1941. Vanessa Bell painted almost a thousand pictures. Even E. M. Forster, who is traditionally regarded as having written very little, has fourteen books to his credit. As a group they seem, in retrospect, to have been as industrious as Victorians.

"I stay myself—"

These are the opening words of Julian Bell's poem, 'Autobiography', which appeared in his second and, as it proved, his final volume, *Work for the Winter* (1936). The remark is characteristic of his strong sense of individuality: "I stay myself—" Yet at the same time he recognizes that he is also

> . . . the product made
> By several hundred English years,
> Of harried labourers underpaid,
> Of Venns who plied the parson's trade,
> Of regicides, of Clapham sects,
> Of high Victorian intellects,
> Leslie, FitzJames.

This, of course, is the Stephen inheritance. And it is equally characteristic of Julian that he should acknowledge it with a kind of sweeping inclusiveness: from the missionary austerities of the

Clapham Sect to the violence of the regicides. We are dealing with something very different here from 'the enlightenment of Bloomsbury'. His mother and his aunt might accept as just the praise accorded their father, Sir Leslie; they would be less likely to respond to praise for their uncle, Sir James Fitzjames Stephen, who, as a conservative Utilitarian, had a decidedly more authoritarian cast of mind. Bloomsbury, with Lytton Strachey in the forefront, had attempted to discredit at least the immediate past, while Julian, one might almost say, revels in it, revels in it all. "I stay myself, the product made . . ." On the one hand there are "high Victorian intellects"; on the other, "not among such honoured, marble names"

> That cavalry ruffian, Hodson of Hodson's Horse,
> Who helped take Delhi, murdered the Moguls . . .

He was "At least a soldiering brigand"—a category for which Julian would always entertain a certain fondness. "There were worse," he goes on to say,

> Who built a country house from iron and coal:
> Hard-bitten capitalists, if on the whole
> They kept the general average of their class.

This, of course, is the Bell inheritance, his father's side, very different from the Stephenses, representing a family which had made its money in coal, and at whose large, ugly, Victorian country house, at Seend in Wiltshire, the Clive Bells and their children spent some vacations and Christmases. To his parents, Clive appeared a wild radical and a dangerous advocate of a new aestheticism: thus they interpreted the fame he had won as the author of such books as *Art* and *Civilization*, as an exponent of the idea of "significant form", and as a sponsor of the notorious exhibitions of Post-Impressionist painting which introduced Cézanne, Matisse and Picasso to England in the years before the First World War. But if he seemed a black sheep to his own family, to the Stephen side he seemed almost a little too conventional—in his 'huntin, shootin, fishin' interests, some of which he conveyed to his son, and in his comparatively conservative political views. Virginia Woolf, in a memoir of Julian written for Vanessa immediately after his death, felt he owed a great deal to the Bell inheritance.

This differentiated him from her beloved Thoby, whose death, thirty years earlier, had had such a profound and lasting effect upon her. "In fact Julian was much rougher, more impulsive, more vigorous than Thoby. He had a strong element of the Bell in him. What do I mean? I think I mean that he was practical and caustic and shrewd . . . He had much higher spirits. He was much more adapted to life. He was much less regularly beautiful to look at. But then he had a warmth, an impetuosity that the Stephens don't have."

This is to give the Bell inheritance its due. But it must be said that Julian's family, in its loyalties and intimacies, almost seemed to exclude the non-Stephen part of it. Clive did not completely fit into the Stephen inheritance of "Clapham sects/Of high Victorian intellects", nor did Leonard Woolf. Clive and Leonard were certainly original progenitors of Bloomsbury, of undoubted brilliance and importance; nevertheless one feels the slightest sense of unease in their relationships with their wives, the Stephen sisters, who were, whatever its Cambridge intellectual masculine origins, the heart of Bloomsbury. If Clive was a little too much to the right in his political thinking, perhaps Leonard went a little too far in his interests in the practice of radical socialism. And if Clive's squire background did not exactly fit with the Stephen inheritance, neither did the London professional and mercantile background of the Woolfs. In her memoir of Julian, Mrs Woolf speaks of "L's family complex which made him eager, no, on the alert, to criticise [the Bell] children because he thought I admired them more than his family." But it seems not to have occurred to her that this preference of hers was almost certainly the case, and, more importantly, that there was a Stephen 'family complex', of mutual affection and admiration, that must have appeared formidable (as well as enviable) to an outsider.

The most important person in Julian's life, from its very beginning to its very end, was his mother, the gifted and beautiful Vanessa Bell. Theirs was a relationship without a break and without concealment: in it the full implications of Bloomsbury candour were taken to their limits, and the connection between mother and son never weakened. It was an extraordinary rapport which one cannot but admire, and impressive testimony to Bloomsbury's belief in personal relations. Yet in some ways the relationship was so perfect that it may have truncated others, provided a standard impossible to achieve elsewhere. The possibility will have to be considered in its place, many years later, in the history of Julian's grand and casual passions; here it can be disregarded.

From the first his mother took great pains with his upbringing, intending it to be as 'natural' and undogmatic as possible: he was not to be Victorianized, a miniature grown-up, seen but not heard, in a spotless pinafore. Yet for all their intellectual adventuresomeness, the Bells were still a well-to-do upper-middle-class family in the comfortable years before the First World War. There were maids, and a series of governesses—one of whom Julian got rid of by pushing into a ditch. And whatever they might think of religion 'upstairs', Julian found it impossible to escape completely the religion of his country 'downstairs'—although it would leave no permanent mark upon him. In a fragment of autobiography written shortly before going out to Spain, he remarks: "I remember as independent ideas—more or less—a Darwinian argument with Mabel and Flossie—our nurses—which must have been very early—pre-war Gordon Square." In other words, this memory dates from before Julian was six. "Though obdurate I was secretly frightened of Jehovah, and even asked to be taught prayers. (Later, learning the Lord's Prayer, I used it as a magic defence against ghosts, and still do: or as a soporific.)" But religion was hardly very significant in Julian's life. Far more important was the education he received from his mother. He writes of this same pre-war time, "The great liberating influence was the reading aloud by Nessa of elementary children's astronomies and geologies." And there was a similar intellectual excitement when she read aloud to him a shortened translation of the *Odyssey*. Before he was able to read himself, he made Flossie read to him a school textbook of history. History, like astronomy, was a passion. "There was also the famous occasion when Roger [Fry] demonstrated a home chemistry box, and brewed coal gas; Mabel was sent out and bought a clay pipe from a pub; it was tamped with plasticine, and, being cooked over the fire, eventually produced a jet of flame." In 1916, when he was eight years old, he had what he called his "first, definite, independent idea. It was a solution of the desire for immortality. I worked out a possible cycle by which a human body would return through grass and sheep, into another human body."[12] But it would be very misleading to give a picture of a male blue-stocking pondering his science, classics and history at a tender age. Rather, it would be more accurate to see him as an extremely adventurous, reckless child bounding from activity to activity, with his parents anxious to introduce him, through explanations and discussions, to the Bloomsbury dictum of rationality, which held that even irrational behaviour should be understood.

David Garnett, in a memoir of Julian, describes him as "a wilful child, swift and erratic in his movements; he looked at one from large eyes and planned devilment . . . Julian was shrill, sometimes noisy, always rather catlike and quick. My first row with him was when I found him standing, unconscious of evil-doing, on some vegetable marrow plants that he had trampled to pieces . . . He had in those days often to be exhorted to reason, often to listen to tedious explanations about the consequences of his violent experiments. He flung newly-hatched ducklings into the pond and after they had raced ashore flung them in again and again until one or two were drowned. He was not punished as a child, but reasoned with: one saw on his face the lovely sulky look of a half-tame creature."[13] And Mrs Woolf had a similar memory of about the same time—or when Julian was slightly older: "We were packing up the tea things. He took a bottle of water and smashed it. He stood there in his knickerbockers with long naked legs looking defiant and triumphant. He smashed the bottle completely. The water or milk spread over the path . . . He stood quite still smiling. I thought This is the victorious male; now he feels himself the conqueror. It was a determined bold gesture, as though he wanted to express his own force and smiled at the consternation of the maids."

One should not make too much either of the enthusiasm for astronomy and history, or of the mischief and high spirits, of a little boy, although it is of some interest that Julian himself should remember the former, and those of his parents' generation the latter. Still, it does not seem too fanciful to read into the division the first hints of a theme that was to figure importantly in Julian's life, and in the lives of many of his contemporaries: how to reconcile the conflicting demands of the life of the mind and the life of action.

The Bells made their home in Bloomsbury, but they were often in the country, and Julian, in his attachment to the land, grew up much more a child of the country than of the city—there would always be something equivocal about his feelings for London; certainly they did not go very deep. Whatever the attractiveness of Bloomsbury for the grown-ups, the children found life more exciting and memorable in the country: at Seend, the house of their Bell grandparents, and at a variety of rented houses—Asheham, near Lewes in Sussex, rented by the Woolfs from 1912 to 1918; Wissett in Suffolk, rented briefly in 1916 by Duncan Grant; and finally, Charleston, a short distance from Asheham, which the Bells began to rent in the autumn of 1916, and was thereafter their place in the country. For Julian, as for his brother Quentin, two years younger than he, and his sister Angelica, born in 1918, Charleston meant childhood.

In his poem 'Autobiography', he recalls "the passage of those country years". England was at war; and his, as he acknowledged, was "a war-time boyhood"; but apart from this reference, the details he chose to record (in the poem) were timeless, of

> . . . orchard trees run wild,
> West wind and rain, winters of holding mud,
> Wood fires in blue-bright frost and tingling blood,
> All brought to the sharp senses of a child.

These are the simplicities of a child's (and a poet's) world. For his parents and their friends the war brought a more complex experience: a true crisis of conscience. On the whole, Bloomsburyans, as we have earlier suggested, tended to live at a certain aloof distance from the world. (This attitude is not to be mistaken for unworldliness. If they had little desire for luxury, or even the creature comforts, they did not scorn the world in its more amiable, civilized aspect: civilization, as they defined it, taking in the pleasures of food and wine and conversation. And Clive Bell was a great believer in *savoir vivre* and *savoir faire*, with an English Francophile's conviction that living and doing were done better across the Channel.) Apart from Keynes and Leonard Woolf, they were indifferent to the day-to-day or even the month-to-month practice of politics: the demands of the private life left one no time for that sort of public interest; one lived *au dessus de la mêlée*. The war changed all that—at least for the duration. After 1914, an attitude of aloofness became increasingly difficult to maintain, even untenable.

Maynard Keynes, Bloomsbury's authority on the subject, predicted a short war brought to an end by economic causes. This must have been some consolation in the beginning, for Bloomsbury was opposed to war in general ("the worst of the epidemic diseases which afflict mankind and the great genetrix of many of the others"[14]) and to this war in particular. But Keynes's optimism was confounded by events. The war was prolonged from one year to the next, and it required increasing tough-mindedness to withstand popular pressure to conform to the war enthusiasm. Not unexpectedly, Bloomsbury, with its belief in the importance of the private life and private convictions, proved extremely good at this. But in 1916, for the first time in British history, conscription was introduced, and thereafter the men of Bloomsbury were compelled to make public their consciences: that is, to declare themselves Conscientious Objectors to military service.

As such they came to public attention. At Trinity College, Cambridge, for example, Bertrand Russell's lectureship was not renewed, and it is hard to avoid the impression that his unpopular pacifist opinions had something to do with the College's action. Lytton Strachey, called before the Hampstead Tribunal to prove his conscientious objections, made in passing his celebrated reply to the Military Representative ("What would you do, Mr Strachey, if you saw an Uhlan attempting to rape your sister?" "I should try to interpose my own body"), and he, like various other members of Bloomsbury, was ordered to do work of National Importance. He and Russell both sought refuge at the farm attached to Garsington Manor, the home of their friends Philip and Lady Ottoline Morrell, outside Oxford. Clive Bell was at Garsington also. A pacifist, who had argued in his pamphlet *Peace at Once* (1915) that "the war ought to be brought to an end as quickly as possible by a negotiated peace", he was working on the land, under the provisions of the Military Service Act. And Duncan Grant and David Garnett (who earlier had been with a Friends' Ambulance Unit in France) rented Wissett Lodge, outside a remote little village in Suffolk, where they meant to become fruit-farmers.

That summer (1916) Vanessa, with Julian, Quentin and the maid Blanche, came down from London to Wissett to keep house for Duncan and Bunny. The Lodge was "a little early Victorian house with numerous small, exceptionally dark, rooms",[15] shadowed by an enormous ilex, which Julian and Quentin called "the safety tree", for there, in its branches, they were safe from the grown-ups. Life went cheerfully at Wissett. Vanessa painted; the men worked hard in the orchard, kept bees, kept fowls—a large flock of white Leghorns: there were frequent visitors: Oliver and Lytton Strachey, Saxon Sydney Turner, Lady Ottoline Morrell. For Julian it was a memorable time: "orchard trees run wild, West wind and rain . . ." Long afterwards, with astonishing vividness, he recalled his first evening's fishing at Wissett, "when I must have caught a couple of dozen roach . . . Bunny was fishing also: Clive advised me. They started to bite hard in the evening: that pond had never been fished before. I think my second was a big one—perhaps an eighth of a pound; impressive enough to a child. We filled a bucket, slimy, fishy smelling; there is something extraordinarily sensual and thrilling about a fish's body in one's hand: the cold, the vigour and convulsive thumping, the odd smell, the gasping open mouth you jag the hook out of."

It was at Wissett too that he read Gardiner's *History of England from Henry VIII to the Corn Laws* ("God knows how much I understood"), and it was there that he first developed "a passion for war and war games".[16] The irony of this, a war-minded child in a conscientiously objecting household, needn't be insisted upon: Julian himself saw it as "a reaction". He knew, of course, that his family and their friends were C.O.s: it explained "the isolation, and later, at Charleston, the expectation of hostility". The war game, which grew increasingly complex and took a variety of forms over the years, originated with Quentin, with Julian as an enthusiastic and inventive collaborator. In one version it was played on a board, moving counters about; in another, it was played 'life-size'. Perhaps its very beginning can be traced back to an afternoon when Bunny Garnett mounted fire-crackers on shingles and sailed them across the pond. There was the normal desire of little boys to play soldiers, to re-enact historical battles ("the Armada . . . the Roman wall with oak-apple armies"), although, out of deference to the household, contemporary history was not drawn upon: the opposing sides were never English and German. What is remarkable about the war game is that the interest in it should have continued well beyond childhood, and that war and military strategy fascinated Julian until the day of his death.

The fruit-farming at Wissett proved unsatisfactory: it had been entered upon, at Keynes's suggestion, to ensure the two men exemption from military service. But the Appeals Tribunal, to which their cases were referred, "declared that though the Wissett Lodge holding might qualify as work of national importance, it was out of the question for us"—we are quoting from Garnett—"to be our own employers". The solution appeared simple enough: to continue doing work of National Importance, that is, to continue farming, but on someone else's farm. So Wissett was abandoned. It was thought "preferable", Garnett explains, "to go back to the neighbourhood of Asheham, where Leonard and Virginia were living, and where Vanessa had pre-war acquaintances among the Sussex farmers, rather than to seek work in Suffolk".[17]

Thus it was that the Bells came to Charleston.

Charleston was rented by the Bells in the autumn of 1916. Until 1918 they lived there without interruption, having given up Gordon Square; thereafter they divided their time between Charleston and London, and in the later 1920s, a house in France, at Cassis on the Mediterranean. But for Julian, Charleston came to represent childhood, holidays from school as he grew older, the long summers: it was the place in which he was most happy, the most loved of his homes.

Charleston, which is owned by Lord Gage of Firle Place, is at the end of a dirt road off the main Lewes-Eastbourne road, right beneath the looming green eminence of Firle Beacon, the highest point on the Sussex downs. At the turn of the century the house had been a simple country hotel, and many of the small, low-ceilinged rooms still retain porcelain number plates on their doors. There was an orchard, a walled garden, and, across the patch of lawn from the front door, a small pond—large enough, however, for naval engagements. There was also, fulfilling the immediate needs of the household, a farm near by, and there the conscientious objectors loyally carried on work of National Importance until 11 o'clock on the morning of November 11, 1918.

In the first decade of the post-war period, Charleston became the centre of what Quentin Bell calls "Bloomsbury-by-the-Sea". It was a triangular outpost, populated by the Charlestonians (the Bells and their frequent visitors, such as Duncan Grant and Roger Fry), the Tiltonians (Maynard and Lydia Keynes, who took up residence at Tilton on a branch of the dirt road leading to Charleston) and the Rodmellians (Leonard and Virginia Woolf, who moved from Asheham to Monk's House at Rodmell, on the other side of Lewes). The house, rambling in its construction and haphazard-seeming in its additions and outbuildings, was full of many oddly placed and sized rooms (not a disadvantage) and provided (apart from the usual bedrooms, sitting-rooms and a dining-room with an immense fireplace) a library for Clive Bell, and studios for Vanessa Bell and Duncan Grant, who, when they were not busy painting canvases, were busy painting walls, bedsteads, cupboards, tables, chairs, plates and almost any other flat surface they could find. The result of their industry was to give the house a colour and a magic (in its unexpectedness) that is unlike anything else: one has no sense, nor is one meant to have, of the self-conscious work of art, as in the Peacock Room of Whistler, or even, perhaps, in the rooms at Kelmscott. The children found the house, its grounds, and the surrounding countryside a perfect place for endless activity: for adventures, walks, war games, butterfly hunting, capture of animals—when older, shooting of birds—and noise: so much noise that poor Clive Bell, in desperation, built himself a little study apart from the house, in which he hoped to gain some quiet.

The children, along with the grown-ups, were at the centre of life at Charleston: that is its immediately distinguishing quality. They were not put to one side, categorized, or patronized, taken up enthusiastically and unceremoniously let down. That this did not happen is a tribute in part to their own charm, which appears to have been considerable, and even more to the character of the grown-ups, who had not only the ability to love children, but also, which is rarer, the ability to respect and to sympathize with them, to educate and to entertain them. Of all the grown-ups, it was Vanessa, naturally, who came first in their affections; and after her, Aunt Virginia. Mrs Woolf's arrivals "were a signal for rejoicing on the part of Julian and Quentin who had secrets to share with her. Thus she was always led aside and from the corner of the walled garden where they were ensconced came her clear hoot of laughter—like the mellow hoot of an owl—and Julian's loud explosions of merriment, protests and explanations."[18] There were relationships of rare closeness, too, with Clive, Bunny, Duncan and Roger Fry. (Indeed, all that seems to have been lacking in this childhood was the presence of other children. When the Desmond MacCarthys came to visit, they would bring their daughter Rachel; one hears also, when Julian was eleven, of the daughter of a woman who was at Charleston to help in the house: with her, the daughter, Julian fenced and wrestled. But such encounters were the exception not the rule. On the whole, the children depended on each other, and the grown-ups, for company.)

Something of the spirit of Charleston can be glimpsed in the daily newspaper that Julian, the Editor, and Quentin, the Illustrator, put out quite regularly whenever they were in residence throughout the twenties, although one feels that in its later period it was carried on with more devotion by Quentin than by his elder brother. Only one copy was printed—i.e., typewritten—and it was handed round for the enjoyment and edification of its readers, usually at the lunch table. There were weather reports, nature notes, news of arrivals and departures ("Today Mr Raymond Mortimer arrived to the great joy of the family"), accounts of Duncan's difficulties in building an ornamental pool ("Grant's Folly"), Clive's search for peace, the foibles and adventures of the servants, with particular emphasis on the attraction of Grace, the housekeeper, for most of the male population of Lewes and the surrounding countryside. Mortality was not neglected ("We regret greatly the death of Marmaduke, the perroquet, who expired suddenly through unknown causes this afternoon. We fear he will be much missed"), daily events were chronicled ("Angelica triumphed again yesterday, she succeeded without difficulty to persuade Nessa to cut her hair short. Afterwards, she danced a triumphal 'black-bottom' to celebrate her victory.") and there was even an occasional advertisement:

The Life and Adventures of J. Bell by

VIRGINIA WOOLF

profusely illustrated by Quentin Bell, Esq.

Some press notices.

. . . a profound and moving piece of work
. . . psychological insight.
WESTERN DAILY NEWS

. . . superb illustrations . . . unwavering truth . . . worthy of royal academy
. . . clearly the work of a pupil of Professor Tonks
ARTIST AND CRAFTSMAN

The paper, which began as the *Charleston Bulletin*, changed its name quite early in its history to the *New Bulletin*. It did not, however, until a later issue, state its credo: " 'The Bulletin' is unique among daily papers in being controlled by no millionaire or political party. It is not perhaps unique in having no principles."

The *New Bulletin* did not confine itself to the activities of the residents of Charleston and their visitors, but spread the circulation, and coverage, of its single copy to Tilton and Rodmell:

> The local countryside is now menaced by a new peril. Following Nessa's sensational purchase of a Renault the Woolves have purchased a Singer. And the denizens of Tilton are now the proud owners of a secondhand Morris Cowley. Whatever we may think of the problem of pedestrian traffic and the missuse [sic] of motor-cars, we must all agree that the car will be a great asset to the house and a permanent source of instruction and amusement to the rats in the duck shed [at Charleston, which was being used as a garage].

Towards Tilton, where the style of life was somewhat grander than at Charleston and Rodmell, the young Editor and Illustrator maintained an attitude of amused tolerance: "We learn that Mr and Mrs Keynes are putting their chauffeur in livery. We remind our more absentminded readers that the Keynes arms are as follows: Innumerable £s rampant, numberless $$$ sinister in concentric circles *or*; Field black. Crest St George Killing the Dragon." Julian and Quentin were quite aware of Keynes's importance in the world: hence the references to Economic Consequences and Conferences that are slyly introduced into accounts not only of the "Squire and his lady", but of the major-domo of the household, Harland, who assumes mythological proportions in the paper as a drunkard, bore and unsuccessful suitor for the favours of the alluring Grace. In 1925, while at Charleston for Christmas, they recorded a pheasant shoot in Tilton wood:

> We have heard from certain sources that Mr Maynard Keynes & some of his business friends formed the party. From the same source we learn that the bag consisted of: 2 pheasants, 4 rabbits, a blackbird, a cow, 7 beaters, 19 members of the party (including leaders, onlookers, etc.) and 1 dog (shot by mistake for a fox).

In the next number, along with the familiar teasing, there is a clear reflection of Keynes's bitter and justified opposition to the return of Britain to the Gold Standard: "We learn that the story that the Keynes are at Tilton has now been fully authenticated. The reason they are not flying a flag to indicate that they are in residence (as, we believe, they intend to in future) is that the price of Union Jacks has risen owing to the introduction of the Gold standard, & only red flags are obtainable."

Towards the Rodmellians, Leonard and Virginia Woolf, the *New Bulletin* was more benign, although it entertained a somewhat equivocal attitude towards their dog Grizel. (Tiltonian dogs, too, were looked at askance: "A stray mongrel, possibly the property of the Keynes's, appeared in the orchard this evening. If seen again it is to be shot at sight and the remains returned to its presumed owners.") Perhaps Mrs Woolf appears most memorably in these pages as

THE DISAPPEARING AUNT

On August 15, 1925, the *New Bulletin* reported

> On Sunday the Woolves paid a visit to the Squire. Virginia, unable to face a Tilton tea with Harland in the offing, decided to walk over to Charleston. She was seen on the road by Angelica and Louie, and her voice is thought to have been heard by Duncan. She failed to appear at tea, however, and did not afterwards return to Tilton. The most widely accredited theory is that she had a sudden inspiration and sat down on the way to compose a new novel.

The next day a sequel was given:

> Nessa and the Illustrator visited the Woolves this afternoon and found the disappearing aunt safe and sound. It appears that for some whim she decided to eat her tea under a hay stack instead of in Charleston dining room. The difference, however, is not great, and it is even possible that she mistook the one for the other.

Let this stand for what, in fact, it was: the charming world of the private joke, the private reference, the intimacy and reassurance within a closely-knit family, the glorious private world of childhood; and let it also stand for the *badinage*, the chaffing, yet the deep sense of intellectual and emotional community that existed among the Bloomsbury family and friends—and most particularly at the very nucleus, Virginia, Vanessa and the Bell children. It was in precisely this spirit of playfulness and affection that Mrs Woolf, in the splendidly ironic Preface to *Orlando* (1928), acknowledged, along with a galaxy of famous names, "the singularly penetrating, if severe, criticism of my nephew Mr Julian Bell . . . my nephew Mr Quentin Bell (an old and valued collaborator in fiction) . . . Miss Angelica Bell, for a service which none but she could have rendered."

But Charleston, pleasant though it was, was not the whole of Julian's childhood and youthful experience. He had also, from the age of eleven on, to experience the unpleasantness of school. Earlier, there had been the informal lessons with his mother in astronomy and geology and Greek mythology, and presumably in other subjects as well; and those governesses and nurses who were not pushed into ditches must have imparted some knowledge. David Garnett, in the years when he was living at Charleston, taught him "a little elementary science: biology, the evolution and principles of heredity in animals and plants, their physiology and anatomy; the elements of physics and astrophysics, the calendar and the weather . . ."[19] As Julian grew older, Clive began to direct his reading; he proved, in his son's words, to be "a most admirable educator". And of course there was the education to be got from listening to the conversation (which he was permitted to do, and did) of Clive Bell and Roger Fry on matters of aesthetics and philosophy. So that if, at eleven, he was officially unschooled, he was not entirely uneducated. But an education at home, unfortunately, in the eyes of the state and of most parents is not judged sufficient, and so Julian was sent to school.

Unlike most male children of his class and age (or a year or two younger), he was not sent away to boarding school to be prepared for Public School, but attended a day grammar school in London. Owen's, the school chosen by the Bells, was one of the best known City of London schools, founded in 1613 by Dame Alice Owen and administered since that time by the Brewers' Company. Technically, Owen's was a Public School, taking boys until they were eighteen; Julian, however, was only there for two years. He entered in September 1919, at the age of eleven and a half; and for a boy for whom childhood had been unusually pleasant, it was his introduction to the darker side of life. He had not been often in the company of other children, except for his brother and sister, and so had little experience or expectation of the cruelty that children *en masse* are capable of. He did not even have an older brother to warn him, or, more likely, to give him a foretaste of the bullying that is endemic among schoolboys: as the eldest child in his own family he was probably accustomed to being able to subdue Quentin and Angelica. But he seemed to adapt quickly to this aspect of school life. "Owen's," he wrote in his memoir, "after a first day of utter horror, and a bad week or so, grew not intolerable." On that first day he was "mobbed", the inevitable fate of being a new boy, especially one whose hair was thought too long. But his childhood had not been either so gentle or sheltered that he had not learned to wrestle and box a little, and, as he was heavier and taller than his contemporaries, he soon discovered that he could hold his own. Looking back upon the experience some eighteen years later, he wrote, "I was able to beat off individual bullies, and even, on occasion, intimidate mobs. My natural nervousness, very much increased by isolation and unpopularity, is consequently counteracted by a belief in the efficiency of force and the offensive. When things come to the point of violence I find my nerves under control and my spirits rise."[20] This belief in force—so at variance with the rationality of Bloomsbury as to be a bothersome problem to him thereafter—was learned outside the classroom; inside, in the true business of the classroom, he was less demonstrably affected, perhaps because, as the present headmaster tactfully suggests, "the special interests of Bloomsbury were not in line with Owen's". Although the school was more progressive than most at that time, it still emphasized "the acquisition of facts above all else",[21] and Julian was exposed to them in a wide range of subjects: English, Divinity, Latin, French, Mathematics, History and Geography. He also received instruction in Drawing, Choral Practice and Woodworking, as well as in Games. But he did not do well. At the end of his first year, he was ranked eighteenth in a form of twenty-three boys; at the end of his second and final year he was still eighteenth, but in a form of thirty-three. His one official distinction was to win one of the Reading Prizes given to the Junior part of the school—about 150 boys. Julian himself was prepared to acknowledge that Owen's "taught me what little arithmetic and algebra I know, and football-soccer", but he thought it "dreary, dingy, and a baddish education", a verdict that must be considered in the light of the phrase that immediately followed: "at home . . . was a refuge".[22] What institution, one wonders, devoted to the education of prepubescent males, could possibly compete for fascination, charm and intellectual stimulation with a household like the Bells? That Julian needed to be schooled is not in question; but it seems highly unlikely that any school to which he was sent would have pleased him. Owen's had not, nor would Leighton Park, the Public School to which his parents, conforming to the educational pattern of their class, sent him in January 1922.

There was no tradition of particular Public School in Bloomsbury, as there was a well-defined tradition of Cambridge, and even within Cambridge, of Trinity and King's. Clive Bell had gone to

Marlborough, but there was no compelling reason for Julian to follow him there. The choice made was Leighton Park School near Reading. On paper it must have looked a particularly appropriate choice, as it was, and is, the leading Quaker Public School in England, founded in 1890 in succession to the defunct Grove House School, Tottenham. Both schools have their historic interest, as they can be seen to represent, in the earlier instance, the liberalization of English life, and, in the later, its increasing class-consciousness. Grove House School had been founded in 1828 to prepare boys of Quaker families to take advantage of the new University of London (1827) which, unlike Oxford and Cambridge, was open to Nonconformists. Leighton Park, founded some seventy years later, was clearly intended to be a school for the wealthier Friends, and as such formed a rather late addition to the boom, largely for social reasons, in Public School foundations in the second half of the nineteenth century. But the fact of its being Quaker made it somewhat different from other schools: more serious and more 'guarded' in its education, more unified in its student body (in the 1920s half the students were Quakers), smaller (under 100 boys), less obsessed with sports and games, and, in theory at least, more tolerant of the individualist, the nonconformist who, like the Quakers in society itself, wishes to go his own way. It was also free from the traditional Public School activities of beating and fagging; and one would have had reason to expect, thanks to the Quaker background, a minimum of bloody-mindedness.

There were other more particular circumstances to predispose the Bells to the school. Although they were not Friends themselves, Vanessa's aunt Caroline, a sister of Sir Leslie Stephen, had become one, and had long been interested in their educational activities. Roger Fry (quite irreligious himself) was a member of the famous Quaker family and would have known Leighton Park: junior Frys and Cadburys were usually in attendance there. But most important was the attitude of conscientious objection to war which the Quakers and Bloomsbury shared, although perhaps not for the same reasons. In 1914 the Headmaster, Charles Evans, had resisted pressure to set up an Officer Training Corps at the school (an omission that Julian with his military interests rather regretted). He did establish an ambulance training scheme, however;

and it should be noted here that twenty-five Old Leightonians lost their lives in World War I. The Bells had had dealings with Evans, on matters having to do with conscientious objection, during the war, and had found him impressive; he was still Headmaster in the 1920s. In short, all the omens were favourable.

But as it happened, 1922 was not a particularly good time to go to Leighton Park. The school's official historian regards the period 1920 to 1928, the last eight years of Evans's headmastership, as a period of decline. Evans was an exciting, imaginative man, and the years of moral crisis—particularly for Quakers—of the war had brought out the best in him, but expansion of the school (which became, officially, a Public School in 1922) and many of the educational problems that arose after World War I needed more of an administrator than Evans was: he tended to let the affairs, and particularly the discipline, of the school get slightly out of hand. At some schools, Eton being a notable example, the years immediately after World War I were marked by a kind of radicalism on the part of the boys, a demand for greater liberalization and less stodginess. At Leighton Park too the boys were demanding more power and influence than they had previously had, but there the situation took a rather odd turn: the boys appear to have been less liberal than the masters, more philistine and sports-minded, more interested in chaos and rags than intellectual activity. This was particularly true in Grove House (named after the predecessor school), the perennial winner in school athletics, where the tone was aggressively hearty. Unfortunately, it happened to be the House to which Julian was sent.

He came to the school late in the academic year: a bad beginning. Rather than entering in the Michaelmas term of 1921, he was allowed to spend the time, undoubtedly much more enjoyable, with his family at St Tropez, and on his return to England he fell ill with influenza, so he did not enter Leighton Park until January 1922 in mid-Lent term. On the day after he left Charleston, Quentin, aged nine, reported in the *New Bulletin*: "Yesterday Julian departed for Layton Park to the great grief of the household. 'The New Bulletin' has suffered greatly by his absence since he is the joint editor of 'The New Bulletin' and founded the 'Charleston Bulletin' this household will never forget the invaluable services he rendered to the 'anti kitcheners army'

During the last ware when he held the office of Generall in cheif." [*sic*]

His late arrival put him at an obvious disadvantage: the other new boys would have had a chance to settle in during the first term, and would gang up on him as a logical victim. Then, as part of his recuperation from influenza, he was not supposed to play games or take cold baths—the *sine qua non* of a Public School—and so gained immediately, or felt he had gained, a reputation for dirt and weakness. Then, having been placed in a form too high for him, he did badly even in his studies. But his "chief memory" of the school was of "bullying by the mob":

> . . . although I sometimes managed to hit back [he wrote in his Notes for a Memoir] I was pretty permanently terrorised and cowed. I lived, often for months on end, in a state of misery and nervous tension. It was not only the pure physical suffering: there were also the horrors of expectation and insecurity. I defended myself to some extent by becoming expert in mob psychology and distracting attention with alternative acts of naughtiness or with other victims. I suppose there were periods of peace, but never of much happiness, though when Quentin came [in 1924] we could, in summer, escape on bicycles butterfly-collecting. But up to the very last I was always nervous and always subject to attack.[23]

That this should be his "chief memory", and that he should record it so vividly and with such urgency fifteen years later, is highly suggestive. But looked at objectively, the four and half years that he spent at Leighton Park were not quite as lamentable as one might infer from this fragment of autobiography, nor were his responses to them as bleakly despairing as he remembered them to have been.

In fact, he could hold his own, not only in rugby but also in rags, pranks, "alternative acts of naughtiness", to which he may have resorted as a way of "distracting attention" from himself, but which he enjoyed for their own sake. "When things come to the point of violence I find my nerves under control and my spirits rise." He may, as he thought, have been bullied "to the very last", but there is reason to suspect the worst was over long before then. J. Duncan Wood, who came to Leighton Park two years after Julian, and looked up to him as an older boy, envied him his bulk:

"For one thing it protected him against attack." His spirits seem often to have been exhilarated. One evening he conducted a raid on School House (one of the two other boarding houses) passing through the dormitories, overturning beds and creating chaos, then leading his followers down the housemaster's private stairs and out by the front door before there was any possibility of reply. "The whole affair, which cannot have lasted more than ten minutes, was a brilliant piece of strategy and caused School House considerable loss of face."[24]

But for all his skill at ragging, and in spite of the advantage of his large size, he did not intend to conform to the stereotype of the Grove House 'tough'. In his studies, in his thinking, even in his pranks, he was determined to go his own way, to be markedly individual, even idiosyncratic. This, though he does not say so, may have been a source of unhappiness, for, as the official historian points out, "Julian Bell was at school at the wrong time . . . a time when freedom for the unusual boy hardly existed . . ."[25] Yet he managed to survive, more or less on his own terms, and he did not do badly. By December 1923, he was a member of the Junior Literary Historical and Archaeological Society, one of the leading clubs in the school. Doubtless he participated fully—as he was never afraid of discussion, indeed revelled in it—in meetings dedicated to topics about which he must have heard a great deal at home. There were four meetings, for example, on the general topic of 'Civilization', two given to the question, 'What is Wrong with Civilization?' one to 'Utopia', and one to a subject that was to be of much greater interest to Julian towards the end of his life: plans and ideas for a model town. He became a member of the Debating Society. He participated in theatricals. In July 1926, when he played Sneer in Sheridan's *The Critic* he received a slightly mixed notice from *The Leightonian*: "The perfection of the performance was marred by a kind of laziness. His sarcasm was too amiably delivered . . . he deserved praise for his clear and natural elocution." His greatest accomplishment, which he considered "the best part of my education", came in 1925, when he won Honourable Mention (actually the second prize) in the J. B. Hodgkin Competition in public speaking. Speeches were delivered to an audience of boys and parents, and heckling was encouraged: this meant that, to be successful, one needed not only a talent for declamation, but a good deal of poise (nerve) and skill in repartee. In Julian's first try in the Competition—not a success—his subject was 'Socialism' and he declared for a "bloody revolution". (Shame!) But he triumphed with a speech extolling the virtues of alcoholic liquor. (Hear hear!) This was his reply to a series of temperance talks to which the school had been exposed at regular intervals throughout the term preceding the competition. He secured his Honourable Mention, *The Leightonian* felt, in a mock-heroic conclusion drawn from Cromwell, which he addressed directly to the temperance fanatics: "In the words of a great brewer, 'I beseech you in the bowels of Christ think it possible you may be mistaken.' "

On the whole, this is not an uncommon Public School history—a diversity of extra-curricular activity, a fair performance in the classroom—yet Julian at Leighton Park was truly uncommon, out of the ordinary, a rare bird (as he would not so conspicuously have been if he had gone to Eton): a self-declared intellectual, with a few intimates ("Fellow dims") to whom he taught the war game; very strong likes and dislikes vehemently expressed; holding forth on post-impressionist theories; writing essays on Wordsworth and the English naturalists, and the Art of War; reading Shaw, Wells, Belloc, Chesterton, Galsworthy, Kipling, the *Encyclopaedia Britannica*; and after the General Election of 1922, a convert to socialism. He was uncommon enough to be remembered. Writing of him more than thirty-five years after he had gone from Leighton Park School, his French master, T. C. Elliott, recalled him as

> Very untidy, careless of his appearance, interested in ideas in a much more evident way than his schoolfellows. I think he did not scruple to indicate that they were not quite up to his level. By this I don't mean that he was a snob, but the Bloomsbury atmosphere was not really the best preparation for the rough & tumble of a boarding school. He certainly came in for a good deal of teasing. He defended himself with a caustic, but not unkindly tongue, and I should think he was not on the whole very happy. I don't think he found many kindred spirits among boys or Staff.[26]

But however much Julian disliked his school, and however much his masters there were aware of it, the truth of the matter, as Elliott suggests, is that he was unprepared for any Public School, that somewhat primitive form of life which the English middle and upper classes seem to think essential for their sons. Julian himself, in the same memoir in which he wrote of being "pretty permanently terrorised and cowed" admitted that "Leighton Park . . . probably was no worse than most schools", although he regretted not having gone to College at Eton, as many of his friends at Cambridge had done. Such a rigorous mental training, had he been qualified for it, might have served him better. But Julian came from so unusual a home that, one feels safe in saying, no Public School would have been satisfactory—unless he had been in revolt against the freedom, unconventionality and seductive colour of his home environment, and longed to become a business-man, a barrister, a colonial administrator, a civil servant: any of the professions for which the Public Schools serve as a first rung.

In fact, Julian loved his home life with almost an unhealthy adoration. Given that, no school could provide anything to equal the intellectual and artistic stimulation, the sheer pleasure, of continual discussions, serious and gay, with Clive and Vanessa Bell, Leonard and Virginia Woolf, Roger Fry, Duncan Grant and David Garnett. In the alternations between Charleston (and Gordon Square) and Leighton Park, the advantage would always be with the former. Home, for so many budding intellectuals the crucial battlefield of adolescence, for Julian was the great good place, the source of all those ideas that had, as John Lehmann says, "the authority of graven tablets of the law: the tablets of Bloomsbury".[27] There is a measure of irony, then, that he should have been thought more unusual, unpredictable, uncommon, at school than at home: it seems not to have occurred to the elders of Bloomsbury, themselves usually so alert in such matters, that his, conceivably, was the sensibility of an artist; that he might, one way or another, prove to be an artist himself. Not that he gave evidence of precocity in these respects: "It must have been in my early years at L.P.S. that I dropped my own efforts as a painter—encouraged of course by family." And his contributions to the *New Bulletin* were exuberant and charming but in themselves do not count as 'first flights'. (From a high-handed affectionate parody of Mrs Woolf's manner: "But then things were like that, she thought.

The children had just run upstairs with the scuffle of a pack of hounds, and her freed mind floated gently, like a goldfish basking in the autumn sunshine, amid the pale, starlike blooms of the waterlilies. The new refrigerator would cost thirty pounds, she thought.") So there was no evident reason to anticipate a burst of creative activity. Yet it seems odd that the possibility should not even have been entertained.

On Saturday, August 2, 1924, at Monk's House, Virginia Woolf wrote in her diary, "Julian has just been and gone, a tall young man who, inveterately believing myself to be young as I do, seems to me like a younger brother; anyhow we sit and chatter, as easily as can be. It's all so much the same—his school continues Thoby's school. He tells me about boys and masters as Thoby used to. It interests me just in the same way. He's a sensitive, very quick witted, rather combative boy; full of Wells, and discoveries and the future of the world. And, being of my own blood, easily understood. Going to be very tall, and go to the Bar, I daresay."[28]

Julian was not yet eighteen when he left Leighton Park, and it was decided that he should have another year of preparation before going off to the University. Clive had an ideal of making his son a man of the world: a feat plainly outside the scope of any English Public School. A season in Paris was indicated: where better to achieve the result? As a Francophile and man of the world himself, Clive was frequently in Paris, spoke the language perfectly, and had a large number of friends in French literary and artistic circles. Among them was a nephew of the painter Renoir, who was teaching at one of the great *lycées* of Paris, Louis le Grand. Renoir recommended that Julian be sent to his colleague Pinault, who would take one or two young men each year for intensive study. It seemed an ideal solution: accordingly, from the autumn of 1926 until the summer of 1927, he was in Paris, living with the Pinaults in their flat at 96 Boulevard Port Royal (at the corner of Boulevard Montparnasse). It was an interesting place to live, a perfectly respectable boulevard on the left bank, near the Observatory and above the Luxembourg gardens. At the same time, it was right next to the Latin Quarter: ideally situated for Julian to venture, experimentally, into *la vie de Bohème*, if he had so wished—but he did not: or did not dare, it came to the same thing. Although he went to the Sorbonne as a student, he took no exams, "followed lectures, steadily less attentively, and presently spent much time walking the streets". Apart from this he did not seem to participate much in Parisian life, nor, according to his own account, did he acquire the social graces that his father expected him to learn in Paris. That was not his style, then, or afterwards. He was a casual country child, and never acquired a city polish. His aunt testifies to this: "He was entirely unself-conscious: I doubt if he ever looked in the glass or thought a moment about his clothes or his appearance. Nessa used to mend his breeches. He was always patched, or in need of patching."

What he enjoyed most in Paris were his discussions and arguments with Pinault ("one of the nicest human beings I ever knew") from whom he learned a considerable amount about French literature, art and politics. He had read Corneille, Racine and Molière; now, along with much else, he added two particular favourites of Pinault's: Voltaire, who destroyed whatever was left of the religiosity of 'downstairs' or Leighton Park, and Anatole France. Pinault was a lively, genial, very charming radical of the old French school. A countryman come to the capital, once a German teacher, he was now secretary of Louis le Grand, but still had time to demonstrate in left-wing causes and vent his antagonism to the Church in the classic tradition of French anti-clerical republicanism. Pinault "called himself a communist", but this seems to have been more a radical stance than an actuality: "there was nothing of the modern party line about him". As might be expected, he had a fondness for the great romantic painters, Courbet and Delacroix, and introduced their work in the Louvre to Julian, who hitherto had only looked at the Impressionists in the Luxembourg. And, to conclude with the lessons *chez* Pinault, he reinforced Julian in his theoretical socialism, adding to it a more romantic continental idea of revolution than he might have acquired at home in England.

At the same time Julian was reading a great deal on his own: Rimbaud, Heredia, Mallarmé, "generally discovering Parnassians and symbolists and moderns". He made "first efforts at Proust and Gide". He "developed a passion for Giraudoux". Indeed, his reading among the modern French appears much more adventurous and advanced than anything he had thus far done in English. There, except for the works of Bloomsbury, he had not yet got beyond the Edwardians. But the crucial influence of that year's reading in Paris was Maupassant. He "provided to a large extent" —Julian wrote—"an introduction to 'life'—I had no experience at first hand. But I became familiar with, and instinctively accepted, a Latin-sensual view of *amour* which, though I have modified it, I think I still keep in essentials, and have found works." That, of course, was written a decade later, when theory had been translated into practice. In Paris, as at Charleston, he was still leading a sheltered existence in which anything and everything could be read about and thought about and talked about (those splendid discussions!) but none of the economic or the sexual realities of the world were actually experienced. "Experience" apart, however, it was a time of great intellectual value, in reading and ideas, and left Julian with a command of bad French which he spoke with great gusto. Matured and enriched, he rejoined his family: Renoir's recommendation had been well given.

In only one respect had Paris fallen short of expectations: even after his prolonged exposure to it, Julian had not been transformed into the man of the world his father would have liked him to be, a man of his own style, so to speak. But it should be emphasized that neither then nor later did Julian wish to be so transformed. There was a duality in Clive that found a parallel in the ambivalence of Julian's feelings towards him. On the one hand, worldliness and suavity of Clive's sort did not seem to him admirable, or a model to emulate. On the other hand, Clive in his aspect of country squire greatly attracted him. It was there, in the natural world of birds and dogs, fields, woods, streams, the changing seasons; and the masculine pursuits of the countryside, shooting, fishing, beagling—all very plain and four-square—that father and son were closest to each other in spirit. And it was this world that Julian would evoke in his earliest poetry.

In Paris he became a poet.

For all the intellectual excitement and stimulation, the pleasures of discussion and argument with "old Pinault", he was profoundly unhappy there—it was his "first experience of a large town"—and he pined for the country, and reacted to the capital of civilization to which his father had sent him in a way that he characterizes as "fiercely naturalist". In his memoir, written ten years later, when the poetic impulse had spent itself (or been thwarted), he gave only a sentence to the event, perhaps the most significant of his life, concluding: "this unhappiness, sending me to watch all the gulls and sparrows of Paris, sent me also to writing my first poems: pure nature descriptions".[29]

Does unhappiness, absence from a landscape passionately loved, force a poet into being? Before Julian comes to Paris, there is no mention of poetry—no serious attempts at writing it, not even of reading it. Yet now, in an almost unpremeditated way, he discovered that he was a poet—interestingly enough, something Bloomsbury had not produced before. (T. S. Eliot was a close friend of the Bells—Clive admired him most among modern poets—and a close friend also of Virginia and Leonard Woolf, who published *The Waste Land* at the Hogarth Press; but he came into their lives, or they into his, at the end of the war, when he was already a 'formed' poet. Eliot's connections and affiliations with Bloomsbury were social and literary, rather than spiritual and philosophical, and it would be misleading, even by proximity, to describe him as a Bloomsbury poet.) These first poems of Julian's, "nature descriptions", are not at all the usual juvenilia of the period: mere Georgian echoes. Nor is the nature he describes in them what he observed in Paris: the flowering parterres and espaliered hedges of the Luxembourg Gardens; the artful wilderness of the *Bois*. In spite of the titles he affixed to these poems, 'Vendémiaire', 'Brumaire', 'Frimaire', 'Pluviose' (the names of months in the French revolutionary calendar), they are descriptions, as exact and truthful, as "fiercely naturalist", as he could make them, of the countryside he knew best and vividly evoked in absence, the Sussex Downs, the landscapes of south-east England.

He recalled how in winter, "wreathing white misty fogs" from off the sea drift across the land, hiding "the pale sun's sky", and how

> On moonless nights, when the whole sky is dark,
> There comes a sudden rush of intense black,
>   Then, terrified, the sheep
>   Break hurdles and escape.

And from the air comes the full cry of hounds,
Mixed with the rushing noise of a high wind,
As, from the coast, the geese
Sweep inland, clamorous.

('Brumaire')

In 'Frimaire', describing a pheasant shoot in autumn, there is a deliberate absence of emotion, but what the eye sees and the ear hears are set down with impressive conviction:

. . . Far-heard the tapping, distant and gentle,
Through the wet, quiet wood, of
The beaters' sticks. A throbbing, whirring rustle,
A pheasant high above.

Grey timid rabbits come forward, hop along.
The beaters' line draws in.
Sudden tumult of pheasants rising strong.
The thudding guns begin.

Pale, ghostly woodcock, pointed wings wandering
Through the trees, in and out.
Wild sudden excitement, beaters calling
And long, random-wild shot.

And the pheasants hit in their rocket flight
Come awkwardly tumbling down.
Blue-white, bead-green and black on gold-bronze bright,
Feminine mottled brown.

John Lehmann, who has written with great sensitivity of Julian and his poetry (they were to become friends and fellow-poets at Cambridge) in his volume of autobiography *The Whispering Gallery*, sees in these early poems "an attempt to let the countryside, the moods of wind and weather and life outside the cultivated human pale, speak for themselves without any interference of the poet's moralizing thoughts".[30] The result, as the quotations we have given perhaps bear out, was a highly original and authentic poetry, too quiet-voiced and unassertive ever to call much attention to itself, and closer in its affinities to painting than to other nature poetry. That image in 'Frimaire':

Pale, ghostly woodcock, pointed wings wandering
Through the trees, in and out.

reads like a transmutation into words of a detail from a Chinese painting. And the final stanza, with its determination to see things exactly as they are, its meticulous notations of colour ("Blue-white, bead-green . . . black on gold-bronze") calls to mind similar notations, a comparable purity of vision, in passages in the Journal of Delacroix, and the letters of Van Gogh.

One does not wish to make excessive claims for this poetry, although it is of a sort easier to underrate than to overpraise. The fact is indisputable: during his year in Paris, and for the next two years in Cambridge, Julian was truly a poet. Thereafter he was a poet intermittently, at widening intervals, until, towards the end of his life, he wrote no poems at all. Among the older generation of Bloomsbury only David Garnett appears to have recognized his quality: "Julian was first of all a poet," he wrote in 1938, "hard thinking never made him a thinker; but his poems are exact, clear, and perfectly expressive. In his poetry he has escaped from all his turmoil. He is the poet I like best of his generation."[31]

2 A Young Apostle

In the autumn of 1927, after his educative year in Paris, Julian Bell went up to King's College, Cambridge. He was eighteen years old, a budding poet, a socialist, a rationalist in matters of life and love, about which he had a large theoretical knowledge but no experience: Bloomsbury's principles were "inscribed on his banner". Yet in Paris he had been more independent of these enlightened principles than he perhaps realized. The act of writing poetry was his own choice, prompted by his own need, and the poetry itself followed no precedent of idea or form set by his elders. Bloomsbury's prime commitment was to man, to man in the world, his works, his civilization; yet in Julian's early poems the primacy is given to nature, and man is of no interest. When, in 'Vendémiaire', a "covey of brown birds" is brought down, the hunter is not even noticed except obliquely, as

> . . . Blue barrel and black dot,
> Thud and thin smoke of double shot.

Then, like an image of dying nature in Courbet, comes the lingering, carefully observed, impersonal centre of the poem:

> Feathers drift down
> Slowly, from breast and wing.
> The chestnut horseshoe bodies bleed

At beak and shattered joint, opaque
Drops, shot unsmoothed
Plumage . . .

Whatever its merits or defects, this is poetry in a different tradition (or mode) from Bloomsbury's, and it was written in a time of absence, when Julian was in Paris, away from home territory. Cambridge, of course, was very much home territory, and King's particularly so. Although most of the first generation of Bloomsbury had been at Trinity, the connection had not been maintained. Keynes, however, had continued in close touch with King's—in 1924 he began his spectacular career as its first Bursar, so arranging its investments that for the first time the College had an income commensurate with its buildings and pretensions—and gradually, over the years, it had become a kind of Bloomsbury outpost at Cambridge. So there was no question where Julian would go.

His first year, when he lived not in college but in lodgings just across the street (12 St Edward's Passage), he afterwards summed up as "a failure on the whole". He was rather shy to begin with; he was eager for "intellectual society", never easily come by, even at King's; and of course, one's earliest undergraduate alliances are almost certain to be mistakes: mutual loneliness and unfamiliarity proving the most tenuous of bonds when one is no longer lonely and knows where one is. Yet "failure" seems a relative judgment; if the second and third years were vastly more exciting, it was in his first year that he formed the closest and most enduring of his friendships: with Eddie Playfair, and the only friendship of which he wrote at length in his memoir. "Eddy [thus Julian's invariable idiosyncratic misspelling] I first scraped acquaintance with in Hall, under a misunderstanding. We discovered a common knowledge of, and interest in, French literature, and very rapidly became intimate. During our three years we met every day, and most evenings, and talked on till one and two in the morning. (Our most extreme effort in this direction was once at Charleston, when I expounded my view of ethics to him until we suddenly noticed that it was six.) Eddy was very much the Etonian [he had been in College there], in spite of the miseries of his school life—hardly, if at all, less than mine. Although at first I reacted very much against it . . . I think he did a great deal to civilise me, and give me whatever social graces I possess."[1]

From the first Julian responded to the diversity and possibility of Cambridge life: he would write poems (but not show them or publish them, that was to come later), form friendships, talk until dawn, read a good deal "in scattered fashion", go out fortnightly with the University Beagles, speak at the Union—and with all this, found time even for his academic responsibilities. He had decided to read History, a continuing passion since childhood, and he went to tutorials with John Clapham, the great economic historian. He worked hard, but, to judge by the result, he ought to have worked harder: bright and imaginative though he was, he was not likely to discipline himself more than he wanted in his studies (there was so much else to do) and Cambridge, like Oxford, tends to put the burden of responsibility for getting work done upon the student. Julian managed to achieve a thoroughly respectable degree—not, however, the First that would have allowed him, almost automatically, to have an academic career. (At the time, it did not matter to him; later, as we shall see, it was a cause for some regret.) He studied History his first two years, and in Part I of the Tripos, the series of three-hour examinations which he took in the late spring of 1929, he received a 2-1: that is, the first division of the second class of the honours degrees—a degree which reflects ability and work of some distinction, but not enough of either to achieve a First. In his third year he made a not uncommon change, and read English for a year with F. L. Lucas. "Peter" Lucas was a much more congenial, much more Bloomsburyan figure than Clapham: although of a younger generation, somewhat between Julian's parents and Julian himself, he was a friend of Keynes and the Bells. His literary sympathies were of admirable breadth, ranging from the Elizabethans to the moderns: he was preparing an edition of Webster; he was an authority on the eighteenth century; he was informed in the French Enlightenment, he was curious about the psychological aspects of literature. Unlike the older generation of Bloomsbury, he had had a military experience of World War I, about which he would write powerfully in the 1930s. He and Julian got on extremely well, and it was as pleasant a tutorial and personal relation as one could wish, yet it achieved precisely the same result as the tutorials with Clapham (no doubt for the same reason). In Part II of the English Tripos Julian received, as he had earlier received in History Part I, a 2-1. Nevertheless King's deemed him worthy of support, and he received studentships in the gift of the College in 1930-1931, and in 1931-1932, while he was a research student. Such, briefly, was his academic career.

But for Julian, as for many other undergraduates, the official academic aspect of things was not a dominating concern. He had his political, philosophical, poetical, emotional and sensual interests, and Cambridge was prepared to minister to them all, in that order.

During his first year he spent a fair amount of time at the Cambridge Union. His interest in politics was long-standing, and went back to his earliest days at Leighton Park; he had been a Socialist since the General Election of 1922, when the Labour Party became the official opposition; he had talked politics with Pinault in Paris, and in Bloomsbury with his Uncle Leonard, and with Keynes. His success at Leighton Park in the Hodgkin Competition had increased his interest in public speaking. Hence the Union. It was a logical starting point for a politically minded young man with a taste for public speaking. But although it provided a place to be heard, and in that sense was not without value, it offered little in the way of a serious confrontation and discussion of political issues. Its motions for debate tended either to be frivolous, or, if serious, to be dealt with frivolously—on occasion, debate on an important but non-political issue, such as birth control, might attract a large and presumably attentive House, but generally, not. Of course, it was a slack time in politics in England—the period 1924-1929 when the Conservatives under Baldwin were in smug possession and making a futile attempt to restore pre-war 'normalcy'—and, as one would expect, that slackness was reflected in the Union. Tories dominated; debates were apolitical; and the rather bogus, would-be Victorian style the Union affected—which would wilt noticeably under the onslaught of the 1930s—was still in full flower.

What is surprising about Julian's brief career in the Union is that it should have lasted as long as it did: this can hardly have been the "intellectual society" he craved. But it was his first year, and other alternatives did not present themselves. He spoke for the first time about a month after the beginning of term, against the motion 'That England thinks too much of her athletes and their doings'. He argued that sport was a sort of opiate, and was a good thing for keeping a democracy quiet. The reporter for *The Cambridge Review* characterized his speech as "excellent". The motion was carried 207 to 144. Two months later, in January 1928, he spoke against the motion 'That the Application of Socialist principles to the National Finances would be disastrous'. *The Cambridge Review* reported that, "Mr J. H. Bell, looking every inch the Kingsman, was interesting and distinctive." The motion was carried 196 to 118. Later that month, he was again on the losing side, when he attacked the cult of efficiency as a menace to civilization. In April, however, he argued in favour of machine civilization, and the small House agreed with him. The Summer Term of his first year was his most active in the Union: he spoke at almost every meeting from the end of April on. At the meeting of May 15, he was the first, the 'on the paper' speaker for the Opposition, on the motion 'That the time has now come for the decent burial of the Savoy Operas'. Gilbert Harding, reporting the event for *The Cambridge Review*, described Julian as doing extraordinarily well, particularly considering that before the formal discussion got under way, there had been an hour-long debate during which it was decided that women would not be allowed to come to the Union as speakers. "Mr Bell concluded . . . with a plea against the burial of the living, after some literary arguments which were too intelligent for the House to appreciate." Musical arguments seem not to have been adduced—music was never a Bloomsbury speciality. In any case, Julian's side won the debate, in a House much reduced by the discussion of feminist questions, 59 to 11. On October 30 he spoke in favour of the motion 'That the sciences are murdering the arts'. As reported in the *Review*, he maintained that, "The scientist, the inquirer, the interrogator, was innately incapable either of creating or appreciating art. The business man, the waste product of Science, was the immediate murderer." The motion was not carried. In the middle of November, towards the end of his active participation in the affairs of the Union, he spoke in favour of the motion 'That the foreign missions have outlived their justification', arguing that "it was monstrous to use a monopoly of medicine and education in order to secure conversion"—a proper Bloomsbury retort to a Claphamite tradition, and, for Julian, a properly iconoclastic note on which to conclude. Even though, at the end of that term, and again at the end of the next, he was elected to the Standing Committee of the Union, his interest in it had not extended much past the first term of his second year. By then he had found his alternatives. "Intellectual society" was elsewhere. He spoke just once more in the Union, in April 1929, and then, significantly, in favour of a political motion that genuinely interested him: 'That this House condemns the policy of the Conservative Party as contained in the Budget and the Prime Minister's speech on April 18.' The motion was not carried.[2]

If his first year had been (in his own eyes) "a failure on the whole", his second was an unqualified success. At its very beginning occurred what he described as "the most important event of my Cambridge life . . . being elected to the Apostles". In fact (and certainly as he recalled it) "the whole period was one of great expansion and a feeling of richness and possibilities in the world. I published my first poems, in *The Venture* and *Cambridge Poetry* [actually, in *The Cambridge Review*] that autumn [actually, that winter]: I had a car, and my own rooms [he had moved into college] furniture, pictures—all the amenities of Cambridge at its best. There was an extraordinary *douceur de vivre*, a combination of material wealth (part boom, part credit-system), the general ease of college life, a certain relaxation of work [with the academic result we have already noticed] and a great many new friends . . . a steadily widening and varying circle."[3]

Taking Julian at his word, that "the core of this was the Apostles", we shall turn our attention first to that aspect of his life. He would, of course, already have been familiar with the Society as the great progenitor of Bloomsbury, and he must have approached it with high expectations. He was not to be disappointed. After attending his first meeting, he "really felt" that he had "reached the pinnacles of Cambridge intellectualism". At those weekly Saturday evenings, Julian was truly in his element, for there was nothing he loved more than discussion—"at that time . . . the greatest passion of my life"—and was prepared not only to talk but to listen, and even, perhaps too easily, to defer to another opinion. A paper was presented, and discussed (dissected) —just as in the past—and there was a traditional form linking the Apostolic generations, from Tennyson and Hallam, to Strachey and G. E. Moore, to Julian and his friends, Anthony Blunt, Andrew Cohen, Hugh Sykes, Richard Llewelyn Davies and Alasdair Watson. Subjects for discussion changed, inevitably, from generation to generation: the Apostles did not live outside time. In the Julian period they discussed "a classic, post-impressionist view of the arts" and "anarchism . . . in the mode of Blake and Dostoievsky". These were the 1920s: one is not surprised to be told that, "Practical politics were beneath discussion." Yet certain of their discussions were peculiarly Apostolic and timeless, restatements of restatements of the concerns of their predecessors. The echo is unmistakable, for example, in this surviving fragment of a paper Julian presented to the Society: "Tho' I know only too well that in reality everyone is more or less blinded by prejudices, I do believe that people have only to see clearly in order to know what is good or bad, and the legitimate means of persuasion are enough to show them clearly the nature of any state of mind or life." Did he really believe this innocent simplification, or did he believe he believed it, for the sake of discussion? As an undergraduate Apostle he thought himself a disciple of G. E. Moore, although he hadn't actually read *Principia Ethica*, and when finally he did, it was "in a very critical spirit". But that was not until some years later, when he was attempting to construct a philosophy of his own. In the memoir he describes the "intellectual climate" of the Society as "Bloomsbury *un peu passé*", but if it was chiefly warmed-over Moore that was served up at meetings, there was also a dash of contemporary spice: "the mild troubles", in Julian's phrase, of I. A. Richards and of Freud. Yet one has the sense of the tail-end of a tradition. In the 1930s, when events in the world outside had thrust themselves upon the consciousness of Cambridge, and of the Apostles, the Marxist views of certain of its members were set forth too passionately (perhaps because believed in) to allow for a gentlemanly exchange of opinion, and the Society was forced to suspend its activities. In 1937, in China, Julian wrote: "From the beginning I took it very seriously, and still do: I think the bitterest thing about the communist hysteria at Cambridge has been the virtual death of the Society; my hope is that it is only a temporary coma." Of the importance of the Society in his life there is no question; that its effect upon him was entirely to the good is less certain: it did encourage him in his philosophic bent, it did encourage him to think, but perhaps at some cost to his instinctive gift.

The immediate effect—we are returning now to the second year—was to enlarge his circle of friends, or perhaps it would be more precise to say, to provide a new category of friends—the Apostles—to be added to the politicians and sportsmen of the first year. And soon there would be the poets. Eddie Playfair, still, as he would always be, his closest friend and confidant, early in that successful second year introduced him to John Lehmann, who had been with Playfair in College at Eton, and who was now at Trinity. Like Julian, Lehmann was an aspiring poet. They met at a time when each was in need of a sympathetic reader, equally able to praise and to criticize, of his own age, at his own level of accomplishment, a colleague with whom to discuss problems of craft and theories of art. Thereafter John Lehmann was Julian's chief 'literary' friend, and they carried on, in conversation and correspondence, a remarkable literary dialogue. Lehmann, in his autobiography twenty-five years later, describes the letters that he and Julian "exchanged in such numbers at that time" as "full of the most detailed arguments and theories about couplets, quatrains, blank verse, free verse, caesuras, rhythm and counter-rhythm, realism and romanticism, dialogue in verse and description in verse, clarity, obscurity, ambiguity and all the other subjects that two eager apprentice craftsmen in poetry can find to discuss with one another." Then, with a valedictory sigh that does not seem quite fair either to himself or to Julian, he concludes, "The light has faded from them, the ashes are dead. And yet"—and this is the heart of the matter—"it was the most exciting colloquy in the world: the whole future of poetry, we felt, depended on these arguments; we were remoulding English literature nearer to our own hearts, and even our great differences of approach seemed to promise a spark of fusion out of which the new way of writing, the completely modern poem would be made."[4]

Until now, in Paris and in his first year in Cambridge, Julian had been writing poetry for himself: unhappiness, it will be recalled, had sent him to writing his first poems. And he had continued, at Cambridge, writing in the same genre, not poems of personal unhappiness but of the natural world, as remote as he could make them from the sentimentality and anthropomorphism of the Georgian tradition. Somehow, in spite of the number of his activities and interests and distractions, even in his first year—the beagling and the debates in the Union, the tutorials with Clapham—his poetic production had been remarkably high. So that when the time came to emerge from the cocoon and to publish—at the beginning of his second year—he had a large assemblage of poems, quite uniform in quality, to draw upon. Whatever diffidence he may have felt in the past, preferring to keep the poems out of sight, he felt none now: he wanted to be read. And the question, more theoretical than pertinent, what is the proper age to publish for the first time, never troubled him. His aunt Virginia, in her 'Letter to a Young Poet'—written to John Lehmann—would recommend thirty as the minimum allowable age: three years younger than herself when she published *The Voyage Out*, her first novel. But most young poets get their first books into print long before this: Julian's *Winter Movement* was published in 1930, when he was twenty-two. Of course, to publish a lyric or two in an undergraduate periodical is not quite as compromising as to bring out (with Blackwell's, say) a whole collection of them: one is not yet irredeemably a 'writer'. But London editors and publishers have a way of keeping their eyes on undergraduate poets, especially at Oxford or Cambridge: so many careers have begun in just such fashion.

As it happened, the late 1920s were a fertile time in the literary life of both the Ancient Universities, although, in a retrospective view, the activities at Cambridge are less likely to be noticed than the more glamorous poetic ferment at Oxford. W. H. Auden, Stephen Spender, C. Day Lewis and Louis MacNeice were all at Oxford between 1927 and 1929, all in their turn were contributing to the annual volumes of *Oxford Poetry* (Auden and Day Lewis were its editors in 1927, Spender and MacNeice in 1929); all would go on from Oxford to constitute a movement: Thirties Poetry. At Cambridge the most conspicuous, and certainly the most influential literary achievement was the revolution in the practice of criticism that was being led by I. A. Richards, a Fellow of Magdalene. This would seem to bear out the stereotyped contrast: impassioned artistic Oxford; detached scientific Cambridge. Yet poets abounded in Cambridge, among them some of Richards's brightest pupils; and there was an abundance of periodicals in which they could place their work—here we shall mention only the quasi-official *Cambridge Review*, a weekly, and *Experiment* and *The Venture*, competing 'little' magazines, both of which were founded in the autumn of 1928, in the first term of Julian's second year. *Experiment* was more or less a Magdalene College enterprise, with five editors: Hugh Sykes, a friend of Julian's and a fellow Apostle, William Empson, J. Bronowski, Humphrey Jennings and William Hare. Seven numbers were issued, the last in May 1931. Judged by the standards of *transition*, it was hardly experimental at all, but these things are relative: it professed to be experimental, considered itself the chief organ for contemporary writing at Cambridge, and regarded its rival, *The Venture*, as neo-Georgian. Although it published, as one would expect, the kind of undergraduate facsimile-poems that reflect the fashionable advanced taste of the period—echoes from *The Waste Land* or *Mauberley*—it also published apprentice work by a number of gifted writers, among them Richard Eberhart, Malcolm Lowry and Kathleen Raine. Its most memorable contributor was Empson himself, who seems, on the evidence of these early poems ('To an Old Lady', 'It is the pain, it is the pain, endures', 'Legal Fiction' and several others) to have created his own extraordinary style at the very beginning of his career. Its rival, *The Venture*, was edited by Anthony Blunt, like Sykes of *Experiment*, an Apostle and a friend of Julian's, H. Romilly Fedden and Michael Redgrave. There were six numbers in all, the last in June 1930. Much more handsomely produced than *Experiment*, it was also more conservative in policy, more aesthetic in taste, more sophisticated in its interests. The contents of the final number are not unrepresentative: an essay by Anthony Blunt on Cubism, an essay by Martin Turnell on 'Donne, T. S. Eliot, and the Symbolists', an essay by Julian on Poetic Obscurity; then, in a self-conscious gesture to the enemy—it was thought worthy of editorial comment—two of the *Experiment* regulars, Empson (a poem) and Malcolm Lowry (a story). If, as a table of contents, this is not particularly venturesome, neither is it jejune: indeed there are moments when the tone of *The Venture* suggests a premature middle-age. From the third number (June 1929): "Founded originally to supply a need in Cambridge, *The Venture* has withstood the violence of a too sudden 'Renaissance' [presumably, *Experiment*] and will continue for another year as a protest against the more licentious forms of Free Verse, Surréalisme, and Art without Tears!" Julian, who tended to see literary life in terms of controversy, cast his lot with *The Venture*. He first appeared in its pages in February 1929 (the second number) with a poem, 'The Moths', and was represented thereafter in each of the four succeeding numbers. He considered himself very much a member of *The Venture* party. It was not necessary that he do so; he might have published in both magazines. Others did—John Davenport, for example. But this would have been less exhilarating; battle was in the air, and he called the writers who contributed to both "the mercenaries". In fact, his enthusiasm for *The Venture* was not as frivolous as this may suggest: he thought it sympathetic to the literary principles (or prejudices) in which he was coming rapidly and dogmatically to believe.

In Paris, writing his earliest poems, and afterwards, at Cambridge, in his first year, Julian was happily free of literary principles and theories. Since boyhood he had admired the prose of Richard Jefferies, the late Victorian essayist and novelist, and he wanted to achieve a comparable clarity and accuracy in verse. The influence of Jefferies is unmistakable. And there is a detachment and absence of sentiment that he might conceivably have learned from the Parnassians he was reading in Paris. But these early poems were not written to conform to a doctrine, whether borrowed or invented: he was still too innocent to be doctrinaire, in a stage, as he described it, of "self-conscious virgin naturalism". Then, in his second year in Cambridge, the ambience became explicitly and flatteringly intellectual. There were discussions of aesthetic and ethical principles at the Saturday evening meetings of the Society; there were discussions of metrics and the principles of versification with John Lehmann (like himself a contributor to *The Venture*); at the same time he was becoming "more and more consciously and conscientiously literary". Rather belatedly, he advanced from the Edwardians to the moderns. He read Eliot and I. A. Richards, Huxley and Wyndham Lewis, disliking Eliot, whom he found obscure (the unforgivable sin of modernism). He set about becoming, in literary matters, "a thoroughgoing classicist reactionary".

It was very odd. He was, he thought, a convinced Bloomsburyan, yet he diverged sharply from the creative practice of his elders. Unfortunately he could never deal with this divergence: it would have been disloyal to single out for criticism the work of anyone who 'belonged' to him—his Aunt Virginia's novels, for example. It is doubtful if he was even aware of the contradiction. Hence, the almost obsessive nature of his dislike for Eliot, the symbolic enemy, who was made to bear the burden of all the resentments Julian was unable to express, even to himself. Bloomsbury's practice in the arts was determinedly new. Mrs Woolf was the outstanding experimental novelist in England. Clive Bell wrote admiringly of Eliot and Proust, of Matisse and Picasso. Vanessa Bell and Duncan Grant were unquestionably modern painters—as late as the mid-1930s they were able to shock the *bourgeoisie*. Specifically, the directors of the Cunard Line, who commissioned Grant to decorate a room on the *Queen Mary*, and then, having seen the work, decided nervously that it would not do. The point hardly needs elaborate documentation. Bloomsbury was a part of the modern movement; Julian, its first poet, who had grown up in its midst, for whom its ideas and beliefs were "tablets of the law", was setting out at the same time to become "a thoroughgoing classicist reactionary".

As a statement of principles upon which his own poetic practice was based, the essay 'A Brief View of Poetic Obscurity', which he wrote towards the end of his third (and last undergraduate) year, and which was published in the final number of *The Venture*, is admirably clear and explicit. Since, in effect, it was the critical credo he would hold to, with just a few variations and modifications, throughout his life, it deserves extensive quotation:

> By obscure poetry I mean poetry that the well educated "common reader" who after all is the juryman giving the final verdict of posterity finds hard or is unable to understand.
>
> My argument is that such obscurity is a defect, though admittedly some poems are great in spite of a certain obscurity . . .

> The reductio ad absurdum of obscurity is nonsense, which in its ideal state towards which our contemporaries are rapidly approaching, consists of a series of totally unconnected words . . . Though I think that obscurity often results from subtlety of thought, I do not know that this is much of an argument in its favour. Truly, it is an admirable quality to be able to express an exact shade of meaning neither more nor less. But this is just what obscurity does not do. It is the cardinal merit of a perfectly clear style to express subtleties without confusion, as witness a hundred writers from Herrick and Jane Austen to Racine and LaFontaine.
>
> Moreover it has yet to be proved that the subtlest, most curious, most hidden and exquisite thoughts and feelings are in any way the most valuable. Without wishing to compromise myself in any way with the grand simplicities, I should say that the best poems had been written clearly and comprehensibly about simple feelings and ideas.[5]

The mark of good sense is upon this, the rationalist view of life and art, the plain sensible Englishman's view—Julian was perhaps more of a Bell than he realized, and his no-nonsense, straightforward attitude had much in common with that of either a nineteenth-century businessman or a country squire. (He himself would have placed it back a century earlier: the good sense of Dr Johnson and Pope.) But without contradicting the intelligence of Julian's argument, one might observe that life and art include more than "simple feelings and ideas", and that the more passionate the commitment to a dispassionate clarity, the more art and life have to be ruled out. This was precisely Julian's situation by the end of his third year. He had "finally reached the point," John Lehmann tells us, "where he would have liked to blot out the whole of the romantic movement, and the century and a half of poetry that followed it".[6]

The dilemma was only beginning to appear, however, in his second year: he was still able to write those poems of "virgin naturalism" in which his gift is most unmistakable. Between February and June 1929 he published nine poems (some very early), two in *The Venture*, and seven in *The Cambridge Review*. The technique is increasingly adventurous and far-ranging: new forms, no doubt talked over with Lehmann and put to him as a challenge, are explored, even the ballade (not very deftly, however). But the range of subject is as circumscribed, by choice, as it has been from the beginning. Except for the 'Ballade of the Dancing Shadows', which is manifestly an exercise ("Princess, if you should complain/I shall put it down to spite"), he is still "fiercely naturalist", an artist who observes:

> Into the north the tall black poplars rise,
> Already the straight upper limbs are bare.
> Like easy fishes, out of cold brown skies,
> The dropping redwings glide through ice-bright air.
> Winterstript, black, fine lines austere and spare,
> Colours half gone, and each green mouldered brown,
> Like stalk-grown depths of stagnant water, where
> Dead leaves decay as they come drifting down,
> In the wet winter days autumn's bright colours drown.
>
> (from 'The Hedge')

The most ambitious of the nine was 'Winter Movement', very close in subject to 'The Hedge', but a "formal ode" of almost 200 lines, wherein Julian moved, not always dexterously, through a variety of stanzaic and metrical forms—"the metre of two stanzas," his prefatory note explains, "imitated from Gerard Manley Hopkins", whom he and John Lehmann had recently discovered. Julian's ear was not really attuned to the peculiarities of sprung rhythm, and the chief effect of the discovery was to encourage a tendency, already latent, to use too many adjectives. And indeed much of the poem is turgid, prolix, even ungainly: it would appear that Julian thought too much about writing it. Somehow, among the complexities and ingenuities of technique, the true poetic impulse was lost, although there are two passages of great beauty, each describing the song of the thrush in winter, of which we quote the first:

> Clear cold,
> Unfold
> Long liquid note
> On note,

Cadence and trill
    That fill
A thrush's throat.
    Black spot
On neck and breast
Sienna apricot,
    Splash'd, shot
With olive-gold.
    At rest,
    Despite
The storm and night,
    Unstirred,
Lets fall the bright
    Music far-heard.

Yet if 'Winter Movement' falls short of being the major poem it was so clearly intended to be, there is no question of the seriousness and dedication it represents. Its publication in *The Venture* at the end of his second year marks a climax in Julian's life. He was now beyond question a poet, accepted as such by himself, by his friends, by Cambridge. Added to this, he was or had been a figure at the Union; he was an Apostle; he was a sportsman; he had his books and pictures, an old car which he liked to drive as though it were a racing car; and a large number of friends and acquaintances; he had even done well enough academically. Attractive, charming, intelligent, gifted, he was dangerously close to being one of those golden youths—Rupert Brooke is the prototype—whose years at the University are a kind of conquest, splendid but short-lived. One by one he had got from Cambridge the gifts it had to offer—summed up in his phrase "an extraordinary *douceur de vivre*". There remained only the discovery of women. That too, in the next year, Cambridge would provide.

In his 'Notes for a Memoir', Julian wrote, "There seem to have been three main divisions in my life: roughly, sensations, ideas and love-affairs." And at the conclusion of the 'Notes' (as published) he wrote: ". . . perhaps I should go back and pick up the story of my dealings with literature, and had also better make an effort to indicate, in outline at least, my early love-affairs. For it is exceeding hard to separate them from the rest of the story." There is the further difficulty that Julian's sensations, ideas and love-affairs seem to have been less clearly separate divisions in his life than he may have realized. Indeed the affairs are themselves such a tangle of ideas and sensations that they exemplify in yet another form the dilemma, or conflict, or problem, of Julian's life.

He had come up to Cambridge a convinced theoretical libertarian. In these matters the Bloomsbury attitude (one "tablet of the law" he would never question) was worldly, tolerant, indulgent but considerate, indifferent to convention, and very much a reaction against Victorian hypocrisy and cant. The initiatory experience that one would have thought (as his father surely did) an inevitable part of his season in Paris had not occurred; but he had brought away from his reading of Maupassant at that time "a Latin-sensual view of *amour*". The opportunity to translate this idea into action was not immediately evident in Cambridge. Now that he was away from Paris, he rather wished he were back. To Quentin, who was in Paris studying painting, he wrote, "I should be furiously jealous, if I weren't suffering from a profound melancholia which only a day's good beagling could cure . . . Three miles of Cambridgeshire fen, thrice weekly, are essential to one's sanity."[7] (On the whole, an Anglo-Saxon rather than a Latin notion—brought on perhaps by "profound melancholia". David Garnett, who lived near by and attended a meet of the University Beagles, offers a more cheerful glimpse of Julian as he then was: ". . . far bigger, noisier, and more raggedly dressed than any of his companions. He was bursting with happy excitement, absolutely unconscious of himself or that anyone present was caring about wearing the right clothes or doing the correct thing, and his primitive delight warmed them so they also forgot their fears . . . Late in the afternoon Julian turned up with his ragged clothes torn to tatters, which flapped about his white thighs. He put on some clothes of mine and lay panting and sighing after the luxurious enjoyment of so much exercise."[8]) He had contrived to fill almost every moment of his waking life: beagling, speaking at the Union, writing poetry, reading at random in literature and purposefully in history, talking long and late with friends. Still, he was curious about women, and in November, very man-of-the-worldly, he wrote to Quentin that he was "beginning an investigation of Newnham and Girton—purely scientific, for except as bottle snakes they are really not possible." These investigations came to nothing, not even a tentative experimental attachment, perhaps because he did not pursue them wholeheartedly, prompted more by curiosity than by a deep emotional need, and because he hadn't time enough, when so much else was attractive, to give to them. Still his virginal state bothered him, especially as he suspected that Quentin, younger than himself, might already have had a woman, and he had not. He brought the question to Aunt Virginia: did she *know* whether Quentin had actually had a mistress in Paris or Austria? She, of course, did not know, for Quentin was close-mouthed in these matters, to Julian's annoyance, and unlike Julian himself, who, as we shall see, was frank to the point of indiscretion. When he finally caught up, it was not at all as he had imagined it would be. The first of Julian's girls, 'A', an undergraduate at Girton, entered his life in his third year. Theirs was an intensely romantic relationship, very different from the idea of such things he had entertained since Paris. Soon he was writing to Quentin, describing himself as being in "a state of outrageous and to-the-rest-of-the-world-intolerable happiness".

This, the most enduring of his attachments, lasted a little more than two years. It was succeeded by others significantly like it: a pattern had been established. As David Garnett observed, "there was always some woman with her eyes full of him". One affair would end, another would begin. Some were of prolonged duration, few (at least in the early years) were entered into lightly or promiscuously or without considerable feeling, and in almost all of them, from the first to the last, there is a pattern of intense involvement followed by withdrawal. Against this must be set his affection for his mother, unvarying and in many ways the richest and finest thing in his life, yet a difficult obstacle to his emotional development. He never felt that he could find a woman who compared with her, and starting with that supposition he found that he never could. "Jane Austen's really the only woman, except Nessa," he wrote lightly to Playfair, "whom one can have much respect for—I mean of course intellectual respect."

Vanessa Bell was one of the beautiful women of her time; she was sensitive and cool and tranquil and imbued with the intuitive wisdom of the artist. Julian, obedient to an intuitive wisdom of his own, chose women who were very different from her, physically, temperamentally and in their intellectual style: they would be interested in history or science or politics, which certainly were not Vanessa's interests. (Her indifference to politics was legendary. Once at a dinner party, she was seated next to Mr Asquith, the then Prime Minister. Thinking that he looked familiar, but unable to place him, she began the conversation with "Are you interested in politics?") Then, either by chance, or, more likely, by an act of recognition, he was drawn to women who, however cool they might appear at first, would prove to be more erratic, more undisciplined, more emotional than his mother. In all his affairs there was an operatic aspect, which Julian thought he disliked, but almost certainly unconsciously encouraged. He was attractive to them, more lovable than loving perhaps, and his women fell very much in love with him, more than he wished ultimately, and they asked for more than he was prepared or able to give of himself, and it was necessary to get free. This, with appropriate variations, was the pattern.

In the first attachment, of course, simply by virtue of its being the first, there was no pattern: everything was new, one discovery after another. In love, he was in "a state of outrageous and to-the-rest-of-the-world-intolerable happiness", yet as much in the world as ever: all the activities and preoccupations of his second year were continued unabated in the third. Love, like poetry and philosophy and politics, was simply another aspect of the total idea of himself. Now that it was happening, he could not have been more pleased; but he did not mean to allow this passionate attachment to dominate—that way led to the romantic heresy.

The preceding spring he had spent his vacation alone at the family house in Cassis. In a letter to John Lehmann, he wrote of "the most incredibly romantic views, with hills, pines, sea, sunsets and distant mountains. Yet the whole affair done in the best grave, sober, French classical style, laid out by Cézanne, with the ghost of Racine at his elbow. So I get the best of both worlds, to say nothing of first-rate French cooking and red wine."[9] He was still at a time of his life when he really did believe he could have the best of both worlds, indeed of all worlds: everything was delicately in balance. Then, almost at once, the scales were heavily weighted in favour of the classic disciplines. The romantic, "the non-rational intuitive side of his nature" (John Lehmann's phrase), was to be controlled, suppressed, denied expression until almost the very end of his life.

The process begins in his poetry (afterwards in his affairs), and there is a concatenation of themes and circumstances that must be kept in mind if one is to understand how it came about: the dislike of modernism; the disapproval of obscurity; the commitment to the rationalism of his elders; the Apostolic preference for abstract ideas; the shift, at the end of his second year, from history to literature. Bloomsbury (especially Strachey) had always had a fondness for the eighteenth century; Julian went a giant step further and became an ardent enthusiast, ready to wage war. His premises were simple: twentieth-century modernism originated in, or resulted in, obscurity; nineteenth-century romanticism exalted the impalpable and irrational; eighteenth-century classicism was clear, precise and disciplined: in its enlightenment a forerunner of Bloomsbury, and in its technique a model to emulate. Romanticism was the enemy. "Above all, we ought to clear our minds of all poeticality," he wrote to Lehmann in the summer of 1929. "Julia's petticoat or the Rape of the Lock are better subjects at the present day than the grand simplicities, Love and Birth and Death, Heaven and the giant wars and all the rest of that old curiosity shop. Down with the romantics, both deluded and disillusioned." Thus he argued, and there perhaps he ought to have stopped. But his admiration for the eighteenth century led him to believe that the heroic couplet, that neat pair of ten-syllabled lines joined by a rhyme, was still the ideal vehicle for the expression of ideas in verse, as it had been for Dryden and Pope, encouraging one to be apothegmatic, antithetical, allegorical and transparent. This notion began to shape his practice as a poet in his own place and time. Lehmann grew alarmed: "I think there is something to be said for taking *certain* 18th century writers as *models*, as a counterbalance to Romantic licence and exaggeration. But it would be disastrous I think to *imitate* them."[10] Julian, however, was too caught up in his enthusiasm to be dissuaded.

> Timid, I venture on a doubtful field
> The heaviest weapon in our verse to wield

Presume with Dryden's couplet to engage
The wild philosophers in all their rage.

These are the opening lines of his first published exercise in the 'new' style: an eight-page assemblage of heroic couplets, which appeared in *The Venture* in February 1930. 'An Epistle on the Subject of the Ethical and Aesthetic Beliefs of Herr Ludwig Wittgenstein (Doctor of Philosophy) to Richard Braithwaite, Esq., M.A.' contains rather more ideas than poetry—the couplets are not so elegantly managed as to justify their revival. It is at its best as comic invective, at its weakest when Julian opposes to the notions of the Viennese philosopher then resident in Cambridge some notions of his own. Predictably, he declares his allegiance to

Good Sense and Reason; for the rest I hope
Voltaire had owned them, and adorned them Pope:
The rational Common Sense, the easy rule,
That marked for centuries the Cambridge school.

Perhaps the most disheartening moment comes somewhat later in the poem when Bloomsbury's cardinal philosophical principle is translated and trivialized in the diction and style of the eighteenth century:

If further you should ask, I take my stand
On an old creed, that all can understand,
Well knowing we this truth shall certain find
"Value resides alone in States of Mind."

As clever undergraduate mimicry, this is creditable enough; as the 'new' style of a young poet of authentic talent, it is downright ominous.

What is puzzling about this descent into the manner of the eighteenth century is that Julian was highly conscious of the problem of style. He knew that style was not something to put on and take off like a peruke, but an integral part of the poetic process. Only three months before he had stirred up something of a controversy in *The Cambridge Review* when he attacked a book of verse then just published and long since forgotten. While he found in it "a great deal of metrical skill and a surprising fancy", he complained that "too many of these poems are versified letters to *The Times*, an expression of the prejudices of a middle-aged, vaguely mystical reactionary". And he concluded: "His verses are valueless, because not being a man of genius, he cannot invent a new technique, while what he has inherited is utterly decayed."[11] The moral would seem clear enough.

The 'Epistle' was Julian's most ambitious effort in his third year, and it was followed in the next (and final) number of *The Venture* by his 'Essay on Poetic Obscurity', almost as though he intended to justify, or to explain, his 'new' procedures. In the early autumn he had been represented by two poems in his 'old' manner, descriptive nature pieces, in *Cambridge Poetry 1929*. (This was the first appearance of an annual collection of undergraduate poets, Experimenters and Venturers alike, offered as a counterpart to *Oxford Poetry*, but which proved to be less durable: only one further number appeared, in 1930. The publishers were Leonard and Virginia Woolf at the Hogarth Press.) Here, and in similar enterprises in the future, it was Julian's misfortune not to stand out among the company. His two poems have admirable passages, but they are lesser work; and F. R. Leavis, in a favourable review of the volume in *The Cambridge Review*, quite rightly reserved his warmest praise for Empson and Eberhart.[12] To discover Julian at his best one must read him in his first book, *Winter Movement*, which Chatto and Windus would publish the next autumn, a few months after the close of his undergraduate career. Since all the poems it contains were written by the end of the first team of his third year—that is, before the publication of the 'Epistle'—and since it includes some of the earliest attempts in the 'new' style, it seems proper to describe its contents here, and to defer until somewhat later an account of its reception.

The book, with its dedicatory stanzas 'To Richard Jefferies' ("You are our master . . ."), consists of twenty-seven poems, some very early, but the major portion written during his first two years at Cambridge, among them 'Brumaire', 'Vendémiaire', 'Frimaire', 'The Hedge', 'Winter Movement'. The intention, as described in the dedicatory poem, is

> To catch those instants in a net
>   Of words; those minutes, crystal clear,
> Which the mind can never forget
>   When all the world stood bright and near.

And indeed, in all but the latest of these poems there is brightness and nearness, a remarkable clarity of seeing and hearing: the consequence, it would seem, of Julian's determination not to allow sentiment or conceit or preconception to distort what he describes. There is 'The Goldfinch in the Orchard':

> In the top branches of the dying pear,
> Almost invisible, despite the bar
> Of yellow gold across his wings,
> And his bright crimson crest,
> The long, sweet whistle carrying far,
> High perched, he sings . . .

There are 'The Moths', glimpsed in an autumn twilight:

> Among the flowers, soft blurs of misty white
> Poised steady on their slow, vibrating flight . . .
>
> The darkness deepens still. Clouds hide the sky.
> And on the pond the moorhens splash and cry
> With their wild voices of an unknown world.
> Crunching the flints, a shepherd passes by.
>
> The smoking lantern throws its moving rays
> Across the orchard, and the warm light plays
> On all the silver undersides of leaves
> Of pear and apple trees beside the ways.
>
> The lantern closes, leaves an instant's dark
> Then lights the brown beads on the pear tree's bark
> And the drugged moths, with softly quivering wings
> Or drowsy, like some lichened knot or mark . . .

Even when he comes indoors, which he does only once, in 'Still Life', there is the same clarity and detachment. Presumably it is the kitchen at Charleston, that house of painters, that is being described as though it were itself a painting:

> Plain, scrub-grained, angular, bare deal,
> Littered with Wednesday's groceries
> And meat, stands the kitchen table.

Enamel basin, sink, brass tap,
Dish-cloth, white plates, circling small flies.
The kitchen tap leaks, drip, drip, drip.

A warm grey afternoon. Upon
The window-sill drowned wasps in jars.
Black range and grate are cold as stone.

Poured from the basket they were in,
Straw criss-cross, bellying, handle tied
With string, dark shadow powdered green,

The apples piled, one rolled astray,
The others mass, wet light, round shade,
Where in a heap confused they lie.

A prism's angles curved and squeezed
In an indented globe. The round
Sides black bright red to white-green washed.

In white glazed dish, a square cup flat,
Five eggs before, below them stand,
Cool, heavy, porous, brown and white.

In many ways the most remarkable poem in the book is 'Marsh Birds Pass Over London'. An 'irregular ode' of more than a hundred lines, it is very consciously an attempt to get beyond the limitations of the descriptive poems Julian had until now been writing. Unlike them, it is a poem based on an idea (suggested to him by an episode in Jefferies' novel *After London*) and it is meant to express an idea; but the idea was not at odds with Julian's poetic imagination and sensibility, it was oddly consonant with the "non-rational intuitive side of his nature", and it could be bodied forth in a true poem. In its opposition of the world of man and the world of nature, the one transient, the other enduring, the idea takes its place among the "grand simplicities". Yet it is translated into a prophetic vision of remarkable intensity.

High over London—
So far and high
That none can see them, few can catch and know
Their wailing cry

—fly the wild birds of the marshes: Curlew, Whimbrel, Grey and Golden Plover, Lapwing and Dotterel. Their cry is a prophecy of fear:

The Seven Whistlers, as they fly,
Tell of who follows presently.
Loud warning all that they beware
Of armies hastening in the air,
That sweep in with a droning flight,
Continually, by day and night.
All through the night great houses flare,
The tattered walls that the bombs tear
Seem broken tins and jars left bare
In muddy sewers, when the sea
Ebbs from the tide-swept estuary.

There follows a lament for the ruined city:

Fallen, fallen and fallen,
The city fallen and gone.
The marsh birds' desolate calling
Comes menacing from the sky,
The city is falling, falling.

A final apocalyptic vision shows

Grey clouds from the north-east,
Where the river mouth is wide;
The waters piled in a tattered hill
Sweep in on the spring tide . . .
Each ruined bridge comes tumbling down,
The waves pour through each gap
That bombs have torn in great stone dykes,
Steadily rise and lap
Against what doors and window-panes
Men had the time to close,
Cascades down every flight of steps,
And still the flooding grows . . .

The tides sweep in and out again,
  Fret and grind at the walls
Already shattered: splashing
In the spreading marsh each falls.
A muddy island, small and low,
Where purple, tall sea asters grow
    On the columns of Saint Paul's . . .

Whether read as darkly romantic prophecy or as a fable of human experience, 'Marsh Birds Pass Over London' is a considerable achievement; and in its fusion of nature and nightmare a reminder that "the black blood of the Stephens" was not only a part of Julian's inheritance but an essential element in his poetic gift. Yet it was precisely against this element that he steeled himself. By the middle of the third year he could write to Quentin, "I feel that the classical reaction is at length getting under way", and to Lehmann, the preceding summer, he had written, "Clarity, precision and above all common sense are the real virtues of poetry." Yet he failed to recognize that the qualities he admired were already present in the poems he had been writing. Dissatisfied with merely descriptive poems—"If one means to do anything more than describe—I am sure one ought to"—he left unexplored the very real possibilities for development from a poem like 'Marsh Birds Pass Over London'. Instead, beguiled by the notion of a countermodernist offensive conducted in classical style, he began a programme of eighteenth-century imitations. Its early results comprise the final pages of *Winter Movement*. Only one example, 'Winter Trees', need be given here:

Gay-decked with flowers the trees arose,
Fair maidens, from their sheets of snows,
The blossoms' ribband, and green leaves' light lace,
Flung bashfully, in spring, round each sweet face.
Then, as the sun hotter and higher grew,
Changed airy robes for staider fashions new,
Full-leaved in summer, dully green,
Wore a Victorian crinoline.
This, too, cast off, startle whoe'er beholds
With gleaming panoply of reds and golds:

Their autumn fashion-plates ablaze
With warmer colours for cold days.
Now, in the winter naked, they're most fair,
Most loved, like other nymphs, when they stand bare.

The antithesis of his earlier poems—which, as John Lehmann has said, created "a new kind of poetic 'stuff', the precipitate of an unusual and difficult, but exciting way of experiencing the objective world"—this trivial and sentimental verbal conceit is evidence enough of the extent of his misapprehension.

The first attachment was rather more romantic than neo-classic. When Julian, in mid-winter, wrote to Quentin, "I find the difficulty of achieving classical restraint and serenity is very great, when you are bubbling over with the wildest metaphysical fancies," he was referring to his literary dilemma. Yet the remark might have applied equally well to the conduct of his emotions. Especially when he added, "I feel very sure of my central thesis—that the only hope is the Golden Mean and good sense." What this meant, in a practical way, was that one fell in love, but not to the point of irrevocable commitment. And in this early stage of the relationship, when he was outrageously happy, 'A' herself seems to have been sensible enough and understanding enough—that is, she understood Julian—not to press for what she knew he was not prepared to give. Thus the Golden Mean was maintained.

In June of that year, 1930, he received his B.A. A period in his life—perhaps the happiest—was at an end. What was he to do next? He had almost too many pursuits to choose from—from poetry to philosophy, from academia to journalism, from politics to criticism—and this very richness of possibilities, a reflection of the successes of his undergraduate career, would dog the rest of his life. He seemed unable to commit himself definitely and wholeheartedly to one particular pursuit, and would move along various paths, either not finding them satisfactory or for some reason or other being deflected from them. In the autumn of 1930 his first book of poems was to be published, but not even then did he choose to think of himself as a poet, *only a poet*: there was so much else to be. (His dissatisfaction with poetry, his own in particular, would continue to deepen as he became increasingly involved in reactions to the decade of the 1930s, to the poverty and depression that surrounded him in England, and, in counterpoint to them, the pleasures and complexities of his own life.) But what, in particular, was he to do next? More or less for want of something better, he decided to continue on at Cambridge, pursuing his interest in Pope, and he received a research studentship from King's. The solution, though temporary, had much to recommend it: it meant, for one thing, that the romantic attachment could be continued on approximately the same terms as before, for 'A' would still be in Cambridge. He himself, in a position now to satisfy his passion for the countryside, would take a cottage in Elsworth, some miles distant from the turmoil of the University. The prospect was pleasing. Yet inevitably there was a sense of anti-climax: the golden undergraduate years were finished; the friends were dispersed. In September, from Charleston, he wrote to John Lehmann, who was travelling abroad:

> The fifth symphony is going on, much against Clive's will, but really just now Beethoven is the only musician I can endure, for I'm suffering from—not melancholy but black blood, the black blood of the Stephens, I suppose, that Virginia talks of, and only hardness, strength, tragedy are endurable. In fact I've had an overdose of romance and beauty. Cures: Beethoven and ten mile walks in big boots, and the slaughter of innocent birds . . .
>
> I've got to save my soul if it's possible. I've just woken up to the fact that effectively I've done nothing except indulge in erotic emotion this last two years. The last really respectable piece of work I did was Winter Movement—Wittgenstein [the 'Epistle'] was all right in its way, but not good enough. The trouble is partly that one—I, I mean—needs friends, or at least fairly intimate acquaintances to talk to, and a mistress to sleep with—the latter I find it impossible to do without now. I spend far too much time thinking about the subject. But both take a fearful lot of time and energy, and leave one incapable of writing well. One's friends—mine, at least—are worth the expenditure of energy. But also, they can be dropped and recovered to a certain extent. One can see them—particularly when one feels at all at ease—and yet go on writing. But a

mistress involves . . . the devil of a lot of energy, besides taking up time with her presence, and being a constant preoccupation away. And really, a great deal of the summer, I was going about in a dream, without attending to anything properly, which is a wretched state of mind, for which I'm still suffering. In the end, I think I shall have to give up being romantic about love, and turn into a common sense sensualist.[13]

But a month later, writing to Lehmann again, this time from the cottage at Elsworth, he was in his more usual high spirits:

. . . Then there's ['A'], two or three days a week—a very happy relationship now. Cambridge and conversation when I feel inclined. And work . . . I contemplate a satire—Cambridge 1930—but that's dubious . . . D. has been made dean—he'll be made vice-provost before long. Shades of the combination room about the golden lad . . .

and so on, very gaily. Yet, towards the end, an equivocal note is sounded:

Here am I, solidly attached to monogamous ['A'], ready to start affairs, if I were free, with half-a-dozen young women. Not of course, that they'd be successful, but at least I shouldn't languish in despair . . . Perhaps it's only that success and security make one feel that all adventures are worth trying.[14]

The first 'romantic period' of the relationship, when he had been in a state of outrageous happiness, had given way to a quasi-domesticity, which he truly enjoyed—but only for two or three days a week. Here, as in other parts of his life, there were strings and reservations (fantasies, it would seem, that made him "languish in despair"), a reluctance or an inability to commit himself wholeheartedly—to 'A' now, and afterwards to 'B', to 'C' . . .

Rather surprisingly, he made no mention to Lehmann of an event that must have been much upon his mind at this time: the approaching publication of *Winter Movement*. He may have decided to appear unconcerned—one possible strategy for a young writer—and thus appear undisturbed if the book should fail. But there is evidence to suggest that these were weeks of anxiety. He wrote to Lehmann:

> For the first time in my life, I fainted on getting up out of a chair. Curious, and unpleasant. I shall never make a man of action—I live too much on my nerves. Or at least, not a great one. I daresay I could lead a cavalry charge, or fly an aeroplane, but I couldn't sit still for days under fire.[15]

At last the day came. It came and went in silence. Then the letters began to trickle in, rather fewer than he might have expected, there was a brief notice in a Sunday paper. One of the first letters he received was from John Lehmann, who had just returned from Paris:

> Here I am, immensely glad to be back, in time to see the last act of an English Autumn. *And* in time to see the publication of *Winter Movement*: I have seen a copy, and I think it looks admirable—Chatto have not failed you. I re-read the first twenty-six pages—to which I am deeply devoted—on the spot. You must let me know what reviews there are—keep them for me. I have not seen anything myself yet, but the Lords of Reviewdom take their time about poetry—if they condescend to notice it at all. I must say I think in some ways Keats was rather lucky to have so many important pages of abuse devoted to him.[16]

Julian answered at once. His letter was very odd in the circumstances. The larger part of it was a thoughtful and straightforward statement of his poetic beliefs. Without pausing to invoke the example of the eighteenth century, or to prescribe the use of the heroic couplet, he set forth a view of poetry that prefigured much of the work that would be written in the 1930s, although he himself would play only a peripheral role in the coming movement:

> I do believe that poetry must interest the common reader by talking about human beings and about events that he is acquainted with, or of a kind similar to those he is acquainted with. I believe we must abandon everything fantastic, distant and other-worldly . . . concentrate on the natural and the reasonable. Equally, I begin to believe that poetic beauty must never be pursued for itself, or sought anywhere but in the natural life and events of our subject matter. I mean, we must not strain after beautiful effects, and be for ever opening magic

> casements and journeying to Xanadu, but discover beauty accidentally.

Only at the end of the letter, and then with an offhandedness that failed to conceal his true feelings, did he mention his book:

> Winter M. had a little puff in the Observer—all so far. Peter [Lucas] will do it for the Review, [James] Reeves, I think, for the Granta. Blunden wrote me a charming letter, and so did Morgan Forster and Angelica. I've sold 44 copies—more than I expected.[17]

Lehmann, of course, was right: reviewers do take their time about poetry, especially about first collections, and *Winter Movement*, over the next several months, would be occasionally noticed, temperately on the whole, but at least not unfavourably. Then, in February 1932 there was a belated act of recognition. Michael Roberts, in his 'Notes on English Poets' written for *Poetry* (Chicago), linked *Winter Movement* with Auden's *Poems* as "the outstanding achievement of the younger men in 1930". But this was too long after the event, and at too great a distance from it—who in England would have seen the tribute?—to mean as much to Julian as it would have earlier: by then his expectations had cooled. At home, from the quarter where praise (one feels) would have been most welcome, there was rather less than he might have expected. Those who adhere to the theory of Bloomsbury as a conspiracy dedicated to self-advancement will find no support in this instance. His elders were admirably restrained: there was no hint of a public or subterranean campaign to bring on the next generation. One has the feeling that, dote on Julian though they did, they were not quite prepared (except for David Garnett) to take him as seriously as a poet as he deserved. After his death, Mrs Woolf wrote: "This is the one thing I regret in our relationship: that I might have encouraged him more as a writer."

Since childhood Julian had always been vulnerable to the opinions of others. Lacking the singlemindedness of vocation so evident, for example, in the young Stephen Spender, he could easily persuade himself that there were other, more important things for him than poetry, and strike out in new directions. Encouragement from his elders might conceivably have determined him to continue in his original course; yet it is quite possible that he had already gone as far in that course as he was able to go. *Winter Movement* is not one of those first books of verse that are more exciting in their promise than in their accomplishment: it is admirable in itself, a self-contained achievement. Michael Roberts, having declared, quite justly, that, "Mr Bell infuses a new vigour into English pastoral poetry . . . he can make poetry where the Edwardians made dull verse," concluded: "[his] technique is so appropriate to his chosen subject that probably he is too careful a craftsman to fail in any field he may attempt, but his strict application makes it impossible to forecast his development."

In the summer of 1929, writing to Lehmann, Julian had prescribed "a settled and orderly life in which certainty and precision rule". In that tranquil summer, which might be compared to the summer of 1914 as the end of a period—thereafter one would live and think differently—a life such as Julian prescribed was, if one wanted it, still available. Eliot might see the post-war world as a waste land, but it depended on one's point of view: the 1920s could be an exceedingly pleasant time to live, especially if one had come of age in that careless decade, and were not haunted (as one's elders were) by all that had followed upon the summer of 1914. Although he himself thought he was expressing a "thoroughly 18th century point of view", Julian was in fact being very much a young man of the late 1920s when he told Lehmann that there were "plenty of interesting and pleasant things left to do and write about without the Romantics' illusions. They might learn with Candide to cultivate the Garden of Epicurus." Then, with an assurance that recalls Keynes writing to Strachey in 1906, he concluded: "Our elders, whose romantic illusions were smashed for them by the war, have an excuse for writing like Tom Eliot and Huxley. But we, who have never believed falsehoods, have no need to be shocked at truth."[18]

That was in the late 1920s. In the 1930s one began to live and think differently. Even if one had wanted "a settled and orderly life in which certainty and precision rule", it would have seemed, as an ideal, an anachronism, and as a reality difficult to obtain. A famous poem of the period—by Stephen Spender—which appeared in the anthology *New Signatures*, begins

> Oh young men oh young comrades
> it is too late now to stay in those houses
> your fathers built

and John Lehmann's poem, 'Travel Bureau', which was published in *Cambridge Poetry 1930*, concludes

> No track returns through time to what has been,
> No wagon-lit is scheduled to the place
> Where twigs begin to cloud with whorls of green
> And purple flags are bursting from their case.

On the whole, it was a time, figuratively speaking, when one was more likely to stand at the barricades ("advance to rebel"—Spender) than to cultivate the garden of Epicurus. Julian, like Spender and Lehmann, a contributor to *New Signatures*, objected to what he considered the "romanticism" of their position, yet he was himself a man of the 1930s: his life, almost until its end, was unsettled and disorderly, uncertain and imprecise.

One sees him in this period, between 1930 and 1935, trying on, as it were, a variety of roles. Given his interest in poetry and politics, and his ability to practise both, he might have played an important role in the literary life of the decade, if he had wished to. With *Winter Movement* he had achieved a small but firm reputation, more than firm enough for a first step; he might have gone much further. But he did not know precisely what it was he wanted yet, and he refused to commit himself to a position just because he might have it. He remained in Cambridge, writing poetry *and* preparing to write about Pope, on the fringes rather than at the centre of literary life. The literary nucleus of *The Venture* went off in other directions. Lehmann, whom he may have regarded as a disciple and certainly regarded as an ally in their own, Cambridge-based 'movement', became more and more in himself a literary figure, and in part the literary figure that Julian might have become. Towards the end of 1930, Lehmann had submitted his first book of poems, *A Garden Revisited*, to Leonard and Virginia Woolf at the Hogarth Press, and not only did Julian's aunt and uncle want the book, but also John as well, to come to work for the Press as an apprentice-editor-partner. "I expect you know substantially what the offer of the Woolves was going to be," he wrote to Julian. "I was surprised when they made it to me—on Friday, at tea, when I met them both for the first time, and thought them most charming, Virginia very beautiful . . ."[19] Thus it was that Lehmann, in his own right, entered Julian's world of Bloomsbury, and he brought with him some of the despised Oxford poets—most particularly Stephen Spender, who became a great friend of Virginia's.

The first significant meeting between Oxford and Cambridge poetry occurred during the Christmas holidays of 1930, when Lehmann's sister Rosamond brought Spender to Fieldhead (the Lehmann family home on the Thames). The two young poets walked by the river, and Spender talked, with the utmost candour, about life and poetry, and Lehmann listened, and was a good deal more impressed than he thought it diplomatic to admit to Julian. To him he wrote: "Romantic of the wildest sort I have ever met (you would have ground your teeth, I fancy)."[20] In fact, with that flair for 'new writing' that was to make him a commanding figure on the English literary scene in the next three decades, he had recognized an authentic poet.

Appropriately enough, Lehmann, as a Cambridge man who had established a connection with the Oxford group, was instrumental in presenting the new young poets to the world. Soon after the publication of *A Garden Revisited*, he tells us in his autobiography, he received a letter "from someone I had never heard of before, called Michael Roberts". (Roberts, himself an interesting figure of the 1930s, as a critic and poet, was a poor boy who had finally managed to go to Trinity College, Cambridge, in the mid-1920s, and at the time of his meeting with Lehmann, was a mathematics master at a London grammar school.) "He wrote that he admired the poems," Lehmann continues, "had been watching my work for some time, and asked if I would care to come in to see him in his flat one evening to discuss them. An irresistibly flattering call for a young author: a few days later, after dinner, I knocked at his door . . ."

> We plunged into talk about modern poetry at once, and I discovered that he had read all my contemporaries, and what

was more had an idea that they belonged together more closely, in spite of the wide apparent differences, than I, in the middle of the *mêlée* which Julian made so dramatic, had detected. The more he talked, the more flattered I felt at the thought of belonging to a revolutionary movement in the arts, and the more my fresh publishing ardour was inflamed by the possibility, which began to grow in my mind, of presenting all of us in some way as a *front*, so that the public, notoriously sluggish in its appreciation of individual poets, should be obliged to sit up and take notice . . . During the next few days I talked it over with Leonard and Virginia, proposed an anthology of poetry by all the young writers whose names had been mentioned that evening, got their sympathy and provisional support, and then wrote to Michael Roberts and suggested he should edit it for us and write an introduction.

The project that was eventually to take shape as *New Signatures* was on.[21]

The book would be a new departure, and the question was whether Julian would join the train, or remain behind in the garden of Epicurus (or Charleston). He was, of course, one of the young writers who had been mentioned that night at Michael Roberts's—the others were Auden, Spender and Day Lewis, from Oxford; Empson, Eberhart and Lehmann, from Cambridge; and two poets Lehmann had met since coming to London, A. S. J. Tessimond, and William Plomer. Julian was not likely to be happy about joining any group that was not of his own making, and Lehmann, when he wrote to him about the anthology—"We want to know at once whether you'll contribute"—made a point of saying, "it will definitely be a flag for 'us' to rally round." Unfortunately, he cancelled out the effectiveness of the point (so far as Julian was concerned) by adding, "Spender, Auden, Day Lewis will be asked among others."[22] This was not at all an "us" Julian would recognize: he wrote Lehmann "a long growling letter" about what they had stood for hitherto and "the danger of condoning the heresies of Spender and Auden". Lehmann was understandably irritated, and on Christmas Eve he replied:

Thank you for your damned intransigent and intractable letter. I enclose a copy of the blurb for the book . . . which will show you how deeply you will commit yourself if you offer any poems to it. The net is meant to be wide, and naturally the poets are not expected to form a *school*—an idea totally ludicrous. Are we to expunge your name from that provisional list? I hope not—but your letter in tone might have been that of a French General arriving in the Ruhr, 1923.[23]

The blurb read:

These new poems and satires by W. H. Auden, Julian Bell, Cecil Day Lewis, Stephen Spender, A. S. J. Tessimond, and others, are a challenge to the pessimism and intellectual aloofness which has marked the best poetry of recent years. These young poets rebel only against those things which they believe can and must be changed in the postwar world, and their work in consequence has a vigour and width of appeal which has long seemed lacking from English poetry.[24]

This seemed inoffensive enough, and Julian prepared to capitulate. First, though, he was determined to make his own position absolutely clear. He wrote to Lehmann, and enclosed a letter to Michael Roberts for Lehmann to read and hand on.

To Lehmann: . . . I don't know Roberts, and I want to be fairly sure of escaping a nonsense blurb of preface. I don't quite like the look of things from the list you showed me . . . I believe in facts and logic and in nothing else, and about poetry I believe most firmly that what is needed is the most extreme 18th century domination of the intellect over the emotions—and about life and politics too [And so forth . . .]

To Roberts: . . . as to the anthology, I have no lyrics that I want to publish, but I have two satires . . . *But* I should like, before committing myself, to know what line the Editor intends to take in his preface, and what poets are to be included . . . I believe in common-sense, wit and clarity. But all the rest of your group seem to accept a fundamentally romantic view of poetry—in Auden's case perhaps with a Lawrentian tinge . . . Empson would probably agree with me in thinking Pope a better poet than Keats, but would the rest of your group if they were being sincere?

Lehmann was too loyal and discreet a friend to hand on this challenge to Roberts, who, as an outsider, might have been less ready than he to indulge or understand the 'French General' tone. In any event, Julian, having stated a point, felt that he had gained it: he allowed himself to be published in the book, and so became, albeit with much reluctance, a member of the *New Signatures* group.

The slim blue volume, No. 24 in the Hogarth Living Poets Series, which had caused so much fuss to assemble, came out in the spring of 1932, created a mild sensation then, and has since been taken to mark the beginning, the formal opening, of the poetic movement of the 1930s. In a sense it was merely a continuation, a sort of joint issue, of *Oxford* and *Cambridge Poetry*, for only two of the nine contributors, Plomer and Tessimond, had not attended one or other of the Ancient Universities. Several had already published books of verse—Lehmann, Day Lewis (*Transitional Poem* and *From Feathers to Iron*) and Plomer, in the Hogarth Series. Auden's *Poems* had come out (from Faber, where T. S. Eliot reigned, and played, like the Woolfs, an important part in sponsoring the new movement) in 1930, and had had "an overwhelming effect". In that year too came *Winter Movement*, admired but not to be an influence, and Spender's *Twenty Poems*—his first "public edition": the important *Poems* would not be brought out by Faber until 1933. And all the contributors, even those whose first books were still two or three years in the future, had published in periodicals: *The Listener*, *The Adelphi*, *This Quarter* and *The Criterion* (edited by Eliot). In short, they were not entirely unknown and unrecognized, nor was *New Signatures* quite the succession of discoveries that its legend credits it with being. But Lehmann was entirely right in his intuition that the public, "sluggish in its appreciation of individual poets", might be "obliged to sit up and take notice" if they were presented as "a *front*".

> The reviewers were impressed [Lehmann sums up], the public bought it and there was a general feeling in the air that Something had happened in poetry. We even had to print a second impression within a few weeks. Several of the poets were already known individually; but the little book was like a

> searchlight suddenly switched on to reveal that, without anyone noticing it, a group of skirmishers had been creeping up in a concerted movement of attack. Some of us were, perhaps, as surprised as the public to find that we formed part of a secret foray . . . however, an impression had been made . . . that no amount of reservations or protestations on the part of individual contributors could efface, and from that moment we were all lumped together as the '*New Signatures* poets'.[25]

It would be convenient, writing in the 1960s, to adopt a 'revisionist' stance, and describe *New Signatures* as simply a collection of verse, some of it remarkably fine, by nine talented young poets of the 1930s. Here are Auden's "Though aware of our rank and alert to obey orders" and "Doom is dark and deeper than any sea-dingle"; and Empson's "You were amused to find you too could fear/'The eternal silence of the infinite spaces' " and his 'Camping Out' ("And now she cleans her teeth into the lake"); and Spender's 'The Express' ("After the first powerful plain manifesto") and "I think continually of those who were truly great". Can one find a 'group theory' that will really account for them? How, as a 'group', do these poets of the 1930s differ from the poets of the previous decade? Roberts, as we have seen, was aiming beyond a mere sampling of excellence: he did have an idea of the sort of poetry that he wanted for his anthology, and of the direction he felt poetry ought to take in the coming decade. But his Preface is too veiled and generalized to provide satisfactory answers to either question. He begins by saying: "new knowledge and new circumstances have compelled us to think and feel in ways not expressible in the old language at all. The poet who, using an obsolete technique, attempts to express his whole conception is compelled to be partly insincere or content with slovenly thought and sentimental feeling." (Cf. Julian in *The Cambridge Review*: ". . . he cannot invent a new technique, while what he has inherited is utterly decayed".) Roberts continues: "A poet cannot expect to write well . . . unless he is abreast of his own times, honest with himself, and uses a technique sufficiently flexible to express precisely those subtleties of thought and feeling in which he differs from his predecessors." This is so inarguable as to be platitudinous, and as appropriate to the poetry of the

1920s as to that of the 1930s. Roberts is more 'thirtyish' when he advances the notion of the poet as a 'leader'—to lead, he must be understood; therefore "a poem must be comprehensible . . . The poems in this book represent a clear reaction against esoteric poetry in which it is necessary for the reader to catch each recondite allusion." (Cf. Julian, at any and all points.) And he is 'thirtyish' too in his concern for a 'popular poetry'. But his major emphases are given to matters of technique: he notices (correctly) that the poets of *New Signatures* are returning to the older forms and disciplines, turning from the irregular cadence of free verse to explore "the possibilities of counterpointed rhythm". He also claims, with a fine disregard for the achievements of the 1920s, that *his* poets have solved a "major problem": how "to use the material presented by modern civilisation . . . Mr Auden's *Poems* and Mr Day Lewis's *From Feathers to Iron* were, I think, the first books in which imagery taken from contemporary life consistently appeared as the natural and spontaneous expression of the poet's thought and feeling."[26] Yet it is hard to believe that Mr Eliot, writing:

> At the violet hour, when the eyes and back
> Turn upward from the desk, when the human engine waits
> Like a taxi throbbing waiting

is not as "natural and spontaneous" and as "contemporary" as any thirties poet. Roberts's difficulty, one feels, is that he is attempting to define differences in terms of technique rather than content. In this, perhaps, he is too 'twentyish'. The crucial point of difference between the writers of the 1930s and their immediate predecessors has more to do with history (content) than with literature (technique). "Perhaps, after all," Spender decided some twenty years later, in his autobiography *World Within World*:

> Perhaps, after all, the qualities which distinguished us from the writers of the previous decade lay not in ourselves, but in the events to which we reacted. These were unemployment, economic crisis, nascent fascism, approaching war . . . The older writers were reacting in the twenties to the exhaustion and hopelessness of a Europe in which the old régimes were falling to pieces. We were a "new generation", but it took me some

> time to appreciate the meaning of this phrase. It amounted to meaning that we had begun to write in circumstances strikingly different from those of our immediate predecessors and that a consciousness of this was shown in our writing . . . We were the 1930s.[27]

Julian had contributed to *New Signatures* with the greatest reluctance: "I don't quite like the look of things . . ." Preoccupied with technique (rather like Roberts himself), he drew a firm line between himself and the other contributors, but as much as they he was a member of the 'new generation', reacting to events of the new decade: "unemployment, economic crisis . . . approaching war". The manner, however, was very much his own; or rather, his own as he had appropriated it from the eighteenth century. Roberts, not having seen the inflammatory note ("I have no lyrics that I want to publish") assumed that Julian would be sending pieces like those in *Winter Movement*, and wrote his Preface accordingly:

> [Mr Bell writes] of the English countryside in rhythms which show that for him it means no week-end cottage or funkhole from the town: his clear-cut delineations of landscape express neither jingoism nor sentimental affectation but a feeling for the land itself; a sentiment which, though local in its origins, leads to a sympathy with that same feeling in others, and to a love of the earth irrespective of place which is the opposite of militant nationalism.[28]

In fact, none of the three poems Julian submitted fits the description. The first, 'Still Life', a glimpse of an empty room at night and the landscape outside it, is cast to its disadvantage in couplets: it is minor work, less impressive, because more conventional in detail and in phrasing, than the poem of the same title which had appeared in *Winter Movement*. The second of the three, 'Tranquillity Recollected', is in his earlier manner—Mediterranean landscape evoked with a wealth of sensuous detail—and grew out of a happy visit he and 'A' had paid to the Charles Maurons in St Rémy. (A gifted critic and the translator of E. M. Forster, Mauron and his wife Marie were great friends of both the older and younger generation of Bloomsbury. They had the peculiar merit in Julian's case of taking him seriously on his own terms, something that did not always happen on home territory.)

His most ambitious contribution to *New Signatures* was the satire 'Arms and the Man', a fully-fledged example of Julian's later manner, embodying all of his notions of what a poem ought to be, and, as such, a kind of test case for them. Like the 'Epistle to Richard Braithwaite', it is written in Pope's (or Dryden's) couplets, but more dexterously than before, and the pace is unflagging throughout the poem's four hundred lines. (It occupied twelve pages, more than a tenth of the anthology; Julian's was the largest representation; fifteen pages in all; ten for Auden; nine for Spender; seven for Empson. Impact, however, did not prove commensurate with length.) The interest of the poem, it must be said, lies principally in its ideas, which proved to be more representative of the period than its technique. There is an epigraph that would appeal to the cynicism of a generation that had watched Ramsay MacDonald become Prime Minister in the new National government: Dr Johnson's "Patriotism is the last refuge of a scoundrel"; then, 'Arms and the Man I sing'; but Julian's tone thereafter is more Shavian than Virgilian.

The satire is wide-ranging: hardly a branch of the Establishment, Empire and State and Church, is allowed to escape. After a look at "Britain's glory":

> Whatever happens, we shall muddle through:
> We muddle out, when we have muddled in,
> And, if a war lasts long enough, we win . . .

he asks "But what's the use of war?":

> See, in reply, Lord Northcliffe's ghost appear,
> Deny mere facts, and tell us undismay'd
> "What is the good of war? It's good for trade."

Trade; and Prestige ("the helpful second cause/Of our prosperity, and fleet and wars") and Security:

> By armaments alone we sleep secure,
> Unless all nations are for war prepared,
> Within an instant, war will be declared . . .

For, as two mot'rists, insolently rich,
Race side by side, to die in the last ditch,
So, scarce one nation in the world will dare
To face the risk of anything but war:
Courage or common sense we vainly seek,
All to disarm too stupid or too weak . . .

Death's the essential: life and all its cares
Are less important than our future wars,
"Economy" employs each Press Lord's breath,
And what economy so great as death?

The realities of the depression haunt the poem, and call upon Julian's otherwise unused descriptive powers for its central passage:

Down the black streets, dark with unwanted coal
The harassed miners wait the grudging dole;
The sinking furnaces, their fires damped down,
Depress to poverty the hopeless town . . .
On every hand the stagnant ruin spreads,
And closed are shops and fact'ries, mines and sheds.
As one by one the farmers break and fail
And barns are emptied at the bankrupt's sale,
Mark from some hill, across the fertile weald,
The arable retreating field by field,
The waste advancing as the corn recedes
Where the lean bullocks chew the fallow weeds.
See rotting gates hang by the rusted catch,
The unstopped hedges, and the mouldered thatch,
The mildewed hay beneath the August rain,
The fly-pock'd turnips, and the shredded grain.
Thistles and brambles choke the sinking tracks,
And deep corruption rots the tumbling stacks.
Here, in a language all can understand,
See plainly told the history of our land.
In war or famine some could still grow fat,
The capit'list then prospered, and the rat:

But that great age is done: now comes the day
When, for their fathers' sins, the children pay;
Yet, not content with paying for the past,
We seek another war to match the last.

As Julian approaches his conclusion, he seems almost to be answering a question asked by Spender at the opening of one of his poems in *New Signatures*:

Who live under the shadow of a war
What can I do that matters?

Not long before this Julian had written to Lehmann, "I sometimes think we may have to take a hand in the politicians' dog-fight"; now, in 'Arms and the Man', he advises:

Strike then, and swiftly; if the end must come
May war, like charity, begin at home:
Do what we can, and use what power we have,
Confront the ruin, if we cannot save;
Nor leave the politicians to their trade,
To spread the idiot tangle they have made.

This is, as it were, the next-to-last word: the declaration of a believer in facts and logic, in the domination of the intellect over the emotions, in life, politics, and poetry. Surely rational men must see the *stupidity* of war? Yet at the very end of the poem (and how characteristic this is of Julian) there is an irruption of romantic fantasy, an apocalyptic vision of the future:

When war shall break across the world once more,
And force the ancient wilderness restore,
The arches crumble, and the column fall,
Through the high places the rough satyr call,
Empire, and State, and Church their turmoil cease,
And marsh and forest reassume their peace.

Julian, in a sort of filial, or perhaps grand-filial gesture, had intended to dedicate 'Arms and the Man' to Goldsworthy Lowes Dickinson, the philosopher, Apostle and friend to Bloomsbury, who was a prime mover behind the idea of the League of Nations, and whose books, such as *The International Anarchy* (1926), helped to shape the anti-war thinking of the war-generation itself, and that of the 1920s. One might presume that he would have welcomed this gesture of affiliation from the younger generation: in fact, it made him uneasy. 'Arms and the Man' seems to have been much too forceful for gentle Goldie. Pleased though he was to discover "that there is at least one young man who hates war", he wrote to Julian: "I feel that your poem will be nothing but provocative and offensive to every kind of man that reads it. You will reply that you mean it to be. Yes, but I am thinking of the main thing, what will tend to change opinion about war . . . I regret now every escape of irritation, satire and rage which I have let escape, and, to be honest, I feel that, if I accept this dedication from you, I shall be supposed to endorse your methods. Will you understand and forgive, my dear, and perhaps reconsider the whole poem? For I feel it in my bones that if you publish it you may regret it later."[29]

Reading this letter, so tepid and so temporizing, one can understand the burst of irritation that prompted Virginia Woolf to note in her diary: "what a thin whistle of hot air Goldie lets out through his front teeth".[30] And perhaps it was just as well that Dickinson declined the dedication, and so kept the youth of *New Signatures* uncontaminated by connection with the older generation. When the collection appeared, Julian, despite all his earlier reservations and protests, was wholly approving. To Lehmann he wrote: "I thought *New Signatures* put up a very substantial show indeed—it's a real, definite achievement for the Press. I hope we shall get reviewed by the political, as well as the literary, papers."[31] But the reviewers paid no particular attention to 'Arms and the Man'; it stirred up none of the controversy that Julian would have welcomed and that Dickinson had feared. Empson, in his poem 'This Last Pain', suggested that one must "learn a style from a despair". But this was precisely what Julian had chosen not to do: he had grafted his very contemporary subject on to the style of the eighteenth century. The hybrid result might have a good deal of intelligence, wit, clarity and common sense, yet it had failed to quicken beyond verse into poetry.

3 Searching

Julian in the early 1930s: a charming, intelligent and discontented young man. He still kept a good deal of the boyish quality that made David Garnett regard him as something of a puppy, high-spirited, alert and affectionate, and he had never got away from the almost compulsive untidiness of his childhood: his clothes were always in need of repair, he could rarely be bothered to comb his hair, or button his collar or shirt buttons. In scale, in goldenness of aspect, he suggested a dishevelled Greek God, Charles Mauron thought, with his generous laughter, large bright eyes, and great height.[1]

Yet even a Greek God from the Olympus of Bloomsbury must do something with his time: in fact, Julian meant to do a great deal, perhaps too much, in too many directions, although his only formal commitment in these years was to the University and the academic community. He had achieved a respectable result on the Tripos, and he was judged worthy of a research studentship by King's. In the autumn of 1930 he returned to Cambridge. As a research student he would register with the English faculty as a possible candidate for Ph.D.; more importantly, he would be at work on a dissertation which might lead to his appointment as a Fellow of his college. In July, Lehmann had written, "Hooray for the studentship—I felt sure you would get it. Have you settled anything about a house? A fine lonely spot to write masterpieces in, during the intervals of Pope . . ."[2] His expectation of creative and scholarly activity was shared by Julian: one could easily do both, Pope and poetry. Also, if one wanted, politics and criticism.

Thus, he began with a commitment to the academic community that was hedged about with unstated restrictions and ironies. And there was no Bloomsbury tradition of formal scholarship to urge him forward. Bloomsbury's own sporadic forays into the groves of academe had not been notable. Strachey had tried to obtain a Fellowship at Trinity (with a dissertation on Warren Hastings) and had failed. Roger Fry had been put up for the Slade Professorship of Fine Arts at both Oxford and Cambridge, but it was not until the year before his death, in 1933, that he finally became Slade Professor at Cambridge. Of course there was the extraordinary example of Keynes, who managed to be equally at home in Cambridge and the world beyond, but even as he was himself regarded with the very faintest condescension by the rest of Bloomsbury, so he treated most of his academic brethren with a certain sense of distance, particularly as they were likely to act upon his stock market tips with lamentable timing. It followed, then, that if Julian were to become any sort of academic, it would have to be in a special hybrid category—no shades of the combination room about *that* golden lad!—with strong connections to literary and political London, and the most flexible commitment to the disciplines of formal scholarship. (The category is not unfamiliar among the dons of Oxford and Cambridge—especially, the former—who often move out and up into the world outside after having established a place in the University; it is one recognized road to eminence.) At the end of his scholarly endeavours, when perhaps he felt more bitter about it than when he began, Julian gave vent to a diatribe against the method of the academy, but it is hard to believe that he had not held the same views from the first:

> There are few human activities more painful to contemplate than scholarship. A parody of the scientific method in its parade of exactitude and vigour, scholarship has neither the excitement nor the justification of scientific research. The additions to human knowledge made by those who meticulously collate,

annotate, and demolish their predecessors, are seldom of the slightest importance or interest to anyone. And when the scholars turn from the works of the unreadable obscure. . . to attempt the works of greater writers, the result of their labours is too often a dense sediment of footnotes encumbering the text and a bored suspicion in the reader: the poets are concealed from us by crusty, insensitive and priggish old gentlemen.[3]

He came back to Cambridge in high spirits. "Pope fascinates and terrifies—" he wrote to Lehmann. "I must read so much, yet there does seem a real chance of doing something and producing some real criticism."[4] He settled down in a version of "a fine lonely spot to write masterpieces in": a small and pleasant cottage, Martin's Farm, in Elsworth, a little village about ten miles from the University, towards Huntingdon, in sparse, green, slightly rolling country. He had the advantage of being near enough to Cambridge to participate as much as he might like in the literary controversies he had become fond of, to continue to attend meetings of the Apostles, take some part in national political questions as they were felt at the University, be secretary of the Heretics (another intellectual society) and arrange for appropriate speakers at monthly meetings—yet still he was far enough away to be able to work without distraction for days at a time, and to live in close touch with the country and natural life that meant so much to him. Elsworth also had the advantage of being just a few miles from the house of his great friend, David Garnett, at Hilton, near Huntingdon: "he liked to come round," Garnett recalls, "and we would rehearse, always with fresh appreciation, some of the comic saga of the past"—that is, "the old anecdotes recording the foibles of his family and their friends". And at Elsworth he could be with 'A'—perhaps the most satisfying period of their relationship, when it was he who still set the terms and she appeared to accept them.

It was an existence very much to his liking: the cottage and Cambridge, and driving recklessly back and forth between them. (Garnett is only one of many who remember him as "rash and dangerous driving a car". He adds, "he had either no sense of fear—or else, as I suspect, he liked the sensation, but he was slapdash and easily flustered as well as quick and always quite sure every other driver on the road was in the wrong."[5]) He was at the splendid untested time of youth, before experience bears down, just having finished his formal education, and therefore believing, since no one was telling him what to do, that he could do everything. He revelled in possibility. Even after a year of work, his enthusiasm was uncurbed. To Lehmann, in October 1931 (shortly before the inception of *New Signatures*), he wrote: "My plans, at present, besides Pope, who sticks, include translating one play each of Corneille, Racine, Molière and Marivaux, a play to finish, another [play], a novel to write, a set of essays, and a second book of poems of which I have the essentials. Enough for a year or two anyway."[6]

What exactly, as a member of Bloomsbury might say, Julian was doing about Pope ("who sticks") is unclear: very little of his formal thought on the subject survives. He was firmly opposed, as we have seen, to academic scholarship of the collating, annotating, and footnoting sort; at the same time he had great faith in his own critical judgment—very much in the English tradition of the golden amateur—and it appears that this, "some real criticism", is what he intended, rather than an historical or biographical study. He took issue (in a review published in the *New Statesman and Nation* in December 1934) with two celebrated views of Pope, put forth in the 1920s: "Miss Sitwell's view of Pope as a romantic over-sensitive and invalid member of the Sitwell family, has always been most dubious. Strachey's 'fiendishly clever and spiteful monkey', though more plausible, was based on the Victorian view of the facts of Pope's life." His own interest was centred on the work itself: "it has the qualities of great poetry . . . produced not by a genius for taking infinite pains—only charlatans and bores take infinite pains—but by a tried and practised genius."[7]

Part of Julian's dilemma, one feels, was his unwillingness to take infinite pains, as if somehow they would prove him a charlatan and a bore. Genius apart, he wanted to do everything, and, in the academic line, a critical study of Pope, at which he worked hard through the early 1930s; but he was constantly being distracted from it by other things that he wanted to do, and he was never able to give it the single-minded concentration that was necessary to bring it to a successful conclusion. As he wrote to 'B' in February of 1932, "I see I shall soon have to be pulling myself together about old Pope—except that I seem to be equally good at most of the things I'm interested in—which makes it difficult to stick to any one of them." A month later he wrote: "I've turned out my old work on Pope—I must have several bushels of paper—and started with squared paper and a dictionary, which seems a silly—and slow—way of analysing poetry. Still, it's quite fun." But what had plagued him from the inception of the project continued to do so. It was fun to invent interpretations for the poems, to work out *explications de textes*, and have brilliant ideas and theories (as though one were at a meeting of the Apostles), but it was boring (as though one were a charlatan) to set them all down on paper, to find out whether other people had anticipated one's discoveries, and to do historical research, all the journeyman scholarship that he deplored. "The trouble," he confessed to 'B' in that spring—the Pope period—"now seems to be that I'm much too ingenious at thinking of explanations, and too lazy to work out strict tests of them." Yet his interest did not dwindle: six months later he was writing, "There's such a lot to say about every single line of it." More and more the project began to take shape in his mind as an *edition* of the poetry. Again one is not certain of what exactly he intended: presumably not a *variorum* for scholars, but a faithful text with commentary for lovers of poetry. In 1934 there was some talk of sending it to Chatto and Windus, who held an option on his next book. When it came to the point, however, he decided more work must be done; and in fact, nothing appeared, then or later; nothing came into print (except for one or two book reviews) from an interest, really an obsession, of *his* 1930s. He did finish the edition (or at least stopped work on it), and it was tentatively accepted by the Nonesuch Press, but, for one reason or another, plans for publication were postponed until late in the 1930s, when Julian was dead, and then, with the outbreak of World War II, they were permanently abandoned.

Thus, the work on Pope, which had been begun as a dissertation topic, became eventually an important, though inconclusive, intellectual pursuit. The dissertation itself, which he submitted at the end of 1931, was based on his preliminary researches, and it was not a success: that is, it did not result in his being made a Fellow of King's. Lehmann wrote to console him:

> I hope [not getting the Fellowship] wasn't a big disappointment: as far as I'd been able to gather from what you'd said, you hadn't expected it this year at all—I hope this was true . . . I never thought a don's life was the life for you, you're far too interested in what's going on, and I don't think it's going to give you wide enough scope . . . I've felt sometimes since leaving Cambridge that one ought to get half a world away from it—physically and spiritually—for a while, unless one's one of those rare people who are simply made for dondom. But I see the working for it gives one a raison d'être—a line that's thinly held to keep the enemy quiet while the main force concentrates elsewhere.[8]

But Julian was determined to make another try. A Fellowship at King's would give him a firm base in the community and an agreeable life, while he considered whether or not to enter into an academic career. The work on Pope remained his prime interest—he was not in the least disheartened by the unfavourable response to his dissertation, and in time came to agree with it: "Rereading my 18 months old dissertation gives me the cold blush all over my sunburn—what idiotic things I did say and think, to be sure."[9] But meanwhile it was necessary to find another topic, and he decided he would do something not in literature, his avowed subject, but along a philosophical line. It was a choice consistent with his ideal of the eighteenth-century gentleman, accomplished in everything, who would do nothing for gain and was untouched by the professionalism of the market-place. Really, he had only to decide along *what* philosophical line—ethics, aesthetics, the psychology of creativity—and proceed. The year before he had considered submitting to the English Board (for the Ph.D.) a topic on Wittgenstein. But George Rylands had dissuaded him, pointing out that to offer such a topic to the English faculty would be much the same as sending Swinburne's 'Dolores' to Queen Victoria as a birthday ode.[10] So that was abandoned, and he eventually gave up the whole idea, if he had ever entertained it seriously, of working for an advanced degree. What mattered was to win a Fellowship, and for that purpose a dissertation of a hundred pages or so might do.

Here he allowed himself to be misled by Apostolic practice. It was an occupational hazard of the Society that one might come to believe that any problem could be dealt with without too much difficulty and with no special qualification beyond the fact of being an Apostle: merely apply the clarity and rationality which a member had by definition—why else was he elected?—and the result was bound to be good. Julian loved the Society; he continued to regard it as the pinnacle of Cambridge intellectualism, and he came in from Elsworth for its Saturday-night gatherings. Over the past three years he had delivered many papers on philosophical themes, and he had had the benefit of rich full discussion. The thought was inevitable, and irresistible: why should he not take some of his old papers and rework them into a dissertation, or at least make use of some of the ideas that had inspired them? He realized that the competition for the Fellowship would be intense; but he seemed unwilling to acknowledge that scholarly attainments might weigh with the Electors of the College. No doubt there was a strong degree of wishful thinking: the Fellowship more and more appeared an answer to the question of what he was to do—he needed it, therefore he must have it. He did not intend to commit himself permanently to the academic life, of course; but at least it would allow him time to discover some viable alternative. The range of possibilities was narrowing. The publication of *New Signatures* had not materially altered his somewhat equivocal position as a poet. It had brought Auden and Spender conspicuously to the front of a movement to which Julian only tenuously belonged: he was, in the phrase of a recent critic, "in but not of".[11] So, in the circumstances, the idea of the Fellowship was more attractive than it might otherwise have been. But he was determined to win it on his own terms, which, in effect, was to lose it on theirs.

Much of his energies for the next year and a half were given to the new dissertation. His working title was 'The Good and All That', and it disguised a long essay dedicated to the sort of problems the Apostles haggled about, over their anchovy paste and toast. When he finished writing, in the autumn of 1933, he began to think of it not only as a dissertation to win him a

Fellowship, but also as a book. To 'B' he wrote, "I've decided to send in 'The Good' as a dissertation—as it may shock a few of the older electors—and I shall have it finished and typed by Christmas, and ready to try on publishers." Early the next year it was in the hands of the college's Electors, who referred it for judgment to authorities in the field. One of these, as it happened, was Roger Fry, the newly appointed Slade Professor. In February he told Julian that he was reading the dissertation and liked it, with reservations. At the same time, Julian's uncle, Leonard Woolf, was reading it as a publisher: he disapproved strongly of the sort of philosophizing it contained, and turned it down.

Out of deference to the feelings of the Electors, Julian had substituted for 'The Good and All That' a more decorous title: 'Some general considerations on ethical theory, with their application to aesthetics and politics'. But the title was almost the only conventionally academic aspect of the dissertation. Julian did not pretend to be a professional, or trained philosopher. He operated on the assumption that the Electors would prefer to see the quality of mind rather than a display of expertise. Yet he must have known that the dissertation, and the Fellowship it might win, were designed to further scholarly activity, as well as to provide a new member of the college staff. But of course he had no patience with the appearance of scholarship, and declares in his Prefatory Note, "I have made use of no authorities beyond those mentioned in the text: I have stolen ideas wherever I came across them, usually in conversation, and used them without acknowledgement, since I cannot trace their authors. I am writing first and foremost for those amateurs of philosophy who like myself are more concerned with practice than with refinements of theory. I hope what I have said is true: I am fairly sure it is useful." Again, as though to make certain that there shall be no doubt of his academic disqualification, he reiterates his amateur status: "I am not a professional philosopher . . . My claim to be interested in the theory of ethics is that, in a small way, I am a practising poet and politician. As such, I am commonly confronted with ridiculous arguments based on ethical assertions." Given the vigour and forthrightness of his style, one might wish that Julian had attempted a new *Candide*, or a new *Gulliver*. As he himself was quick to declare, he hadn't the qualification to write a systematic critique; hence, the somewhat disorganized, arbitrary and improvisory character of much of the dissertation. His aim is to distinguish between ideas of Good and Bad (or in fact, good and bad ideas) in Art and Life, Politics, Religion, War, Peace—the spectrum of human behaviour. In the working out, he allowed himself the pleasure of expounding, in a very lively style, many of his favourite prejudices. Christianity, for example:

> Most of the human misery not due to capitalism is due to Christianity, either directly, or through the religious muddle about means and ends. The Christian religion, or the traces of it that remain in the minds of politicians, old gentlemen and the great British public, holds that certain specific actions—for instance, making love to a married woman, or the direct removal of coal from a pit to a miner's fireplace—are sins.

Yet for all the entertaining hodge-podgery of the whole, a dominant theme does emerge. More perhaps than he himself realized, Julian was in full revolt against his Bloomsbury philosophical background, and its static conception of "states of mind" as values in themselves, without regard to the effects, or actions, or consequences that might ensue from them. He thought of himself as modernizing a deeply cherished set of values; in fact, he was calling them into question.

In a chapter devoted largely to the ideas of G. E. Moore, he wrote:

> Professor Moore is, in a sense, my spiritual grandparent, though I fear he might question my legitimacy. For I was born into, and grew up in, a world very largely of his making, the world of "Old Bloomsbury". And the hard, vigorous lucidity of mind, the orderly beauty of that view of the universe, seems to me to have been very much the reflection in life of the teaching of "Principia Ethica". And perhaps the society of painters, in particular, may have made familiar and congenial to me the habit of relying, in the last resort, on direct intuitive judgments, and on their apparent application to real, tangibly and indubitably existing entities. Equally, I am familiar with the self-reliant judgment asserted without the faintest regard to the opinions of any but a minute group of friends, or the collected judgments of centuries, if even of those.

Consequently I feel at home with a theory which asserts that there exist certain "states of mind" intrinsically and universally good, good in themselves, good simply, undefinably, self-evidently; which asserts that we perceive states of mind to be good as if we perceived apples to be red, and as if they were good with no more ado about the matter. To anyone of a contemplative turn of mind, averse to moralities of action and strenuous right-doing, to anyone more concerned to enjoy the good life than to reform the bad, to anyone to whom the arts are of the first importance, such a theory naturally recommends itself.

But, alas . . . the belief in universal and absolute good is only too often the second line of defence in priests and tyrants. It is apt to lead to intolerance, interference, misery and error in personal relations, to mistakes, at least, in discussions of aesthetic theory, to Fascism, tyranny and reaction in politics.

Julian could not have made any clearer his break with his parents, with the generation of Apostles who had gathered together before World War I and thought they were discovering values far superior to the didactic moralizations of their Victorian forebears. For a young man of the 1930s, the simultaneous authoritarianism and quietism of Bloomsbury philosophy were suspect and unsatisfactory. How in any absolute sense could one be certain of the rightness of one's values? As a thoroughgoing relativist he asked why choose this particular set of values, and answered, "Because I choose to choose it," which, in effect, is a restatement of what he had written in an earlier chapter: "the only 'ideal' I feel I am supporting against others is that of the toleration of all 'ideals' ". And yet: "The victory is to whoever shouts loudest and, ultimately, I suppose to whoever shoots straightest." Here he is caught in a classic paradox of English middle-class liberalism: all men have the right to believe as they please; yet it is the enlightened Liberal who knows what is best for them to believe. The Victorians had not hesitated to resolve the paradox in favour of "strenuous right-doing" in the public world; Bloomsbury, serenely in possession of its own private values, which were perhaps too rare and special for the commonality, had no wish to proselytize, except, as it were incidentally, by example. In the end, Julian plumps for the 'good' in action: it is better to do something than to do nothing. Writing in a time of "unemployment, economic crisis, nascent fascism, and approaching war", he rejects the quietism of Bloomsbury for the activism of the 1930s:

> We should cultivate all those valued states of mind that are produced by action . . . For one thing, it is obviously prudent to dive in of your own accord rather than wait to be pushed. For another, action is the most potent of drugs, and battlefields and revolutions are usually fairly good at curing romantic despairs—and other diseases incident to life. For another, intellectuals often turn out to be good men of action, and would probably do so more often if they could keep their minds clear—could become intellectuals rather than emotionals—and if they acquired a hard enough outer shell of cynicism and practical common-sense.

As a compendium or anthology or grab-bag of Julian's thought in the early 1930s, or even as a period document, 'The Good and All That' has considerable interest. But it was clearly not a success, nor did it deserve to be, as an academic dissertation intended to demonstrate its author's worthiness to receive a College Fellowship. The system at King's was for the Electors to refer the dissertation to two qualified readers who would make a recommendation which the Electors might or might not follow: the final decision was theirs. Julian, most unusually, saw the comments of his readers. Keynes sent him the mimeographed copies of their reports, noting that he had received their permission to do so. One of them, as has already been mentioned, was Roger Fry, a great friend of all the Bells (and all Bloomsbury), and a formative influence upon Julian's mind. He began his remarks with a disclaimer rather like Julian's own: "I have not read recent works and I gather from his frank avowal that Mr Bell is in the same state of ignorance." He did not allow friendship to inhibit criticism: he found that his pupil had not really learned the great Bloomsbury lesson of clarity, particularly in regard to the definition of terms, and he objected to the unsubstantiated attack on

Christianity. But in spite of these and other objections, he was more favourable than not, and concluded with an enthusiastic recommendation:

> On the whole in spite of the defects which I have pointed out I think this a very praiseworthy and courageous attempt to think out some of the most difficult problems of life. Mr Bell shows a keen desire to arrive at the truth regardless of his pre-conceptions and a much more balanced judgment than some of his rather reckless outbursts might suggest. It is eminently the work of a very young mind but one that should develop rapidly. I cannot help thinking that if Mr Bell were to become a resident Fellow his influence in stimulating and guiding younger men would be of real value to the College.

The other reader, a distinguished philosopher, was not as kind. Like Fry, he too commented on the rather hasty dismissal of Christianity, "a religion for which [Mr Bell] expresses a contempt which would not appear to be bred from any great familiarity with its doctrines". Unlike Fry, who had written quite briefly, he provided an exhaustive five foolscap page summary of the thesis, and did it the justice, which it could hardly bear, of treating it as a serious piece of philosophical writing. After pointing out a succession of errors, omissions and inconsistencies, he concluded:

> Plainly it [the dissertation] must not be judged simply as a contribution to the theory of ethics, and it must not be judged simply as a contribution to aesthetics and current politics. On either ground, taken separately, I should say that it falls definitely below the standard required of a fellowship dissertation. It does not follow that it may not be up to that standard when these two factors are taken jointly into consideration.
>
> It appears to me that Mr Bell inherits from his father the power of writing an absolutely first-rate political pamphlet, addressed to intelligent men, and moving at a far higher intellectual level than e.g., the average leading articles in the most "high-brow" weekly reviews, such as the *New Statesman*. What he claims to do is to produce something more fundamental than such articles, but less fundamental than the work of the best professional philosophers. At the same time he would claim

> that his work is in closer touch with practical problems than that of most philosophers.
>
> Now I think that one must admit that he has largely fulfilled this claim . . . Plainly the dissertation cannot claim to be an important contribution to knowledge. I have tried to explain to the Electors that it is a very intelligent, lively and well-written politico-ethical pamphlet of a rather special kind. It is for them to decide whether they consider that this is the kind of dissertation on which they are willing to award a fellowship at King's.

Clearly, as a serious reader, he would have been happier to recommend Julian to the editor of the *New Statesman* than to the Electors of the college. Even Roger Fry, recommending that he be given the fellowship, did not claim high marks for the dissertation itself. Julian, shortly after submitting it, wrote to 'B': "I've begun, I must confess, to have a quite mad hope—for it will surely be disappointed—that I shall after all get a fellowship." A mad hope it proved to be: the Electors decided against him; his association with Cambridge was at an end. What he had written to Playfair in December 1931, still held true in the spring of 1934: "I must make up my mind what I'm going to do, failing a fellowship, or I shall be in the soup."

He had been leading a poetic, academic, literary-critical, philosophic, political and romantic existence. It was all very crowded, everything contemporaneous and exciting for that reason, but for the same reason not entirely satisfactory in any of its aspects. From the time he began his research studentship until his final rejection by King's, from 1930 to 1934, he was publishing poetry and book reviews, working on a study of Pope, participating (as we shall see) in politics in Sussex and Cambridge, writing his dissertation on ethics, and conducting a full-scale social life, with a generous allotment of time to family, friends and love affairs. He was capable of being in love and in literature and in politics, simultaneously and passionately yet inconclusively. Whichever direction one turns, there are disquieting similarities; his involvement with women and his involvement with politics seem different aspects of the same experience.

We have already described the rare emotional fulfilment that he found within his family circle; school had done very little to disengage him from his family; Pinault was a surrogate father; in a sense, Cambridge was his family writ large. His deepest attachment, unchanged throughout his life, was to his mother: it meant that it was very difficult for him to commit himself fully to other women. A kind of emotional reluctance marks all his romantic involvements.

He found his mother a perfect confidante. "I told Vanessa all about it last night," he wrote to 'B', "somehow I find it very consoling to confide in her. Perhaps because she never does anything to shatter my self-confidence or vanity." He particularly enjoyed talking to her, or writing to her, about his love affairs, which he did with astonishing frankness. "I like to imagine us all becoming very famous," he wrote to her at Christmas in 1935, when he was in China, "and then, in some new Victorian age, our letters being published. The embarrassed comments of Editors. The protests that this is a forgery . . . Stern denunciations of the Sir Leslies . . . I don't get much fun out of shocking the bourgeois, but I should with this . . . . Well, this would have seemed a most improbable letter 50 years ago, wouldn't it? Even now, I suppose, 99 out of 100 people, or more, would consider it appalling a son should write like this to a mother." It was almost as though the happenings of his life were authenticated, only became real and manageable, when reported to his mother, who was certainly the only woman, and at times the only person, for whom he had full and absolute respect, and love; and he never changed in this regard.

Nor did he change in his need to confide. The pleasure of self-disclosure was very real to him, and his list of confidantes, headed by his mother and Eddie Playfair, was not a short one. He did not expect a return of disclosures comparable to his own, although he did rather resent Quentin's reluctance to tell him exactly what he was doing and with whom. "It's a ridiculous state of affairs," he wrote to him in 1930, "when you come to think [and plainly, he wanted Quentin to think as he did] that money and sex, the two most interesting and important subjects, are the things people are shyest about, particularly parents and children". Of course these subjects were not at all taboo between Julian and his parents, whatever might be the situation between himself and Quentin: Julian discussed sex with his mother and money with his father. Clive Bell was convinced that the Crash would ruin them all, but although there may have been somewhat less money immediately available to spend, there seemed to be enough for everything to go on as before, and it was assumed, as it had always been assumed, that Julian would have the advantage of a small private income. (Clive continued to complain and worry; Julian, however, did not take seriously his contention that the family's economic difficulties would force him, Julian, to become an advertising-man or a schoolmaster.) In his letter to Quentin (quoted above) he was ready not only to talk about sex ("The Apostles and Dr Freud are going into the whole matter of sexual life in the modern world") but also about money (a brisk discussion of the expectations of the young Bells, based upon what he had been told by their mother). He was determined to be honest about those "two most interesting and important subjects".

And indeed, given his temperament, it was easy enough to be honest, or at least forthright, in letters to his mother and friends. What was really much more difficult was to be honest with himself. It is unlikely that Julian ever achieved this ideal state. He came rather belatedly to the experience of women; then he found that he could not do without them; at the same time a part of his mind was sufficiently detached to resent the time they demanded, and he felt that his work, his writing, his various intellectual pursuits, suffered as a result. He was in many ways, as John Lehmann suspected, a romantic who did his best to conceal the fact from himself and others. He liked to think of himself as cold and hard and calm; actually he was gentle but passionate, and full of a simmering violence. But this was an aspect of himself he feared and disliked and was determined to curb. Set in this context, his admiration for the eighteenth century comes to seem less a literary eccentricity than the expression of psychological unease. General Wolfe is projected as a kind of idealized counterpart: "A man of his own century in his ability to admit, and to dominate by force of will and intelligence, his extreme and violent passions."[12]

When he first fell in love with 'A' he could think of nothing else: he was outrageously happy; that summer, away from her, he was wretched. He was shocked at his vulnerability. As a Bloomsbury intellectual he tended to look askance at the heart, which, in a community of talkers, he regarded as a rather "inarticulate beast". Romantic and too deeply involved to be comfortable, he quoted neo-classical wisdom to John Lehmann: " 'Minds and bodies are best naked, whereas hearts should be carefully wrapped up in flannel.' "[13]

The same division of thought continued throughout his life. He wanted to discipline himself against emotionalism, and felt that writing in neo-classical couplets helped him to do this; later he recognized that the miseries and storms that entered into his affairs were necessary to arouse the dormant creative impulse. He wrote to Eddie Playfair: "It seems to be one of the few beneficent arrangements of providence that physical satisfaction restores one's equilibrium—one's head grows clear and one's heart grows cold—the only tolerable state of affairs."[14] Yet the ideal of clear head and cold heart was in contradiction to the basic elements of his character. Julian thought he loathed violent emotions, but in everything, in politics and in love, he could not avoid them.

The relationship with 'A' was a very happy one in its middle phase, less romantic than it had been, less tempestuous than it was to become. There were a few weeks, a few months, when he was first at Elsworth, of the desired "golden mean": he would have been content—as what young man would not?—to have had it indefinitely prolonged. But he recognized that 'A' was becoming concerned about the future. While he hesitated and temporized, she grew demanding, difficult, distrustful. She scrutinized his poems for allusions to herself. There were scenes, storms, quarrels, reconciliations. By the spring of 1931 it was clear to them both that they could not go on as they had been: they must either marry, or put an end to the relationship. Twice Julian obtained a marriage licence; he went no further. He wrote to his mother, "I know that I am still very violently in love, though perhaps not very romantically . . . In a great many ways I should very much like to be married. It would put an end to all the nervous strain of the life I lead, and judging from the past I think we should probably be very happy. On the other hand I hate losing my freedom . . . So give me some good advice. You know much better what I'm like than anyone else does."[15] But what he really wanted from her was approval: the choice had already been made, it was implicit in the way he had phrased his alternatives: he would like to be married, he would hate to lose his freedom.

So the break took place; for the next few months he was unattached, which proved more trying than he had anticipated; then, in the autumn of 1931, he began his relationship with 'B'. She was older than 'A' and a good deal more worldly: on the face of it he could look forward to a calm, stable, undemanding love such as he imagined he wanted. It was understood that they would love within limits and without expectations: that was the "golden mean". In March 1932 he wrote to her: "Nessa congratulated us on having such a satisfactory relationship." Nonetheless, 'B' would have welcomed a rather less considered, more spendthrift passion than he was prepared to give. He was working a good deal of the time in the cottage in Elsworth, and he wrote to her often in Cambridge, where she had a house of her own, but his letters were more often bulletins than romantic missives. She complained gently; he replied, "My dear, whatever you say, I really can't break out on paper." That was the point of danger, of course: to break out. A few months later he wrote to her, "I, as far as I am reasonable, am consciously trying to keep my balance in a torrent—fortunately of conflicting emotions." He found it odd that she was not afraid, as he was, of letting go: "you seem both impervious to and respectful of romanticism—which I dread as a vice". He had fallen deeply in love again, and the "golden mean" or the "Latin-sensual view of *amour*" really did not make any provision for this. The conflict of emotions was essentially what it had been in his relationship with 'A': on the one hand, a commitment to love; on the other, a determination to remain free. The next year he was away from Cambridge a good deal, spending much of his time in London and in Charleston, and he was prey to fits of jealousy and depression. The virtue of his relationship with 'B', as he had envisioned it, was the measure of freedom it allowed them both. But it had been *his* freedom, not hers, that he had been principally concerned with. 'B', now, was sufficiently impervious to romanticism to insist upon terms of her own: ironically, she had adopted his original position. She offered him a love that was not completely demanding, and asked of him confidence and affection, which he could have given, albeit with a certain lack of grace.

Theoretically, he ought to have found this perfect, but he did not. For all his rationality, he could not accept the idea that 'B' should be as free as he wished to be himself. Nor was he untrammelled enough to offer her a full alternative commitment:

> It's a great pity [he wrote] we should be the sort of people we are—able to feel seriously, but with our feelings so arranged that we make each other miserable. I sometimes think we reflect the world at large—the way in which it seems that all that is needed is a small, simple change, but really all the devils of the abysses have to be let loose to make it, and suffering and destruction which seems out of all proportion to the case. I can't think why I shouldn't give in, knowing what I do about your feeling for me and mine for you. But I couldn't make myself do it. I should break something inside if I did. The worst of being a rather easy-going character is that if you do get your mind made up you can't change it back again. No doubt it comes of taking too external and dramatic a view of oneself, and of my military fixation. So that I see everything in terms of a struggle and victory and defeat, and get an obstinate "no surrender" feeling. But there it is—I'm like that, and now it's too late for me to change.[16]

A month later, when he was waiting for word about his Fellowship, and entertaining a "mad" hope that he might get it, he concocted a fantasy in which (he wrote to her) he would "come back to Cambridge with a definite life that could be shared with you, and sane enough and settled enough in my own mind not to be jealous or suspicious, but to value you properly for being the sort of person you are, without having to think about myself". But he did not receive the Fellowship, he did not return to Cambridge, and the passionate aspect of the relationship was at an end. They remained good friends, however; and thereafter he would write to 'B' with almost the same frankness with which he wrote to his mother.

As he grew older—but it must be remembered that he was only twenty-one to twenty-six in the years that are being considered here—he became increasingly dispassionate about love in his life, and as he passed from 'C' to 'D' he more nearly achieved the "Latin sensual view" he had aimed at from the beginning. Yet he rather regretted the romantic excitements of the past. "I should like to be eighteen again," he wrote to 'B', when he was twenty-six, "and feel I had everything to learn and everything mattered . . . You say I was deliberately unromantic and so on, but I find it difficult to remember unromantically. But then I suppose one always improves the past."

In the autumn of 1931 Julian was alone at Charleston, intending to "rush through" his dissertation on Pope. But the coming General Election absorbed the greater part of his attention: he set enthusiastically to work to help create some sort of Labour organization in his area in Sussex. "My life's absorbed by politics now," he wrote to John Lehmann. "I spent about 14 hours yesterday canvassing, and drove 200 miles, which has left me pretty tired . . . Most of the Labour workers—a lot of my fellow-canvassers are unemployed dockers—are thoroughly sensible, intelligent, very nice . . . I believe if one troubled one could get a strong pacifist party, or even get men to strike against a threatened war." Unemployment; Opposition to War: these were dominant political themes of the early 1930s, and Julian's interest in them was shared by his fellow poets. But the closer he came to practical politics, the more impatient he became with poetry. "The only thing I'm sure of," he told Lehmann in another letter, "gift and talent aren't enough to save us . . . one may have to take a hand in the politician's dogfight if we're to have enough leisure and freedom to work at all." In the first burst of enthusiasm, he was tempted to turn to politics altogether. "There's action and excitement. I seem to get on well with people and say the right sort of thing. I've a notion I could get at a country village meeting rather more effectively than most of these people. They keep on missing the point through not seeing how countrymen feel, and not knowing what conditions really are. (This may be just my imagination.) I suspect a Cambridge education . . . has its uses."

Working even at the village level of politics in a General Election campaign was exhilarating, and Julian allowed his enthusiasm to delude him that Labour would not do too badly: in fact, in the South of England the number of Labour M.P.s went down from 35 to 5. "What a state the world has got intself into," he wrote to Lehmann, "general elections, financial crisis . . . I feel we should all go out into the streets and agitate for a 75% cut, at least, in armaments expenditure." Lehmann took a bleak view of the aftermath of the election. "I'm all for you being more political," he told Julian, "if you've found you have some gifts that way, whether you do it by articles or by talking. Some of us *must* make a stand against the old gang and shake off the clutch of the drowning before they pull us down." Julian was less pessimistic. Although he shared the disgust and disillusionment felt by intelligent young men of the Labour Party when MacDonald, Prime Minister of the Labour government, chose to remain as Prime Minister of the National government, he believed that the party would survive the "betrayal of 1931", and in the next few months he spent much of his time in attempts to rebuild the local organization. He found it unexpectedly difficult to recruit new members from among the farm labourers. They were terrified of losing their jobs, and therefore reluctant to declare themselves openly. This was not so unreasonable a fear in 1932, a time when jobs were scarce, poverty widespread, and landowners for the most part Tories, although Julian felt that it was not based on "anything more than a general nervousness—I've not yet been told of anything specific." He made the centre of his operations the little village of Glynde, a few miles from Charleston. (It was to come into international prominence in the summer of 1934, with the inauguration of an annual season of opera at the near-by country house, Glyndebourne.) In February, at a meeting in Glynde at which eight people were present, he was made secretary of the local Labour organization. "The people are nice," he wrote to 'B', "and seem ready to treat me as an ordinary human being—tho I'm still horribly shy of them." Four days later he was able to report that he had succeeded in winning over the local publican, which was a great *coup*. And in March the "meeting was a great success—the membership increased. Everyone seeming very friendly and cheerful . . ." Yet enthusiasm for politics on this level was difficult to sustain: "I'm rather 'on the shrink' over my various commitments to an active life," he reported, and "Local politics have been getting almost too much for me," and "Politics . . . laborious." His strongest commitments continued to be given to an intellectual life—although he was "thoroughly distrustful" of his abilities to lead one—to Cambridge, to Pope, to poetry, to philosophy, to political theory. The experience of practical politics, canvassing, gingering up the small Labour group in Glynde, would not issue any practical result—it was clear that he hadn't time or temperament to become a figure in local politics, or to get himself adopted for a constituency. But it had been instructive: "I shall anyway be able to feel practical and effectively revolutionary at Cambridge," he wrote to 'B'.

His satire 'Arms and the Man' was published in *New Signatures* that winter. We have already described it at some length in a literary context: here we would note only how directly it deals with poverty and unemployment, with disarmament and pacifism: in short, with the significant political themes of the 1930s. But the problem of poverty was a more or less obligatory and formal concern for him. He would never respond to it with the intellectual excitement and imaginative identification that he brought to the problem of war. From the games of early childhood until his death in the battle of Brunete, war was in many ways the abiding concern of his life. In the early 1930s he adopted a strongly anti-war position: the folly of 1914-1918 must not be allowed to recur. In this he was at one with his generation. Then, as the threat of Hitler became increasingly serious, his attitude changed, and was crystallized with the outbreak of the Spanish Civil War. Again he was like many of his generation; and surely this was a crucial moment in the history of the 1930s, when young men on the Left abandoned their anti-war position, and some among them crossed the frontier into Spain.

In the late 1920s, when Julian had been an undergraduate, "no one" at the Universities had seemed to care very much about politics; then, as it were overnight, with the coming of the new decade, the situation was reversed and "everyone" was political, arranged on a spectrum from Left of Centre to Furthest Left. On February 9, 1933, when the Oxford Union passed a resolution 'That this House in no circumstances will fight for King and Country', it was expressing largely a political rather than a pacifist objection to war. The members of the Union had not gone over in a body to conscientious objection. But the resolution was dramatic enough to attract national, and even international notice, and it suggested that Oxford was seething with political activity and disaffection. In fact, this was more the case at Cambridge. Student leaders like John Cornford went about their political business very seriously. The old "extraordinary *douceur de vivre*" of a few years back was quite gone, and Julian felt at times that he was the only non-Communist remaining in Cambridge, so quickly and completely had the atmosphere changed. Conflicting political beliefs, too intensely adhered to, brought about the cessation of the Apostles, some of whom had gone Communist—so many of the leading intellectual lights at Cambridge belonged to the party. Julian particularly regretted this; so too did Keynes. His biographer records: "He could not but observe the tendency towards Communism among the young at Cambridge, and most markedly among the choice spirits, those whom thirty years before he would have wished to consider for membership in 'the Society'. He attributed it to a recrudescence of the strain of Puritanism in our blood, the zest to adopt a painful solution because of its painfulness. But he found it depressing."[17] Politics came first, and social life, from the rarefied level of Apostolic Saturday evenings to the more ordinary level of the sherry or dinner party, disintegrated.

Julian regretted the lost *douceur de vivre*; at the same time, he approved of the change in the political temperature. Although he never committed himself very far in a Marxist, and certainly not in a Communist, direction, he did participate to some extent in left-wing activities in Cambridge itself, most particularly in 1933, the last year when he would be there with any regularity, and when the course of political thought, spurred on by the advent of Hitler, was veering Left-wards almost at a dizzying rate. November saw the climax of these activities, and if one were in search of a date to establish when many of the younger people turned Left, a good choice would be Saturday, November 11, 1933. On that day, under the leadership of John Cornford and his friends, a variety of organizations, from pacifists to Communists, joined forces in a manner that suggests the later Popular Front, and staged a massive anti-war demonstration in Cambridge.

Julian was enthusiastically in the midst of it. His attitude in these matters reveals a fine, parochial inconsistency: he was willing to support causes in Cambridge that he would not support nationally; he would repudiate the activities of the extreme Left in the world at large at the same time that he was participating in its activities at his University. (But in this respect he was not untypical.) For instance, at the beginning of 1933, a friend in London asked him to support the British Anti-War Council: "We hope very much that you'll be able to give your name." Julian refused: he felt that the organization was dominated by Communists. His friend replied tartly: "I rather suspected that for party reasons you'd be unable to oppose war." Yet he was not at all reluctant to work for Cambridge organizations that had precisely the same aims, and no fewer Communists at their head. He and 'B' were active in arranging a 'No More War' exhibit, which was put on display in Cambridge early in November: an assemblage of photographs, documents and posters that followed the preparations leading to the First World War, contrasted the idealizations of propaganda with the realities of battle, touched on the disillusionment of the war's aftermath, and concluded with a prophetic look at preparations for the next war. Concurrently, a jingoist film, *Our Fighting Navy*, was scheduled for a local cinema, and Julian and 'B' were part of an anti-war group who went to protest against the showing. A crowd of 'hearties', out to get those they considered effete and cowardly, to 'rag the cads', gathered in the street, and there was a brawl. "Quite a decent amount of fighting," Julian reported to his brother, and although the anti-war group got the worst of it, "the reactionaries smashed up some of the cinema, and the management lost their nerve and took the film off," so the protest had achieved its purpose. But the climactic event was the great anti-war demonstration of November 11. Armistice Day itself, since the inauguration of Earl Haig's Poppy Fund, had become the occasion of pranks and parades intended to raise money for the Fund. The Socialist Society and the Student Christian Movement joined forces to make the day more meaningful. There was to be a three-mile march through the town to the Cambridge war memorial, where a wreath would be placed, bearing the inscription, 'To the victims of the Great War, from those who are determined to prevent similar crimes of imperialism'. The words 'of imperialism' were removed by order of the police, who felt they were not conducive to maintaining the public peace. Even so, the day was tumultuous. Hundreds of students joined the procession through the town; among them, rather more conspicuous than most, was Julian. Nothing would please him more than to be a soldier for peace, and he had prepared for the demonstration with military efficiency. His beaten-up Morris car, in which he had terrified his friends as he drove them along the roads of Cambridgeshire, he now attempted to transform into a military vehicle. "I tried to use the Morris as an armoured car (stript of everything breakable)," he wrote to Quentin. The armour of the car was mattresses, and his navigator was Guy Burgess, a research student at Trinity. They entered the line of march, and as they moved slowly and conspicuously along, they were a tempting target for tomatoes, and got well pelted. But they made a couple of good charges at the enemy—'hearties' again, attempting to break up the parade—before they were ordered out by the police. Julian merely changed his tactics, drove round through a circuitous route and rejoined the march towards its head. His letter to Quentin concludes: "There was one good fight, which I missed, when they stole our banner and gave a man a concussion." At that point the police had intervened again, using their batons. "However, we managed to beat them in the end, and got our wreath on to the War Memorial."

All this was tremendously exciting, and Julian loved being in the thick of things. It appealed to the romantic and violent aspect of his character—how much fun it was to be using the Morris as a sort of battering ram!—and he exulted quite unthinkingly in what he felt. But almost at once the curb was applied: it was not enough to feel; one must also think, clearly and rationally, one must understand. Thus, it was as much in an effort at clarification for himself as to communicate to others, that he wrote a remarkable letter to *The New Statesman and Nation*, less than a month after the excitements of Armistice Day, describing the political situation at Cambridge:

> In the Cambridge that I first knew, in 1929 and 1930, the central subject of ordinary intelligent conversation was poetry. As far as I can remember we hardly ever talked or thought about politics. For one thing, we almost all of us had implicit confidence in Maynard Keynes's rosy prophecies of continually increasing capitalist prosperity. Only the secondary problems, such as birth control, seemed to need the intervention of the intellectuals.

By the end of 1933, we have arrived at a situation in which almost the only subject of discussion is contemporary politics, and in which a very large majority of the more intelligent undergraduates are Communists, or almost Communists. As far as an interest in literature continues it has very largely changed its character, and become an ally of Communism under the influence of Mr Auden's Oxford Group. Indeed, it might, with some plausibility, be argued that Communism in England is at present very largely a literary phenomenon—an attempt of a second "post-war generation" to escape from the Waste Land.

Certainly it would be a mistake to take it too seriously, or to neglect the very large element of rather neurotic personal salvationism in our brand of Communism. It is only too easy to point to the remarkable resemblances between Communism and Buchmanism, the way in which both are used to satisfy the need of some individuals for communion with a group, and the need for some outlet for enthusiasm. Our generation seems to be repeating the experience of Rupert Brooke's, the appearance of a need for "the moral equivalent of war" among a large number of the members of the leisured and educated classes. And Communism provides the activity, the sense of common effort, and something of the hysteria of war.

But this is only one side of the picture. If Communism makes many of its converts among the "emotionals", it appeals almost as strongly to minds a great deal harder. It is not so much that we are all Socialists now as that we are all Marxists now. The burning questions for us are questions of tactics and method, and of our own place in a Socialist State and a Socialist revolution. It would be difficult to find anyone of any intellectual pretensions who would not accept the general Marxist analysis of the present crises. There is a general feeling, which perhaps has something to do with the prevalent hysterical enthusiasm, that we are personally and individually involved in the crisis, and that our business is rather to find the least evil course of action that will solve our immediate problems than to argue about rival Utopias.[18]

The enthusiasm he felt in November waned quickly. What Julian thrived on was a mixture of high principles and the conversation of intimate friends—the Apostolic formula—and he found not enough of either in any particular political movement. The following January he attended a conference of Socialist Societies. "A thoroughly bad show," he told 'B', "all details and reports, no real debate on principles and too large for effective discussion. I daresay I shall go and hunger-march as an unemployed student—more likely not. It made me ill and livid and depressed—the sillier sort of Communists, particularly the rather scrawny, provincial university ones, are not over-sympathetic. I can't get clearly fixed in my own attitude—I don't like either side, but probably one's got to choose sides."

His feelings about Communism were compounded of admiration and suspicion. While he was ready to declare "We are all Marxists now", he considered Communism a "dismal religion" and did not enjoy reading *Das Kapital*, if indeed he ever got through it—not that not reading it was any bar to being a good Communist. But he felt the Marxian analysis to be scientific, and clear, and rational, values he had been trained to rate highly. A Cambridge graduate wrote to *The New Statesman* after Julian's letter was published there to ask in what sense it was accurate to describe undergraduates as "all Marxists now". He answered that they accepted the Marxist explanation for the appalling state in which the world found itself, bankrupt and threatened by war—that the financial slump had resulted, not from the machinations of wicked bankers and financiers, but from the nature of capitalism itself; and that the major cause of war was the contest for new markets between rival imperialisms. "It's really cheering," a friend on the far left wrote to him after reading these public letters, "to see you coming out in a shirt dyed a deeper tint of red at last. I'd been expecting it for a long time: ever since, in fact, you said to me that you saw no point in being a Social-Democrat outside one's own country." But Julian was not likely to become a communicant of the "dismal religion". He was prepared to accept the Marxist analysis; it did not follow that he must accept the Communist solution. He was extremely distrustful of commitment for the wrong reason—that is, to become a Communist romantically, in a swirl of emotion and muddled thought. Analysis proved that his own way of life, the Bloomsbury way, which he valued dearly, and which was based on capitalism, was doomed to disappear. Yet he had no wish to accelerate its disappearance. His position was rather like the Saint's before conversion: "Make me chaste, Lord, but not yet." Keynesian theories and the pragmatic experiments of Roosevelt's New Deal might temporarily patch up the fabric. "It looks as if capitalism was going to weather this slump," he wrote to Lehmann, "even if the Americans do get themselves socialized by mistake. Personally, I shan't be sorry to have a few more years on an independent income of sorts—largely consisting of gambling gains on the New York stock exchange at present. At least until I finish Pope and get a job." This was the candid, unromantic, hard-headed side of himself that he enjoyed exhibiting; at the same time he was troubled by his lack of involvement: "I feel envious of groups and communities, and horrified at the isolation of human beings." When black moods of this sort came upon him, he was unquestionably drawn to the party, and in a set of Prose Reflections that he wrote at about this time (but never published) 'To My Bourgeois Friends in the Communist Party', he conceded:

> No doubt there are emotional satisfactions; the beloved group; fools gold and ignis fatuus of enthusiasm and flags, and the satisfactions of war—a war of attrition under second-rate generals. And no doubt there is an argument—even apart from Marx there is an argument—and no doubt there is righteous indignation against poverty. And finally, and most importantly, you are in an infernal tangle: you can't deal with your own emotions nor with the world outside you.

But he also recognized that the bourgeois Communist, unless capable of an absolute commitment, would "always be out of the beloved group, rather suspect and irretrievably different"; and the search for an alternative position of his own, to which he could commit himself without reservation, continued—but inconclusively. "I *can't*, *can't* get clear about politics," he wrote to Lehmann in the spring of 1934. "Again, there's an emotional contradiction, or set of contradictions. I'm Left by tradition, and I'm an intellectual of the governing classes by tradition, and I can neither quite make up my mind to trying to get an economically intelligent Roosevelt 'Social Fascism', nor give way to 'the Party' with its fanatical war mentality."[19]

He was very much at loose ends. He was twenty-six; he had no definite place in life, in society; and he was not at all sure, now that he had not been made a Fellow of King's, of what he wanted to do. He thought of finding some sort of temporary job in London, and of various book projects. He felt his poetic commitment was not strong enough for him to be a poet; he was merely someone who happened to write poems. In a letter to his mother in which he remarked that at the moment all his young women seemed to have left him, he added that it was not this that was making him unhappy but "the trouble of finding some serious occupation. I don't seem able to write poetry—that's obviously not going to be a reliable thing for me; I seem to have been able to at moments only, not all through my life."

He had no settled scheme for the future. John Lehmann, who had given up his job with the Hogarth Press to write, and was spending much of his time in Vienna, suggested: "Why not travel for a bit, or do something entirely different—a foreign correspondent say—before you make up your mind?" But in his present irresolute state he was not capable of the decisiveness such a gesture would have required, even if it had appealed to him. His family was in London, as were many of his close friends—Eddie Playfair was a civil servant in the Treasury—and he had no reason to linger in Cambridge. He took a room of his own in Taviton Street in Bloomsbury. He thought he might try to become a lecturer at the University of London: "It sounds a heavenly job," he wrote to 'B', "decently short hours and amusing work. Unfortunately I've no notion of their having a vacancy." Nor is there any indication that he ever pursued the job. He found that the various odd bits of journalism that came his way were enough, with his small private income, to support him and allow him to lead if not a satisfactory life at least an interesting one. He did reviews for the *New Statesman*; he worked on his proposed edition of Pope, and also an edition of Mallarmé in translation, continuing the work that Roger Fry had started with Charles Mauron and that Julian helped finish after Fry's death in 1934. (He had already, with Mauron, published a translation of Rimbaud's *Le Bateau Ivre* in *The Cambridge Review*. Fry's translations of Mallarmé finally appeared in 1936, with a preface by Mauron and Julian, who had edited Fry's early introduction to the work and completed his translation—Fry had already done nineteen of the twenty-eight before his death—of Mauron's commentaries on most of the poems.) He edited a collection of reminiscences of World War I pacifists. He wrote poems, and drafts of essays. But all this activity, though it kept him occupied and distracted, was too marginal and haphazard to satisfy him that he had embarked on a career; his discontent deepened: the important work of the generation was being done by others.

One of the poems he wrote in this period is the lightly ironic 'Cambridge Revisited':

> Down by the bridge the lovers walk,
> Above the leaves there rolls the talk
> Of lighted rooms. Across the lawn
> Clare's greyness prophesies the dawn.
> River and grass and classic weight,
> As if the Fellows meditate
> Socratically, the masculine
> Beauty of th' athletic line,
> Squared brow or pediment, and look
> For Greek ghosts out of Rupert Brooke.
> Grey stone, slow river, heavy trees,
> I once had my share of these;
> But now, within the central wood,
> I neglect the wise and good:
> And London smoke, and middle age,
> Open on a grimier page.

The irony is double-edged, turned as much against Julian in his nostalgic "middle age", as against the meditative dons. But there is no comic over-emphasis in the final line: "a grimier page" does go directly to the point of what Julian felt about London. He wrote to Lehmann, "I'm being more or less miserable here: poverty, chastity and the other horrors of large towns." The first complaint needn't be taken too seriously; the second was purely temporary—soon came 'C', and after her 'D', and then 'E'. But the "horrors of large towns" were real to him: he had been unhappy in Paris, he was unhappy in London, in both cases unhappiness sent him to writing poems. Yet he appeared as gay and as cheerful and as exuberant as ever. That was one side of it. The depression came out in the poetry—which, for the first time, was autobiographical and personal and pervasively melancholy—and sometimes in moody, confessional letters. These tended to be exaggerated, as he himself saw: once, having written in a black mood to 'B', he drew back and concluded, "Really I lead, I suppose, an unusually sheltered and happy life, and all my miseries are vicarious." But that also was an exaggeration.

Another poem concludes:

> The world will slowly make us tame,
> And events as they pass provide
> Some object to the game.

These lines might serve as the epigraph for the period in Julian's life which we are now describing: from the winter when he came to London, to the summer of 1935, when he went out to China. He allowed himself to appear tamed: he did his various odd jobs, talked politics with friends, alternated between London and Charleston and Cassis, had affairs, published a few poems, a few book reviews. That was the surface. His interior life of ideas and feelings—was much more turbulent and eventful. Unable to commit himself to his own satisfaction to poetry, or to politics, or to love, he engaged in a kind of strategic retreat, a withdrawal to re-gather his forces, while he waited for events to provide "Some object to the game".

In politics—indeed, in all aspects of his life—he became a party of one. He wanted to be, as his grandfather, Sir Leslie Stephen, had proposed a young man should be, "a partisan of the ideas struggling to remould the ancient order and raise the aspirations of mankind",[20] but he would have to be so in his own fashion. "For my own part," he wrote, "I am proposing to turn myself into a man of action, cultivate my tastes for war and intrigue, conceivably even for town-planning and machines, and, generally for organizing things and running the world. As for poetry, I shall write it more for my own satisfaction, to please my friends or flatter a mistress, and not bother about 'the public'." The quotation is taken from one of the several unpublished essays he wrote during his London period, 'To my Friends in the Communist Party'. (Titles of this sort were very fashionable. *New Country* (1933), the sequel to *New Signatures*, in which Julian did not appear—nor Empson nor Eberhart—included 'Letter to a Young Revolutionary' by Day Lewis, 'Letter to the Intelligentsia' by Charles Madge, and Auden's 'A Communist to Others'. Julian, of course, had earlier written 'To My Bourgeois Friends in the Communist Party'. It was the great age of the open letter and the manifesto. But the most remarkable example was Auden's 'Letter to a Wound' in *The Orators*.)

In the autumn of 1933 he had been resolutely anti-war; now his attitude underwent a series of significant modifications. David Garnett, looking about for things for him to do, had arranged for him to edit a book of memoirs by British conscientious objectors during World War I. The book, *We Did Not Fight*, which was published in 1935, consisted of eighteen short autobiographical essays, a poem by Siegfried Sassoon, a Foreword by Canon 'Dick' Sheppard, the leader of the Peace Pledge Union, and an Introduction by the Editor. Among the contributors were Garnett himself, Bertrand Russell, Julian's uncle, Adrian Stephen, Sir Norman Angell, Harry Pollitt, the foremost British Communist, and James Maxton, the leader of the Independent Labour Party. The discordant note in the collection was Julian's Introduction, which dealt with questions of war and peace in a paradoxical way that must have given his elders to pause. He imagined himself to be modernizing pacificism; actually, he was making one of the first steps towards resolving a crucial dilemma of the 1930s: how to oppose both war and Hitler. He was aware of the immense pacifist sentiment abroad at the time he was writing—1934—and he cited the evidence of the Oxford Resolution and the Peace Pledge Union, maintaining that the 16,000 conscientous objectors of 1914-1918 had now become the 12,000,000 signers of the Peace Ballot of 1934. But he added quite sensibly that, when it came to a test, probably very few of those 12,000,000 would prove to be absolute pacifists—nor did he think this regrettable. While he had only praise for the courage of conscientious objectors during

World War I, and commended pacifists for the independence of their thought, he doubted whether absolute pacifism was appropriate to the situation of the 1930s: "I do not think there is likely to be much chance of the absolutist conscientious objector again becoming an important figure in a campaign of war resistance." From his stance of the unsentimental realist, he looked coldly at the individual gesture, no matter how sincerely inspired, that gained no practical result. He felt that the modern pacifist who genuinely wished to oppose war must do so actively, rather than in the traditional passive style. The solution was not, as in the past, to opt out of a society committed to war—that contest of rival imperialisms—but to try to change society. "The most active and ardent war resisters—at least among my own generation—those of military age—are more likely to take the line of revolutionary action than conscientious objection." By a kind of semantic sleight of hand he blurred the distinctions between war resistance and pacifism, conjuring up a movement that conformed to his own prescription: practical, potentially revolutionary, determined "to bring down, by hook or by crook, any government and any governing class that dares to make war". In the last sentence of the Introduction he completed his modernization of pacifism with a militant paradox that reveals how far he had travelled from the attitudes of his parents and their friends. "I believe that the war-resistance movements of my generation will in the end succeed in putting down war," he declared "—by force if necessary."[21]

This was relatively restrained. As the editor of a collection of memoirs by pacifists of the older generation, he had had to proceed diplomatically. But in an unpublished paper which he wrote at this time, 'The Labour Party and War', he took a much stronger anti-pacifist line: "It is not any more virtuous to hate being killed than to wish to die on the field of battle . . . It needs courage to say 'I am a Socialist, and I am willing to fight for the peace of Europe'." He felt certain that the conjunction of German nationalism and English pacifism was leading to war. Accordingly he objected to the pro-pacifist policies of the Labour Party. "So long as the English people remain content to support either Beaverbrook or the Pacifist in the policy of irresponsible isolation there can be no lasting peace . . . The [Labour] party must once and for all discard negative Pacifism and preach the Positive Pacifism of Pooled Security, Disarmament, and the National control and International inspection of armament firms."

(He was writing in Taviton Street, ostensibly to the Labour Party, or to his Bourgeois Communist Friends, but actually to himself. It was a time of withdrawal, while he waited for events, whatever they might be: manuscripts piled up but were not sent out; he made no effort to translate his ideas into action. In February of that year Leonard Woolf arranged for him to talk with an official of the Labour Party, and the notion was put forward that Julian might have a half-time job drafting party propaganda leaflets, but nothing came of it.)

Though he argued for peace, and proposed a variety of practical ways to maintain it, it was war that fascinated him: civil war—the revolution for Socialism; and international war—the struggle against Fascism. In 1934 he believed in the possibility of one or the other, or both: in the event of either it would be impossible to stand aside as his elders had done. He had already declared his intention of turning himself into "a man of action". The difficulty was that he was also an intellectual, a poet and a son of Bloomsbury: he could not deceive himself that war was a 'good'—however much it might fascinate him, scruples, doubts and hesitations intervened.

> I'm getting rather obsessed about war [he wrote to Lehmann], with a very ambivalent attitude. All my instincts make me want to be a soldier; all my intelligence is against it. I have rather nightmares of 'the masses' trying a rising or a civil war and getting beaten—being wasted on impossible attacks by civilian enthusiasts, or crowds being machine-gunned by aeroplanes in the streets . . . No doubt it's better for one's soul to fight than surrender, but otherwise— . . . One feels that a battlefield's a nicer place to die than a torture chamber, but probably there's not really so much difference, and at least fewer people suffer from the terror than would in a war. Oh, I don't know—personally I'd be for war every time, however hopeless. But that's only a personal feeling.

In spite of his ambivalent attitude, he allowed his fascination with war to go unchecked, and it was characteristic of him that, having admitted the possibility or rather inevitability of war, he should next address himself to the problem of how it ought to be conducted. It was as though the "war game" which had begun when he was a child at Wissett was now to be played with the utmost calculation, sophistication and inventiveness. A game for one player, however: as in other aspects of his life at this time, here he was a party of one. Although he did a few reviews of military books for the *New Statesman* in the early months of 1935, his most ambitious efforts, two long essays, 'Military Considerations of Socialist Policy' and a study of Michael Collins's guerrilla tactics in the Irish rebellion, were not offered for publication (except in a single instance to be noted below). The reviews, written to be read by the public at large, are more straightforward and less venturesome than the essays, yet they are not without point or prejudice. Perhaps the most interesting is of the volume devoted to the German March Offensive of 1918 in *The Official History of the War*. Critical of the stalemate strategy that kept the armies in the trenches, he remarked that, "the generals were quite right in thinking that they could avoid losing a decisive battle, but it was, of course, a peculiarly clumsy way of winning a war". And he went on to advance a favourite theory, that, "the only leaders who showed any obvious brilliance were the civilian soldiers, untrained in classic doctrine, acting in open theatres, and unprovided with limitless reserves: Lawrence, Trotsky and Collins". His conclusion has precisely the note of calculation and sophistication indigenous to the war game: "It will be interesting to see if the present British and German armies, apparently small, highly trained and reasonably mobile, are capable of revising the classic tradition sufficiently to avoid another disastrous and uninteresting deadlock. No doubt it will not be too long before we are allowed to make the experiment."[22] This was in February 1935.

He had an almost obsessive interest in Michael Collins, and for a time even considered writing his biography. But chiefly he was interested in what was to be learned from his career: how a guerrilla war might best be waged in England, if it had to be waged, to achieve some sort of Socialist government. It was a goal that mattered to him, albeit in a rather abstract way; but it is hard to resist the impression that he was most deeply engaged by the phenomenon of guerrilla war in itself, about which his ideas were well in advance of most military thinking of the time. A long sketch, in very rough form, survives of some lessons that Julian felt could be gleaned from the campaigns of Collins, beginning with the creation of a private army—in this case Socialist, to be led (secretly) by heads of the Labour party, and staffed by middle-class intellectuals and a few token workers. The effect, for all its air of practicality, is oddly surrealistic, as in much of the writing of the period: a wealth of realistic detail is called upon to substantiate a romantic fantasy. It is the tone of Auden's 'Leave for Cape Wrath tonight!' Similarly, there is a period fascination with violence: "Prisoners could be mutilated to prevent further active service: this should be made to appear a reprisal", and again, "Prisoners are an important source of information: it may be necessary to use torture to extract it"—though he felt constrained to add, "The revolutionaries will on the whole profit by a humane war." Events taking place at the time that he was writing appeared to confirm his hypotheses. The February fighting in Vienna, the attack on the working-class tenement, the Karl Marx House, proved (to his mind) the need for a private army if there was to be any kind of effective Socialist resistance. He did not waver from this position: a year later he was writing to Lehmann, who was in Vienna, to ask if he knew of any Socialist paper, "legal, or illegal", that might consider publishing his article on Collins. He was convinced that the workers could learn from it "certain military methods and principles which would make all the difference" if they were going to fight again, and he hoped that they would. In his poem 'Vienna', he deplored "The useless firing and the weary ends/Of comrades . . . / Who fought well, but too late." And he asked,

> Can we, from that fate
> Wring to some foresight
> Or will the same lost fight
> Mark too our ends?

He answered by indirection:

> War is a game for the whole mind,
> An art of will and eye . . .
> A hard art of foreseeing,
> Of not too much caring;

> A game for their playing
> Who fall in love with death,
> Doubt, and seeping fear . . .

There is an admirable candour about this: it was easy enough, given his long-standing fascination with war, to describe it as "a game for the whole mind"; it was more difficult to acknowledge that it was also "A game for their playing / Who fall in love with death". The self-confidence and zest with which he recommended the formation of a private army, and, in the event of international war, the re-siting of towns, industries and communications, are somewhat misleading. One gets a more accurate picture of his state of mind from a long letter he wrote to Lehmann at precisely this time:

> I don't mind war as killing, nor as pain, nor utterly as destruction. But it means turning our minds and feelings downwards, growing hard (well, no harm, perhaps) but also savage and stupid and revengeful. You know, the Russians haven't escaped: spies and suspicion and tyranny, and no jobs if your 'class origins' aren't above suspicion. That's war—far more than the battlefields, even, tho' I think I shall live to see the people who talk about 'the masses' in peace using those same masses like Haig and Wilson, until you've knocked the heart out of them. For it's clear that "revolution" is a dream of the nineteenth century: now we shall just have civil war, to the last dregs of modern invention . . . I want to . . . leave the human race free to sit down to think for a bit. It's just another "trahison des clercs" to go into the struggle, whipping up enthusiasm and leading it to war . . . If there must be violence, there must. But let's be thoroughly cold-blooded and unenthusiastic about it . . . As you'll see, I'm not yet clear, and pretty near despair either way. I believe one of the differences in our points of view comes from the circumstances of our private lives. I don't know at all, but I fancy you don't hit back when you're hurt. I do. When one has seen the extent of human beastliness in oneself as well as outside one hesitates to let loose devils. There's nothing in the world fouler than enthusiasm, the enthusiasm of a fighting group, not even jealousy or suspicion, not even open-eyed causing of misery.[23]

Not long after this he wrote to 'B': "Nothing has ever really cured me of my militarist daydreams, and I hope I shall spend at least a part of my life—even the last part—on battlefields."

He had been disappointed by the reception of *Winter Movement*; he had not been one of the conspicuously admired contributors to *New Signatures*. Judged by his own extremely high expectations for himself—one must be distinguished, as were one's father and mother, aunt and uncle, and all their friends—he was a failure as a poet. (And of course just at this time he had failed at Cambridge.) His solution was to be a poet "at moments only" and to withdraw from the literary game. When *New Country* appeared, to which he had not contributed, he wrote to John Lehmann, who had, "I hear dreadful things of *New Country*, which I've asked Bunny for to review." Lehmann's reply was ironic and diplomatic, but quite inaccurate in its prophetic aspect: "Amusing that you've got *New Country* to review. Yes, it's a pretty good mess, & a tombstone for us all, I should think. Don't be too nasty, I quail, I quake." But Garnett had already given the book to someone else to review, and so Julian was unable to put an end publicly to his involvement—however tenuous it had been—with Thirties Poetry.

Paradoxically, once he had committed himself to being a poet "at moments only", the poetic impulse revived. He wrote a good deal: from the work of this period he eventually selected thirty-three poems from a larger number for his second book, *Work for the Winter*, which was published by the Hogarth Press in the spring of 1936, when he had been in China almost a year, and was truly 'out' of the literary game. The poems are markedly different from those he had written in the past. The campaign for the heroic couplet has been abandoned—neither the 'Epistle to Braithwaite' nor 'Arms and the Man' are reprinted—and there is no attempt to maintain the impersonality of the early nature-descriptive pieces. There is, as Lehmann wrote to him, a "new directness and simplicity". Almost without exception, the poems are drawn from his own experience, they reflect the uncertainties and regrets of his time in London—which is at once their virtues and defect: they have less poetic than autobiographical interest.

(Perhaps it should be said that Julian's claims as a poet are based most firmly upon his early poems. In spite of its occasional successes, *Work for the Winter* is the traditional 'disappointing' second book: tentative, pointing towards a new direction not yet firmly discerned. But it is not at all a dead-end.)

Uncertainties and regrets: the elegiac tone prevails throughout.

> Shall we not often remember
> That summer, flowers, garden,
> Shock and flock of white blossoms
> —How white snow will thicken the branches—
> Dotted and golden in green, in deep green
> dancing and burning . . .
>
> But now take stronger tools,
> Axe, fire, plough.
> Metal sheathed in despairs, winter is fast
> come on us.

This is from 'Work for the Winter', included in the section of 'Political Poems'. It is followed by a section of 'London' poems:

> So I shall never in verse put down
> The wringing horror of this town,
> A vision hard to repeat
> Of a long unhappy street . . .
>
> No help now: this town could do
> With some poison gas and a bomb or two.
> ('London I')

> I want—I don't want—the not wanting
> Leaves the need, but stops the acting,
> Nothing worth the winning or saving,
> And the narrow life contracting.
> ('London II')

Then a section of nine 'Love Poems':

> Regret, shake hands, and the dry kiss
> Grating too sharply at the past
> Snaps short what yet remains of this,
> Briefly acknowledged for our last.
> ('Coming to an End')

> Is this an end
> Or is there yet
> Waste time to spend,
> More to forget?
>
> Is this an end
> Of the facile rhyme;
> Mistress and friend
> How runs the time?
>
> Is this an end
> Or must I still
> Spiral descend
> The westward hill?
> ('Finale')

And from the section called 'Constructions':

> Drive on, sharp wings, and cry above
> Not contemplating life or love,
> Or war or death: a winter flight
> Impartial to our human plight . . .
>
> What useless dream, a hope to wring
> Comfort from a migrant wing:
> Human or beast, between us set
> The incommunicable net.
>
> Parallel, yet separate,
> The languages we mistranslate,
> And knowledge seems no less absurd
> If of a mistress, or a bird.
> ('The Redshanks')

These were private poems, written "at moments only", and he had no declared intention of sending them out from Taviton Street for publication. Still, if a friend were to take the initiative, and if that friend were an editor . . . In March, Lehmann wrote to Julian to say that he, along with Denys Kilham Roberts and Gerald Gould, was to edit *The Year's Poetry 1934*, and of course Julian must send poems. The comedy of *New Signatures* was about to be played again. Or did Lehmann imagine that Julian had changed, would allow himself to be included in an anthology, *any* anthology, with a minimum of fuss? At first, however, all was harmonious. Julian sent off a group of poems, along with a slightly defensive note: "God knows what you'll think—highly individualist (no doubt bourgeois decadent) love poems, of sorts." But Lehmann was enthusiastic. Having consulted with Kilham Roberts, he wrote that they had reserved eight, among them 'Autobiography', and 'Visualization of Marxism', from which they would make a final choice. The problem was a surplus of riches—the editors were casting a wide net, and no poet would be represented by more than two poems. But Julian sent along another batch anyway. These Lehmann turned down—"they don't seem to me quite as good as the others"—but he asked for permission to include either 'Redshanks' or 'Visualization of Marxism' in a selection of younger poets he was assembling for *The New Republic*.[24] On the same day, July 28, 1934, he wrote to Julian again, this time in an official co-editorial capacity: "We've decided that, if you will allow us, we will use the following poems by you, which we like very much, in *The Year's Poetry*, viz. 'Visualization of Marxism'; 'Autobiography'. Will you please let us know if you agree . . .' Julian agreed, and recommended 'Visualization' for *The New Republic*, as 'Redshanks', an earlier poem, had already been published in *The Listener*. All was harmonious still.

Then, within a month, he changed his mind. He wrote to Lehmann, who had gone on holiday to Vienna, that he had decided to withdraw 'Visualization'—it was "too Spender-Audenish". Lehmann, justifiably annoyed, for manuscripts had already been sent to the printer, replied that he was writing to London to cancel the poem, but that it was far too late to do anything about *The New Republic*—unless Julian wanted to pay for a transatlantic cable. "Why did you ever let me have the poems? Or not tell me in your last letter definitely *No*? 'Visualization' is not Spender-Audenish. It is Shelley-Fitzgerald-Empsonish."

That was in August. In September, with the proofs in his hands, Julian had second thoughts about 'Autobiography', and decided to withdraw that too. He wrote this time to Kilham Roberts in London, with a fine disregard of the likelihood that co-editors might share their correspondence as well as their responsibilities: "Owing to some extraordinary oversight of Mr Lehmann's—presumably—two of the poems in proof ['Autobiography' and 'Visualization'] are those which I had asked him two months ago, not to print, and I cannot understand why they have been set up . . . I hope Mr Lehmann has not made any further mistake about this . . . I regret the trouble I am giving you at the last moment; I assure you it is none of my making."

He wrote to Lehmann to apologize for the muddle he had caused about the anthology. Lehmann replied: "It was nice to have your word that you realised the mess was largely of your own making. But at the same time, to be quite frank with you, I find it difficult to square with what you say in your letter of about the same date to my co-editor, which was, like all others, sent on to me in copy . . . You must know perfectly well that you did *not* veto 'Autobiography', and when you wrote [about withdrawing 'Visualization'] it was too late to alter what was going to the printers . . . it was always open to you to cut [it] in proof, though we hoped you wouldn't. Kilham Roberts seems to have been too irritated by your letter to answer. He writes, 'It's an awful pity because both *Autobiography* and *Marxism* were good stuff.' "[25]

Nevertheless Julian had his way: the poems the editors had chosen were withdrawn, and in their place he substituted 'The Redshanks' ("the last of my birds", he wrote to Playfair at Christmas 1933) and a lyric of disillusionment, 'Sowing Sand'. He had been prompted by literary scruples to withdraw 'Visualization of Marxism'; he never explained why he vetoed 'Autobiography' and one can only speculate as to his reasons for doing so. In November 1934 Lehmann was back in England, and he wrote to Julian from Fieldhead, "I consider that you effectively prevented me showing the public that you're a damn good poet when you like, and in order that I may say this louder and

LOUDER, let's meet sometime. Next week I plan to be in London."
Perhaps the explanation of Julian's seeming perversity is to be found in that phrase, "showing the public". 'Autobiography' is one of the most impressive examples of his "new directness and simplicity"; it is an intensely personal poem, based upon a crucial conflict in his life that he would never satisfactorily resolve: his emotional commitment to the past against his intellectual commitment to the future which would almost certainly mean, he thought, the end of all that he valued most. For all his pride in the poem as a poem, he also knew that it was a document, and it was only after he had left Taviton Street, left London, left Charleston, that he was able to make it public. He was reluctant to show the poem even to his mother. It had been written by early 1934, and submitted rashly to Lehmann that spring, and reclaimed, unpublished, in September. More than a year later, on October 13, 1935, from China, he wrote to his mother, "Also, dearest, I've found out how much our relationship matters to me. And we both know it. I feel about it rather like Donne going religious after his profane mistresses, except that I can love you without having to believe nonsense. I've tried to say a little about you—and about you and Roger [Fry] together—in one of my new poems, the 'Autobiography'. It's not enough nearly, but it's the only time I've come at all near putting it down."

AUTOBIOGRAPHY

I stay myself—the product made
By several hundred English years,
Of harried labourers underpaid,
Of Venns who plied the parson's trade,
Of regicides, of Clapham sects,
Of high Victorian intellects,
Leslie, FitzJames:

And, not among such honoured, marbled names,
That cavalry ruffian, Hodson of Hodson's Horse,
Who helped take Delhi, murdered the Moguls;

At least a soldiering brigand: there were worse,
Who built a country house from iron and coal:
Hard-bitten capitalists, if on the whole
They kept the general average of their class.

And then, not breeding but environment,
Leisure without great wealth; people intent
To follow mind, feeling and sense
Where they might lead, and, for the world, content
To let it run along its toppling course.
Humane, just, sensible; with no pretence
To fame, success, or meddling with that world.

And one, my best, with such a calm of mind,
And, I have thought, with clear experience
Of what is felt of waste, confusion, pain,
Faced with a strong good sense, stubborn and plain;
Patient and sensitive, cynic and kind.

The sensuous mind within preoccupied
By lucid vision of form and colour and space,
The careful hand and eye, and where resides
An intellectual landscape's living face,
Oh certitude of mind and sense, and where
Native I love, and feel accustomed air.

And then the passage of those country years,
A war-time boyhood; orchard trees run wild,
West wind and rain, winters of holding mud,
Wood fires in blue-bright frost and tingling blood,
All brought to the sharp senses of a child.

Whatever comes since then, that life appears
Central and certain and undoubted good,
As the known qualities of clay or wood
Live in the finger's ends, as tool or gun
Come easily to hand as they have done.

Whatever games there now remain to play
Of love or war, of ruin or revolt,
I cannot quite admit that world's decay
Or undespairing wish it on its way.

For here was good, built though it was, no doubt,
On poverty I could not live without,
Yet none the less, good certain and secure,
And even though I see it not endure,
And though it sinks within the rising tide,
What can for me replace it good or sure?

Part Two

John Cornford

1 Rupert John Cornford

Rupert John Cornford was born in December 1915, in the second year of the First World War. In April of that year, the man after whom he was named, the golden poet of pre-war Cambridge, Sub-Lieutenant Rupert Brooke of the Royal Naval Division, had died of acute blood-poisoning while sailing through the Greek Islands *en route* to the Dardanelles and the Gallipoli campaign. When he had learned where the Division was to go, Brooke wrote to a friend, "I've never been quite so happy in my life, I think. Not quite so pervasively happy; like a stream flowing entirely to one end. I suddenly realise that the ambition of my life has been—since I was two—to go on a military expedition against Constantinople. And when I *thought* I was hungry or sleepy or aching to write a poem—*that* was what I really, blindly, wanted. This is nonsense. Good-night. I'm very tired with equipping my platoon."[1]

A few months earlier, at home at Rugby for a few days' leave just after Christmas, he had written in his sonnet sequence '1914'

> If I should die, think only this of me:
> That there's some corner of a foreign field
> That is forever England . . .

and so it proved: on April 23 he was buried with military honours on the island of Scyros. The Greek interpreter with the burial party scribbled on the back of the cross that marked his grave, "Here lies the servant of God, Sub-Lieutenant in the English Navy, who died for the deliverance of Constantinople from the Turks."[2] The legend of this most romantic and romanticized of soldier-poets had begun.

Three days later, Winston Churchill, then First Lord of the Admiralty, wrote to *The Times*: "Rupert Brooke is dead. A telegram from the Admiral at Lemnos tells us that this life has closed at the moment when it seemed to have reached its springtime. A voice had become audible, a note had been struck, more true, more thrilling, more able to do justice to the nobility of our youth in arms engaged in this present war, than any other—more able to express their thoughts of self-surrender, and with a power to carry comfort to those who watched them so intently from afar. The voice has been swiftly stilled. Only the echoes and the memory remain; but they will linger." Within a year of his death, however, the murderous progress of the war had made the kind of poetry Brooke had written seem increasingly anachronistic and unreal: patriotism and nostalgia, no matter how genuinely felt, gave way to bitterness, irony and pity—to the poetry, in short, of Siegfried Sassoon and Robert Graves and Wilfred Owen.

Brooke had been a close friend of the Cornfords in Cambridge, and as a gesture to his memory they named their son Rupert John. It was no more than a gesture, however: the glamorous name did not take, he was John from the beginning. But even if it had survived into childhood, one can be certain that John, with a firm distaste for Brooke's poetry and legend alike, would have put a stop to the use of the name with his customary assurance.

It is tempting to ascribe this assurance of his, which is so recognizable an aspect of his character, to inheritance. Born into a family of high intellectual distinction—he was the great-grandson, on his mother's side, of Charles Darwin—he may well reflect the confidence and sense of security that such an inheritance conveys to its heirs when it does not thwart or diminish them.

The Darwin family home, Down House, was a plain, oblong, white-washed, three-storied house, large enough for a large family, but in no sense luxurious, indeed almost austere, with an attractive garden, an orchard beyond a row of lime trees and a long walk bordered with flowering shrubs that led through the kitchen garden to Charles Darwin's "sandwalk"—the strip of wood that he had planted with various trees and where he took his "daily pacings for forty or more years". The house was at Downe, in Kent, the home of other solid Liberal families, the Bonham-Carters and the Lubbocks, but the Darwins were also to become increasingly important at Cambridge.

John's mother, Frances Darwin, was part of that small-scale 'population explosion' which took place at the Universities of Oxford and Cambridge in the 1880s. Before that time, almost the only ways permitted to a Fellow of a college to marry were either to become its Master, or a Professor—both rare jobs to come by—or else to receive a college living—very likely in some remote country parish—and there, comparatively late in life, he could start a large Victorian family. From 1878 onward, as a step in the liberalization of the Ancient Universities, one by one the colleges decreed that their Fellows should be allowed to marry. A consequence of freeing academic life from its quasi-monastic restrictions was that the intellectual aristocracy, no more celibate than any other, began to a certain extent to leave London, and to a greater extent the country parishes of England, and came logically to roost in and about Oxford and Cambridge. In Cambridge their commodious family houses tended to be near those other new phenomena, the colleges for ladies, across the river either towards Newnham or towards Girton: in either direction the climate was favourable for scholarship and marriage.

Charles and Emma Wedgwood Darwin had produced seven children, five sons and two daughters, and of these, George and Francis came to Cambridge in the early 1880s to settle down with wives and children to the full Victorian life that Gwen Raverat has described with a judicious admixture of candour and affection in her memoir, *Period Piece*. Presently they were joined by their mother, after Charles Darwin's death in 1882, which meant that there were now three large Darwin houses in Cambridge, one after another along the Huntingdon Road towards Girton, and their continuous expanse of lawns, gardens and woods afforded a splendid playground for the youngest generation. Francis Darwin, the third son, who was to be John Cornford's grandfather, was born in 1848, went to Trinity College, Cambridge, like all his brothers, and later qualified as a physician, although he never practised. A distinguished botanist, he was also within respectable bounds the most aesthetic member of a family that Mrs Raverat, his niece, characterizes as "benevolently Philistine". His four brothers, gifted scientists and professional men, were more limited in their interests than he: they did not concern themselves much with philosophy, theology and religion, and "they would have admitted that they knew nothing at all about music, very little about art, and not a great deal even about Literature, though they all loved reading". Frank, by contrast, had (in Mrs Raverat's words) a good deal of the artist in him; loved music, played the flute, oboe, bassoon, recorder and pipe-and-tabor; had a fine sense of style and a light touch in writing—he was the author of two collections of familiar essays—and his very personal turns of speech and of humour were enchanting. Cheerfulness was not his usual mode, however, especially as he grew older: he was subject to fits of melancholia and depression, "his form of the family hypochondria",[3] which one gathers that he passed on to his daughter, along with a certain gentleness characteristic of her, and that was to be noticeable in John also—especially to those who were close to him. His father, writing after John's death to a friend of the family, the painter William Rothenstein, spoke of his "wisdom and gentleness" which were always there under "the superficial arrogance", and he concluded that "there was a good deal of Francis Darwin in his nature, combined with that astonishing intellectual force & strength of character which F.D. had not."[4]

Taking into account his diffidence and melancholy, it would appear that Francis Darwin remained too much under the shadow of his famous father too long. As a young man he acted as his secretary and assistant, living at Down, and when he married (in 1874) he took a house near by so that the daily intimacy continued unimpaired. Two years later his young wife died in childbirth. The shock confirmed him in his pessimism: thereafter, Mrs Raverat tells us, "he continually expected the worst about everything". With his infant son Bernard he moved back into

Down and lived there until the death of his father in 1882. Only then did he return to Cambridge, where he would become a Lecturer in Botany, and a Fellow—oddly but not surprisingly—of Christ's, his father's old college, rather than Trinity, his own. It was from this time onward that he achieved his not inconsiderable career, making important contributions as a botanist, and writing several books, among them the official *Life and Letters* of his father.

A year after his return to Cambridge he married again, a perfect marriage for the time and the place, to a great-niece of Wordsworth, Miss Ellen Crofts, who was a Lecturer in English at Newnham, the ladies' college her cousin Henry Sidgwick had boldly founded twelve years earlier. Newnham was rather more liberal than the slightly older Girton, and, unlike it, had no chapel, nor did it feel compelled to situate itself three miles outside Cambridge in order to protect the virtue of its girls. We learn from *Period Piece* that Miss Crofts wore her hair short, and even smoked. A reader of Henley and Stevenson, she was much more up-to-date, more modern than the solid Darwins, with whom she did not really get along. Perhaps, although it seems unlikely, this is sufficient explanation for the otherwise unexplained, vague but persistent melancholy that burdened her until her death in 1903.

Frances Darwin, the only child of the marriage, was born in 1886. She had a happy Cambridge childhood; her parents doted upon her; after the death of her mother, she and her father would be particularly close; and there were her Darwin cousins, Gwen especially, from whom she was inseparable. Frances, as one would expect, was very much a Darwin. One of Mrs Raverat's most charming scenes describes herself, aged ten, and Frances, aged nine, crouching under a wooden bridge, while Frances tells Gwen in confidence that "it was not at all the thing nowadays to believe in Christianity any more. It simply wasn't done." But if she was Charles Darwin's granddaughter, she was even more the daughter of Francis and Ellen Crofts Darwin; and they communicated to her something of their own complex and melancholy response to life. In this respect she was very different from Gwen, who saw it simply as a matter of temperament. Writing long afterwards, she comments, "Believing what you can't believe is a kind of exercise which some people like. Others don't. I don't. This is however the religious temperament, and it got Frances in the end."[5]

As the girls grew older, the peculiar advantage of Cambridge as a place of residence became apparent: it offered an ample supply of attractive, intelligent and more or less eligible young men. For our purposes it is necessary to single out only two: Rupert Brooke, a year younger than Frances, who became her great friend; and Francis Cornford, twelve years older than she, who became her husband. Life at Cambridge in those pre-war years was not less than 'idyllic'—at least it has been made to appear so in the recollections of it that have been written since—and if there is one young man who in his person, and even more in his myth, evokes that idyll, surely it is Rupert Brooke. Frances Darwin met him early after he came up as an undergraduate to King's in 1906. They were soon friends—one might even say colleagues—confidantes, admirers: it was she who wrote the famous, ultimately ironic, and now, to our ears, somewhat overblown epigram, describing him as he appeared in his 'great days' in Cambridge:

> A young Apollo, golden-haired,
> Stands dreaming on the verge of strife,
> Magnificently unprepared
> For the long littleness of life.

One can imagine—too easily perhaps—the black-haired young girl with the look of a gypsy and the golden-haired young man with the look (his admirers insisted) of a Greek god, strolling beside the Cam in the long summer evenings, or taking tea at Grantchester, carrying on serious conversations about poetry. For they were both aspiring poets: that was the important thing; and it was poetry, not romantic attachment, that brought them together. Mrs Cornford (as she would soon become) recalled after his death that "he was endlessly kind in helping me with my verses (except that kindness seems the wrong word, because he did it as a matter of course). He would sit for an hour or two at a time, generally on the ground, frowning and biting the end of his pencil and scribbling little notes on the margin before we talked. Of the better things he would only say 'I like that', or 'That's good'. I can't imagine him using a word of that emotional jargon in which people usually talk or write of poetry."

Both young poets intended to have their first books published in 1910. "They will review us together!" he told her. "The *Daily Chronicle*, or some such, that reviews verse in lumps, will notice thirty-four minor poets in one day, ending with *Thoughts in Verse on Many Occasions, by a Person of Great Sensibility*, by F. Cornford, and *Dead Pansy-Leaves, and other Flowerets* by R. Brooke; and it will say 'Mr Cornford has some pretty thoughts; but Miss Brooke is always intolerable' (they always guess the sex wrong). And then I shall refuse to call on you. Or another paper will say, 'Major Cornford and the Widow Brooke are both bad; but Major Cornford is the worst.' And then you will cut me in the street."

Frances Cornford had a small but true talent, and in the course of her lifetime would publish several volumes of verse, all of them characterized by an elegance of craft and an elegiac note that was only slightly muffled by her at times perhaps too conventional, too poetical diction and metres. But if the tone is often elegiac, she is not without humour, lightness of touch and a gentle irony: they are evident, to give a single instance, in her often anthologized piece, the triolet, 'To a Fat Lady Seen from the Train':

> O why do you walk through the fields in gloves,
>   Missing so much and so much?
> O fat white woman whom nobody loves,
> Why do you walk through the fields in gloves
> When the grass is soft as the breast of doves
>   And shivering-sweet to the touch?
> O why do you walk through the fields in gloves,
>   Missing so much and so much?

Her first book, *Poems*, was published, as she had intended, in 1910, but Brooke's was postponed and did not appear until the end of the following year. Meanwhile, in 1909, she had married Francis M. Cornford of Trinity College, Cambridge, a Lecturer in Classics, who was to have an academic career of great distinction. Marriage did not alter the friendship of the two poets:

Brooke was a frequent visitor at Conduit Head, the Cornfords' house in the Madingley Road. (They rented it from Trinity College, and it was named in honour of the well on the property that supplies the fountain in Trinity Great Court, three miles distant.) When Brooke was in Munich in 1911 he wrote to Mrs Cornford, "Oh, I sometimes make a picture of Conduit Head, with Jacques [Raverat, who had married Gwen Darwin] in a corner, and Gwen on other cushions . . . and Francis smoking, and Frances in the chair to the right (facing the fire) . . . It stands out against the marble of the Luitpold Café and then fades . . . But say it's true!" Then, in December, Rupert's book finally appeared. Frances, secure in her role of married woman and published poet, ventured to criticize some of his poems: it was as though the pupil had turned on her teacher. Rupert, deeply offended, gave vent to his feelings in a letter, not to Frances but to Eddie Marsh, his friend and mentor and—as editor of *Georgian Poetry*—ardent publicist: "Mrs Cornford [sic] tried to engage me in a controversy over the book—she and her school. They are known as the Heart-criers, because they believe all poetry ought to be short, simple, naïve, and a cry from the heart; the sort of thing an inspired only child might utter if it was in the habit of posing to its elders. They object to my poetry as unreal, affected, complex, 'literary', and full of long words. I'm re-writing English literature on their lines. Do you think this is a fair rendering of Shakespeare's first twenty sonnets, if Mrs Cornford had had the doing of them?

TRIOLET

If you would only have a son,
  William, the day would be a glad one.
It *would* be nice for everyone,
If you would only have a son.
And, William, what would *you* have done
  If Lady Pembroke hadn't had one?
If you would only have a son,
  William, the day *would* be a glad one!

It seems to me to have got the kernel of the situation, and stripped away all unnecessary verbiage or conscious adornment."[6]

Thereafter the friendship seems to have been more 'official' than 'actual', smoothed over by Brooke's prolonged absences from Cambridge, and commemorated by a graceful, if curiously ineffective gesture: the Cornfords' decision to name their first son after the dead poet.

James Cornford, Francis's father, was a clergyman of the Church of England, author of the *Historical Prayer Book*, and for a time Headmaster of the Cathedral School at Ripon. He took his B.A. at Trinity College, Cambridge, in 1863; thereafter, one might say with only slight exaggeration, he moved through the parishes of England. Between 1863 and 1887—the year Francis entered St Paul's School—the Reverend James Cornford and his family were successively in residence in Hale, in Walcot, in East Claydon, in Eastbourne, in Virginia Water, in Ripon, in Peper Harow and in London. The transient, uprooted character of his childhood was in marked contrast to the life Francis would make for himself as an adult: at the earliest opportunity he put down roots in Cambridge; and Conduit Head, into which he moved with Frances after their marriage, was the one home his children would know.

He was born in 1874, during the family's sojourn in Eastbourne. He was an intelligent, serious child from the beginning. When he was thirteen the family was living in London—where the Reverend James Cornford was teaching at the London College of Divinity—and Francis was enrolled at St Paul's. There he distinguished himself under the famous High-Mastership of F. W. Walker. It has been suggested that the hard driving to which he was subjected by Walker had the effect of fostering his already somewhat withdrawn and solitary nature. In any event, Walker achieved the sort of brilliant academic result with him that he liked and for which he was celebrated: in 1892 Francis Cornford went as a minor scholar to Trinity College, Cambridge—how that name resounds in the lives of Darwins and Cornfords—and soon was a major scholar, with Firsts in both parts of the Classical Tripos, and bracketed for the Chancellor's Medal in Classics. He also wrote a number of humorous pieces for *The Cambridge Review*, of which he was an editor: a pleasant reminder that the young man, though serious, was not oppressively solemn.

In 1899 he became a Fellow of the College. It was an exciting time at Cambridge for someone of Cornford's interests and ambitions. A revolution in classical studies, inspired largely by the work of his great friend and mentor, Jane Harrison, was in full progress. Miss Harrison brought to classics the insights of anthropology and archaeology, and her fundamental contention—that much that was irrational, primitive and religious lay behind the civilization of the fifth century in Greece—was to have a considerable influence upon Cornford's writing and thinking, and the development of his academic career. The salient dates of the latter are quickly given: he was appointed Lecturer in Classics in 1904, Reader in Classics in 1927, and Laurence Professor of Ancient Philosophy in 1931. (Except for the years of the First World War, when he was a Sergeant-Instructor of Musketry at Grantham, and 1928 when he was a visiting lecturer at Harvard, he spent his life in Cambridge.) An exciting teacher—especially for better students—he was eager to restore humane values to the study of classics and to remove the subject from the purely philological concerns which had deadened it in the nineteenth century. As his friend Gilbert Murray has pointed out, "In Cornford the artist and the poet were always lying in wait behind the savant." He was the author of many books, among them a revolutionary work on Thucydides and what has become a standard translation of *The Republic*; and in a less exalted vein, the formidably titled *Microcosmographia Academica* of 1907, an irreverent and much-reprinted little book which treats such subjects as the number of times a beginning academic at Cambridge should be seen walking up and down King's Parade in order to get ahead in his profession.

He and Frances Darwin had met at a tea party given by Jane Harrison for the purpose. It was appropriate that Miss Harrison should introduce them, for she was also a close friend of the Darwin family and she had been at the centre of the distinguished circle of early Newnham students which had included Ellen Crofts. No details of the courtship have been recorded, but as the day of the wedding approached, Francis Darwin became even more melancholy than usual at the prospect of losing his daughter. "Frances thought that something ought to be done," Mrs Raverat tells us, "to cheer him up, and to entertain the uncles and aunts assembled in Cambridge for the occasion. So a river picnic was arranged, entirely for their sakes; a family party, given by the young for the old."

It proved a disaster. The weather was cold; the aunts and uncles difficult to please. "When they had to sit down to have tea on the damp, thistly grass near Grantchester Mill," it was found that the tea had been sugared beforehand. Francis Darwin said, "with extreme bitterness: 'It's not the sugar I mind, but the Folly of it.' This was half a joke; but at his words the hopelessness and the hollowness of a world where everything goes wrong, came flooding over us," Mrs Raverat says, "and we cut our losses and made all possible haste to get them home to a good fire."[7]

Looking back, Mrs Raverat saw Frances's marriage as "the end of an epoch". Thereafter they were "really grown up". She herself was allowed to go off to live in London and study at the Slade School. Frances and Francis—the comic possibilities of whose identical-sounding names had been exploited by Gwen in a family Christmas playlet which she entitled 'The Importance of Being Frank'—went to live in the Chesterton Road; a year later they moved to Conduit Head. And Francis Darwin, like many another elderly widower-father who has 'lost' a daughter, presently fell in love: in 1913 he married the beautiful widow of Professor F. W. Maitland, the historian.

The early years of the Cornfords' marriage belong, of course, to the 'pre-War period', but this is not a crucial distinction: there will be no dramatic 'post-War' contrast. Academic life is relatively timeless: that is its seduction. In the 1920s Mrs Cornford would write,

> Cambridge, my home:
> The figure of a scholar carrying back
> Books to the library, absorbed, content,
> Seeming as everlasting as the elms
> Bark-wrinkled, puddled round their roots, the bells,
> And the far shouting in the football fields.
>
> The same since I was born, the same to be
> When all my children's children grow old men.

In those early years there were the rewards of settling down to a comfortable but unpretentious, bookish but sociable existence at Conduit Head—we catch a glimpse of it in Brooke's nostalgic letter from Munich—the rewards of marriage and parenthood—Helena, their first child, was born in 1913—and of work well done. Mr Cornford published two of his most important books in this period, *From Religion to Philosophy* and *The Origin of Attic Comedy*, and Mrs Cornford, having survived the ordeal of a first volume, was now writing the poems she would gather together in *Spring Morning*.

John, their second child, was born in Cambridge, December 27, 1915. Mr Cornford, who had volunteered for the Army in the autumn of 1914, was stationed near by at Grantham. An expert shot as well as a classics scholar, he had been assigned to train recruits in musketry. Since Grantham was only sixty miles from Cambridge, it meant that he could come home fairly frequently; it also meant that his wife need not worry for his immediate safety. Still, it was a time of anxieties and griefs: there were friends and relations fighting in France; there was the death of Brooke; and in the same year, Ferenc Békássy, the Hungarian poet who had been a scholar of King's and a member of the Conduit Head circle, was killed fighting for his country on the Eastern Front. Imaginative and highly sensitive, unwilling to translate her most urgent personal concerns into her poetry, alone a good deal of the time, Mrs Cornford gave to her children, and to John in particular, a much more concentrated, undivided, continuous love and attention than would ordinarily have been the case. John, in the first three years of his life, was hardly aware of his soldier father; his earliest childhood was dominated to an unusual extent by his mother.

Whether for this reason, or because of the vividness of Mrs Cornford's personality—in many ways the reverse of her husband's—or simply because, as time passes, that is how things are between mothers and sons, it is evident throughout his life that John's relationship with his mother was much more intense, and accordingly more difficult, than that with his father. Although they might disagree fundamentally about politics—and Francis Cornford was the sort of old-fashioned liberal who held as a first principle the right of his son to believe whatever he wished—relations between father and son were warm and affectionate from childhood on; one has very little sense of tension, rivalry or antagonism between them—nor of love at the very deepest, most disturbing levels of feeling. All that was to be much more characteristic of his relationship with his mother—particularly in his adolescence—although here too the dominant note is of affection, not rancour.

The family was large; their life together, congenial. There were five children in all. After Helena and John came Christopher, born in February 1917, who would always be very close to John; then Hugh, in 1921, and Clare, in 1924. John, who is introduced in his father's memoir as "a large, placid baby with very dark eyes and skin and thick black hair [the look of the Darwins] . . . good-tempered and easy to amuse, even when unwell", grew up an intelligent, thoughtful, enterprising and independent child. Yet he was not noticeably gifted or precocious: he took much longer than Helena to learn a game; Christopher was more agile and better co-ordinated than he physically; his juvenile literary productions bore no mark of the *wunderkind*. An unexceptional childhood, one might fairly say; still, in the quite commonplace anecdotes of his childhood one finds a hint at least of the exceptional young man he ultimately became.

The first such anecdote in point of time happens to be as illustrative as any other of what was perhaps most remarkable about him as a child: his determination to go his own way, to do only what reason, *his* reason, told him he ought to do and—perhaps more important—could do. Mr Cornford was walking through a field with John, aged four, and Christopher, aged three, when they came to a stile, which had to be crossed. Christopher dashed at it, "bumped his head, and withdrew howling; then dashed at it again and got over at the third attempt". John, conscious (too conscious perhaps) of his clumsiness, refused even to attempt to cross the stile. He sat down on the grass, and "when asked why he did not try, said slowly, 'I can't; I'm too fat and too stupid.' "

His father speaks of "a blank wall of obstinacy", and reports that John could not be made to learn the piano or dancing; or to fish or sail; or, after learning to swim, to go beyond his depth. During a week of sailing on the Norfolk Broads—with his father, a friend of the family, and Helena and Christopher—he was very reluctant to steer the boat, and preferred to spend "hours lying in the cabin and playing by himself a game of cards which mysteriously determined the course of an imaginary game of cricket". Untalented as an athlete but fascinated by sports, he was almost able to convince himself that the cricket card-game was as satisfactory as the real thing. Professor Cornford sums up, "He refused to attempt what he thought he never could do well."

What he thought: the phrase deserves emphasis. We have already described John as a thoughtful child, but it would be closer to fact (and more literal) to say that he was full of thought. From Professor Cornford's memoir one takes away a vivid impression of the child *thinking*: everything had to be thought out, thought about, thought over. We learn, for example, that "when he was seven, after saying the Lord's Prayer and repeating 'for ever and ever, Amen,' John said: 'How can a thing go on for ever and ever, Mumma?' Either before or after a somewhat lame explanation he replied: 'I think all things must have an end, Mumma.' " His father noticed that "he lived in thought without needing to translate it into action". Fond of drawing up plans for objects to be made, he had no interest in making them himself. One such plan was headed: MAKE THIS GUN. The directions were explicit. "Get 3 FEET of elder then get piece of wood 6 inches long an inch thick then nail see fig. three. Then get piece of Meccano 4 INCHES long. Nail it on piece of wood . . ." His mother, always generous with her encouragement, "said this was splendid: if she got the materials would he try to make the gun? But he was quite content with the directions." Perhaps the most emblematic of such anecdotes comes from 1925, when John was nine. Towards bedtime one night he said: "I feel I want something and I don't know what it is. I've thought about all the things I usually think about. So I suppose there's something I haven't thought about." Professor Cornford adds, "Some light on these meditations was gained a little later. Coming upon him in a reverie, his mother asked what he was thinking. He said: 'Whether Oliver Cromwell was really sincere.' On another such occasion he answered at once: 'I was thinking what Napoleon might have done for France if he had cared more about France than himself.' "

He was, one might say, a thinking rather than an imagining child, responsive to fact, indifferent to fantasy. The world about him was being considered, used and judged, and his large dark eyes were staring out anxious to take it all in, and, through thought, make it his. He saw the commonplace with the unexpectedness and freshness of a child: watching his mother pass out bread at tea, he suddenly remarked, "Brown bread makes more noise than white bread." This, of course, is a very different thing from the fantastication many children delight in: the brown bread was *not* fairy bread; if you ate white bread, you did *not* shrink to the size of a walnut. Mrs Cornford, "with great delight to herself", read him *The Little Mermaid*, the fairy tale she had loved most as a child. When she finished reading, he asked gravely: " 'Is the bottom of the sea *really* like that?' She replied she supposed not exactly. 'Then I think it's rather silly.' " What Mrs Cornford thought at that moment we are not told, but it is difficult not to give her our sympathy. Or again, on the occasion when she sang the ballad of *Lord Randal* to him and Christopher,

> O yes I am poisoned; so make my bed soon,
> For I'm sick at the heart, and I fain would lie down

Christopher sobbed at Randal's death, but John merely said, "Christopher, how silly you are. You know Randal isn't even a real man." This attachment to fact, with its accompanying matter-of-factness, is evident in the stories that he made up but found too "laborious to write out". In March 1923, however, a few months after his seventh birthday, his mother persuaded him to dictate some of them to her, and while the three that she transcribed give little hint of the future poet—nor was Mrs Cornford deceived on the point—they do suggest the factual cast of his mind. The most coherent of the three, 'His Discovery', tells of a ten-year-old boy who ran away to sea, and "just then a storm came on":

> The sky was black—the waves were as big as you could imagine, they were so big that the highest struck away the top mast. But soon there were only three [of the crew] left who, as the ship broke down, started a boat towards the eddy which carried the boat to where it was still raining though the waves were not so high. At last he was the only one left so he steered the boat towards the East, as the storm was coming from the West. Soon the waves were so, so, so big they broke in pieces just behind the boat, and carried the boat southward and as the wind was

> coming on from the s.w. he steered to the s.e. as there he saw a little country far in the distance. He thought perhaps it was part of India, as all the time he felt very hot but it was really Africa, and when he came near the place he saw there were some sort of natives waiting for him. He did not care much about this—as he saw they were shooting arrows at him. But he had an old chest full of food & weapons & he took out an old pistol & first shot —the ignorant men flew for their lives.

This, except for an impenetrable first sentence, is the whole of what John called Chapter One. The second, and concluding chapter, a bit shorter, tells of the hero's escape from a tribe of Zulus, and the final sentence reads: ". . . so he went to Egypt and now he is the man who is discovering all these secrets in Egypt and that is the end of the story and the man's name was William."

If, unlike William, John had no desire to run away to sea, he did want to go his own way. The attitude of his parents, and the life they made available to him at Conduit Head, fostered him in his independence. The house itself, at the bottom of a wooded lane off the Madingley Road, was not large. Altogether in a different category from Down, it was twentieth-century-professorial rather than nineteenth-century-Darwinian: that is, it contained more than rooms enough to enable a family of seven to live together comfortably and sociably, but lacked the Victorian superabundance of attics and box-rooms where a child in search of a hiding-place might find it. Outside, however, there was a considerable hedged-in garden, and better yet, a small wilderness near by in which John could lose himself when he wished. The spacious pre-war days of *Period Piece* were gone for ever, but servants were not yet a vanished race—there were four at Conduit Head—the style of life was still generous and hospitable, and certainly the 1920s were a pleasant time to grow up in a well-off academic family. Both Mr and Mrs Cornford were prepared to allow their children a considerable degree of freedom. In her poem, 'Ode on the Whole Duty of Parents', she writes

> The spirit of children are remote and wise,
> They must go free
> Like fishes in the sea
> Or starlings in the skies,

Whilst you remain
The shore where casually they come again.

An admirable programme—but the difficulty, in the words of another poet, is "to sit still", and it must have been particularly so when dealing with John, who, long before adolescence, was "fiercely defending the citadel of his independence and shielding a sensitiveness that would never forgive intrusion". Professor Cornford, whose observation this is, goes on to say: "If we were to be friends later, the only hope was to give him every possible freedom and never try to force the barrier of reserve." Admirable again; and on the whole this was the view that prevailed. But there were difficulties, since a child's and an adult's notions of freedom can so easily not coincide, and a parent may transgress without even being aware that he is doing so. It did not occur to Mr and Mrs Cornford, for example, that John, although diffident and shy, might mind being called in with Helena and Christopher to meet Professor Gilbert Murray at tea. In fact, he did mind, he did not want to meet Professor Murray, and he ran off to hide in the bushes. "His mother searched the garden, calling and asking him to come but he never appeared. She said nothing more to him and forgot all about it." For the Cornfords it was an episode of no consequence. For John, however, it bulked large: he had asserted his independence, he had not been made to do what he did not want to do, but at the cost of 'disappointing' his mother and thereby risking the loss of her affection.

One evening, some two months later, he was saying his prayers, in which the word 'happy' came at the end.

John: 'I'm never happy now, Mumma.'

Mrs Cornford: 'You seemed very happy after tea.'

(He had been rolling about on the lawn with Christopher, full of laughter.)

John: 'No, not never, really.'

She begged him to tell her why. He hid his head and began to cry, saying only, 'Why did you call me, Mumma, why did you?' She was completely puzzled. At last the memory of calling him to see Professor Murray flashed on her mind. She asked incredulously whether it could be that he was unhappy about this thing she had never thought of again. He nodded, saying once more, 'Why did you call me?', but then, after sobbing a little more, as if with relief, he hugged her happily and settled to sleep content.

One returns to Mrs Cornford's Ode. "You must be suddenly near," she wrote, drawing upon her own experience, "To love and to caress." And she was, and she did, as long as John and custom would allow.

Until he was nine he attended day school in Cambridge. Then, in accordance with that custom peculiar to the English upper classes of separating boys from their parents at the earliest convenient moment, he was sent away to prep school. Mr Cornford, aware of the importance of enrolling his son at a school that would get him off to a good academic start, chose Copthorne, in Sussex. It was qualified to do the job: to prepare a boy for the next and most crucial rung on the ladder: the Public School. John's education, rung by rung, was to conform to the pattern of his class.

The four years at Copthorne are quickly summarized: if there are no records of outstanding scholastic or athletic achievements, neither is there a history of unhappiness. Self-sufficient and self-contained even as a very young child, John became increasingly so as he grew older; he would not have resented being sent away from his parents: it proved that he was 'on his own', always an important concern for him. At school he did well enough to cause no uneasiness at home, and he went, from the first, his own way. We have an early glimpse of him in a letter from a family friend who took John out from school for a picnic with her own children and wrote to Mrs Cornford on February 2, 1925: "John is still inclined to walk 20 yards in the rear, but there is less imaginary bowling! Mr Randall said he was slow at settling down but that he was making friends now . . . I believe John's slight isolation is due to some originality; I believe he thinks more than any of mine."

He did, of course, think a great deal, and read a great deal, and thought about what he read, at home and at school. A year or two before entering Copthorne he had begun to read the historical novels of G. A. Henty, which led in turn to an interest in biography and history: military history in particular. He was fascinated by the campaigns of Napoleon and the American Civil War: while still at day school he asked his father for a biography of Stonewall Jackson. The Great War represented an opportunity missed: "Not to fight particularly," he said when he was nine, "but to go to a military college. Because now I have no military experience, have I, Mumma?"

Military history, however, was not a passion: only cricket was. He had an exhaustive knowledge of the history of the game, spent all his pocket money on books about it, and could produce the most recondite information, such as the names of players for Sussex in 1900 who had the same middle initial. Ironically, when it came to playing the game himself, he was not much good—enthusiastic but clumsy—and his Headmaster told Mr Cornford that John's style was "the most incredible he had ever seen". At football, thanks to his weight and strength, he was somewhat more effective. But the Cornfords had decided not to send the younger Christopher to Copthorne as they were afraid he would overshadow John there as an athlete—that distinction that means so much at school—although Christopher had already recognized John as his intellectual leader. In this respect Christopher was his earliest disciple, and there would not be another for some years. John's emergence as a figure-to-be-reckoned-with takes place, not at Copthorne but at Stowe, his Public School.

These years from nine to fourteen continue rather than change the pattern set down earlier: the 'slight isolation', the 'barrier of reserve', are evident at school and at home; there were limits to the intimacy he would allow, even—or perhaps one should say especially—with his parents. Yet he was not a brooding, unhappy, difficult child, moody and solitary, a kind of baby Heathcliff. In fact, he had friends and pleasures, and enjoyed himself in the world about him thoroughly, but in his own way, at his own prompting. Certainly he enjoyed the holidays at Conduit Head, and the summers at the Cornfords' mill near Hunstanton on the Norfolk coast. There he and Christopher would play war games in the chalk pits; for a time he was a butterfly-hunter; he swam in the sea; in the evenings he would listen quietly as his father read aloud to the family from *War and Peace* and *Pickwick* and *John*

Brown's Body. He was growing up darkly handsome, rather gypsy-like, sultry and swarthy—"the ape-ish good looks of the Darwins made somewhat more magnificent and imperial"—but he was still very much the schoolboy, for all his assurance and ability to know his own mind; and he needed then an older friend, someone outside the family, in whom he could confide. Obviously his parents would not do: against them, as they themselves realized, the "citadel of his independence" had to be defended. And Christopher, though devoted, was too young.

He found what seems to have been the ideal person in the summer of 1928, when Christopher brought home for the holiday a young master from his prep school, Reginald Snell. Snell was immediately charmed by the Cornfords, parents and children alike, and they by him: he would spend every school holiday with them for the next seven years. He was fascinated by the young John Cornford, impressed by the quality of his mind, responsive to the complexity and power of his personality, beguiled by his humour and gurgling laughter. The friendship between them grew rapidly: John seems to have understood from the first that Reg Snell would never condescend to him and would talk to him as though he were an adult. Talk they did, as they tramped across the downs or bicycled around the countryside, about a variety of subjects, from cricket to politics, and there is no reason to believe that John, in the summer of 1928, attached more importance to the latter than the former. Snell discovered him to be a confident 'Lloyd George' Liberal, a bit smug in his assurance that the Welshman had all the answers for a troubled England; and he suggested, teasingly, that John, when he had the time, might look into Marx, whose answers were said by some to go deeper, to get closer to the truth. Then the conversation veered, to poetry perhaps: it would be another three years before John would act upon the suggestion so offhandedly made. But Snell, except as it were by accident, was not to play an important role in his political development. Especially in the years of early adolescence, he was a friend and confidant, and a link between the boy and his parents. At the end of the summer of 1928, when the holiday was over, Mrs Cornford wrote to Snell about John: "He needs your friendship. He needs somebody with whom he *can* be intimate, and shake off that mask . . . I have just ceased to be any use in that way. I have no doubt I shall be some again when he's really grown up. But at present he would rather be remote with me . . . To live in a shell (even later on in a good solid attractive shell) but *never* to be intimate, is his huge danger."

2 Stowe

In October 1929—at the beginning of the Great Depression but in a country that had never really recovered from the effects of World War I—John Cornford entered his Public School. The choice, rather an unusual one, was Stowe, near Buckingham, which was then only in its sixth year of existence, and which the Cornfords settled on principally because they knew and thought well of the Headmaster, J. F. Roxburgh, who had been a pupil of Mr Cornford's at Trinity.

Stowe had been founded in 1923, but not as an experimental or progressive school—in the style of Dartington, say—aiming to cope in new ways with the new problems of education that arose in the post-war periods.[1] Quite the contrary. It was a paradox of the anti-Victorian 1920s that the Victorian passions for self-improvement, self-advancement and self-aggrandisement in education should manifest themselves once again in a fashion oddly reminiscent of the previous century—at least among those who could afford them. In the nineteenth century there had been a demand, backed by money, for more boarding school education than was available, and for this reason many new Public Schools had been called into being, and many old grammar schools had been converted to Public Schools. To some extent this was an expression of the need, generally acknowledged, for more and more education for more and more children; but it also represented the desire of the middle-class parent to provide his sons with an education that would assure, if not augment, their position in class-conscious English society. World War I changed many things, but not parental concerns and ambitions. In the 1920s there was an almost universal belief among the expanding middle classes in the desirability of a Public School education, which had the practical effect of limiting its availability: demand continually exceeded supply. When the time came to go on from preparatory school to Public School, the bright child from the right social background—or sometimes the exceptionally bright child, without the background, or the not so bright child with a family connection to a particular school—could generally find a place; but many middling families with middling connections could find no reputable school for their male offspring.

The solution resorted to was precisely that of the Victorians: enough new Public Schools to satisfy the demand: not modest establishments that might grow splendid and tradition-encrusted with the passage of years, like latter-day Etons and Harrows, but full-blown Public Schools from the start, like such foundations of the nineteenth century as Marlborough and Wellington. In 1921 the great mansion of Stowe, celebrated by Pope, the former home of the Temples and Grenvilles, came on the market, and was ultimately bought by the Martyrs Memorial and Church of England Trust, who there, in May 1923, founded Stowe School. The result was to ensure the survival of the vast neo-classic house, with its colonnades and porticoes and painted dome, and the large park with its scattered eighteenth-century monuments; and Stowe itself has become in the space of forty years or so a Public School of undoubted distinction.

When Cornford entered in the autumn of 1929, it was still very much a new school, still in the formative phase—and favourable therefore to a certain venturesomeness on the part of staff and students. Its curriculum was standard fare, but Roxburgh, who had been an outstanding teacher at Lancing, was mildly progressive in his attitude towards it. In a pamphlet he wrote in 1930 on the future of the Public School he pointed out that modern languages might well confer many of the same virtues as Latin and Greek and prove to be more relevant to the modern world, particularly for schoolboys who would grow up to be businessmen.

But Stowe was not attempting to strike out in dramatically new directions. Indeed, it laboured for some years under the slightly unjust, undeserved reputation of being a school for the not-too-bright sons of the *nouveaux riches* who could afford a Public School but would not be admitted to a more distinguished one.

Stowe was a second choice for the Cornfords. They had been considering Eton and Winchester, and finally decided to put John in for a place in College—a scholarship—at Eton. But the standard there was exceptionally high, and the competition formidable. His father thought it a wise precaution to put him down also for Stowe, which he did in September 1928—at the beginning of his last year at Copthorne—not concealing from Roxburgh that John would enter Stowe only in the event that Eton rejected him. Roxburgh did not demur at the condition: a brilliant boy from a notable academic background was not so easily come by that one worried over precedence. John acquitted himself well on the standard entrance exam; he was accepted promptly by Stowe; he was given the scholarship his father had said would be essential. (The Cornfords, though comparatively well off for the period, were a good deal less than rich, and their expenses were high; as Mr Cornford explained in a letter to Roxburgh, there were five children to be educated.)

But his acceptance by Stowe had not diminished John's preference for Eton, and he went ahead to sit the exam for College in the summer of 1929. He was placed sixteenth on the list of scholars elected to fill vacancies in the Foundation Scholarships. However, by the time a place actually became available for him, he was settled at Stowe and enjoying it. Neither he, nor his parents, nor Roxburgh, felt that he should leave. So the idea of Eton was put aside without reluctance.

Did it matter? The years between twelve and sixteen are crucial in the history of John's intellectual development. One might argue that he would have developed differently if he had been at the older school. In College he would have had to contend with much more of an intellectual *élite* than was the case at Stowe; Etonian traditions might have proved more confining and demanding; at every turn in his thought he might have been more insistently challenged. But the point is speculative. All things considered, the choice of Stowe seems felicitous. A new school, with a headmaster of great charm and intelligence, and a staff of young, enthusiastic and imaginative masters, it provided an atmosphere in which John thrived.

He arrived there on October 7, 1929, a little after the beginning of term, as he had been exposed to mumps and his mother kept him at home. At first, very briefly, there were the traditional uncertainties and hazards of the new boy at an unfamiliar school. But long before he was offered Eton, he had become the master of his situation at Stowe, and continued so thereafter. He seems to have been a boy around whom friends gathered: he was magnetic and impressive; which held true at school and in Cambridge on holidays. In both places he was at the centre, or the leader, of a group, not with any conscious effort on his part to assert himself: it was something that happened.

Although in succeeding years he grew increasingly restless and impatient to be done with Stowe, convinced that he had had from it all it could give him, he was never actively unhappy there—unlike Julian Bell at Leighton Park—and in his first year he was "on the whole, a contented citizen". It was then, of course, that the contrast between prep school and Public School would have been at its most marked: proof that he had got beyond childhood and was no longer to be treated as a child. Compared with Copthorne, Stowe was Liberty Hall. John revelled in the opportunities it afforded him (or did not deny him) to think and do and say as he pleased: his character as a rebel began to reveal itself. He enjoyed walking through the park at night—without permission—when the Temple of the Worthies, the Palladian Bridge, and the other eighteenth-century monuments in their states of ruination seemed to him "far less cheap" than they did in daylight, and he could see "the whole main building lit up and reflected in the lake". He ought to have been inside—which no doubt added to the enjoyment of being outside—but his nocturnal strolls were not detected, or if detected, tolerated. More significantly, he took the courageous step of refusing to join the school's Officer Training Corps. To join or not was officially voluntary, but "I am having a certain amount of pressure put upon me about the O.T.C.," he wrote to his parents. "Mr Timberlake [his Housemaster] is rather keen on it, and but for him I should have no hesitation about not joining it. He is very nice about it, and that is just the trouble. He is not in the least bit militarist, and does not want to compel me in the least. At the same time, I can see that he would rather I joined . . ." But in the end he did not join, and he was not made to suffer for it.

In the first year his time was divided among studies, games, friends and a multitude of interests: somehow everything was kept in balance, and he moved rapidly forward. He was playing cricket, enthusiastically but unskilfully, and rugby, which, he wrote to his parents, "I am really beginning to enjoy . . . though I always thought that I should like soccer better. I am in the top game of the bottom club now, and if I stay there I may get moved up into the middle club next term." He was making friends of all sorts: a few close friends, "intellectuals like himself", but also "a section of the more desperate characters, brainless 'toughs' who had an anarchist and anti-authoritarian outlook which John shared", and also, certain of the masters. (Perhaps the most exciting aspect of Stowe, in part a result of its newness, before the lines had rigidified, was the relative ease of relations among teachers and pupils. Friendship was possible, as between John and Hugh Heckstall Smith, a science master just down from Cambridge, whose enthusiasm for the richness and variety of intellectual life was infectious and illuminating. A lover of music, Heckstall Smith would have informal gramophone concerts at which the boys were welcomed. John had never had much feeling for music: experimenting with foghorn noises during hymns at the back of chapel, he concluded that he was tone-deaf; now, at these weekly concerts, he listened and was moved, especially by the symphonies of Sibelius and Beethoven.) But what is most remarkable about this first year, and typical of John's precocious ability to manage his life, is that somehow he kept games, friends and all other interests in balance with a quite formidable programme of studies—English, History, Latin, Greek, French and German—in all of which he took the School Certificate in July 1930.

It had been a very full, very satisfying time for him. But almost immediately dissatisfaction set in. His "terrific rate of development, his burning energy", gaining momentum in each successive year, led to a predictable result: the school simply could not contain him—he was beyond it long before he left it. "'Forging ahead' is a well-worn expression," his brother Christopher sums up, "but it is the best I can think of to describe his life. Trying to know him was like standing on a railway embankment and trying to grab an express train." His elders—his father, Reg Snell, the masters at school—who had hitherto regarded him as an intelligent but not exceptional child, now began to recognize that his mind had a power and his character a forcefulness that were altogether uncommon. "I was visiting Stowe when he was about fifteen," Professor Cornford recalled. "We were talking about a modern book and I made some very ordinary remark. John replied with a criticism so penetrating that I had an odd feeling as if I had received a blow on the chest. I thought, 'This boy has a better brain than I have.' I had also a profound belief in the strength and fundamental rightness of his character."

In his first year at Stowe there had been a kind of generalized excitement: everything interested him. In succeeding years there he was interested chiefly in poetry and politics, and to a somewhat lesser degree, in his studies. After taking the School Certificate, he would concentrate in History. But he was never entirely happy about this decision, and was continually tempted to the formal study of English. As late as the spring holiday of 1932, at home at Conduit Head, he was still uncertain of his commitment to History, and his father sent him to talk to I. A. Richards (with whose criticism John was already familiar) about the possibility of reading English when he came up to Cambridge the next year. Literature—poetry in particular—seemed at first, when he was between fourteen and sixteen, the direction in which he meant to go.

Why he should have turned to poetry in the autumn of 1930 cannot be precisely determined. Of course he had grown up in a house where poetry was taken for granted as a natural part of one's life: his mother was a practising poet, his sister Helena had begun to write. And the climate was favourable at Stowe: C. R. Spencer, the English master, whom he admired, kept up with the new poetry and brought it to the attention of the very active Literary Society of which John was a member. But for whatever reason, there was a remarkable and highly characteristic burst of poetic activity: "he attacked the subject with his usual voracity", Christopher tells us. Not only did he read a great deal of poetry, once his interest had been aroused, but he also began to write it, to criticize and theorize and presently to talk about it, with friends and teachers, and most importantly, with his mother.

He was fourteen and determined to assert his independence. His father recognized this: "It seemed to be my part to stand aside and give him every opportunity to take his own line." And his mother recognized it too, but found it more difficult to maintain a tactful attitude of detachment. Her love was perhaps too possessive, or was felt by John to be so. He defended himself against it by adopting a brusqueness in his dealings with her—was short, thoughtless, sometimes rude, ungiving, unconfiding. Once, in a letter to Reg Snell, he spoke regretfully of this, and Snell took advantage of the opportunity to reply: "I always wondered, by the way, if you knew just *how* rude you were to, and how deeply you wounded, your extremely sensitive mother. Since you mention it, I will mention (what I've always been too cowardly to say outright to you, tho' I've occasionally wanted to) that it's the one thing about your home that embarrasses me, and makes me feel awkward when I'm there. Possibly, you being you, and your mother being your mother, it's unavoidable, but since it so obviously pains her, and since you are both so fundamentally fond of each other, I wonder whether it couldn't be avoided . . . Your mother is so very much the wisest woman that I've ever come across, that I think I instinctively take her side, so to speak, in any difference of opinion that she may have with any member of the family. But then, I grant you, I haven't been brought up by her."

It was an aspect of the classic warfare of adolescence that goes on quite apart from, and without doing injury to, a fundamental fondness. If Mrs Cornford was too sensitive not to be wounded by John's behaviour, she was too wise not to recognize in it a kind of protective veneer and she never wavered in her conviction, expressed in a letter to Snell, that "Deep down, emotionally and spiritually, John is one of the most generous people I've ever known."

For each of them, in very different, contrasting ways, poetry was meant to and did serve an extra-literary function. For Mrs

Cornford it was a way of bringing John close to her: there was a continual exchange of letters on the subject between Stowe and Conduit Head, and when he was at home on holidays, long serious thoughtful conversations. For him it was a way of declaring his independence from his mother, since his views were dramatically opposed to hers. This became apparent at once. The divergence between them went deeper than the expected antipathies of the older and younger generation—she, for example, admiring Tennyson and Browning, he finding almost nothing in them to admire ("I detest nearly all Browning and I am more annoyed by Tennyson's artificiality and Victorianism than I enjoy his occasional really good verses")—and got down to essential questions of subject and technique. Mrs Cornford never condescended or lectured to him, or presumed upon her achievements and position as a poet to lend weight to her opinions. Very wisely, she treated him as an adult; very bravely, she sent him her new poems, as she wrote them, for criticism. At times their roles reversed: it was he who seemed the older and more experienced writer; his tone was serious, knowledgeable, judicious and severe. In the early autumn of 1930—that is, when he was not yet fifteen years old—he was writing to her:

> Here are your two poems. I don't like either of them as much as the previous short one: though I think that in both of them you are getting much closer than in any of your earlier poems—except a few lines now and again—to a live language. But in the first, "as it tells the birds" grated on me at any rate unpleasantly. They seem to be utterly false to the image-structure of the poem, which is surely as important as the music of it. I wonder, how much of your poetry is shaped by tradition: are the poems that you write really your most important experiences? or has your view of poetry been so much moulded by the traditional view that the more important experiences are too repressed to occur in poem-form at all? I don't know in the least myself: but it always seems to me that you have a great deal that needs to be said more urgently but can't because of the limitations of your view of poetry—because I should guess (though I don't know) that until fairly recently you would have denied (and perhaps still do) that every subject is equally "poetical". It may be, of

> course, that I am trying to substitute another and equally narrow concept of poetry; but I think it can include all that yours could and more besides—though I think that language is fantastically limited at present, and the more psychology I read the more I am convinced in this: in short I believe in a much stricter vocabulary and a much wider range of subjects; and writing unselfconsciously on a subject enormously depends on whether anyone else has before. To say something not only new, but that will enforce in most readers, if they are to accept it, an extended definition of poetry, is almost impossible to do without some sort of flourish and defiance of the stupider reader in advance: it is there that tradition is so important, that your tradition has gone so utterly wrong.

The tradition to which Mrs Cornford belonged, and which in John's eyes had gone "so utterly wrong", was that of Georgian Poetry, the movement that had been christened, sponsored and publicized by Eddie Marsh, her great friend and a frequent visitor at Conduit Head. Its most famous exemplar was Rupert Brooke, after whom John had been named, and of whom he was now to write, in a paper to be delivered to the literary society: "Rupert Brooke developed an individual use of language that might have been perfectly adequate to communicate any experience of any value; but he had none, only vaguely noble emotions, and had therefore no excuse whatever to publish." What is of particular interest in this summary execution of his namesake, as in the missionary letter to his mother (whom he would have been pleased to convert to *his* tradition) is not the degree to which Brooke and Mrs Cornford approach or fall short of John's standard, but that he should have so early determined upon a standard. He knew what he wanted poetry to be. There are key phrases in the passages we have quoted—"A live language", "A much stricter vocabulary", "An individual use of language"—that, taken together, comprise a programme for achieving verse that will be honest, accurate and significant, the qualities he valued most. These notions of style—the manner in which the poem is written—were inseparable from his conviction that "every subject is equally poetical", and that the poet must write "unselfconsciously" on a "much wider range of subjects" than in the immediate Georgian past. He was particularly scornful of the Georgian's "beautiful" subjects which had, he would have insisted, little to do with "any experience of any value". Christopher, who joined him at Stowe in the autumn of 1930 and thereafter was a constant companion, recalls that he "loathed all false lyricism and romanticism. 'Beauty' was a word unmentionable in his presence . . ."

Mrs Cornford was secure enough in her own tradition not to be converted to John's, and went on writing and sending to him poems that she must have realized he would object to. Perhaps she enjoyed stirring him up. Surely she cannot have imagined that he would approve of 'Tapestry Song', which she sent him in May 1931:

> O here is Paradise for me
> With white Does bounding,
> And here the fair immortal Tree
> With various fruits abounding. . . .
>
> O sweeter, sweeter, every one
> Than mead the Gods have drunk,
> And all are for the Shepherd's Son
> Who leans against the trunk . . .
>
> See where the Tiger to destroy
> Doth roam with ebon stripes.
> O Shepherd, O Arcadian boy,
> Play, play your pipes!—
>
> *How sweet the shepherd his pipes doth blow—*
> *Sing Ut Hoy, Tirlee, Tirlow—*
> *How silverly, silverly whistle and play*
> *Like drops of dew at the break of the day.*
>
> *Like drops of dew where cowslips are,*
> *Sing Ut Hoy and echo it far,*
> *Drops of dew where periwinkles blow*
> *Ut Hoy, Tirlee, Tirlow . . .*

The poem continues for another fourteen stanzas, listing the various animals who come to dance to the shepherd's pipe, and concludes:

> *All Creation, safe and free,*
> *Sings around the Happy Tree.*
> *Tirlee, Tirlow, and Ut Hoy,*
> *Play for ever, Shepherd Boy.*

John's response was predictably severe. "I have just finished reading the 'Tapestry Song', which I did not like in the very least. I did not think it one-tenth as good as the 'Autumn Fantasia'. which I nearly liked."

The 'Tapestry Song' was a kind of studio piece, an exercise in Georgian pastoral written (it would seem) with a minimum of emotional involvement, and so Mrs Cornford could offer it up without pain to John's rigorous disapproval. (And indeed to her own—in the final version which appears in her *Collected Poems* [1954], she has removed all those arch "ut hoy" stanzas.) Disdainful of mere 'prettiness', he reported to her that "our English set had a competition as to who could find and quote the worst piece of English poetry". John's choice—he does not identify it, but it might come fitly from a minor Georgian—was cited as co-winner:

> The river dawdled silver clear,
> A lane of mirrored sky
> Thro march and lawn of jewelled green
> And restless fields of rye,
> Thro haze and heat and round the feet
> Of meadow sweet July.

Given his preference, it may seem odd that she should not have sent him the admirably simple and expressive poems that she was writing at this time:

> 'Where have you been? You look queer,
> You look black.' 'O my dear,
> All alone to Hell and back,
> By my known, my desert track;
> Though once I might, like you, have gone
> By candlelight to Babylon.'

'What have you seen?' 'No flame or fires,
But such a stream of terrors and desires.
O my child, nothing's there
Like your fingers, like your hair,
Nor this table, nor this chair;
Nothing certain but despair.'

But as she admitted to Reg Snell, she was vulnerable to John's criticism, and it cost less to sacrifice a fanciful studio piece, however technically ambitious, than to risk his dismissal of a poem in which she spoke, however indirectly, of her own deep feelings. Yet his attitude towards her verse was not wholly negative. He had "almost liked" 'Autumn Fantasia', and when she wrote to him in a mood of discouragement about her poem 'Mountain Path', he told her "I think it is really really good"—perhaps one more "really" than he really felt. At the same time he made a number of detailed criticisms of particular words and rhymes—"I don't like 'fire' rhymed to 'higher' " etc.—although if one compares the final version of the poem and the suggestions he offered, it would appear that Mrs Cornford knew her own mind and had enough trust in her own experience not to kowtow to her assured, schoolboy son. But intellectually, their discussion is very much on the level of two adults; whether it was on that level in an emotional sense it is of course impossible to say.

For the exchange was not one-way—her poems, his criticism. As he criticized the poems his mother sent to him, so he sent poems to her to be criticized, but with more protection for himself than he would allow to her—at first they were shown as by a friend of his at Stowe; and always he was careful to disparage them in advance. The strategy is evident in a letter he wrote to her that winter. He begins, with undoubted sincerity, "I hope you have liked the poem I sent you." Then, bringing up reinforcements: "I sent it to Reg to criticize, and he was distinctly pro." Then, since it was her opinion that he valued, and fearing that it might not be favourable, he concluded, "It isn't particularly good." Yet even when her opinion was enthusiastic, as very often it was, he was likely to disparage the poem she had praised. Once when she wrote to ask his permission to show to friends one or two poems he had sent her, he replied, "You may show that other thing to all the people you want to, if you like. I disown it absolutely. It appears to me a complete failure in almost every respect."

John's difficulty as a beginner, not an uncommon one, was that he was considerably more assured in his reading and theories of poetry than in the writing of it. It was only some five years later, at twenty, in the last year of his life, that he wrote a handful of poems that approached the standard he had set for himself from the beginning. And by then, ironically, it was no longer a challenge that mattered to him as, at fifteen, it had. In his discovery of poetry, reading had led to theorizing, and theorizing to writing. The gap between theory and practice—the kind of poem he wanted to write, and the poems he actually wrote—was a source of continual dissatisfaction. His view of what poetry ought to be was based principally upon his reading of Robert Graves, T. S. Eliot and W. H. Auden, the poets whom he most admired, in whose work he found "a much wider range of subjects" and a much more "individual use of language" than in the tradition he associated with his mother. He wrote to her in February 1931, "I have just come to an end of the Robert Graves [*Poems 1926-1930*]. I found them exceedingly good, though intensely obscure. I don't think you'd like them a bit, as according to what I think your definition of poetry is, you won't find them poetry at all." Mrs Cornford no doubt was acquainted with Graves's early work, some of which had appeared in *Georgian Poetry*, but it was his "later and more intellectual style" that John admired and attempted to emulate. (In his essay on Graves, he dismissed the early work as belonging to "the *London Mercury* branch of the Georgian movement, that dead movement which Graves himself condemns in the *Survey of Modernist Poetry*".)

Graves was the first influence; Eliot was the second (and most powerful); Auden was the third. In an essay he wrote in the summer of 1931, he described Graves and Eliot as attaining "a successful artist's practice of poetry". Of Auden's first book, which had recently been published, he declared: "whatever its ultimate value, it is already of the greatest historical and literary importance". It was not surprising that their voices, echoes of their cadences, diction, and stylistic devices should be heard in his poems. He thought of himself as belonging to their tradition, post-war, post-Georgian and new. "Thanks to Eliot and Graves I think I am able to tackle a far wider range of subjects in a more direct way than you were when you were at the same stage as I am," he told his mother. He disagreed with her that "the most any poet can do is to write a few individual lines for himself in every poem and let the tradition he writes in write the rest for him". Eliot and Graves were admirable because they wrote so carefully that "hardly a line of either of them could be confused with another poet". Yet there was the risk of his being drowned out (in his own poems) by their unforgettable voices; it was essential to draw a line between admiration and imitation. He was determined upon an individual use of language: "I am only just beginning," he wrote in the summer of 1931, "to find out a little about the correct use of English: and still find it abominably hard to get an absolutely accurate expression of what I want to say."

1931 was the first, and also his most productive year as a poet. It was a year of experiment, trying out various forms and styles, one voice and then another. And he wrote a great deal: at times as many as several poems a week. It was characteristic of John that whatever he did, he did wholeheartedly—he was never a dabbler, or dilettante—so now he was a beginning poet and critic, deeply in earnest, and the role contented him for a time. That year, from September to September, Mr Cornford's sabbatical, his parents were living in Switzerland, at Glion above Lake Geneva, and John and Christopher went out to spend the school holidays with them there. The discovery of poetry, and of himself as a poet, had very recently occurred; in his own eyes he now had an identity quite apart from being his parents' schoolboy son, and this made it easier to be less guarded and more openly affectionate with them. "John put off his armour of scepticism," Mrs Cornford reported happily to Reg Snell, "and talked most charmingly with FMC and myself on all manner of subjects." As one might expect, she found him much more sympathetic and splendid as a poet than a critic. Toward the end of January she wrote to Snell again: "John the last three days wrote 3 poems, all good—doubtless he'll show them to you. The difference in his whole being when he creates and stops criticizing, is astounding."

The poems of 1931 seldom rise above the level of 'juvenilia', and then only slightly, and we shall not quote from them extensively here. (None were included in the memorial volume brought out after his death.) John copied a number of them into a blue-covered student's notebook, presumably those he liked most, or else, considering the scathing comments he made about some of them, those he disliked least. There is a title page, complete with epigraph drawn from a contemporary poet whom he admired:

A SLAB OF TRIPE

Poems 1931

JOHN CORNFORD

Between the marble and the metal
I hear their reedy voices pipe,
Where the blue burnished angels settle
Like flies upon a slab of tripe
—*Roy Campbell*

The epigraph is appropriately chosen, for most of the poems that John preserved in this notebook are ironies and satires, albeit of a rather obvious kind:

The clink of empty glasses in dim bars,
Hoot of the foghorn bawling out to sea,
The klaxoning of twenty million cars,
Is this thy chosen music, liberty?

Or again, in 'Machine':

Man conquered nature; then I conquered man;
I laid him low before he could resist . . .

The time when he could fight my ways is past,
For years ago he had become my slave,
Fed, clothed and carried by me: at the last
Murdered by me and driven to his grave.

A power house is his fitting burial ground,
Whose wheels turn ceaselessly above his head,
Chanting his epitaph as they spin round
"He sold his soul to progress and is dead."

Religion, of course, was a favourite target, in these early poems, and in his life at school. He wrote to his mother, "I have just come from a really superb argument with the School Chaplain in which I defeated him rather heavily. The unfortunate man has to take us in 'Divinity' every week, in which we read a hopelessly incompetent book about the Christian religion, on which I and one or two others (sometimes) attack him furiously. The good man is fairly intelligent but extremely slow, and it always ends by one forcing him to the most extravagant statement, or else losing his temper." 'Divinity' entertained him; it also provided him with subjects for poems. In this same letter he told his mother, "I have only one poem to send you this week—a very weak one, which is meant to convey the terrific and disorderly impression I obtained from reading Ezekiel—which, I think, must have been written under the influence of drugs, as some of the visions correspond so closely to the descriptions of men's visions under drugs." Of the poem itself, 'Ezekiel Saw the Wheel' ("In the red depths of a hashish hell" etc.) he remarked with disarming candour, "It fails rather badly—seeming somehow to be too obviously an imitation of I am not quite sure what."

'Divinity' precipitated at least two further poems—one, with its title from Eliot ('This is the Way the World Ends') and an epigraph from Graves ("We are also gradually tending/To be less philosophical") rings ironic changes on the idea of a God-created universe. In its opening stanzas, one hears (presumably) the argumentation of those weekly meetings with the School Chaplain:

In the beginning the Word, or if you like
In the beginning vast perpetual lakes,
Tall rocks, dull marshland drained by squelching dyke,
Half riddles. Is man one of God's jokes?
And should I ask what came before the rocks
You say innumerable electric sparks
Fusing together with unfeeling shocks . . .

> What came before the sparks? Why, Sir, the Word—
> *Caetera fecimus*—the very essence of God—
> But, Sir, your questionings become absurd.
> Since all things work together for the best
> This problem does not touch us in the least,
> Leave to your God to order all the rest.
>
> Electric sparks; then rocks and sucking mud
> Then the first trees of the primeval wood,
> Apes and then men: and after that the Flood
> And why? Because the Lord our God is good . . .

On the whole, John seems to have enjoyed the argument more than the poetry it gave rise to: he decided to exclude 'This is the Way' as well as 'Ezekiel' from *A Slab of Tripe*. But 'Miracle', a satiric anecdote of human rather than divine fallibility, pleased him more, and he copied it into the notebook in May. Its direct, unadorned speech suggests the kind of unpoetical, Gravesian poem John valued, where the poetry is not in the decorative properties (nymphs, shepherds, bells, and roses) but in the play and interplay of sound and idea:

> The candle which the priest held upside down,
> Flickered, guttered, went out in one slow second.
> Who then, triumphantly, with smile or frown:
> 'This is or is not just as I had reckoned.'
> Either 'the flame before it faltered out
> Burnt upside down until I let it fall.'
> Or else 'the faith which shifts whole hills about
> Does not expend itself in deeds so small.'

The characteristic note of irony or satire is entirely absent from his most ambitious poem of that winter, 'Garret', which he thought well enough of to include in the notebook, but repudiated as soon as his mother praised it. It is a long, romantic, one might even say Georgian, descriptive poem, written in quatrains, that tells of a sick man in an attic bedroom, who lies awake throughout the night, listening to the sounds in the street outside. It begins:

The ugly gaslights' dim persistent burning
Flared with a hideous brilliance for sick eyes,
While on the wall huge shadows unreturning
Flickered and shuddered to a monstrous size.

All night he lay too dazed with pain for feeling,
Groping for drink, his throat too parched to swallow,
But with the dawn, the cracks along the ceiling
Made a cool pattern for his eyes to follow.

At ten o'clock he heard a street dog bark,
The plaintive undulations of a tram.
Mouth open, he breathed husky in the dark,
Wincing with pain to hear the front door slam.

And so, stanza by stanza, through the hours of the night, from twelve, to one, to two, to

The darkest hour, the hour before the dawn,
He lay in silence, too afraid to speak.
Only he heard a rattling lorry's horn,
Only a window blind began to creak . . .

Aroused, at length he staggered from his bed,
Tormented by his night of useless pain,
Then clapped his cool hands to his burning head.
To ease the angry drumming in his brain.

Then fumbled in a drawer for shirts and braces,
In the dim squalor of the city room,
While from the street below a sea of faces
Tossed ever onwards, upturned through the gloom.

It was a perfectly respectable piece of work by a boy of fifteen who had been writing verse for no more than two or three months at most, and Mrs Cornford was understandably pleased. But John was not pleased by her praise. In fact, this is the poem, alluded to earlier, that he disowned absolutely. "It appears to me a complete failure in almost every respect," he told her. "The metre is utterly unsuited to the subject, and very clumsily handled. I'm sure that no sick man ever would behave in the least like that. There are 7 or 8 good lines which redeem the poem from being sheer drivel, but not enough to make it the least good. Besides, it's almost a crib of Robert Graves' 'Down'. Do you know that brilliant poem?"

Now, it is true that 'Down' and 'Garret' (and how many countless other poems!) are written about a sick man lying awake in the night: there, however, the resemblance between them ends. But if John was determined to measure his own effort against Graves's, the one truly enough "that brilliant poem", the other a bland assemblage of familiar poetical counters, it is not surprising that he was irritated by praise from his mother. Yet whenever she praised him, Mrs Cornford was neither insincere nor doting: it was simply that, if she felt it advisable to do so, she applied a relative standard to his work, keeping in mind his youth and inexperience; whereas John without fail applied a high and inflexible standard to himself (the Graves standard, so to speak) and found himself wanting. But in the case of this particular poem Mrs Cornford's admiration for it was such that she decided to submit it for publication to Middleton Murry's *The Adelphi*, where her own work often appeared. In the early summer of 1931 she reported to Reg Snell, who was then in Germany teaching that "The Adelphi says it *may* publish John's 'Garret'. He says he is perfectly indifferent about this, as long as his name is not allowed to appear; it would be disastrous to have his name attached to such a romantic work, for his first published one!" But in the end the poem was rejected, and the problem of choosing a pseudonym did not have to be dealt with.

He was very serious about poetry, and about himself as a poet; he threw himself almost too wholeheartedly into the role—that is, the *intellectual* role; he was never the aesthete in a cape, drinking absinthe. As Christopher remarked in his memoir, there was an element of dramatization and self-consciousness about John at this period that was sometimes a little absurd. Yet he was aware of this himself. "I am always considering not what I want to do, but what impressions my actions will make on other people, and on myself afterwards," he wrote to a friend. And he added firmly, "That can, and is being cured." Still, the sin seems venial. "We were all serious," Christopher observed, and it is not seriousness but the strategy of *how* to be serious that makes for difficulties in adolescence: whether to be covertly serious and appear frivolous; or to be openly serious and appear solemn. John had an exceptional mind and was eager to use it, nor was he prepared to apologize for it: he hadn't time to be stupid. In part this would explain the ease with which he entered into friendships with people many years older than himself—Reg Snell, for example, and Hugh Heckstall Smith.

Perhaps the most remarkable of these friendships was with Sidney Schiff, then in his sixties, whom he met in Switzerland the winter of 1931 when he had gone out to spend the holidays with his family. An Edwardian figure from the plutocratic world of Anglo-Jewish banking, and a friend of writers as various as Katherine Mansfield and Marcel Proust, Schiff at the age of fifty had decided to dedicate himself to the literary life. He possessed a small dignified talent, and under the *nom de plume* of Stephen Hudson he had gained a small dignified reputation as a novelist and translator of Proust. (When John wrote to Reg Snell about him, he replied, "I keep mixing up Stephen Hudson, W. H. Hudson, and Stephen Graham, but I know they aren't really all the same men.") Schiff and his wife Violet were wintering at Glion, and inevitably, given the interconnectedness of English intellectual society, proved to be friends of friends of friends of the Cornfords, with whom they were now acquainted. He fell into conversation with John and Christopher one morning when they were walking along the snow-banked Glion-Montreux road. As Christopher recalls it, Schiff was "instantly impressed by John's rebel character and amazing maturity". John, dissatisfied with his life at Stowe, was full of admiration when he learned that the elderly writer had run away from Wellington almost fifty years before. They talked of books and writings; and a friendship was begun that continued for the next year or two—really until John transferred his allegiance from poetry to politics.

In May Schiff was back in England and proposed coming down to Stowe on a Saturday to visit. John replied, "I am extremely sorry to say that I don't think either Christopher or I could manage to see you if you come down on Saturday for any reasonable length of time: since we have both been roped into various cricket teams, and on that particular day we shall have to play from about two to five in the afternoon. I have tried hard to get permission off the game from the authorities, but, since I have been harassing them on almost every conceivable subject this term, they are only too glad to refuse me anything. I think Sunday is probably the only day on which we are both always certain to be free: on Saturdays there is generally cricket or something equally nauseous, but on Sundays we are always free from 12 to 6." Another letter from about this time evokes the tone of "*cher confrère*" that John imparted to the relationship: "I sympathize with you about your work. I too am in something of the same position: several times this term I have had a poem utterly ruined by not being able to write it down at once: and the mood is impossible to recapture. I suppose it is somewhat the same in prose writing but I have never yet tried seriously."

Schiff was clearly taken with John's talents, and did his best to bring him on and make his name known to a wider public. John himself professed no urgency about having his work published. In May he enclosed a poem in a letter to his mother, "not because I think you will like it, but if you think it good enough please give it Dadda for his birthday. Personally I am vaguely pleased with the earlier part, and I think it is the only thing that I have done that is worth keeping, but you won't like the theme or the language. Certainly I shan't attempt to get it published, or at any rate, not for a long time." Which, of course, is a not unfamiliar way of saying that he would not have been averse to publication. Schiff was generous in his praise, and constant in his encouragement. He believed very seriously in his young friend as a writer. In the winter of 1932, when John sent him his essay on modern poetry, he thought it so impressive that he decided to send it on, unbeknownst to John, to his friend, T. S. Eliot, who was then editing that most exemplary of intellectual quarterlies, *The Criterion*. In the essay it is perfectly clear that Cornford knew his Eliot backwards and forwards, and placed him first among modern poets. Did Schiff send it to Eliot simply to inform him of his standing with the youngest generation, or to establish an interest in Cornford, or even for possible publication? One can't be certain. It is probable that he himself, convinced as he was of John's talent, thought it worthy of publication, and took care to make his covering letter sufficiently ambiguous, so that if Eliot by any chance wanted to publish the essay, he could. Eliot in his reply was splendidly judicious:

> He is obviously a boy of whom much may be expected, but at present alarmingly precocious. On principle I should never willingly publish anything by a boy at school or even by an undergraduate at college, because I feel that nowadays there is a tendency for young talents to blossom before they have taken deep root. I doubt if I should have accepted this even if I had not known the age of the author because it seems to me that he has not yet learned to manage the English language with great ease, and he is inclined to use cumbrous words and cumbrous constructions. But I do not suppose that you yourself wished to see this particular performance in print, and I can sincerely say that I am very much impressed by the boy's abilities and I should like to be kept in touch from time to time with his development.[2]

There is no reason to believe that John ever saw this letter—at least there is no mention of it in his correspondence. But at approximately the same time, Spencer, the English master and patron of the Literary Society, sent one of John's poems to W. H. Auden. Auden, who was then teaching at Larchfield Academy, a preparatory school for boys in Scotland—he had succeeded Day Lewis in the position—wrote to John directly:

> Dear Mr Cornford,
>
> A poem of yours has come to me with the suggestion that I shall say something about it. This, as you can imagine, is not easy, as I know nothing about you but your name and age. I think the only useful criticism is the personal kind—if I could say 'Get into the first XV' or 'Shoot your French master with a water-pistol', I might really be of use—but as I can't you must forgive me if anything I say sounds too like a governess.
>
> First of all, I think your power of writing, of using words is very good indeed. Considered as a craftsman, you have nothing to fear. My only suggestion here (which I daresay is unnecessary, as I haven't seen anything else of your writing) is that you might do more with stricter verse forms. I think it is easier to find what it is that *you* want to say . . . as the very nature of the form forces the mind to think rather than to recollect. (Incidentally while on this question of originality, of course being

> influenced by others doesn't matter. One damn well ought to be. And you must cheat and quote verbatim.)
>
> The real problem though for you as for every other writer, but particularly for people like yourself who come of literary stock, and are intelligent and well-read, i.e., certainly developed, is that of the Daemon and the Prig. Real poetry originates in the guts and only flowers in the head. But one is always trying to reverse the process and work one's guts from one's head. Just when the Daemon is going to speak, the Prig claps his hand over his mouth and edits it. I can't help feeling you are too afraid of making a fool of yourself. For God's sake never try to be posh. I can't say anything more about this because I don't know you or your life. If it's a choice between reading and doing something else, do something else and remember that everything your housemaster says about the team spirit and all that (perhaps he doesn't but suppose it) is absolutely right but that it is the tone of his voice which makes it such a lie. He always forgets to put on the crown of thorns. May I anyway wish you every success and happiness.[3]

Unlike Schiff, who had been exposed to the force of John's personality, Eliot and Auden, in each case judging solely upon the basis of one sample of his literary production, felt him to be a talented and precocious schoolboy who might very well become a writer—or again, who might not. Their view, so much less flattering than Schiff's, and more realistic, was also closer to John's own. The dissatisfaction and discontent he felt in his last years at Stowe flowed out to colour almost every aspect of his life and certainly his activities as a poet. The poems of this later period—from the autumn of 1931 to December 1932, when he was finally allowed to leave Stowe and went off to London—differ in quality and kind from the earlier ironies and satires. They are more ambitious, more serious, written out of conviction and with deep feeling. But they do not communicate as much of their meaning as he intended; clear in their language, they are often obscure, slightly out of focus, as though he had said only part of what he meant to say. *The Waste Land* was an intimidating precedent. He believed it to be a great poem, read it not as a religious allegory (which Heckstall Smith, who had been introduced to it by John, claimed it to be) but as an anatomy of capitalist society in decay; it shaped his style, but more important, it was a preface to his politics. He had only to look beyond the confines of the splendid eighteenth-century park and there was England, in 1931, in the grip of the depression—the waste land:

> This is the land [he wrote] Take stock of our inheritance . . .
> In sidings disused coaltrucks rusting . . .
> Ships drifting in and out of silted harbours
> Where the gutted dogfish sprawls on sandbank . . .
>
> This was a giant's castle, and here was done
> Such and such, magnified and dimmed by legend
> Till it means nothing to us. Now these legends
> Shall no longer interpose their meaningless language
> Between us and the fact.
> This land is not worth even the trouble of claiming.
> We will disinherit ourselves, and stranger knocking
> At the door of this ruined castle, must turn back, finding
> This is ghosts' house, there is no one to answer the bell.

Which, for all its echoes of Eliot and Auden, was not ineffective, but not quite what he wanted to write. Had the Prig edited the Daemon? Or was it that the tradition made no provision for certain subjects—politics, for example—that were important to him? He thought the latter. He told his mother "there are still a number of poems which I have in my head intrinsically as good as any other, which, because of the history of poetry during the last ten years, I can't and never will be able to write." He never would abandon poetry entirely, but even at Stowe his interest in it began to diminish, the while his interest in politics grew. He drew a line between them: one could not give oneself wholeheartedly to both, and politics counted for more. In his last year at Stowe, he wrote only a few very personal poems. Except for one love poem, none is overtly autobiographical, but all, it is clear, have their source in "a growing feeling of restlessness and dissatisfaction with the limitations of his life". In February 1932 he wrote to a friend, "Here is my latest and I think my best poem." In fact, what he enclosed was a suite of four poems, written at different times, and put together with no regard for their order of composition. "I don't know whether you can find any coherence in it. There is none intellectually," he said, "but I feel it as a whole, and I hope you can find the connection too." No doubt there are connections, or clues, to be found in the events of his life at this period, but the poems, especially I and II, which John himself liked best, exist quite independently of them, and can stand alone.

I

At least to know the sun rising each morning
And see at least a sunset's punctual glory
Is at least something. And at least to hear
Water over a rock, all night dripping,
And at least sometimes to walk the mountains all day
And stain our lips with bilberries. In the winter
Snow falling at least covers the earth, gives promise
Of at least something more than for ever sitting
Here, in darkened rooms frowning back a headache.

Hand on the tiller and the flapping sail
And brows contracted, the blessing of concentration
On a single time and place, this boat, this sail.
Wind in the roots of the hair, eyes see no further
Than the small circles of the rain downwards falling
Silently into the sea, and far enough.

II

Leave off loving and be hating;
Complete the final well-worn round.
Practised in all the arts of hurting
Satisfy the will to wound.

Whirled by wind the cold sleet falling
Smoulders rage, hinders its stroke.
But even now, with anger falling,
Exploit your mood for its own sake.

Carry your hatred to its limit,
Expose to wind and sleet those sores,
And when exhaustion comes to end it
With no pride show healing scars.

Auden had written to John both as a young poet, which he was, and as an English Public Schoolboy, which he also was, although he threw himself a good deal less wholeheartedly into the latter role than the former. At the end of his first year as an "on the whole contented citizen" at Stowe, he became restive and would have been glad to be elsewhere—not at another school for they were all equally confining, but to be free. In short, he wanted what he could not yet have: his independence. The pattern of the upper-middle class, to which he belonged and was being made to conform to, offered no feasible alternative: a boy was at school until a certain age—at least seventeen. Hence the discontent and restlessness that were inseparable from his later years at Stowe. But although he was increasingly and understandably dissatisfied, it was not his style to brood, sulk or languish. He was impatient, not unhappy. He had so much energy, curiosity and *élan* that one feels he would have found something to enjoy, or at least to interest him, in almost any situation. Certainly this was the case at Stowe, where he was actively engaged in the life of the school at all its levels, from sport to music to high-spirited anarchy. Although he objected on principle to organized games and was not very good at them, he was nevertheless passionately interested in sport: he played hard, walked for miles, swam, and never abandoned or forgot his amazingly detailed knowledge of cricket, past and present. He was a prime mover of the Literary Society, and a member of the Debating Club. As a leading rebel and non-believer, he figured importantly in a campaign (successful) to put an end to compulsory attendance at evening Chapel. He had many acquaintances, and it has been said that everyone who knew him liked him. But he allowed only a few to know him well—his chosen friends—and of these perhaps the two closest were a slightly older boy, here called 'Hugh Evans', who was to influence his politics, and his brother Christopher, who joined him at Stowe in his second year.

John's role toward his friends was somewhat that of a 'father figure'—one who was consulted and confided in—perhaps because there was a certain austerity, a certain aloofness about him, or a certain wisdom, that kept him from the kind of emotional situations in which they found themselves caught up, confused and let down. His one romantic attachment in these years—innocent but intense, and perhaps the more intense for being innocent—was to his cousin Elisabeth, whom he saw in the holidays, in Cambridge and in Norfolk. Christopher in his memoir tells us that, away from Stowe, "John was the leader of a small circle of which I might say that I was the chief priest. While I was with him at Stowe, and for a long time afterwards, John meant everything to me: I thought and lived through him and was with him whenever I was able. To varyingly lesser degrees this was the case with all of us; with my cousin, with those schoolfriends of John and myself who stayed with us during the holidays, with a girl friend of my sister's, and to some extent with my sister. We were all rather conspiratorial, and talked a lot about the Younger Generation Breaking with the Past, and of course about Art, Sex, Psychology, Politics and what we called Life." There were picnics, swimming parties, bicycle trips, sunbathing in the dunes and games of soldier-stalking about the Cornfords' windmill at Hunstanton: the ordinary joys and jubilations, to set against the misunderstandings and grievances of adolescence.

The situation of the two brothers had dramatically changed from what it had been only a few years earlier, when their parents had decided against sending them both to Copthorne. Now there was no danger that Christopher would outshine his older brother because of his greater ability at games. He was almost too contented serving as 'high priest' for John and his rebellious views. The atmosphere was highly charged, and Christopher was keyed up rather more than his parents (and Roxburgh) thought good for him. John "admitted that he'd rather overbalanced Christopher with his constant ratiocination last term," his mother wrote to Reg Snell, and at the end of the year the Cornfords decided that Christopher should not return to Stowe. Thereafter he attended a day school, The Leys, in Cambridge. As it happened, at the end of that academic year (1931), Hugh Evans also left Stowe—which meant that John's two closest friends were gone—and at about the same time there was a crisis in his relationship with Elisabeth. Her mother felt that the young people were becoming perhaps a bit too intense, and that it would be a good thing if they should not see each other alone quite so frequently. Elisabeth acquiesced, which allowed John to claim that he cared more deeply than she. Undeniably there was an element of self-dramatization in his avowals and demands upon her, which presently he would recognize. A poem he wrote to her some months later is, in effect, an apology "For how I have wronged you and wronged myself"; and it concludes, "Now no longer see me/As I once wished you to, but as I am." His feelings for her henceforth were intermittent and unresolved: "At times I miss Elisabeth badly; at other times scarcely at all. There is certainly nothing more to be done."

One consequence of the departure from school of Christopher and of Hugh Evans, and of the changed relationship with Elisabeth, was that his discontent crystallized. Then the whole Stowe thing hardly seemed worthwhile, and one can sense something of the dissatisfaction he felt as he faced the camera that year for the photograph of the History Sixth. But he broached to the history master, MacLaughlin, the possibility of his trying for a scholarship for Trinity College, Cambridge, the next year. "His chief argument against it," John reported to his mother, "seems to me to be that I would have almost two years with nothing to do if I got it, as Trinity would not want me till I was nineteen and they wouldn't want the two years' gap between scholarship and coming up. Also, singularly childishly, he says that Trinity would ask me why I wanted to leave early and if they found it was because I disliked Stowe it would be a bad advertisement for Stowe!! But he says if he can get a 'guarantee' from Trinity that they wouldn't mind the two year gap he is prepared to do it. Anyhow FMC [his father] could find out about that. I wish he would write to MacL. as I don't look forward to 7 terms more. 4 will be quite enough." But by spring even four terms were more than he could contemplate with equanimity. He could adduce any number of reasons to justify his dissatisfaction with Stowe, but they were all slightly beside the crucial point: he wanted his independence. Historical circumstance—the fact of England in political and economic crisis—pointed up the contrast between the world outside, and the artificiality and constriction of life at a Public School. He wrote angrily to Reg Snell of the "futility" of his present existence, and blamed his parents for having sent him to Stowe. Reg replied, "I don't see how your parents can fairly be blamed, or anybody or anything except an intangible (but tremendously tough) social convention, which lays it down as absolute law that people of your class, and of your age, shall go to one or another of a limited number of extremely similar Public Schools for 5 years 'education'. After all, what else could you be doing? If the accident of birth had brought you into the world in a mining village instead of a university town, you would now be working underground during most of the hours of sunlight (29,000 boys *under sixteen* do this, and they are killed off or maimed . . . at the rate of 251 per 1,000—a quarter of their number—each year)." But this was not an argument that would make John any the happier about being at Stowe—as Snell realized: "I hope all the foregoing sounds convincing; I don't really believe it, and what is more," he added incautiously, for he was putting ammunition into John's hands, "I argued against your going to an orthodox public school, with your father and mother, the first time I came to Conduit Head. We had a protracted session, and eventually I was convinced by the Olympian logic and fairness of F.M.C."

The Cornfords were dismayed when they realized the extent of John's "very true and real hatred of public schools", which, of course, he did not attempt to conceal from them—he told his mother that, on principle, he broke every school rule, if he was sure of not being found out. During the spring holiday, at Glion, Mrs Cornford "tackled seriously the idea of his leaving Stowe", only to discover "it was *quite* clear he didn't want to". What she failed to realize was that the alternative she proposed—that he come back to live at Conduit Head and work under various coaches there—would seem to John only an exchange of one form of dependence for another. In the circumstances, Stowe was preferable, for what fifteen-year-old boy would not feel freer at school than at home, under the eyes of his doting mother? Rather touchingly, Mrs Cornford brought the conversation round to "the necessity of freeing yourself psychologically from your parents—only so could you return and have a perfectly free and happy relationship with them". She was thinking so entirely of "mental and spiritual independence" that she was nonplussed by the vehemence with which he said how much he wanted this freedom, and how impossible it was while he had to depend on his parents for every penny. "You can't separate body and mind, it's impossible!" he told her.

In September 1931 John began his third year at Stowe. He was in a bleak mood: Christopher and Hugh Evans were gone; there were few friends left whom he wanted to see; among the masters, only Heckstall Smith. In the spring he had been "distinctly enjoying" his work in history with MacLaughlin, and decided that he liked history "very much more than classics", but now he wondered if he wouldn't be happier doing English with Spencer. He wrote to Hugh Evans that he was suffering from "loneliness in the worst sense—not being able to come into any reasonable contact with 500 people who are nevertheless unavoidable". It was precisely at this time that his mother provided him with the opportunity to reopen the question of his leaving Stowe. In the course of a very cheerful letter, which began "this is after supper & at any moment Stewart Wilson may begin to sing on the wireless, whereupon I shall run. So if this ends abruptly—its stamped envelope awaits it—you won't think the abruptness has dark psychological causes," she had referred in passing to the family finances: "I still feel it's our scale is more wrong than our income, if you know what I mean—so we are not really the deserving poor. But at the same time we are heavily in debt to the bank at the moment."

John replied immediately: "I should like you to consider rather seriously the idea of my leaving at the end of this term." He was now ready to accept the proposal his mother had made in the spring: that he return to Conduit Head. "Because I think that by doing so we should (a) save a certain amount of money. I don't know how much, but I shouldn't think CH would cost as much as Stowe, even though I am a scholar. And all the inane expense of clothes would be cut down enormously; (b) that I think I should be able to learn as much or more than I do now in less time: and would leave myself a great deal more spare time to read and write what I wanted to . . . My objection to Stowe is that I spend a good deal more time of the day than is necessary working and the day is so organized that I don't have time to do very much with my spare time . . . Also, rather important, since I have to be in bed by 10 o'clock here, which means altogether 9 hours in bed, since I need so little sleep I have to waste about two hours a day doing absolutely nothing, not even sleeping. In the summer I could read in the early morning but this term I can't . . . Also I'm beginning to feel rather badly the need for interesting people."

But his parents had either forgotten or changed their minds about the proposal of the spring, and insisted that he must remain at Stowe. Had they not done so, had they allowed him to come back to Cambridge, it is not inconceivable that his life might have taken a somewhat different course than it did: for he was now, at a time when his various discontents had crystallized, to experience the most significant year of his intellectual development.

Christopher, in the memoir, asks, "Exactly why and how did he become a Communist?" And answers, "Everything tended towards it: study of history, literary criticism and an inner drive which caused him to revolt against the restrictions of his life, and also made him unsatisfied until he had found, in everything on which he focused the power of his formidable intellect, the essential element, the key to action." One must also add that the times were favourable. In 1932, in a period of international economic and political crises, it did not seem either unreasonable or unusual to look to Marxism for answers, to find them there, and to believe in them.

"I have found it a great relief to stop pretending to be an artist," he wrote to his mother in 1932, and in this same letter he told her that he had bought "*Kapital* and a good deal of commentary, which I hope to find time to tackle this term. Also *The Communist Manifesto*." He was turning to politics, and Marxism in particular, as the area for his beliefs, and where his abilities would fuse so that he might achieve his great potentiality. In many respects his literary endeavours, as well as his personal dissatisfactions, had been crucial in pointing him in this direction. Hugh Heckstall Smith, in his autobiography *Doubtful Schoolmaster*, points out that it was John's insistence on the greatness of T. S. Eliot's poetry that led him to read, study and appreciate what Eliot was saying, and so finally to become a Christian. He cannot understand how John could reconcile his admiration for Eliot's poetry with his Marxist politics. But there is reason to believe that the black vision of the world that Eliot presents in *The Waste Land* may well have provided the original impetus for John to try to change the world.

Once his interest in politics was thoroughly engaged, he moved rapidly Left. At Copthorne, he had been as much as he was anything, a Liberal of the Lloyd George variety. At Stowe for a while his interest in politics simmered. He wrote to his mother, "I have at long last been elected to the Debating Society. I made a very brief and violent speech, mostly quoting Disraeli and I did not once mention the motion, but merely jeered at the opposing speakers and compared the audience to a communist mob." In this same letter he spoke of making "the acquaintance of one [Evans], a rather magnificent character, with whom I can argue for hours". Evans, whose father was a prominent figure in Whitehall, knew the inside nature of Establishment politics at their most personal and nasty. He could present such a picture of them to John, no doubt a powerful and instructive one, reinforced on Hugh's part with some Oedipal pleasure in doing the old man in —certainly in the next few years as the father moved to the far Right, his son was at the other end of the spectrum. Hugh and John talked and gossiped politics—still very much as schoolboys —and John was 'for Russia', seeming to share the opinion and the attitude of his History master: "He is the only person I know who has really got the thing in its right perspective & he is an admirable Liberal. He thinks that . . . the Five Year Plan will succeed. If it does, it will leave Russia infinitely the most prosperous and well organized country in the world."

When Christopher came to Stowe in the autumn of 1930, he found that John had become a Socialist sympathizer. He recalls: "As we strode together through the school grounds, among the great beech trees and lakes, the rotundas and monumental obelisks, in shiny blue serge Sunday suits and stiff collars unloosed, he explained to me the principles of the 'nationalisation of industry' and the injustices of our economic system. 'But don't go shouting about it,' he said, 'or you'll make yourself unpopular.' "

Of course, it was just at this time that John's outburst of poetic activity began, and for the next several months politics had only a peripheral claim on his attention. In February of that year, between discussions of poems, he wrote to his mother of the New Party, Mosley's last effort on the Left, and its demand that the Government do something radical to deal with the growing economic distress. His own half-serious scheme, as he described it to her, was that a "band of enthusiasts" would march around England with great placards marked "DISARMAMENT, P.R., LIMITATION OF FRANCHISE, BIRTH CONTROL, NEW UPPER HOUSE, DESTRUCTION OF SLUMS" etc.; then, a petition to the Houses of Parliament signed by ten million would threaten to refuse to pay taxes, obey laws or in any way co-operate with the Government.

In the autumn of 1931 he came into full political consciousness. As a result of the general election in October, Labour's Parliamentary representation was cut from 287 to 46. The 'National' Government, with MacDonald, Baldwin, Chamberlain and Simon at its head, had 556 seats in Parliament; 472 of these were Conservative. For John, as for so many others, the collapse of Labour and the triumph of the National Government seemed to represent the total bankruptcy of British politics, and the end of any hope to do very much with the sold-out and antiquated machinery of parliamentary democracy. In November he wrote to Sidney Schiff, "The election seems to me a piece of sheer political lunacy on the part of the electorate. The government has no sort of programme or policy whatever—and it takes into office nothing whatever except a record of political dishonesty almost as great as the Socialists, or greater. I think there'll be trouble in the North before long, if the Communists organize the unemployed as well as the suffragettes were organized in 1913."

He became increasingly serious about politics, and at the same time, more and more dissatisfied with the poetry he had been writing. It was as if he felt that as a poet he could no longer express himself fully, and needed a wider stage on which to do so. His estrangement from his mother's literary tradition was complete; and he seemed anxious to put an end to the dialogue on poetry they had been conducting for the past two years. "I don't know whether or not I like your poem; or rather, whether or not I understand it; because words seem to have a totally different meaning for us." But although he no longer seemed willing to share his literary interests with his mother, particularly as they were in a state of decline, he did not hesitate to write to his parents about his political views, and a lively debate, or rather, interested parental replies to enthusiastic letters, dominated much of the last year's correspondence from Stowe. Urging upon them a pamphlet, *Wage Labour and Capital*, a summary of the economic argument of *Das Kapital*—"(only 50 pp., do buy it and read it with FMC if ever you have time, as it is perfectly intelligible)"—he remarked, "It seems to me dishonest for men like Laski to dismiss the Marxist interpretation of history and yet proclaim Marx as a great prophet, because his wonderfully accurate prophecy is dependent on his interpretation." Mrs Cornford replied, "*Certainly* we'll get that shorter Marx thing & read it," and under John's guidance his parents did read some Marx, Maxton on Lenin, and other similar literature; but it had discouragingly little effect on their views.

In the summer of 1932 Hugh Evans was in Russia, sending back enthusiastic letters which served to bolster John, at Stowe, in his convictions. By the autumn of that year, in his thinking if not in actual fact, he had become a Communist. At the age of sixteen he had come to a view of the world which he found fascinating and sustaining, complete and good. But he was still at Stowe, cut off from the 'realities' of the world outside: this accounts for an occasional air of closet speculation about some of his thinking at this time. But there is also an admirable toughness and absence of sentimentality. When his mother wrote to ask if the term 'Hunger Marchers' was not sentimental and unjustified, he answered: 'I think the Hunger Marchers were really hungry. I don't think it's sentimentalism. B. Seebohm Rowntree calculates that the price of living for a family of 5—*without considering rates or rents*—is 31*s*. 8*d*. I don't know how much a baby costs to feed—certainly it must be more than the 1*s*. it's allowed under the present Means Test; once rents and rates have been deducted, it might be possible to buy enough food for the week: but there is still the cost of lighting and fuel, as well as occasionally doctors, unemployment insurance, etc. In Stoke some families that had been evicted erected huts out of their furniture, and stretched sheets on top. They were *fined 10s.* and told that it wasn't allowed. And the iniquity of the Means Test is that, while formerly the dole was fixed, so that wages had to be a few shillings above, or else no one would work, the new provision is that benefit shd. be below the rate of wages—so that where one employer is able to enforce a wage-cut, the benefit level in the whole district must come down. So I think they really were Hunger Marchers."

Eager though he was to enlighten her, he finally despaired of bringing his mother very far down the revolutionary road. He felt that she would always regard Communism as a 'religious movement' and never consider it from an intellectual standpoint, which meant that she would be making "objections that aren't at all relevant to the central problem". And he became a little irritated, albeit in a perfectly indulgent way, with her concern for "inner spiritual freedom". As it was, the intellectual position had to be clarified and settled, and this was done in long letters to Hugh Evans. (On G. D. H. Cole: "His preface to *Das Kapital* immensely weakens his position, by his [as far as I can see] purely negative rejection of the Marxian Theory of Value. [For Cole, the only source of profit is co-operation; for Marx, not only co-operation, but the labour time embodied in the surplus product.]") John apologized, "Sorry my letters are so like manifestoes." But perhaps it was inevitable that they should seem so: not only did Marxism offer him an explanation for the lamentable state of the world, but also the possibility that it might yet be saved.

During the summer and autumn of 1932, when this tremendous intellectual resolution was in progress, John was also studying for the scholarship examination for Trinity College, Cambridge. In December he took the examination in History, and was awarded a hundred pound exhibition, at "the preposterous age of 16", as his Headmaster wrote. The usual thing, then, would have been to return to Stowe for the Spring and Summer terms, to enjoy those last 'golden months' when he would be free of academic pressures, and Public School life could be lived to the full extent of its romantic mythology. That was hardly John's style, however. As he could not go up to Trinity in the middle of the year—indeed, the college would be stretching a point to admit him in the autumn when he would be only seventeen and a half—he persuaded his parents to allow him to enrol for the remainder of the academic year at the London School of Economics.

Meanwhile Roxburgh, the Headmaster of Stowe, was writing in headmasterly tones—affectionate and a little patronizing—to J. R. M. Butler, the historian and Fellow of Trinity, to apprise him of the remarkable young man who was soon to descend upon Cambridge. "He is very 'advanced' as Sixth Formers are apt to be nowadays and I cannot keep pace with him at all in his views on politics, economics or literature. But he is very charitable in his attitude to elderly schoolmasters, and though he disapproves entirely of the public school system, he takes no active steps to interfere with its working at Stowe.

"In personal appearance he is very striking and he wears his dark and curly hair startlingly long and has a contempt for people who bother at all about their clothes. But he is a delightful person to have in the place, and I should have liked to keep him here for some time longer."[4]

3 London

In January 1933, a few weeks after his seventeenth birthday, John Cornford came to London. At last he was to be free—after the restrictions of Conduit Head, and Copthorne and Stowe—to live as he had long wanted, away from parental or quasi-parental supervision. On the point of leaving Stowe, he wrote to his mother that he was "particularly anxious to be alone for a while". He knew that she would have preferred that he "be with a 'responsible' person for the first few months". The Darwin connection extended into London; or there were family friends there with whom he could live. But this was precisely what he did not want. He reassured her: "I really don't think you need worry. I know myself when I am living the right sort of life; the silly things I have done in the past were because I haven't yet begun to find the right organization of life."

He had had more than three years at Stowe; a Public School education was expected to prepare one for the world as well as the University; and in any case John was so evidently able to take care of himself that there was no thought of interfering with his plan to enrol at what his mother called "that odd London School of Economics". Professor Cornford, impressed by the quality of his son's mind and character, felt that he could be trusted to act in a responsible, adult manner. At the end of January he wrote to Roxburgh gratefully: "I think Stowe has helped him through a period in his life in which he might have been dangerously warped and driven into a wasteful sort of rebellion. As it is, he is coming through all right and I have no anxiety about his future."[1]

He was to be in London until midsummer of 1933, a period of little more than half a year of his life, and his attendance at L.S.E. was thought to be a way of passing the time usefully—Mrs Cornford was under the impression, false as it turned out, that he might do Moral Science—until he was ready to take up his scholarship at Trinity College, Cambridge, the next autumn. Yet however brief the period, it was not insignificant: he came up to London with an already formidable theoretical knowledge of life, art and politics; to it he would now add an almost equally extensive experience of all three.

It must be said at the outset that his academic experience counted least with him. He did enrol at the London School of Economics. He did, when he had time—which was not often—attend lectures. His tutor was the distinguished nineteenth-century social historian, H. L. Beales, an assurance that, whatever work John did for him, he would have been offered a solid grounding in the connections of Government and economic conditions, and a dispassionate account of the inequities of the Industrial Revolution. But for John, the importance of the London School—which had been founded by the Webbs and whose best-known teacher in 1933 was Harold Laski—was as a base for his activities. It enjoyed an undisputed reputation as the centre of the student movement on the Left, in London certainly, and in the country at large—although by that time the movement was under way at Cambridge and at Oxford. For a convinced young Marxist like John, who had had no chance to put his ideas into action at his Public School, it was the logical place to go. And the time was also peculiarly favourable. The Depression was at its worst; Hitler had just come to power in Germany; the unthinkable war began to loom. Thus, the three principal battles lines of the Left in the first half of the 1930s—say, until the outbreak of the Spanish Civil War—were established in the winter when John was in London: to fight against poverty (or Capitalism); to fight against Fascism; to fight against War. (It was not yet apparent that the second and third might be in contradiction.) And of course, for a young man who believed, as John did, that Communism held the solution to the world's problems, there was a fourth: to fight to establish Communism in England. The student movement had been, one might say, in its latency period; from now on it would grow rapidly, and John would be in the thick of it. He came just at the right moment from the converted country house of the Dukes of Buckingham to plunge into a maelstrom of activity. Soon he was writing to a friend:

At the moment I'm
Secretary FSS
Editor *Vanguard*
Sec. L.R.D. Group
Sub-editor *Young Worker*
L.S.E. Anti-Fascist Committee
Marxist Society
Anti-War Committee, etc.
So you see I haven't time to write.

He took a room not far from the school, off Red Lion Square, in Parton Street. Like all the rooms he would occupy thereafter, it contained a minimum of furniture—mattress, table and chair—and a maximum of mess. This did not represent a new development. Towards the end of his time at Stowe he had shared a study with two friends, which, as Christopher put it, "he kept in a state of sordidness and bareness which would be difficult to describe; not because he liked it like that, but because he was too preoccupied to care about his aesthetic surroundings or bother to improve them". Nor did he care about his personal appearance. Once, Mrs Cornford in a superb understatement ventured to write to him about his "untidiness", and he replied, "The stage I object to is when a room gets so untidy that one can't find where anything is. I don't mind things getting out of place and dusty as long as I can find them as soon as I want them. For instance, I don't (as you do) mind books lying crooked open and shut, as long as I know where each one is. I don't believe chaos begins till things get lost."

He had not come to Parton Street by chance, but was drawn there by the presence, only a few doors down the street from his own lodgings, of David Archer's Parton Street Bookshop. This landmark, since obliterated, of the 1930s, was a haunt of young poets and young revolutionaries. (Sometimes, as in John's case, they were one and the same.)

It was to this shop in January 1934 that Esmond Romilly, aged fifteen, came to "hide out" when he ran away from Wellington, and it was from its back room that he published his magazine, *Out of Bounds*, "against Reaction, Militarism, and Fascism in the Public Schools". Philip Toynbee, inspired by *Out of Bounds*, ran away from *his* school, Rugby, in June of that year, and naturally went straight to Parton Street, hoping to meet Romilly. He did, and the story is told in his memoir *Friends Apart*. There he recalls the Parton Street Bookshop: "The solemn red-backed classics of the Marx-Engels-Lenin Institute, the mauve and bright yellow pamphlets by Pollitt and Palme Dutt, the Soviet posters of moonlit Yalta and sunlit tractors—the whole marvellous atmosphere of conspiracy and purpose."[2] But this was only its political side, and Archer, with equal assiduousness, made it a point to stock all the newest poetry: Auden, Spender, Day Lewis, MacNeice, *New Signatures*, *New Country*, *New Verse* . . . He was also, in a small-scale, brave and unprofitable way, himself a publisher of poetry, and it is to his credit in literary history that he brought out the first books of Dylan Thomas, George Barker and David Gascoyne, all of whom were haunters of his shop. John hadn't time to be a haunter at leisure—there were too many other places where he must be—but he would hurry in on the way to and from his lodgings to borrow books of verse and politics—Archer was a generous lender—and indeed, the shop does symbolize neatly, although not in the proper proportions, the range of his activities in London. It was as a poet that he was remembered by George Barker, coming into the shop "filthy and consumed with a ferocity of nervous energy"[3]. But politics dominated his life, and poetry was made subordinate to them. As one would expect, his politics influenced his critical attitudes, his expectations of what literature should be; but the poetry that he continued to write, though subordinate to his politics, was not subservient to them, and was kept to one side of his life in a separate minor compartment of its own.

At Stowe he had been a theoretical Communist; in London he was introduced to the Communist movement in action, approved of what he saw, and wanted to become a part of it. On March 17, 1933, little over a month after coming to London, he joined the party—more precisely, the Young Communist League, a branch of the party open to those from fourteen to twenty-five. (His first membership book, which expired in December 1935, survives, and it shows that he loyally paid his dues of twopence a week: all the stamps in his book are there.) Presumably he fully subscribed to the programme set forth in the membership book. It states as the aim of the Young Communist League "The winning of the workers for Communism and the revolutionary struggle of the working class, to educate and lead them in their struggles against capitalist exploitation and against imperialist war." It points out that "The Young Communist League as a section of the Young Communist International is bound by its decisions and must unreservedly carry them out." It prescribes that a member belong to a cell of three or more which should meet once a week, that he will form fractions within other organizations, and that he must adhere to strict party discipline. John, believing in the objective these rules were intended to help bring about, would have no reason to take issue with them.

The Young Communist League was the beginning, or perhaps one should say the centre, of his political life in London, from which fanned out all his other activities. He was endowed with a prodigious energy which seemed never to run down. The almost telegraphic letter or memorandum, quoted earlier, apologizing for not writing, lists seven organizations in which he was simultaneously working; and there were many others. His list begins, "Secretary FSS"—the Federation of Student Societies, which was formed at a conference held in London on April 9. Invitations were sent out by the Marxist Society of L.S.E. (John, of course, a member); the Socialist Society; and the October Club, Oxford, to student societies all over the country, and the response, according to *The Student Vanguard* (John, an editor) was "excellent". Such a conference was perfectly in keeping with the movement within the Comintern towards a Popular Front, which had got under way that March. Delegates came from as far as "Aberdeen University, from Bristol, Newcastle, and Liverpool, and many others. In all, 16 university colleges, from 10 universities, were represented, standing for more than 1,000 students." The Federation was formed, John was elected secretary, there was a lively discussion, and it was decided—again, as reported by *The Student*

Vanguard—that the Federation would "combat all military and reactionary propaganda in the universities and lead the fight against the growing forces of fascism, and against militarisation of the students, who in this fight above all must join in with the workers in every form of action against imperialist war and in support of the Soviet Union."

There was "Secretary FSS", "Editor *Vanguard*", "Marxist Society", and the several others, of which the most important, he felt, was "Sec. L.R.D. Group". This last, spelled out, was Secretary of a student group working for the Labour Research Department, an independent organization founded by the Webbs in 1912, which, among other research functions, put together statistical and analytical reports, and provided expert speakers for local branches of trade unions, co-operatives, and the various political parties of the Left. Always in need of funds, it relied largely on volunteer labour, mainly students. John's "L.R.D. Group", of which he was secretary and which he had helped to organize, was made up of volunteers from L.S.E. When Mrs Cornford wondered if his political work was being done at the expense of his academic work, he reassured her that the two often dovetailed. Certainly this was the case with the L.R.D. Group. John had made the economics of the transportation industries his subject, he had done a fair amount of research, and now he was allowed to put his theoretical knowledge to practical use. "On the whole question of the relation of party work to anything else," he wrote to his mother, "if I am to explain the nature of the work I'm doing for the L.R.D. it might help you to understand my position. What happened was this:

> after I had collected the materials for my research work, the L.R.D. wrote round to the Trade Union Branches (not Co-operatives) saying that they had a speaker on the Transport Act [namely, John himself] who was prepared to speak at branch meetings . . . It's far the most important job I've ever done in my life, or, most likely, will have for another three or four years. I'm tremendously lucky to have got this job, as it ought to go only to an experienced speaker and research worker, and I must make full use of it.
>
> If you put yourself in my position you can see why I think

> it's so much more important now than anything else. I have to speak to a working-class audience, usually for the most part consisting of men twice my age, on a highly complicated technical subject. I'm almost without previous experience as a speaker or as a research worker. So you can see that it needs all the power I have to make a good job of it . . .
>
> So far I've done as well as I could expect. The first meeting I undertook I was very nervous and also shaky on my material, and I was only saved from making a mess by the fact that I had a very sympathetic audience. Luckily I retrieved my failure as a speaker by making friends with the Secretary, who invited me to attend any branch meeting I liked, which is a big privilege for a non-unionist—almost like being admitted. The second time was much better than the first. The third time I was lucky enough to be at the top of my form; the branch secretary stood me a drink beforehand, with the result that I wasn't nervous before speaking! and spoke much better than I ever have anywhere before.

John's job in these talks was to present simply and convincingly a mass of facts and figures that would prove to the transport workers what they already felt: that they were being exploited by their employers, and hence would be justified in going out on strike. Here was experience of yet another kind: not only could he help to "educate" the workers, he could also, in the most direct and practical way, participate in their struggles—if there was a strike, he wanted to be there. He gave activities of this sort precedence over everything else, especially social engagements; as a result, his mother was always uncertain as to whether he would or would not be at Conduit Head for the week-end. "It may be that I shall have to call off this week-end again," he would write, "as there's a strike situation developing in one of the tramway depots, so that I may be wanted down there." He carried the struggle into the pages of *The Student Vanguard.* For the May number he wrote a one-page polemic, 'Students—Not Scabs', in which he called attention to "the imminent prospect of a transport strike in London, and the probability of a nation-wide rail strike". In that event, students must not allow themselves to be used, as they had been in the General Strike of 1926, as "scabs and strikebreakers".

But the fight against student scabbing was "not an isolated question of political opinion". Very shrewdly he linked the strike to the major concerns of the student movement: "it is directly connected with the fight against reaction, against Fascism, against education cuts, against war." And he concluded, as usual now, with his eyes fixed on the possibilities of practical action: "We shall have to explain and popularize the aims of the strike as widely as possible. We shall have to prevent scabbing by any means in our power, from peaceful dissuasion to picketing in force. And we shall put our services, as individuals or as organised bodies, at the disposal of the strike committees for whatever purpose they are most needed."

Mrs Cornford was still uneasy about the intensity of his commitment to his new, political life: she felt that he was doing too much, and she suggested that he go with Christopher for a brief holiday in the South of France. Some of their friends and relations from Cambridge would be there at the same time; it would be a pleasant change of pace for him. Finally he agreed, and they set out from London, immediately after the conference that called the F.S.S. into being. Mrs Cornford wrote to Reg Snell: "It takes John away for 14 days from the extreme tension of Communism. He's *very* happy, but it's rather too great a burning for seventeen." Back in London at Easter, he reported to his mother that he was "safe after a most fantastic journey, though what should have been the worst part—the 3rd class from Toulon to Paris for 15 hours—I slept [through] almost perfectly. Then for no apparent reason as soon as I got on to the boat, I was sick for the rest of the way, although the sea was absolutely calm." There is an oddness about the letter: it is quite long, but only one brief perfunctory paragraph—at midpoint—is devoted to the holiday. The South of France had been "well worth it, though not perfectly successful". He had been ill at ease in the hotel; there hadn't been "quite the right selection of people . . . which was no one's fault". And once more: "it was worth it for the sake of the sun and the sea and (sometimes) the hills".

That was all that he chose to say. He had walked among the Mediterranean pines with Christopher, "inveighing against the orthodox economists of the L.S.E. . . . forcing home each point with a characteristic gesture of the bended arm and clenched fist".

He had written and sent off to his mother a long polemic against the unorthodox Communism of Middleton Murry ("Forgive my addressing you like a public meeting"). He had thought about her news that she might undergo treatment with Jung for the anxiety from which she suffered, and wrote to her now, "I think you should go to him as soon as you can. What I always feel about psychologists—at any rate looking through Adler's case books (I don't know about Jung)—is that in general they only get the dregs of the unemployed rich to work on, who aren't a representative cross-section of humanity, and who are mostly incurable from birth. Anyhow that's true of his European cases; I suppose the American rich have alive blood in them a much shorter time back. So from the point of view of psychology, the more real people with real problems who go, the better. And I'm pretty certain that it would do you more good than anything else . . ."

He had also seen Elisabeth. On April 24, he wrote to Hugh Evans in Oxford, "I've had to break with Elisabeth, and I should think for good. I've seen it coming for some time back, but waited to see her to make certain. She can't lead the sort of life I do; and I neither can nor want to give it up. She's born in the wrong century; the fault for our failure isn't in ourselves so much as in the time we're living in. I tried to hope all the time that when she saw the real issues, not in terms of arguments around the fire, but among the workers, she'd feel that she'd have to come in. And I left France in a pretty inconclusive state. But when I saw the Y.C.L. at the Young Worker Conference, I felt that the gap's too hopelessly wide. I am very sorry in one way, though I am always glad of any break with the past that reflects my own position from a new angle. If one's ready to kill and be killed for the revolution, this kind of break shouldn't make too much difference. Heil, Rot Front!"

This letter, in which romanticism and priggishness, solemnity and bravado are so curiously mingled, serves to remind us of what we often forget: that John was still a very young man, and that his experience or knowledge of women, calf-love apart, was still a total blank. Now, almost immediately upon his return from his holiday in Southern France, that blank was to be filled.

A favourite place of John's to eat and to meet friends was an inexpensive Chinese restaurant, the Nanking, in Soho. It was there, on a Saturday afternoon, having lunch with Christopher, who had come up for the day from Cambridge, and with Hugh Evans, who had come up from Oxford, that he met Ray. She was sitting at a near-by table with an acquaintance of John's, a party member, and John went over to speak to him. Introductions were made. A beautiful Welsh girl, dark and (like John) rather gypsy-looking, Ray too was a member of the party—hence, a comrade—but the attraction between them was immediate and powerful and had little to do with 'the real issues'. They met again. Very soon she came to live with him in Parton Street, and they lived together, in London and Cambridge, for the next two years.

Ray's experience was not uncommon in the period. She had come from Wales, where unemployment was at its worst, to London looking for work, found a job in a shop, met friends who were party members, and eventually had joined the party herself. A few years older than John, she had a warmth and a womanliness that suited him, and a shrewd intelligence; but at no time in their 'marriage'—for such, virtually, it was—was there ever any question but that John was leader.

This new relationship did not slow down appreciably the tempo of his existence. Away from Parton Street there was as much activity as ever. A note to Evans in connection with a demonstration on behalf of the transport workers suggests the pitch of urgency at which he lived. There was a lot of work to be done; he thought it foolish to waste words over it:

> Elect 1 marshal for 50 demonstrators.
> Get out at least 100 somehow.
> I've revised the slogan list—4 on Fascism and not one on scabbing—Red Front! also omitted—overweights it heavily.
> There'll be a marshals' meeting . . . at 10:30 on Sunday.
> Get someone along if you can. If not, it doesn't matter desperately.

Meanwhile he and Ray lived very simply and happily together. It was not all politics. They went to concerts, and football matches, and on Sunday afternoons to the British Museum. Walking back to Parton Street, they played hopscotch along the sidewalk, indifferent to passers-by. At home John was as absorbed as ever in cricket, in cricket scores and cricket history, and played a cricket card game, a variant of patience, that he had invented. Also, he wrote poetry.

His literary ideas and attitudes had undergone a Marxian change. In the May number of *The Student Vanguard*, he published under the title 'Art and the Class Struggle' a reply to an article by Rayner Heppenstall which had appeared in an earlier number. Heppenstall had attempted to separate Eliot's poetry from his criticism, and thus, John argued, subscribed to "the myth of the detached artist". But "Art like any other expression of man, such as science and politics, cannot be divorced from reality, i.e., from man in relation to his material surroundings. The idea of a detached, impartial artist is therefore utterly false. The classic struggle is a conflict between the dynamic force of revolution and what Engels called the 'inertia force of history'. Any 'detachment' from this conflict means siding with the 'inertia force'." On these grounds—a flight from reality, "the separation of art from reality" —the poets of the 1920s, T. S. Eliot, Richard Aldington, Ezra Pound, D. H. Lawrence, Wyndham Lewis and James Joyce, were examined and found wanting. Thus, *The Waste Land*: "It is of great importance not for the pleasure it gives, but for its perfect picture of the disintegration of a civilisation. Its second section as a picture of the two classes, could hardly be bettered. But something more than description, some analysis of the situation is needed. And it is here that Eliot breaks down. He refuses to answer the question he has so perfectly formulated. He retreats into the familiar triangle—Classicism, Royalism, Anglo-Catholicism. He has not found an answer to the question in resignation. Rather he has resigned himself to finding no answer." Did this mean then that Eliot was no longer a great poet, as John had declared only a year or two before? He did not allow the question to obtrude. He was only concerned in putting forth, or putting down these writers as they might demonstrate the validity of the Marxist analysis of society. And he concluded, "These, then, are the best poets of their generation; and all they have to offer is collapse and retreat under the stress of decaying capitalism."

But he did not, or could not yet, allow the implications of his criticism to affect his own practice of poetry. The poems that he wrote at this period are intensely subjective and cryptic: much more a private than a social poetry. He thought highly enough of them to send some out to periodicals, and one, 'Unaware', was accepted by *The Listener*, although it was not published until the next year:[4]

They keep their nerve on ledges still
And climbing granite wall
Carry no fear
Of lightning's stroke on face of rock
Or depthless falling.

Homing at evening tired after sailing
Beyond boats' foamwide wake
Eyes unsurprised
See over dunes first sign of rains
And skyline blacken.

Yet eyes' clearness bring no awareness
And compromised with fate
They'll hear in fear
The clock's strict time tick out their doom
Who has fallen better.

This poem he signed with a pseudonym, 'Dai Barton'. When his mother had proposed to send out 'Garret', he had said it must be done under a false name: as a modern poet, he could not suffer the liability of making his first appearance with so old-fashioned and romantic a poem. So perhaps now as a Communist, he did not want to publish in his own name a poem that existed outside the canons he drew up for a new, revolutionary poetry. Or again, he may have decided already to keep his identity as a poet separate from the rest of his life, and it is true that very few of his friends in the party knew that he was writing verse.

The academic year ended beautifully for John. He and Ray were in London until the end of July. Then, in August, they camped in Horsey near Great Yarmouth on the Norfolk coast, an area familiar to him from family holidays. An American student leader at L.S.E. and his girl came with them, and presently they were joined by Christopher. T. H. White, whom John had known as a master at Stowe, was near by, working on a novel.

"We are camping in the last field before you get to the salt marsh," he wrote to his mother, "and behind there are some high sandhills and then the sea . . . T. W[hite] is writing a book inside a railway carriage in a back garden in the village, where we have been able to dump our things, so I see very little of him except in the evenings, when we go to the pub and play snap with the landlord. Otherwise I am doing very little; bathing, playing hide and seek with the children from a near-by cottage, walking, reading a little, and eating. Sleeping 9-12 hours every night."

Reassured by this letter, and relieved that his London experience was at an end, Mrs Cornford wrote to Reg Snell: "I do think the fact of his being tuned in to the world's vibrations of violence, and to a certain extent of brutality, is awful. But he's essentially all right."

4 Cambridge

In October 1933, at the age of seventeen, John Cornford went up to Trinity College, Cambridge. Doing so, he was continuing a family tradition, and it had never occurred to him to try for a scholarship elsewhere: at Oxford, or one of the provincial universities. Trinity was one tradition of which he approved: he meant to take advantage of the excellent education it could offer him. That he would be in Cambridge again, only a few miles distant from Conduit Head, did not seem to disturb or please him, or make any particular difference to his way of life. Living in college, he could see as much or as little of his family as he chose: since he was on affectionate terms with them all, it would be a question, chiefly, of finding the time. His first evening in Cambridge he met Christopher in the street by chance, and they stood in the lamplight talking. John, fresh from the freedom of life in London, had already adopted a patronizing attitude towards University regulations: he especially disliked the short academic gown that students had to wear in the evening if they were out of college. Nevertheless, he was wearing it—that night it was still in pristine condition—and, no doubt inspired by it, he assured Christopher that the University was "A lunatic asylum—run by the lunatics!" But very soon he was leading his life on his own terms, with little official interference. He even managed to make a mockery of the detested gown, which grew ever more decrepit, since he was always pulling loose bits from it, until, as a friend has recalled, "the Proctors declared him academically nude".

Now and then John would bicycle out from the Madingley Road to Conduit Head; sometimes he would bring a friend with him: more often not. His new friends, unlike the earlier Cambridge circle of which Christopher had been high priest, were not altogether at ease there, although the Cornfords did their best to welcome them. There were musical evenings and at homes and teas that John might have attended but rarely did. In order to do all that he wanted to do—more each year!—he could not afford to sacrifice his time to social occasions of that sort, where he would quickly grow bored and restless. His parents reconciled themselves to his unannounced arrivals and abrupt departures, and learned not to count on him.

John had always got on well with his father, and continued to do so now—perhaps because on neither side was there an attempt at extravagant gestures of intimacy. They liked and respected and felt no need to confide in each other. Whatever Professor Cornford might have thought of his son's opinions and activities, he would not allow himself to interfere. John's relationship with his mother was, of course, a good deal more intense and complex, but now that he was indisputably free, he was free to be fond of her: there was no longer any of the brusqueness and rudeness that had been so painful a few years earlier. Theoretically at least, she too believed that he must be allowed to go his own way. Yet she could not help regretting that he had already gone so far, and clearly meant to go further.

His parents knew about his living with Ray. In fact, John did not attempt to make a secret of it. When he was first in Cambridge, she stayed on in London and he would come down for week-ends. But this proved an unsatisfactory arrangement: presently she came to Cambridge to live, in the beginning in a room she rented from Maurice Cornforth, the Marxist philosopher, and his wife; afterwards in a little flat of her own in Ainsworth Street, and John would live there, and in his room at Trinity.

Ray represented an extreme test for the liberal attitudes of the Cornfords. It might almost be said that it was easier for them to come to terms with John's ardent Communism than to accept this serious, settled, monogamous attachment—so obviously very different from the conventional undergraduate 'wild oat': indeed, that might have been preferable. The Cornfords were intellectuals, and members in good standing of the upper-middle class. Such things are relative, of course. Still, among the younger faculty, and more especially among the wives of the younger faculty, they were sometimes referred to as the dukes of Cambridge. Conduit Head was a simple house and the Cornfords lived in it very simply; but at a dinner party there, even during the Depression, there were certain things taken for granted: a maid to serve it, fine linen, china, silver . . . There would be conversation of a certain kind, and whatever the subject, one's accent would be of a certain kind: the accent of one's class. The Depression might have affected the quality and quantity of food and wine that one's maid served at a dinner party, but in England in the 1930s the differences between the classes were still clearly marked and easily recognized. The Cornfords were too intelligent to be consciously snobbish. The fact that Ray was working-class was only another regrettable aspect of a situation that seemed to them to be regrettable in every respect: John at seventeen committed to a woman older than himself, at a time when his undergraduate career had only begun and his future was wholly unresolved. But liberalism triumphed, and they were able at least to tolerate the relationship. John would bring Ray to tea, at wide-spaced intervals, and it would go pleasantly enough. Mrs Cornford held to her principle of non-interference: when John would spring up to announce that it was time to go, she would never press them to stay for dinner. Ray had her partisans in the family circle. Christopher, then fifteen, adored her, and would not hesitate to tell his parents so. Reg Snell, who met her for the first time in March 1934, liked her very much and wrote appreciatively of her to Mrs Cornford. Her reply was splendidly ambiguous: "Yes, such a lot of the best of RJC is being used on Ray. That's why it's not *essentially* distressing (though so full of danger) as it would seem on just hearing the facts."

His experience in London had prepared John to play a leading role in the development of the student movement on the Left in

Cambridge. The very notion of a 'student movement', politically aware and committed to political action, belongs to the 1930s. Hitherto, in accord with a distinguished tradition, an interest in politics at Cambridge and Oxford expressed itself in gentlemanly speechmaking and debate at the Cambridge and Oxford Unions, some of whose more dedicated members went on as a matter of course to participate in the politics of the country. There was hardly a Cabinet Minister who had been at Oxford or Cambridge who had not been in the Union. But politics at the University were regarded as a form of training for the 'varsity of life', in much the same way that academic studies—traditionally, classics at Oxford; mathematics at Cambridge—were meant to train the mind to deal with problems of the 'world'. In effect, the Unions were the 'talking shop in Westminster' writ small; or annexes of the Establishment: party leaders, Conservative and Labour alike, often came down to take part in their debates, and kept a watchful eye on them for promising material. But the student movement that John and others like him envisioned was to function as a distinct political force of its own.

Again, 1931 was the crucial year, with the Depression steadily worsening, and the new National Government under MacDonald incapable of dealing with it in a constructive way. It was a time when, as Edmund Wilson has pointed out, "the whole structure of American society seemed to be going to pieces", and a comparable sense of collapse, of having reached a terminal point, was beginning to be felt in England. It was in this ambience, in the third year of the Depression—when John Cornford at Stowe, was writing to his mother, "I think the Hunger Marchers were really hungry"—that a Communist cell was organized at Cambridge, in the University.

There had long been Marxists in Cambridge—J. D. Bernal and Maurice Dobb, for example—but they had worked with the cell that had been established in the town. In 1931 the desirability of making a more concentrated effort in the University itself became apparent. This was the task set for themselves by the forerunners, among whom was David Haden Guest. Guest, who was later killed in Spain, was at Trinity. He had studied at the University of Göttingen, and, like so many others in the late 1920s and early '30s, he had been deeply impressed with the intensity of political life in Germany: the struggle that was being fought there between the Right and the Left. He returned to Cambridge in 1931, and shortly thereafter became a Communist, and one of the founders of a cell of four dons and six undergraduates in the University. At first the movement grew slowly—"The mass of the students were as yet untouched by the crisis and apathetic"—and the group continued to work "chiefly 'in the town', directly among the working class".[1] But "University Socialism", which later became "the main thing", also engaged their attention. Much of their activity—a welcome for the Hunger Marchers, peace demonstrations on November 11—prefigures what would be done on a grander scale in Cambridge from 1933 on. Guest went as the representative of the group to an anti-war Congress in Amsterdam. (John, at Stowe, had read of its proceedings, and wrote to his mother, "You're right that it's impossible to be a pacifist and a Communist. The Amsterdam Congress declared itself anti-pacifist. And I really don't see how any pacifist organization wd. be strong enough to fight the Armament Firms, the Banks, and the Newspapers.") He also founded a Marxist 'study group' in the non-Communist Cambridge Socialist Club, which was firmly anti-Fascist and theoretically revolutionary, and whose membership by the autumn of 1933 had grown to approximately 200, ranging from orthodox Labourites to Communists such as Guest himself.

Guest, who left Cambridge in the autumn of that year, was one of the forerunners; John, arriving there as he was departing, was one of the brilliant generation of student Communists who came into prominence in the universities in the period 1933-1936. They represented, and were able to put to use, both the dissatisfaction with the political *status quo*, and the belief that action must be taken—if not by politicians, then by students—to prevent war, stop Fascism, and cure unemployment. In the early 1930s it was not yet clear that these three urgent goals might prove irreconcilable; it was felt, though seldom stated so simplistically, that a mixture of pacifism and Marxist economics would somehow make possible the attainment of all three. The time was opportune for the student movement to gain in momentum. Massive unemployment, like an incurable blight on the land, year after year after year, had finally dissipated the political apathy of Julian Bell's

Cambridge. Even the Union, only a few years earlier a stronghold of inanity and burlesque, was affected. As a former president has written of this period, " . . . the rise of Hitler and the persecution of the Jews did not affect us as much as the discovery of what was happening in our own country. Hitler and the Means Test drove Jews and the unemployed together in our minds as fellow victims. They had this in common: no one could make a joke about them."[2] Students were prepared to think seriously about the world and their own relation to it: this was an atmosphere in which John could flourish. At the very least, by the power of his personality he made the movement more intense and effective. It would have existed without him, but not as successfully or as memorably.

John's apprenticeship to real, rather than fantasy, Communism, had taken place in London, where the party was at its most tough-minded and experienced. He had quickly shed the somewhat romantic, conspiratorial view of revolution which he had held while at Stowe: as when, assuring his mother that revolution would not lead to a prolonged and bloody civil war, he had written, "I think all that is needed is enough force to hold up communications—telegraph besides roads and rails—and get wireless stations and newspaper offices. Army must be managed with fairly clever moderate propaganda. After that all fighting would simply be a function of the enemy resistance . . ." Or, as he told Victor Kiernan, a fellow undergraduate who became a close political friend, he had begun by thinking that "all that was needed to overturn society was a surprise raid on police stations and telegraph offices. These notions he had already got beyond, but," Kiernan observed "traces of them lingered in his manner and tactics,"[3] and also, so far as respectable Cambridge was concerned, in his appearance. He had spent the years of his adolescence at what was said to be "the second dressiest Public School in England"; thereafter his style was his own, and it became a style of the student Communist, as in an earlier version it had been a style in Bohemia, and has since reappeared among the Beats—in short, among those who choose to disaffiliate themselves from the middle class. The cry, consciously or not, is "*Epatez les bourgeois!*" To which must be added that John simply did not have time to be bothered with dress. He wore what came to be regarded as a uniform: stained trousers, black shirt, ragged raincoat, and what the *Trinity Review* described as "those dirty sweaters". In the memorial volume a group of his contemporaries wrote that "Of a whole generation of pioneer Communists he was a kind of symbol—the most brilliant, the most sectarian, the most conspiratorial, the most devoted and full of animal energy," but they did not neglect to add that he was also the one "most in need, at times, of a haircut and a shave". Kiernan admits, "It was no wonder he struck Cambridge in general as 'odd'. The College magazine had a humorous description of him tramping through [Trinity] Great Court wrapped in portentous gloom and an antique raincoat." But he makes a significant qualification: "There was nothing in the slightest degree affected in his oddities. He would use a bread-knife to clean his finger-nails with complete naturalness, and his indifference to clothes was wholehearted."

This was the outward aspect. Cambridge was soon to discover that he was a good deal more than merely odd. He had an extraordinary conviction and power as a true believer, and the ability to convince others of the rightness of his beliefs. Meaning to continue as he had begun in London, on a level of urgent action, he was impatient with the gentility and theoretical character of Cambridge politics as he first encountered them. Very soon after his arrival, Kiernan heard him make "what was probably his first speech in Cambridge, at one of the Sunday Teas of the Socialist Society in a café near the Market. He was accusing the Government and the universities of a policy of cutting down entries and scholarships. He sat at one end of a long table, his right hand all the time tapping jerkily. 'Shades of opinion,' as one respectable pillar of the Society expressed it, made themselves felt on the spot; the speech was extremely uncompromising. Conservative Socialists were already shaking their heads. They felt that this new young man was very young and wanted to go far too fast." In fact, John was too tough-minded to compromise with gentility, believing that it trivialized whatever serious concerns it touched. Respectable opposition toughened him in his resolve: clearly, there was a lot to be done; the times were critical. Soon after this, Kiernan attended a meeting in John's room in Trinity; John, as usual, sat on the floor, frowning. The room was long, sparsely furnished, "lit with naked electric bulbs". When the meeting ended, John, who wanted advice from Kiernan on academic matters, asked him to a meal, "but in such a nervous mutter that I could not hear, and asked him to tea instead. On the day arranged he left a hurried note to say he could not come, as 'A crisis has arisen in the town.' He came next day, and sat on a sofa for several hours eating hunks of bread-and-jam and arguing about History. He stayed so long that he missed his Hall, which he dismissed as a trifle, saying that bread-and-jam was enough in the way of food." From this beginning, their intimacy grew, but always, essentially, in a political context. To Kiernan, John "had an odd way of laughing, a chuckle that seemed extorted from him against his will, as though he felt the world was too serious a place to laugh in. Nobody would have dreamed of calling him 'Jack', in spite of his, in many ways, simplicity and youthfulness."

Like any portrait this is at once truthful and misleading. The difficulty is that John was many-faceted, but preferred to behave as though he were not. He wanted to appear single-minded, which made for efficiency at least. "He never spoke of his own verses", and he was "far from self-explanatory about his own life". Friends who knew him in one context took away a totally different impression from those who knew him in another. From the time he was at Cambridge, he was seen by most people in the context of politics, and it is in this context, chiefly, that he is portrayed in the memorial volume—with the result that some who had known John best and longest found the portrait there unrecognizable. Too much of him that they had loved and valued and enjoyed had been omitted. For Mrs Cornford, "the early photographs were the only things that came out not quite false".[4] Yet this was inevitable. Politics had become the central fact of his life since Stowe, and provided the impetus for most of his relationships and activities in what were truly, for him, the political years. But this was the part of his life that had least to do with all those whom he had been closest to in the past. Even Christopher was to have no more than "a few encounters with him in Cambridge", although their affection for each other remained undiminished. The need of a break with the past, in order to assure himself of an unimpeded course of action, is unmistakable.

John arrived at Cambridge at a time when the movement on the Left was entering a markedly more active, more popular phase. Its appeal was based upon a mixture of pacifism and Socialism, neither very precisely defined, and rather more of the former than the latter. For more than a decade, in poems, plays, memoirs, novels and factual studies, the horror and folly of the war of 1914-1918 had been impressed upon the generation that had grown up in its aftermath; whereas the 'sickness of Capitalist society' had only recently been called to their attention, and as a cause still hadn't the emotional charge of 'being against war'. In the preceding winter the Oxford Union had conducted debate on the 'King and Country' resolution, and the motion was carried 275-153. Its impact was extraordinary; very soon the resolution was being debated at other universities—at L.S.E. it was carried with only thirty dissenting in a house of more than 300—and stirring up headlines and controversy in the country at large. Colonel Blimps, pacifists, and Communists alike tended to exaggerate its significance, reading into it support for their respective preconceptions: it showed a yellow streak in the younger generations; a recognition by the younger generation that war is an absolute evil, not to be tolerated under any circumstances; a refusal by the younger generation to participate in a class war on the side of the bourgeoisie against the proletariat. Such shadings of meaning apart, the 'Oxford Resolution' was the most dramatic evidence, thus far, of a strong anti-war sentiment among undergraduates, and it hastened the growth of the student movement. In May, *The Student Vanguard* reported that the provisional Anti-War Committee at Cambridge earlier in the term had "decided to call a demonstration which turned out a great success in spite of the hasty preparations. Some eighty students took part, mostly equipped with gas masks or with posters bearing slogans, and marched round the town on a Saturday afternoon, finishing up with a meeting on Parker's Piece."[5] But looked at realistically, as John would be certain to look at it, a demonstration by some eighty students would appear to be less a "great success" than a promising beginning. By autumn 1933—John's first term at Cambridge—anti-war sentiment, spurred on by the coming to power of Hitler in Germany, had grown sufficiently to attempt a demonstration on a much grander scale, under the aegis of the

Socialist Society, of which John was already a member, as he was also a leading member of the Communist 'fraction' within the Society. The time chosen was Armistice Week, with its climactic Poppy Day, when undergraduates traditionally swarmed through the streets of Cambridge, parading, and selling paper poppies, for the Earl Haig Fund. It was essentially a carnival occasion, during which a considerable amount of money was raised, and the tragic associations of the poppies—the fields of Flanders—were easily lost sight of in the general hilarity. There was no more appropriate time for a demonstration against war, nor one better calculated to attract a maximum of publicity and perhaps even a good fight.

Student Communists before 1933 had worked principally in the town, attemping "to organise the unemployed to protest against the scales of allowances; to enrol workers in trade unions . . .; to raise protests against the high rents in Council houses; to get inadequate schools repaired or rebuilt". These were clear-cut, well-defined, practical objectives. One made one's poster and went off to picket, knowing what it was that one was picketing for, or against. But within the University, the cell had had to proceed much more tentatively, and had accomplished much less. Essentially, it had been feeling its way: " 'The line on students' and 'the line on culture' had to be worked out more or less from first principles. Hence the tremendous energy which the group brought to theoretical reading and discussion; hence, too, a hundred sectarian mistakes due to over-reacting against Cambridge liberalism and Cambridge culture." Reading and discussion groups, dedicated to a careful study of Marxist classics, were not likely to break down the apathy of the uncommitted. Since 1931 the party had made little headway; Communist students felt themselves "completely isolated from university life". But the political events of 1933—in particular the establishment of a Nazi Germany whose Führer nine years before had spelled out a plan for world conquest—provided "the conditions for a great anti-war and anti-Fascist movement". Now there was the basis for establishing a "line". With a "feeling of desperate haste", we are told by 'A Group of Contemporaries', "the student Communists in the Socialist Club in 1933 set themselves two main aims. One was to build a mass anti-Fascist movement among students; the other was to form a big revolutionary Socialist organisation."

Anti-war sentiment, hitherto without political connotation, could be harnessed to anti-Fascism; but first, as John realized, the mass of students must be made politically conscious. The proposed Armistice Week demonstrations offered a splendid opportunity to put into effect the new policy of action—carried out under John's direction and very likely inspired by him—"to provoke clashes, to make a stir . . . to put politics on the map and into university conversation; to bounce, startle, or shock people into being interested".

As a kind of preface, it was decided to hold a small demonstration earlier in the week inside the Tivoli Cinema—in the heart of the town—where the film *Our Fighting Navy* was being shown. It was perhaps not the happiest choice for Armistice Week—and the Socialist Society denounced it as militaristic propaganda. News of the planned demonstration got out—no doubt by design, for what would be gained if it went unnoticed? It will be recalled that when the small group of demonstrators, among them Julian Bell and 'B', emerged from the theatre, they were confronted by a crowd of 'patriotic' hearties, out for a good time, shouting, jeering, waving Union Jacks and accompanied by a brass band. It was not quite a 'lark': very soon the ragging turned nasty, a free-for-all fight began, although it was almost impossible in the crowded dark to distinguish pacifists from patriots. "One demonstrator was debagged in traditional style, and escaped on a lorry. Finally the band struck up and 'tough' Cambridge, having dealt with 'cranks' in the time-worn manner, marched back in mock procession."

The result of this counter-demonstration, which its organizers could not have anticipated, was to ensure the success of the anti-war demonstration of November 11, a few days later. The kind of beefy philistinism represented by the riot outside the Tivoli incensed many among the undergraduates who otherwise might have remained aloof. "There were many students who had never been active on behalf of their vaguely peace-loving convictions, but who intensely disliked a victory for the anti-intellectual jingoism which many of them had learned to know and hate at their public schools." They felt that something should be done to show that the defenders of *Our Fighting Navy* were not representative of the entire University. On the other hand, they, having triumphed at the Tivoli, were not likely to stand quietly by on the sidelines. "It seemed certain that attempts would be made to break up the demonstration; and that in itself gave a sense of urgency and importance to the whole affair."

The Socialist Society secured the full co-operation of the Student Christian Movement, a notable portion of whose members on the basis of their experiences that day became Socialists. The plan was simple: a march to the Cambridge War Memorial, with a wreath bearing the inscription, 'To the victims of the Great War, from those who are determined to prevent similar crimes of imperialism'. It was the Socialists who insisted on the second part of the inscription, losing thereby the support of the League of Nations Union who felt that it was too provocative. But ultimately the police interfered, and insisted that the words 'of imperialism' be removed: they might lead to 'a breach of the peace'. Passions were already so aroused that it was unlikely that so subtle a modification would calm anyone. Hundreds of students —looking rather dapper and well-dressed in the photographs of the occasions that have survived, as if to emphasize the respectability of their enterprise—Christians, pacifists and Socialists together, first held a meet at Parker's Piece; then formed a procession to march to the memorial. There were aspects of the morning that suggested battles in the streets of Paris, oddly juxtaposed with the traditional, larking aspects of Poppy Day which were never quite dissipated. But in a riot, as had been proved at the Tivoli, it is extremely easy for high spirits to turn to ugliness. As the procession came abreast of Peterhouse, where the road narrowed, fighting broke out. An attempt was made to set up a barrier of cars across the road, and it was almost certainly here that Julian Bell and Guy Burgess were able to put Julian's car to effective use as a battering ram. The banner pole of the Socialist Society, at the head of the line of march, was broken. Flour was thrown on the demonstrators; white feathers rained down on them— which they wore as badges of honour; town toughs pelted them with eggs and tomatoes, and as they went along the pavement they became adroit at "knocking bags of eggs out of the enemy's hands before he could fire". Finally, despite the efforts of the toughs of town and gown, the procession reached the memorial, and the wreath was set in place.

John's contemporaries, reflecting on the event, did not question its value: it had made those who took part in it "feel that there was a need for protest and action on behalf of peace in a way that no orderly meeting would have convinced them. A large number of the demonstrators became from that time very active in the anti-war movement. But the effect (like that of the 'King and Country' debate at Oxford) was magnified by the press. The demonstrators were denounced as 'young hooligans who had got what they deserved for desecrating a holy day'; they were defended as 'idealists' who had brought back the true seriousness into what had become in Cambridge a disgusting and tasteless occasion for carnival; one side was as bad as another; and so on. . . . The sensational nature of the whole thing made it very widely discussed: that was its importance, that it brought a physical clash on war and peace into the sleepy atmosphere of bored and cultured Cambridge, with permanent effects." One effect that, rather strangely, John's contemporaries failed to mention, is that the event marked the effective beginning of a militant student Socialist movement in Cambridge. John, at the University barely a month, had been one of the principal leaders of the demonstration; he was ready now to capitalize on the united front that had come into existence to strike this blow for pacifism and Socialism, or alternatively, against war and Fascism.

It should be mentioned that at Oxford on the same day, Michael Foot led a crowd of 300 to its War Memorial, and there laid a wreath, inscribed, 'To the victims of a war they did not want, from those who are pledged to fight against all such crimes and their cause'.[6]

The Armistice Day demonstration of 1933 marked the beginning on a significant scale of political action and consciousness at Cambridge. What had begun 'underground' two years before as the concern of a handful of secretarians was to become in the years between 1933 and 1936—Cornford's years—the public commitment of impressive numbers of undergraduates. This, of course, was one of the objectives that John had set for himself and his fellow party members upon his arrival at the University; indeed, it was the essential objective upon which the others depended. There could be neither a mass anti-Fascist movement, nor a big revolutionary Socialist organization, without first a large number of students who were politically conscious and prepared to act—if only to march in a parade and risk a barrage of tomatoes and eggs—for what they believed.

In 1933 the membership of the Socialist Society numbered 200; in 1936 it had increased to 600,[7] and this was after the Society had in fact gone considerably further to the Left in its outlook. The Armistice Day demonstration had attracted to the Society a lot of attention, curiosity, sympathy and new members. It justified the policy of action that John and others had insisted upon, and continued to insist upon despite the uneasiness of the 'pillars'. They called for action again at the time of the Hunger March of February 1934. From all over the country groups of the unemployed were to march to London to protest against the inadequacies of the dole and other relief measures resorted to by the Government. The aim of the Society was to arouse a maximum of student support for the north-east coast contingent of marchers, who would be coming through Cambridge on their way to London. For many students it would be a first encounter with the realities of unemployment, met face to face, and the ravages of poverty and hunger, more meaningful when seen than when read about, and hence more positive in their impact: there was reason to anticipate a surge of response, expressed in humanitarian terms, and also in new conversions to the cause of Revolutionary Socialism.

Several days before the advent of the marchers, meetings were held to explain their grievances, explaining again and again "why students should be concerned with the militant working-class movement". There were collections taken in all the colleges to provide them with food and clothing, and 120 pounds were raised —"an unheard-of thing in Cambridge at that time, before the sufferings of Spain made the raising of such sums almost an everyday matter." On the day, an advance party from the Society went out to Huntingdon to meet the marchers, and led them to Girton—the college farthest out from town—where a demonstration had been organized, and girl students handed out refreshments. Most of the demonstrators waiting in the cold February afternoon "had little personal knowledge of the working class, and of the militant working class almost none. It was a thrilling moment for them," 'A Group of Contemporaries' recalled, "when their demonstration met the tired, shabby, cheerful column whose progress on the road they had followed day by day. Then the students and the unemployed formed up together and marched back down the long hill into Cambridge. At first, some of the students were a bit shy and self-conscious, wondering whether they had a right to be there, wondering whether it would be cheek to buy a pack of cigarettes for the men. Gradually they began to enjoy it, singing *Pie in the Sky* and *Solidarity for Ever* and the rest of the marchers' songs. Going through the town, shouting 'Down with the Means Test!' you would see some student you knew slightly, standing on the pavement, staring, a little frightened, at the broken boots and the old mackintoshes."

On this occasion, unlike the demonstration in November, there were no attempts at interference: the town authorities provided a bivouac for the marchers in the Corn Exchange; and the next evening there was a public meeting on their behalf—spurredon by the Socialist Society, it proved to be "the biggest and most enthusiastic that Cambridge had seen for many a day". The next morning, when the unemployed resumed their march, a number of undergraduates marched with them as far as Saffron Walden; and later in the week a group went up to London to join them in Hyde Park—"the first of many such 'solidarity' contingents".

Thus, as with the anti-war activities in November, the campaign of the Socialist Society to enlist the sympathy and support of Cambridge for the Hunger Marchers was "extraordinarily successful". But in the course of preparing for it, the Society experienced a good deal of internal dissension. There had been turbulent meetings at which those on the furthest Left (Cornford and his group) wanted the campaign based on *their* argument that "slave-camps" (work camps for the unemployed) and "low relief pay" were paving the way for "War and Fascism". Against them were the more conservative Socialists who felt that the camps might not be as evil (apparently no one in the Society had actually seen them) nor the Government as bent on war as claimed, and who wanted the campaign based on humanitarian rather than political considerations. Somehow a split on the question was avoided, but it left a legacy of discontent that was not laid to rest by the continual agitation of the Communists within the Society, forming 'study groups', seizing upon opportunities to clash with the University authorities, adopting a logical Marxist, as opposed to what they regarded as a sentimental Socialist, position on political issues as they arose, and committed to a belief in unremitting political action on all fronts. There had been no rival organization, specifically Marxist or Communist, set up for students on the far Left who would find the policies of the long-established Socialist Society too namby-pamby; instead, they had joined the Society, and, in the perhaps too simple phrase of 'A Group of Contemporaries', "had simply won leading positions and majority support". As a result, they were able to impose on the Society "a very radical programme of action and speakers". This, of course, was a year before the 'United Front' became the slogan of the Communist International, and no attempt was made to conciliate the minority: "the Communist students, confident in their new interpretation of events, were inclined to be overdogmatic and to insist on 'the line, the whole line and nothing but the line'". Finally, the more moderate members of the Society, "in particular those closely attached to the line of the Labour Party", could not tolerate the situation any longer, and in the summer term of 1934 they broke away to form a new, orthodox Labour Club. John's immediate reaction to the split proved to be too 'sectarian', for he, like a number of other student Communists, welcomed it, thinking that since it had been effected by Labour party members, "it would discredit them and show the correctness of the left-wing line". But the new Labour Club affiliated itself, on the national level, to the University Labour Federation; the Socialist Society was affiliated to the Federation of Student Societies, of which John was secretary, and which had been founded the year before in protest against the torpid policies of the U.L.F. There was a danger—recognized at the high party levels where a policy of co-operation on the Left was then being worked out—that the student movement, so promisingly begun, might yet be immobilized by 'sectarian divisiveness'. It was only after the fiercest discussion, in committee and in private, that John and the others became fully convinced that their aim must be to heal the split, both in Cambridge and nationally, before it crippled the whole anti-Fascist movement. This, 'A Group of Contemporaries' informs us, "was a turning point for the movement in Cambridge. It was before the Seventh World Congress of the Communist International had clarified the need for the broadest unity as the first aim of all Communists. Once the leaders [i.e., John and his friends] were convinced, however, they applied their decision whole-heartedly."

If John had erred, it was on the side of zeal. He was a zealous Communist; he was a dedicated Communist; he was also a Communist who enjoyed being a Communist. He was not dour. He could talk sports for hours, comparing, for example, the merits of the Australian and the American all-in wrestlers; or he would play cricket in his long room at Trinity, using a coal shovel as a bat. But he had no interest in 'social life' as a diversion: he did not want to meet people, or go to parties, unless it served some useful purpose—usually something connected with the party. He chided his colleagues in Trinity, and himself, for taking the easy way of sitting together at dinner in Hall, rather than spreading themselves out among the undergraduates they knew only slightly or not at all: it was a chance to proselytize and should not be neglected. He lived at a pitch of urgency. At lunch, one talked business first; then, if there were time (usually not), one might gossip—but even that would have rather a dedicated flavour. Personal relations, which are, after all, the important requisite for gossip, and which Bloomsbury had explored in all their ramifications, counted for very little with John and his colleagues: Marx, not Moore, was their philosopher. Conversation, that prime element of Cambridge *douceur*, still had its importance, not as a civilized art, however, but as a technique for forwarding the work of the party. The 'politicizing' of Cambridge had not only put an end to argumentation in the Apostolic style—people had begun to care too much to tolerate disagreement—but had made amiable, superficial, cultivated chatter an anachronism. *The Cambridge Review* paid due satiric notice to the new solemnity in a piece called 'Conversation with Communists' which was answered two weeks later in 'Conversation with Conscience', a reminder that Communists had more important concerns than the preservation of the airs and graces of a dying culture.[8] Subtle discriminations of personality were abandoned in favour of categories. "Elaborate lists were kept of sympathisers, near-sympathisers, and in general of everyone a Socialist student knew; and systematic collection and recruiting and converting were his main occupation." John would speak to Ray, of those who were dedicated—that is, were already in the party—those who were on the brink, and those who were friendly but in the need of encouragement. The last category was the most challenging: to encourage those who were friendly—such as the members of the Student Christian Movement who participated in the Armistice Day demonstrations—to approach the brink, and, if one were very skilful, even to go over. In pursuit of a likely convert, he would put in an appearance, usually with Ray beside him, at some of the larger literary-Bohemian parties; but he had an invincible distaste for small talk, and while the conversation flowed about him—of Auden and Eliot, Lawrence and Yeats—he would go briskly to work. And after he had made an appointment for lunch, or extended an invitation to a meeting, he would signal to Ray and they would leave. Perhaps it was after one such party that he wrote the poem "Keep Culture Out of Cambridge":

> Wind from the dead land, hollow men,
> Webster's skull and Eliot's pen,
> The important words that come between
> The unhappy eye and the difficult scene.
> All the obscene important names
> For silly griefs and silly shames,
> All the tricks we once thought smart,
> The Kestrel joy and the change of heart,
> The dark, mysterious urge of the blood,
> The donkeys shitting on Dali's food,
> There's none of these fashions have come to stay,
> And there's nobody here got time to play.
> All we've brought are our party cards
> Which are no bloody good for your bloody charades.

In December 1933, John published in *The Student Vanguard* a second polemic on poetry, 'The Class Front of Modern Art'. Like the earlier 'Art and the Class Struggle' (*Vanguard*, May 1933) it declared against the decadent-bourgeois idea that the artist must choose, in Yeats's words, "Perfection of the art or of the life". As before, the major writers of "the period of bourgeois decline"—

Yeats, Eliot, Pound, D. H. Lawrence—are found to be in the service of reaction, committed as they are to "the idea of the artist as a lofty and impartial observer". But "for those who realize that the class conflict in society is a struggle between the dynamic and vital forces of society against the reactionary inertial forces, the idea of the 'impartial' artist is an absurdity". It is also an escape-hatch: it allows the artist to condemn the bourgeois society in which he lives (as in the case of D. H. Lawrence) at the same time as it excuses him from taking an active part in the revolutionary struggle to change it.

In his earlier piece John had been content simply to proscribe the writers he had once admired; now he advanced an affirmative and optimistic conclusion:

> Meanwhile all over the world there is growing up a revolutionary movement in literature which flatly denies that there is a contradiction between art and life, which rejects the theory of artistic 'impartiality'. Its writers do not regard themselves as isolated and detached observers of history, but as active participators. Their work is born out of struggle. Ernst Toller, the workers' councillor of the Bavarian Soviet, who was forced to escape with a price of 10,000 marks on his head, wrote his first plays secretly in prison. Theodor Plivier, the novelist of the revolt in the German navy, took an active part as an able seaman in the event he describes . . . Everywhere a revolutionary literature is being written with a crude and violent energy comparable only to the force of the earlier artists of the bourgeois revolution, men such as Kyd and Marlowe; but with this difference, that the hero is no longer the great king or successful general, but the working class as a whole.
>
> In England [he conceded] the movement is not as advanced as elsewhere, but the same stirrings can be found in some of the work of the younger poets, Auden, Madge, and a few others. And although the very youth of these writers, and their consequent inexperience of the revolutionary movement, means that the work still has largely the content of a literary revolt against the concept of the contradiction between art and life, the only possible logical development is towards a consistently revolutionary standpoint.

Polemical writing invites response, and it came in the next number of the *Vanguard* (January 1934) from Julian Bell. In the same number there was a rejoinder by John. And in March, Julian replied to the rejoinder. It was a lively and illuminating exchange. John was writing as an orthodox Marxist. Julian was writing as a Marxist of a sort—his own sort really, with a strong commitment to Bloomsbury's belief in clarity, rationalism and the primacy of art. Both, of course, were engaging in polemic, a form in which niceties of fact are made subordinate to the course of argument; both were highly selective in what they chose to notice the other was saying; and both wrote with a touch of characteristic arrogance, John of the true believer, Julian of the true Bloomsburyan, which has always so irritated its critics—and certainly in this instance it irritated John.

"Dear Sir," Julian began, "Surely John Cornford has something better to give us in the way of a Marxist analysis than this . . . grotesque piece of false over-simplification and verbal indefiniteness . . . Cornford seems to be very far from clear as to the part to be played by contemporary poets in the revolutionary movement. I would suggest . . . that poets, as such, have very little part to play in the movement." This was his crucial contention, and one to which John paid curiously little heed, perhaps because he was so distracted by Julian's supporting argument:

> Whatever their class origins, anyone who acquires enough literary training and practice to be able to write poetry at all becomes interested in his own emotions, and looks to the arts as a form of self-expression. And he finds ready to hand a highly developed technique for expressing his more personal and intimate emotions. Naturally, writers like Auden are only able to write what it feels like to be a bourgeois intellectual who is politically on the Left. And writers like D. H. Lawrence are only able to write about what it feels like to be an educated proletarian.

Having provided John with a splendid target, he now returns to the main, practical, pragmatic point:

> It is certainly desirable that anyone with abilities for doing so should take part in the revolutionary movement, but it is highly

> improbable that anyone who does will have time and energy enough to carry out a literary revolution at the same moment. For if poetry and imaginative literature are to be directly used in the struggle, and there is no very good reason why they should be—the most far-reaching reforms are necessary . . . which practically amount to a return to classicism and the development of a new plain style, something precise and clear and immediately comprehensible to any literate person. This is probably out of the question by now for poetry . . .
>
> With prose, on the other hand, there is a certain amount of hope. At present the propaganda of the Left is conducted in a technical and incomprehensible language: it should be possible for the intellectuals to produce a persuasive prose that would be understood by, and that would affect, anyone able to read. What is needed at the moment is clear thinking and the clearing away of muddle—an intellectual counter-attack by the scientifically minded on the mistakes and deceits of Fascism.

John, in his reply, concentrated his fire on the supporting argument. Observing that "Comrade Bell, in his first paragraph, accuses me of a 'grotesque piece of false over-simplification'," he addresses himself to a restatement of "Comrade Bell's subjective formulation". Julian's argument is now discovered in John's words to be as follows:

> Literature stands above or outside the class struggle. The struggle for power between bourgeoisie and proletariat which has included every other field of human activity, has somehow kept clear of the sacred precincts of literary traditions. It is therefore unreal to look for a corresponding division between revolutionary and reactionary writers . . .
>
> There is one single literary tradition, the precious heritage of a cultured, educated, sensitive minority, which includes all writers who, whatever their class origins, acquire enough literary training and practice to be able to write poetry . . . It is ridiculous to analyse their art in terms of the class struggle. They are so busily engaged in analysing what it feels like to be themselves and telling the world about it by a "highly developed literary technique" which they find "ready to hand" that they can have no concern with objective reality . . .

> Consequently, literature can play no important part in the class-struggle. It is the exclusive affair of a minority, who, to use F. R. Leavis's words, "keep alive the subtlest and most perishable parts of tradition. Upon them depend the implicit standards that order the finer living of an age." They haven't time to carry out a literary revolution and so it is impossible to expect them to write anything intelligible to anyone who hasn't the leisure to study literature carefully.

Then, having set forth "this assortment of abstract dogmas", he concludes:

> Comrade Bell is quite right that this tradition cannot be used as a revolutionary weapon in the class struggle. That is exactly why it is not the only tradition. There is today everywhere a tremendous spontaneous development of working-class literature, although as yet little is published and most is technically backward. More and more younger writers realising that the logical direction of bourgeois art in decline is towards a kind of artistic sophism, a super-subjectivity, realising that the art of the future is the art of the ruling class of the future, go over to the revolutionary movement as the only possible solution to their cultural problems.

Not surprisingly, Julian, caught up in the pleasures of controversy, was unwilling to allow John the last word. Again, he wrote to the editor of the *Vanguard*:

> I must make a protest against Comrade Cornford's attributions to me of the opinions of Mr Leavis. What he calls an objective restatement of my case is in part a repetition of points of fact about the present intellectual situation, as to which we are agreed, in part an attempt to show that I approve of that situation, which I do not.
>
> I attempted to show: (1) that it is almost impossible in England today for anyone to write poetry that will be read by the present English working class; (2) that the younger revolutionary poets are in fact simply writing romantic-subjective poetry about their revolutionary feelings; (3) that this is not a particularly useful activity from the point of view of anyone wishing to bring about a revolution; (4) that it should be pos-

Vanessa Bell–bust by Marcel Gimond

Julian and Vanessa, 1910

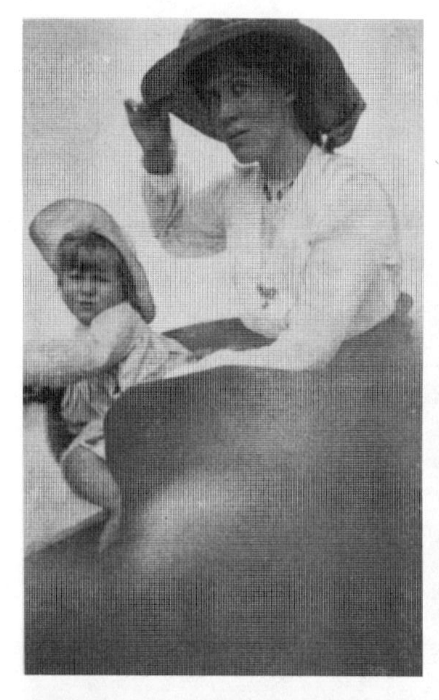

Duncan Grant, Clive Bell, Julian and Vanessa Bell–Tea at Charleston

Julian at Charleston

Julian at Rodmell, 1923

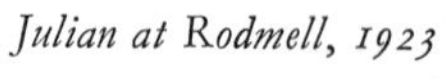

Julian and Clinker

Julian at Cassis

Cambridge, November 11, 1933

In front of Peterhouse

Frances Cornford with Helena, Christopher and John

Frances Cornford in the late 1930's

John at Copthorne

'The Islanders'

History Sixth at the Vanburgh Rotunda, *Stowe, 1931*
(John at extreme left)

12 Mon—Michaelmas Law Sittings begin

13 Tues

14 Wed—Michaelmas Fire Insurance ceases

OCTOBER 1936

15 Thur—● New Moon, 10.20 a.m.

16 Fri

'The Last Mile to Huesca' in John's diary

John at Dartington, 1936

sible to write prose that would be directly useful and that would be read by the working class.

John had been writing hopefully of the future; Julian was writing realistically of the present. John, in effect, acknowledged this in the last extended statement he was to make about poetry, 'Left?', a study of "the revolutionary fermentation in the work of the younger poets", which appeared in *Cambridge Left* later that spring.[9] His subject is the question of his title: are these poets authentically 'Left'? Or again, to what degree are they writing true or false revolutionary poetry? Have they really made common cause with the revolutionary class? How, as poets, are they taking part in the class struggle?

He begins with some generalizations that are, in fact, convictions by which he ordered his own life: "As the crisis deepens, the situation more and more urgently demands a choice between revolution and reaction." And: "The traditional artist's 'impartiality' is unmasked as a denial of the class struggle."

By definition, then, a revolutionary poet is one who chooses "revolution" and aligns himself in the class struggle with the proletariat.

But the work "even of the genuinely revolutionary and leftward moving poets" suffers from a contradiction: "although politically they have rejected their class, they are still writing mainly for it. Their training as writers has been a direct barrier to the writing of straightforward revolutionary poetry which can only be overcome by direct participation in revolutionary struggles." Given this prerequisite, it is not surprising that John should find it difficult to point to examples of which he can approve. The most he is prepared to say is that "there are hopes that, in spite of the obscurity and crudity which are the growing pains of every vital movement, by certain of these poets a clear and powerful verse is being evolved". But he singles out for favourable comment only a poem of Auden's, 'A Communist to Others', which first appeared in the *Twentieth Century*, and then in *New Country*, and finally in his book *Look, Stranger*. (Auden was not a Communist, however. His liking for the poem, which, according to Spender, was simply "an exercise in entering into a point of view not his own",[10] diminished over the years, and he excluded it from his *Collected Poems* with the marginal comment, "O God, what rubbish!"[11]) Spender's 'The Funeral' is dismissed as "only a kind of wish-fulfilment. It is not the poetry of revolutionary struggle." Against its highly concentrated, subjective, metaphoric style is set Louis Aragon's

> I am a witness to the crushing of a world out of date,
> I am a witness drunkenly to the stamping out of the bourgeois.
> Was there ever a finer chase than the chase we give
> to that vermin which flattens itself in every nook of the cities
> I sing the violent domination of the bourgeoisie by the proletariat
> for the annihilation of that bourgeoisie
> for the total annihilation of that bourgeoisie.

"There can be no doubt," John concludes, "that the future is with the revolutionary and not the 'impartial observer' nor the romantic-utopian idealist. And just as out of the rise to power of the bourgeoisie, out of the violent shattering of the feudal remnants, out of the violent expropriation of the independent producers, was born the tremendous revolutionary movement of the Elizabethan drama, so out of the violent struggle for power between the bourgeoisie and the proletariat, as the Communist Party in this country develops from its sectarian beginnings to a mass revolutionary party, there will arise a revolutionary literature stronger and more various than any which preceded it."

That John meant to be, and indeed was, a "revolutionary participator" is not in question. He believed in the revolution; he had chosen sides; in the coming struggle for power as he envisioned it he meant to fight side by side with the proletariat. But did he mean to be a revolutionary poet? This much can be said: to be a poet mattered less to him than to be a revolutionary. A poet might be of use to the revolution; but the likelihood of his being so was slight; and the barrier against it formidable. The political situation was daily becoming more urgent: one must participate in the revolutionary struggle first, before one could write about it. Having declared himself on poetry in 'Left?', he regarded the subject as closed, and went on to matters of more immediate interest. For the next number of *Cambridge Left*, he wrote on 'The Struggle for Power in Western Europe' ("We are heading straight for war;

it is on war that the 'recovery' mongers are speculating, and on no fundamental chance of improvement within the existing system.")

While at Cambridge he wrote, so far as we have been able to determine, only nine poems. Seven were published in the memorial volume; two more from this period have been found among his papers. Nine poems in three years—at a time when young poets are traditionally at their most prolific—is a rather meagre production. But for John the need to write poetry was less insistent than to participate in the revolutionary struggle as he recognized it and helped to shape it at Cambridge.

Poetry had become a marginal activity, and a private one. He never discussed his work with his friends in the party; most of them did not even know until after his death that he had been a poet. The exchanges of verse and criticism with his mother had ended, by his wish, even before he had left Stowe. At Cambridge he had no acknowledged mentor. There (as afterwards in Spain) in the rare moments when he was free to do so, he wrote both personal and political poems. The latter represent a conscious effort to 'objectify' his ideas and attitudes as a revolutionary participator, and to transform them into revolutionary poetry:

> Should spring bring remembrance, a raw wound smarting?
> Say rather for us fine weather for hurting,
>   For there's no parting curse we fear.
> Here we break for good with the old way of living,
> For we're leaving only what wasn't worth having,
>   And face turned forward, for there's no life here.
>
> . . .
>
> You know at what forge our purpose was steeled,
> At what anvil was hammered the hammer we wield,
>   Who cut the sickle to a cutting edge.
> And under the light of our five-point star
> The faces you see here are different far
>   From those at the closed works, or fallen bridge.
>
> . . .
>
> Not the dreamed-of battle on the windy plain,
> But light slitting the eyelids in the cold dawn.

The old world seen in a new light.
And see! the fist of the silent defender
Is clenched to strike as we gather under
Our banner, 'Students and Workers Unite!'

Now the crazy structure of the old world's reeling,
They can see with their own eyes its pitprops falling,
Whether they like it, or whether they don't.
Though they lie to themselves so as not to discover
That their game is up, that their day is over,
They can't be deaf to our shout, 'RED FRONT!'

The poem, a lively example of the propaganda verse of the 1930s, was a revolutionary gesture John had enjoyed making—much as he would enjoy leading an anti-war demonstration or chalking anti-Fascist slogans on the pavements of Cambridge—but he was careful not to overvalue it as poetry. His standards were very high, and he would apply them as rigorously to himself as to other young poets of the period. After London, he seems to have made no effort to have any of his verse published. Perhaps none of it ever quite satisfied him: the propaganda falling short of the level of poetry he aimed for; the personal lyrics revealing too much of himself. In any case, his day-to-day involvement was with the practice rather than the poetry of politics.

The Communist group had gained the ascendancy in the Socialist Society: a minority of moderates had broken away to form the Labour Club. John's first impulse was to pursue an uncompromising Marxian line. But the result of this would be to isolate the Society at the furthest Left of the Cambridge spectrum and reduce to a minimum its effectiveness in the University youth movement. The times, the issues, the objectives, were all against sectarian austerity; it was a matter of practical politics to move towards *rapprochement*, to co-operate with the Labour Club, or indeed with any of the other organizations, whether mildly on the Left or firmly at the centre, that might be persuaded to take part in the struggle against war and Fascism.

The first important co-operative effort was a demonstration on Armistice Day 1934 organized by the Cambridge (town) Anti-War Council, in which members of the Socialist Society, the Labour Club and the Anti-War Movement participated. The day happened to fall on a Sunday—"By a sort of kindly intercalation," the editor of *The Cambridge Review* intoned, "we have more than one Armistice Day this year. An Armistice Day that is also a Sunday has, by this added prestige, managed to save itself from being the occasion of a grand rag into which the two minutes' silence makes an unwelcome intrusion."[12] The grand rag, the Poppy Day solicitation, took place on the Saturday, and gathered in more than £2,000; on the Sunday, the anti-war demonstrators marched through the town to the War Memorial, without so much as an egg or a tomato to mar their progress. The demonstration was becoming respectable: "by 1937 it was carried through—shades of 1933!—after consultation with the University Poppy Day Committee!"

The second effort was in response to a comment in *The Cambridge Review* in February 1935: "On March 6th Sir Oswald is coming to Cambridge to attend a dinner of the University Branch of the British Union of Fascists. To most people this may seem a trivial event unworthy of their attention, or at the best a subject for mild humour. But Mosley is too readily dismissed by intellectuals. It was not so long ago that Hitler was dismissed with equal equanimity. The visit of the Fascist leader to Cambridge University should be the occasion for serious reflection on the prospect which Fascism offers to the intellectual and education world." It was also the occasion for an anti-Fascist demonstration organized jointly by the Socialist Society and the Labour Club. There were the inevitable disputes on procedure—a crowd shouting slogans, or a single file of silent pickets—but arrangements were finally made, and on the night of March 6 the demonstrators assembled outside the University Arms. British Fascism, in the words of *The Cambridge Review*, was "only a small cloud on the horizon",[13] but Mosley, emerging from his black limousine, in his black costume, surrounded by his black-shirted young men, was the enemy personified. There was a howl of disapproval; the leader hurried in to his disciples; the demonstration came to an end "with a speech by John, very excited, on the fountain in the market-place, and a fine joint drinking and singing party". The end result of all this co-operation was that the two organizations united again as the Socialist Club late in 1935—the era of the Popular Front was well under way—"with a double secretaryship corresponding to the two groups" and John as one of the two secretaries.

He had enjoyed the demonstration against Mosley, and he made it a point to be on the alert for Fascist activity in and about Cambridge. Victor Kiernan has a recollection of him "sitting in the middle of a hall at a Fascist meeting in an outlying village, like a captain amidst his troop of hecklers. After this last affair he confessed respect for the speaker, who had taken his grilling well: very reluctantly—his hatred of Fascism amounted to physical loathing, and to break up a Fascist meeting was perhaps his highest enjoyment." But in Cambridge at large at this time (1934-1935) war and Fascism had not yet been indissolubly linked as one cause; it would be another year before anti-Fascism would serve as an effective rallying cry for the Popular Front. Whereas in the winter of 1935 anti-war sentiment had become a passion—almost, one is tempted to say, an obsession, judging by the proliferation of organizations dedicated to the cause. There were so many of them that in February the editor of *The Cambridge Review* was moved to remark, "By now every sort of pacifist must be catered for," and he listed the League of Nations Union, the Anti-War Movement (Left), the New Commonwealth Society (international police force) and the New Peace Movement ("combines advocacy of peace between nations with opposition to revolution by violence and to dictatorship"). There were also the Anti-War Council, the Christian Peace Society, the Scientists' Anti-War Group and the Society of Friends. Many of these organizations had their subdivisions: the New Peace Movement, for example, held monthly University-wide meetings that were addressed by such men as Sir Norman Angell and John Maynard Keynes, and also weekly meetings in the colleges—"It is only to be hoped that such zeal does not wear itself out,"[14] the editor of the *Review* concluded.

Communists were not pacifists, as John had explained to his mother some time before, but they were unalterably opposed to war for Capitalism or Fascism. ("There is nothing revolutionary about Fascism. Although the forms of rule may be different, the class-content is the same. Fascism develops quite logically out of

capitalist democracy—it is in no sense a revolutionary break with it."—'The Struggle for Power in Western Europe', Spring 1934.[15])
Accordingly, it was entirely consistent for them to co-operate with the various pacifist and anti-war organizations, "irrespective of other political disagreements". Fighting for peace was a first step towards the Popular Front, the anti-Fascist movement that came into being after the Seventh World Congress of the Communist International. By 1936 the slogan had become, "Socialist students the most active upholders of peace, democracy and civilization."

The energies of the anti-war movement that winter were given principally to the Peace Ballot, or the National Declaration on Peace and Armaments, sponsored on a nation-wide basis by the League of Nations Union. The Ballot has been taken to stand for the absolute pacifism of the British electorate during the 1930s—as more than eleven million people over the age of eighteen voted—and at the least it indicated a high level of interest in questions of peace and war. But, as with the Oxford 'King and Country' resolution, the significance of the Peace Ballot has been exaggerated: its results fall far short of an endorsement of the pacifist position. Five proposals were offered to be voted upon.

First, an endorsement of the League of Nations. (More than 90% voted Yes.)

Second, a reduction in armaments. (More than 90% voted Yes.)

Third, the abolition of military and naval aircraft by international agreement. (85% voted Yes.)

Fourth, opposition to the manufacture of arms for private profit. (More than 90% voted Yes.)

The fifth proposal was divided into two parts: "Do you consider that, if a nation insists on attacking another, the other nations should combine to compel it to stop by economic and non-military measure?" (94.1% voted Yes.) And the second, perhaps the most crucial of all, for it proposed military action under certain 'justified' conditions: "Do you consider that, if a nation insists on attacking another, the other nations should combine to compel it to stop by, if necessary, military measures?" (74.2% voted Yes.)

More than sixty undergraduate organizations, ranging from the extreme Left to the extreme Right in political attitudes, participated in the Ballot activity. Early in February, as the voting got under way, *The Cambridge Review* published a letter from J. Cornford, Chairman, C.U. Socialist Society:

> At the present time members of the University are being called on to vote in the Peace Ballot, and in view of the extreme urgency of the international situation the C.U.S.S. wishes to make an appeal to all sincere opponents of war. It is idle to think that the National Government will consider itself bound by the outcome of the ballot, which does not touch many of the most important issues at all. Nevertheless the outcry against it in certain reactionary circles shows that even such limited action as supporting the Ballot is in some degree an act of opposition to the war-policy of the Government, and the C.U.S.S. calls on every undergraduate to register an emphatic 'Yes' to the first four questions. The fifth question is on another footing. Wars between Imperialist capitalist Powers are not caused by unprovoked attacks of one nation on another, but are the outcome of economic struggles for markets and raw materials which are inherent in capitalism, and every Power is an "aggressor". The plea that Military action by one Power against another is needed to "maintain peace" would be merely a propaganda excuse for declaring war with the approval of the countries which happen to be members of the League at the moment.
>
> We do not want another 1914. Many are tempted to vote 'Yes' to 5a, because they imagine economic sanctions are less liable to result in world war than military sanctions. But experience shows that boycotts, blockades, offensive tariffs, etc., etc., *lead directly to war*. We call on all undergraduates to vote 'No' to sections 5a and 5b . . . To express our attitude clearly we advise the following declaration for the blank space at the bottom of the paper.
>
> "War is the outcome of the economic rivalries of capitalist imperialist Powers, and can only be ended by the abolition of capitalism. The only effective way of fighting against war is *mass resistance* by the united front of the working class and their allies against all forms of militarism and war-preparations."[16]

The forthrightness of this declaration makes it evident that for John, co-operation was to be undertaken on his terms: one opposed a capitalist war for Marxian reasons. Oddly enough, his opposition to the fifth proposal of the Peace Ballot was echoed by the most dedicated of pacifists: those who opposed war (any war) for religious reasons. The *Review*, reporting a joint meeting of pacifists held at this time, noticed that the spokesman for the Christian Peace Society, "expressed his sympathy for other peace movements, but said that he was unable to go beyond his own principles. Individual pacifism was a necessary outcome of Christianity; the correct moral state must be attained before war can be prevented by international agreement. The Christian faith was a sufficient basis for internationalism and, like Communism, had in itself an ultimate aim beyond the prevention of war: it was an alternative to militarism, since it was better to destroy enmity than to destroy enemies. The speaker objected to sanctions, as he considered the method of war unjustifiable whatever the end in view."[17] On the preceding day, the Christian Peace Society had expressed its disapproval of 'Question 5'.

Communists were not pacifists, of course, but the united Front could accommodate such alliances. Pacifism, or anti-war-ism, in the winter of 1935 was the chief, really the only serious political concern of most Cambridge undergraduates, who were otherwise berated for their irresponsibility. A writer in the *Review* complained that, "Most of the talk about politics and social question is, consciously or unconsciously, influenced by the irresponsible attitude of the undergraduate who feels that he is not called upon to test his theories by practice."[18] John and his fellow Communists were the notable exceptions to this generalization, committed to political action not only within the University, but also in the town, where they handed out leaflets, sold the *Daily Worker* and their own *Cambridge Red Front*, joined picket lines, helped organize tenants to strike for lower rents, agitated on behalf of college servants to get them higher wages, and on the occasion of a bus strike, staged a demonstration at the terminal to prevent students from driving 'black-leg buses'. In the general election of 1935 John worked quietly behind the scenes to enlist student support for the local Labour party candidate, but the result of the election was a disappointment. There had been a by-election in 1934 when the Conservative candidate had won with a majority of approximately 2,000; now he was to win again, this time with a majority of about 5,000 in a total 31,000 votes. Whatever the reason for the

Labour defeat, it was not likely to have been for want of student support. After the campaign was over, the Labour candidate wrote to John to thank him; his letter is an interesting illustration of the amicable but tentative relations that were possible between Labour and the Communists in 1935:

> My dear Cornford,
>
> In case I do not see you immediately I wish to thank you personally for the magnificent work which you and your friends did for us in the election. In many ways my policy must have fallen short of what you would have liked it to have been, and there were difficulties in the way of giving your support the publicity which it deserved. These facts were not allowed in any way to affect the keenness of your work and I appreciate tremendously what you did for us.

Victor Kiernan has recorded that John would work at politics as much as fourteen hours a day. "He never seemed tired, and conveyed an idea of enormous physical vitality." He had the ability to fix his attention upon a given subject at a given moment and not be distracted from it by irrelevancies. Working, doing party business, whether at a meeting or in private conversation, he had no small talk, and disdained it. "When he determined to spend an evening 'working on the masses', as he called it, he would come into someone's rooms with a muttered apology, and stand or shuffle in a painfully awkward way for a minute or two; then he plunged without preface into an argument on politics or Marxist theory, and quickly lost his uneasiness, talking well, even aggressively."

His life at the University was shaped by his concern to help the cause. He was never completely at his ease as a public speaker, as his own feelings about his earliest experiences with the Labour Research Department testify, but he managed to become an effective one, making up in intellectual force what he lacked in grace. Victor Kiernan remembered him, "perpetually swaying back and forwards on his feet". His father felt that his gestures managed, unconsciously, in their shape and abruptness, to suggest both the hammer and the sickle. Margot Heinemann has written of him:[19]

> When he began, he talked too fast
> To be heard well, and he knew too much.

> He never had, though learned a little at last,
> The sure, sincere and easy touch
> On an audience: and his handsome head
> Charmed no acquiescence: he convinced and led.

For the sake of the cause, he spoke at meetings, large and small, at street rallies and demonstrations, and even, most trying of all, at the Cambridge Union—of which, in the autumn of 1935, he became an active member. In March of that year he had left the Young Communists League to become a fully-fledged member of the Communist Party of Great Britain.

He was perhaps happier writing than speaking, and took advantage of the opportunities that were offered to him to set forth his political ideas. He proved to be an admirable pamphleteer. He wrote in a clear, straightforward style, expressing a tough Communist view of the contemporary world as seen by a very young man—he was nineteen—of powerful intelligence and unshakeable conviction. In 1935, his reputation as a leading student Communist had already spread beyond Cambridge, and he was asked—he was the only undergraduate who was asked—to contribute to a symposium on *Christianity and the Social Revolution*. Divided into three parts—Socialism in Historical Christianity, Communism and Religion, and *Dies Irae*—the book itself is a characteristic document of the period: edited by John Lewis, Karl Polanyi and Donald Kitchin, and with an eminent editorial board of Joseph Needham, Charles Raven and John MacMurray, whose concluding essay, 'Christianity and Communism: Towards a Synthesis' suggests the prevailing spirit. Among the contributors were W. H. Auden, Conrad Noel and Reinhold Niebuhr, as well as the two sets of editors, and Julius Hecker of Moscow University. John Cornford had been assigned the task of expounding the doctrines of Communism. His article, 'What Communism Stands For,[20] is not particularly ambitious, and makes no attempt to deal with the central theme of the symposium. John is specific on the point: he has no wish to determine whether or not the early Christian church was communistic. He is only concerned with Communism in its modern context—as the Marxist theory dealing with the rise of industrial capitalism—and he states the problem succinctly: "Capitalism can no longer solve its problems peacefully; each successive crisis in the imperialist epoch is a prelude to a more desperate world war." He is careful to dissociate Communists from the Christian 'sense of injustice', and, by implication, from the sort of judgment that Christians might use as a basis for deciding that contemporary society must be changed. For him it is the course of history that proves the correctness of the Marxist analysis. "It is not simply that it is unjust that Communists work for the overthrow of capitalism. They do not judge anything by abstract ethical standards."

The bulk of the essay is a demonstration—conducted by a succession of historical steps, one to a section—of the need for revolution in England. Briskly he whisks the reader along from Primitive and Contemporary Communism Contrasted, to Why Capitalism Declines, to The Period of Permanent Crisis and War, the Limitation of Production under Capitalism, The Rise of Scientific Socialism, The Character of a Reorganized Society, The Capitalist State, the Dictatorship of the Proletariat, and finally The Preconditions of a Revolution. These last are all too evident: he points to the disadvantaged situation of the working class in contemporary Britain—seen most clearly in the General Strike of 1926, when the machinery of state was overtly mobilized against the workers, but essentially still unchanged. Hence, if in 1935 Britain has not become a Fascist state, it is simply because the need for it to become so has not yet arisen. "Every capitalist constitution admits of the 'democratic' introduction of Fascism when necessary. In England the machinery already exists. If there is not yet an open rule of violence against the working class, it is solely because the capitalist class can manœuvre well enough to maintain its power without it." (This is very similar to the point that John had made in his essay in *Cambridge Left* a year earlier: "What we are witnessing is a process of fascisation through the democratic machinery. Bruning, von Papen and Schleicher 'constitutionally' prepared the way for Hindenburg to invite Hitler—also 'constitutionally', through the single loophole in the water-tight Weimar constitution—to power. At no period was there a revolutionary overthrow of democracy.") The capitalist class has its machinery, then, to keep it in power; but, "for the working class to take power by the existing machinery is impossible". Therefore, a revolution becomes necessary, and for the revolution to be brought off successfully, for the civil war to be won, it is essential that it be controlled, organized, inspired and maintained by the Communist party—"Without a powerful and experienced revolutionary party," he concludes, "victory will be lost."

'What Communism Stands For' was an informed and competent presentation of the Marxist 'case' for revolution, which might have been presented with equal effectiveness by any number of other Communist intellectuals, well read in Marxist literature, and dedicated to furthering the cause. But John occupied a unique position in the student movement, and for that reason his essay 'Communism in the Universities' is of more than ordinary interest.[21] The essay—his contribution to a symposium *Young Minds for Old*, published in 1936—begins with a brief history of the movement, emphasizing the influence of the Communist Party, then offers an explanation for the 'swing to the Left' among students in recent years:

> This swing to the Left has not come primarily because students are interested in politics in the abstract. It has come because the actual conditions of their lives, the actual problems with which they are confronted, force them steadily though hesitatingly to a revolutionary position. Because a student does not have to be interested in politics before he comes face to face with one great reality. The existence of the capitalist structure of society means that there is an ever-widening gap between the potentialities of science, technique, culture and education, and their application in the world today.

By this, he is not making the traditional Philistine point that what one learns in the University has nothing to do with the life one lives in the world; rather, that what has been learned in the University for the effective betterment of the world can't be put to use. Capitalism intervenes:

> The whole field of British industry and agriculture today presents a picture of productive waste that capitalism cannot overcome, of preventable deaths and preventable accidents that are not prevented because no employer profits from preventing them, of preventable diseases that are not prevented because our present rulers find it more important to spend money on

> interest on war debt and on huge rearmament than on the health of the English people.

Then, there is the more immediate concern, that graduates with good degrees are finding it increasingly difficult to get jobs ("I have known one case of a graduate with first class honours in Zoology with a job as a ratcatcher at 30*s.* a week"); badly off now, in "the 1935-1936 'boom' ", they know they will be worse off yet in the next inevitable depression:

> This general economic insecurity has its effects. Of course it does not of itself make revolutionaries. But ultimately all the secure prejudices and traditions of the English middle and professional classes depended on a stable and more or less well-provided environment. This comfortable life is breaking up, and with it the comfortable illusions which it fostered.

Undoubtedly these explanations, and a variety of others that John set forth, had their validity for the student movement in general, and for himself too; but one may wonder how deeply they applied in John's own case. After all, he had been a Marxist at sixteen, when he was still at his Public School, a long way from the possibility, so to speak, of taking a job as a ratcatcher. It is only at the conclusion of the essay, with its overtones of a personal emotion, that one catches sight of what it was that John was looking for and found in the Communist party:

> The transformation of a worried intellectual into an effective member of a revolutionary party does not take place overnight. It is a long and sometimes a painful process . . . It is very easy and to some people very comforting to sneer at youthful fanaticism. A movement so young as the Communist movement is inevitably at times naïve, immature, over-enthusiastic, and provides a splendid field for the peddlers of second-hand witticisms. But it is none the less a serious movement. Out of the break-up of the standards of an entire class before changing conditions of life, a compact revolutionary core is being formed —a small minority still, but the most organized and efficient of the minorities. The changes that are going on now, often imperceptibly, but none the less steadily, will perhaps later assume a national importance that very few of the actors in the present

> small-scale events realise. But when the next crisis that will shake the whole system explodes, whether it is war crisis, economic crisis, or political crisis, the relatively quiet and petty developments of these pre-war, pre-crisis years will emerge in their real significance.

John believed in the seriousness of what he was doing as a Communist in the youth movement; he believed in the seriousness of the revolutionary role he would play in the future; he believed in the seriousness of his academic studies. It is easy to forget, with so much else happening, and the energetic, seemingly all-consuming nature of his political activity, that he was also reading History (he had apparently given up any thought of reading English): and, indeed, was a brilliant student. Here we should note that the party was anxious that students should not immerse themselves in political action at the expense of their studies: they were to demonstrate that being a Communist helped rather than hindered academic endeavours. John was active in encouraging the development of study groups within the Socialist Society, which would apply Marxist doctrine to various academic disciplines; he himself founded the History study group, It was a period with a fondness for slogans, and the relevant one in this context was 'Every Communist is a good student'. At Oxford, the parallel slogan was rather more authoritarian: 'Communist students must be *good* students'.[22] But John was a good student not because the party 'line' decreed it, but because he was an intellectual—a member of the intellectual aristocracy—and it would not have occurred to him not to work hard at his studies. He did do extremely well, receiving a first on Part I, and a starred first (a first with distinction, the highest honour Cambridge gives) on Part II of the History Tripos. He received excellent, non-Marxist tutorials from the Trinity historians, F. A. Simpson, J. R. M. Butler and G. Kitson Clark, who did not find him too easy to teach, as he was convinced that he had discovered the key to history in Marx, and continually subjected them and the past to Marxian analysis. He enjoyed his arguments with them, however—perhaps more than they did. Recognizing the force of his personality, they must have hoped that this remarkable son of a colleague would recover from his youthful 'enthusiasm' and put his good brain to some other use than fomenting the revolution. Perhaps in his case too the *douceur* of Cambridge might work a transformation, as it had in the past with other embryonic revolutionaries. But John had been inoculated against such a possibility by early exposure to the charms of the University. In fact, he found what he was taught not entirely satisfactory—chiefly because it did not take into account the truth of Marxian analysis—and he wrote, as so many students write or are tempted to write, an essay exposing the inadequacies of his education, which was found among his papers and published in the memorial volume.[23]

He was not at all solemn, however serious he might have been, in his attitude towards his studies. One afternoon, at the end of his second year, Victor Kiernan met him on his way back from lunch to the Tripos hall, where he was to take the last of the three examinations for Part I. "He and a Canadian friend had been priming themselves with brandy during lunch, and were marching along singing ribald snatches, clearly fancying themselves as a pair of Wild West tough men. That evening he called on me with three pints of beer inside him and stamped up and down the room, shouting like the man in the *Beggar's Opera*, '*I want women!*' When I enquired why he didn't look for some he declared that one woman at a time was his rule—he was a 'monopoly capitalist'." He was quite willing for his friends to believe that his success on the Tripos had been "a mixture of luck and brilliance", and he told them his recipe was to know four thousand facts and a hundred dirty stories, but hard work had also contributed to it: "He could be seen on most mornings sitting concentratedly over a book in the college reading room"; in his first year, in Ray's flat in Ainsworth Street, he had been able to get a good deal of reading done without interruption, which was not the case when he was in his rooms at Trinity.

Neither he nor Ray had any use for the bourgeois conventions. They made no secret of the fact that they were living together. They would go about in the town, to meetings and demonstrations, and, on very rare occasions, to parties. There was the inevitable gossip: it was said by tea-cup Cambridge that the Cornfords' eldest son, who was said to be a Communist, was keeping a Russian mistress in the town. They made a very handsome and dramatic-looking pair: so much so that Lettice Ramsey, the photographer, at one of her parties asked them if they would be willing to be photographed by her. Ray was pleased at the idea, John was not but yielded to please Ray, and their dual portrait was exhibited in a show of Mrs Ramsey's work under the title, 'The Islanders'. Much of their time was taken up by party matters: most agreeably on one occasion when they went together to Paris to attend a Youth Conference. They were deeply fond of each other, and so, when Ray became pregnant, that did not disturb them; in fact, they rather enjoyed shocking the more 'respectable' of their friends. Three months before the baby was due, Ray went to live with relatives in London, and John would come down to see her when he could, and there the child was born. Soon afterwards he summoned them back to Cambridge to a new flat in Mill Road with an enormous sitting-room that could be used for meetings.

They found themselves in a quasi-respectable and inevitably domestic situation that brought into focus the differences between them: intellectual and emotional differences, and even, Ray felt, class differences, which had inadvertently manifested themselves in all sorts of little ways. The arrival of the child simply hurried the process of separation, which had actually begun some months before. But the inevitability of a separation does not diminish its sadness. Something of what John felt at this time is reflected in the lyric which is included in the memorial volume under the title 'Sad Poem':

I loved you with all that was in me, hard and blind,
Strove to possess all that my arms could bind,
Only in your loving found peace of mind.
But something is broken, something is gone,
We've loved each other too long to try to be kind,
This will turn to falseness if it goes on.

Though parting's as cruel as the surgeon's knife,
It's better than the ingrown canker, the rotten leaf.
All that I know is I have got to leave.
There's new life fighting in me to get at the air,
And I can't stop its mouth with the rags of old love.
Clean wounds are easiest to bear.

Else feel the warm response grow each night colder,
The fires of our strength in each other ash and smoulder.
Nothing that we do can prevent that we have grown older,
No words to say, no tears to weep.
Don't think any more, dear, rest your dark head on my
  shoulder,
And try to sleep, now, try to sleep.

He was to fall in love again, this time, as it turned out, for the rest of his life, with a girl much more truly similar to himself, a member of the middle class, who was now a Communist—as Ray had been also: but Margot Heinemann was a Communist of a much more intellectual sort. They might have met first at Conduit Head, where Miss Heinemann was one of the Cambridge undergraduates who came to play in an informal chamber music group organized by Professor Cornford. Such a meeting would not have been inappropriate in the pages of *Period Piece.* As it happened, they met through the party. Christopher, who had regarded her with admiration and some awe as she played the cello and talked politely but distantly at tea, was somewhat taken aback to learn that the 'Miss Heinemann' he knew at Conduit Head was also the 'Margot' with whom John had fallen in love. She had been at Newnham, and received firsts in both parts of the English Tripos. Now she was doing a year as a research student. She was active in politics, and an occasional contributor to *The Cambridge Review*—it was she who rebuked the author of 'Conversation with Communists'—where she published a very favourable review of John Lehmann's book of verse, *The Noise of History*, and a graphic account of unemployment and poverty in the collieries. In fact, mining was her particular interest—during the summer of 1935 she did a report on the distressed areas for the Labour Research Department, while John worked for their London office.

That autumn he returned to Cambridge for his last year as an undergraduate; Margot, her research studentship at an end, went to Birmingham to teach, and John would often visit her there. Undoubtedly her absence contributed to the restlessness he had begun to feel—"Before the end he was tired of student work, and wanted to be out in the world." Still, there was a great deal to be done, and although he might be "tired of student work", he was as actively engaged in it as he had ever been. He was always ready to branch out in new directions that might prove useful to the cause, and he made his first speech at the Union in November 1935. Considerably more serious than it had been in Julian Bell's day, the Union was still capable of an occasional descent into undergraduate fatuity, but it offered an audience widely diversified in its political allegiances; it was conceivable that one or two among them *might* be converted. Accordingly, John was prepared to endure its pseudo-parliamentary formality, its elaborate fossilized mannerisms so lovingly preserved, and even to undergo the ordeal of wearing a dinner jacket (required of all speakers) which he borrowed from his friend Michael Straight.

Straight, who had recently come up to Cambridge—he too was at Trinity—was perhaps the closest friend John was to make, after leaving Stowe, who was not a member of the party. Straight was on the Left in his sympathies, and, as the son of an extremely wealthy Anglo-American philanthropic family—his parents had founded at Dartington, their house in Devon, the experimental school of that name—he must have seemed an excellent prospect for conversion. But he was bored by Marx. Talk of the 'class struggle' did not enliven his imagination, or reproach his conscience, although he was willing to concede that, having grown up in the hills of Devon, he could not appreciate the miseries of factory life. On one occasion, John spent a futile hour trying to instil in him the idea of the 'class struggle'. He turned in frustration to a newspaper, and seized on a story about a strike. "There it is!" he said triumphantly. "I see," Straight replied, "you mean that this strike is a symbol of the class struggle." "No, dammit, it *is* the class struggle!"[24]

Nonetheless, their friendship flourished. Perhaps, at that moment, when so much of his life was given over to politics, John needed a less political friend: and he was fascinated by a young man like Straight who was so dedicated to the idea of freedom in his own life that he would surrender none of it, even to a cause as right and as inevitable as the revolution. For Straight the attraction was immediate: he was drawn to John, as so many others were, by his extraordinary gifts. But he was better able to estimate them at their worth than most undergraduates, for he had a standard of comparison: in spite of his youth, he had already met and numbered among his friends many who were gifted and celebrated in the world beyond Cambridge, and he recognized in Cornford someone truly remarkable.

As it happened, Straight took a more active part in the Union than John, who soon wearied of it, felt it had little to offer him (or the party) and turned to more important things. John spoke first on November 5, 1935, when Guy Fawkes Night inspired a motion that might have been debated either facetiously or seriously: 'That this House, regarding Parliamentary institutions as an obstacle to progress, deplores the failure of Guy Fawkes.' John, in moving the motion, made a serious speech in which he pointed out the unfairness of the allegedly democratic institutions under which Englishmen lived: rural areas were favoured in Parliament; election expenses kept members of the working class from running for office; in times of depression people were prevented, fearful that they might lose their jobs, from participating in local elections; and in any case, the Press made free choice in elections a farce. The Union reporter for *The Cambridge Review* was respectful: "He is to be congratulated on a sensible and well-argued maiden-paper speech. He is the first Communist to have spoken on the paper for some time."[25] John was seconded by another member of Trinity, Peter Kemp, who supported the motion for reactionary rather than revolutionary reasons, arguing that Parliament should be abolished and its functions taken over by the monarch and the aristocracy. (Interestingly enough, Kemp was to be one of the very few Englishmen who fought on Franco's side during the Spanish Civil War.[26]) But in spite of revolutionary and reactionary arguments, the motion was defeated, 160 to 49.

John spoke again later in the month, in support of Michael Straight's maiden-paper speech on the motion, 'That Downing Street is too close to Fleet Street', and the motion was carried, 115 to 95.[27] John's attitude towards the Union is made clear in a note of introduction he wrote for Straight (who never used it) to a journalist friend: "The bearer of this note is Michael Straight, who wants to get some dope on the question of the ownership and control of the press. The reason why is this: He has to move a motion in a fool debate in the Cambridge Student Union. 'That Downing St. is too close to Fleet St.' or some such nonsense. The importance of this otherwise silly debate is that it is important to get him elected into the Committee which he can do if he makes a speech that goes down well. So it is absolutely necessary to get hold of the dope on the question of the ownership of the press and its political connections, also, if there is any, of the control of the press by Government departments."[28]

In December, both Straight and Cornford were elected to the Standing Committee. This was the beginning of the route to higher office, and Straight went on to become president of the Union. But John had already had his fill of it, and spoke there only on two more occasions, first, unsuccessfully, against the National Government's agricultural policy, and the second time, successfully, against the motion 'That the least attempt to tamper with the integrity of the British Empire would be disastrous for the Peace of Mankind.'

The Christmas vacation of that year he and Margot and a few friends spent at the mill in Hunstanton. Afterwards, they went their respective ways: Margot to Birmingham to teach; John to Cambridge, but first for a few days to Cardiff, where he went as a 'fraternal delegate' from the Federation of Student Societies to the conference of the University Labour Federation. It was a time when the party was working strongly for unity in the student movement. Earlier in the year the F.S.S. had offered to dissolve and allow its sections to affiliate again with the U.L.F. At the Cardiff conference the proposal was accepted, the two groups were amalgamated, and John became vice-president of the new, enlarged Federation, which had a total membership of 1,500 and fifteen affiliated societies; thereafter it grew rapidly to a total membership of 3,000 and twenty-eight branches.[29]

John had reason to be pleased in Cardiff; but at the same time, the memory of his holiday at the mill was fresh in his mind, and he was acutely conscious of Margot's absence. Alone, he was desolate. As though to bring his feelings under control, he wrote the brief, very moving lyric to which he affixed the ironic title, 'A Happy New Year'.[30]

> All last night we lay so close,
> All completeness of the heart
> The restless future will efface;
> Tomorrow night we sleep apart.
>
> The eyeless shutter clamping out,
> Dear, the certainty of your touch,
> All the warmth and all the light;
> O don't think, it hurts too much.
>
> Though your nerves are frozen numb,
> Your sorrow will not make time stop,
> You're not a statue but a man;
> O don't grieve, it doesn't help.

That winter and spring of 1936, he spent as much time as he could in Birmingham. Chiefly he was there to see Margot; but he took advantage of being in an industrial city to further his political education, getting experience beyond the student movement. Once, handing out trade union recruiting leaflets outside a factory, he was arrested and brought into court on a charge of wilful obstruction: "Not very much fun," he wrote to Michael Straight, "but quite interesting." In April, he and Margot spent a week with Straight at Dartington. Michael Chekhov and his theatre group were using the estate as a base of operations at this time, and one evening they all joined forces for a party. John got happily drunk. When the company launched impulsively into a succession of high-spirited and athletic Russian dances, so too did John, flinging himself about enthusiastically. It was a happy time for them all.

But even an undergraduate as remarkable as John Cornford must consider what he will do in the year after he receives his degree. Very likely he saw himself as eventually becoming a leader in the Communist party—Reg Snell expected London to become Cornfordgrad—but that did not solve the problem of the immediate future. He did receive from his college, Trinity, a studentship, the Earl of Derby Research Scholarship. This was hardly a surprise after his starred first on the second part of the History Tripos: he had done as well as a major scholar on the foundation could be expected to do. To become a research student did not necessarily mean that he would be committing himself to an academic career; it was the common thing for a student who had done particularly well to stay at Cambridge for a few more years to consider if he might want to try for a fellowship. He had had a long-standing interest in the Elizabethans, ever since Stowe, when he had written to his mother that they could write "equally freely on everything", unlike the writers of succeeding ages. Victor Kiernan recalls his fondness for " 'explaining the Elizabethans' in terms of the expansion of merchant capital". There, possibly, might be a line of research for him, and he discussed the subject with his father—whose Greeks John found "insipid"—at some length, but inconclusively. The difficulty was that he would not know about the studentship until after his examinations in June. So that much of the spring was given over to a consideration of alternatives.

Politics, for example: at the organization level, working within and for the party. But he could not afford to go directly into political work of this kind, and there is no indication that the party, although doubtless valuing him highly, would support him in London. The leaders might well have wanted him to remain in Cambridge and to continue his work among students. Finally he applied for a job as an organizer with the Workers' Educational Association in Birmingham—a sensible thing to do, as it meant that he could be with Margot. Professor Ernest Barker, the political philosopher, whose seminar John had been attending, wrote an enthusiastic testimonial for him, but the selectors may have been put off by his remark that John had "A good range of knowledge about current social and economic conditions, and especially about contemporary Russia." Presently he received a formal letter of rejection from the Birmingham office of the W.E.A. to tell him that he had not been awarded the job he had applied for. But by then he had been awarded his studentship, and he was quite content to spend another year at Cambridge: he was twenty years old, there was no urgent need to commit himself to a particular pursuit at the moment.

After all, whatever he did, his main object would be further to train himself as a revolutionary leader, further to harden himself for the struggle. More than three years before, when he was at L.S.E., he had written to a friend, "It would be interesting to see how long one would remain a Communist inside a Nazi barracks. That's the final test. I feel already I could stand any other. That one I don't know about." The theme recurs in the political poems that he was writing at Cambridge:

> For all but suicides and slaves
> This death is background to our lives,
> This is the risk our freedom has us take.
> Some may die bold as Schulze died,
> Many will live to avenge our dead,
> But this fear haunts us all. Flesh still is weak.

Yet he answered firmly:

> Though flesh is weak, though bone is brittle,
> Our sinews must be hard as metal,
> We must learn to mock at what makes readers wince.

And again, writing of Kirov's assassination:

> Nothing is ever certain, nothing is ever safe,
> Today is overturning yesterday's settled good,
> Everything dying keeps a hungry grip on life.
> Nothing is ever born without screaming and blood.
>
> Understand the weapon, understand the wound:
> What shapeless past was hammered to action by his deeds,
> Only in constant action was his constant certainty found.
> He will throw a longer shadow as time recedes.

Victor Kiernan has recalled him "telling, with genuine relish, a story of Bela Kun machine-gunning five thousand prisoners during a forced retreat in the Russian Civil War: he told it not in a spirit of sadism, but of appreciation of an act of political necessity firmly carried out. I also recall his saying one day, when he had been reading of torture of political prisoners abroad, that he knew he could rely on his will-power as regards fighting, but that he was not sure how well he would be able to resist physical pain. There was no self-delusion."

Part Three

Julian Bell in China

Julian Bell in China

By the winter of 1935 Julian Bell seemed to have come to the end of a line in London: until now his life had fallen far short of the great expectations he and others had entertained for it. The thought occurred, perhaps if he made some break with life in England . . . He might get away from his dissatisfactions, strike out on his own, loosen himself from the environment and heritage that meant so much to him, and had done so much to shape him and perhaps to restrict him. For some time he had been attracted by the possibility of teaching in a foreign University, preferably in the Far East. As early as May 1934 he applied for a job in Siam, and also for one in China, through the Cambridge Appointments Board. He even put in (unsuccessfully) for a job in Japan for which a Methodist was preferred. He was anxious to move, to achieve some aim which was not at all clear in his own mind. Sometimes he thought that he wanted to go away in search of excitement: to a place where the Communist party might really be interesting—China perhaps, where there might even be a small-scale war where he could test his military theories. At other times he felt that he must leave England because he had got, without trying, an agreeable second-generation Bloomsbury existence—poems, women, good conversation—in which his successes were not important nor significant enough to satisfy him. In this mood, going to China seemed an escape, indeed a form of suicide. "My own feeling about China," he wrote to 'B', "is that it's about all I'm fit for now: a genteel form of suicide. Getting most of what I wanted has been bad for my morale, I think. Either I must have stability, or misery, if I'm to get much done."[1]

On July 16, 1935, the job he had applied for a year earlier, Professor of English at the National University of Wuhan in China, suddenly materialized. He wrote on the same day to his mother, who was in Cassis:

> Dearest Nessa
>
> I hope this letter won't be upsetting to you. No, I've not got married. But I have accepted a job in China—the English professorship I tried for last year.
>
> It happened completely unexpectedly—I went for an interview this morning, expecting nothing, came away without having taken it seriously—and heard this afternoon I'd got the job. It sounds amusing enough—as a job: £800 a year, one year certain, 3 probable: it could be renewed after that, but I don't want to spend my life away from you.
>
> The bore is that I have to be there at latest by the end of September: this means sailing at latest by August 20. I should like to leave by Marseilles and visit you at Cassis for as long as possible: you can imagine I've a busy month ahead. I shall know in a day or two more about dates, sailings, etc., and will let you know.
>
> I might have foreseen things happening like this: one's preparations of a couple of years ago taking effect at last.
>
> It felt rather appalling at the moment of hearing—since then I've stopped being sharply conscious of it all: it just stays a day-dream. I shall have to go on making arrangements like anything—the confusion will be frightful in an already busy life.
>
> I'm appalled at the thought of leaving you all for three years—it seems a terrific slice out of life. I shall be thirty then—1938. Angelica and Quentin settled down. It's the most drastic step I've ever taken, I think, after getting born.
>
> I'm sure that it's a good thing to do—what I wanted to do also, somewhere. I knew that for the time I'd got most of what I wanted from London. When I come back I should have got straight internally, and also have seen enough of the world to

be pretty clear about that . . . And somehow I'm convinced that it will produce a kind of peace of mind I now want above all things.[2]

He was full of excitement. As John Lehmann wrote to him, his going to China might turn out to be "a thing . . . absolutely decisive in your life". It was certainly the most decisive step he had taken in his career thus far. Going to Leighton Park School, going to Cambridge, working for a Fellowship at King's, living the London literary life, had all been more or less fore ordained, and what many a bright young man might do: what a Bloomsbury young man was almost bound to do. But to go and teach in China —that was something different and comparatively adventurous, a step of his own. It is tempting to think that the final poem of the London section in *Work for the Winter* was written after Julian had heard that he was going to China; it very much has the feeling of a new direction taken:

> Resurrect, resurrect,
> The senses and the intellect,
> Swing and stride and march again
> In thundering charges down the plain.
> Carry the dry logs to the fire,
> Relight pride, resurge desire,
> And spin the dead leaves down the wind,
> And let in winter on the mind.
>
> Out with old banners, let them fly,
> Nor care a hang for symbolry:
> I am I, and close to hand
> My world to shape or understand.
> Life goes on, once more I live,
> Once more the open skies can give
> Some native force, some natural power,
> And flaming triumph through an hour.

It was all rather sudden: he had been given the job on July 16, he was to sail no later than August 20, and he proposed going out to Cassis to see his mother: it would be the last time for them to be together for three years. She replied that she was cutting short her vacation, and returning to England, and of course he was delighted: "I've wanted you very much this last week." They said their good-byes at Charleston. Later, from on board ship, he wrote to 'B' about their parting: "Nessa and I both have about the same notion of how to behave, but it isn't easy. As it happened, it was her giving me some money as a present that broke me down. Then a bright, cheerful, grim little drive into Lewes and Newhaven. You know, I'm almost the only person I know who has an adult relationship with their mother. It's about the most satisfactory human relationship I have, perhaps because it's the only one where I've deep emotions uncomplicated by power-sadist feelings."[3]

The psychological reasons which impelled him to China seem to be very clear: intense dissatisfaction with his life in the present, the hope of making a fresh start in the future. There were practical reasons too. He imagined that life at a Chinese university would be stable and uneventful enough for him to get a great deal of work accomplished: he intended to write a series of long essays which would clarify his position *vis-à-vis* his generation, and perhaps allow him to play a more central role in the life of England when he returned. Also, there was the attractiveness of the salary he was offered. He did have small private means, which were beginning to improve in 1935 as the effects of the Depression lessened, but he welcomed the money from a regular job, at a good wage at a place where living expenses presumably would be low. But in the end one comes back to his situation in London, where he no longer wished to be. The moment was opportune. Wuhan University had wanted an English Professor of English; Julian had wanted such a job. At the end of August he sailed from Marseilles on a Japanese ship, the *Fushimi Maru*.

Wuhan University was not, as one might perhaps expect in the circumstances, a missionary institution with official ties to the West, but a creation of the state, one of fifteen National Universities scattered about China. Somewhat removed and out of the way, at a considerable distance from the great coastal cities, Wuhan is on the Yangtze River about 400 miles up river from Nanking. Even before the 1911 revolution, it had been a centre of education, but in very much the provincial sense, a worthy rather than a sophisticated *milieu*, and as such not particularly Julian's style. In 1895, a Government School of Mines was opened in Wuhan; and the reforming Viceroy Chang Chih-tung inaugurated the system of which Julian was a part: the regular importation of professors from the West. The revolution which overthrew the Manchu dynasty actually began at Wuhan in October 1911; two years later, a National University was founded there, with departments of Chinese Language and Literature, Russian Language and Literature, History, Philosophy, Physics, Chemistry, Biology, Law and Library Science. By the 1930s it had become one of the more prominent universities in China, but it was still very small and provincial.

Chinese higher education in this period was neither adventurous, ambitious—the B.A. was the only degree awarded—nor widespread. Altogether, as of 1931, there were fifty-nine universities, with an enrolment of 34,000 students. Most of the twenty-seven private universities were missionary sponsored, and, though comparatively free of government interference, might be inhibited by the doctrinal principles of their sponsors. Even so, they were believed to offer the best education, and attracted almost half the entire undergraduate enrolment. The rest were divided among the government's Provincial and National Universities.

State education was of doubtful merit and badly hampered—or so a League of Nations investigating team decided in the early 1930s—because of its hierarchical structure, with everything depending on the whims of the Central Ministry and its politically-appointed head: students and faculty alike might find themselves thrown out for the most trivial political reasons; faculty members were jeopardized by every change in administration. (Professors from abroad, like Julian, would be somewhat removed from this sort of pressure.) Teaching was primarily done by lectures—students might be attending as many as twenty a week—but there were also a few smaller classes and supervisions. (Julian was to do some of these, as well as lecture.)

The National University of Wuhan—there was also a private university in the town—consisted of approximately 700 students and 150 teachers. Most of the students came from the local area, as the University, except perhaps in Library Science, had no particular *cachet* that would attract anyone to it from a great distance.

It was divided into a School of Letters, a School of Law (which included politics and economics), a School of Science, and a School of Technology; and, in all but the last, girls as well as boys were allowed to register. Almost all of them studied English and English Literature: it was particularly emphasized in the School of Letters. There, there were the expected courses in Shakespeare, Shelley and Keats, as well as a survey of the novel—it was to teach these courses that Julian had been hired. The University was dowdy-to-respectable, rather than distinguished-to-brilliant: it must have regarded Professor Bell as quite a catch. He himself had been somewhat diffident about his chances, particularly as for one reason or another his various other efforts to leave England for a teaching post abroad had failed. But he had done well at Cambridge, he was the nephew of Virginia Woolf, he was *au courant* in London: who better to bring Western culture to the Chinese?

The voyage out was long, leisurely, uneventful and entirely enjoyable. He was on board the *Fushimi Maru* for almost six weeks, with brief stop-overs at a number of outposts of Empire. Along the way he wrote his mother very lively, colourful, gossipy 'traveller's letters' about his fellow passengers (the inevitable "charming tea planter from Assam" whom Julian summed up, just as inevitably, as "pure Somerset Maugham") and places seen ("We're in Singapore for the night . . . We came in this afternoon through archipelagoes and palms and sampans and junks: mangrove swamps growing out into the sea: single trees sticking out of the water a hundred yards from the bank") and shipboard happenings ("It's said the laundryman who was ill in the Red Sea and then recovered has gone mad and jumped overboard. However, I don't feel at all concerned about that, since any of us might easily go mad"). The tone is unfailingly exuberant, and oddly boyish—a schoolboy let out of school for an unexpected holiday. In Colombo he was entertained by a friend of Leonard Woolf's, who at the moment was Acting-Governor. "I got a lot of fun out of the grandeurs," he reported. "Sentries to present arms. Two sets of uniformed servants, upstairs and down . . . And, which really pleased me immensely, I was lent an enormous Humber saloon, with chauffeur (native, extremely competent) and royal arms on a flag on the bonnet! It was terrific fun." Phrases of this sort abound: "I feel a good deal excited and fascinated." In Singapore he went ashore with a fellow passenger and wandered around the amusement parks: "It was fascinating beyond words." Hongkong "was great fun: a lovely mountain town with a long fjord of a harbour alive with fascinating junks. I was given lunch at the Government House and taken round the town in a car, thanks to Leonard's introduction." In Shanghai occurred his "first real adventure", a classic encounter with a pimp—"Russian girl, yes?" "No, no, no time"—who attempted to extort payment for services not rendered:

> "Go the devil" (I really did say that.) Then, to rickshaw man, "North Station." Rickshaw man hesitates. Pimp: "I shoot, I kill you." "Don't be a damned fool." So far very heroic. But then, fool myself, I got out, and saying to rickshaw man, with vague honesty, "you come," started to walk out. (Thank God for good visual memory and sense of direction.) Attack by pimp, vaguely and weakly supported by rickshaw man. First dive for my balls got home, and I fell, dropping papers carried. However, attack not pressed, and I got up. Second attack, attempt to dislocate my jaw, painful but unsuccessful; another ball dive, some vague hitting by me, and they drew off. I turned and walked out. One picked up a stone, but it never came. I walked back, a long-seeming way, waked a Sikh policeman at traffic lights, asked for taxi place, found one, took a taxi to the station, found my American express man waiting, and a hard sleeper, drank queer-tasting mineral water, and sat down to write to you.

Finally, on the first of October, suffering from a mild attack of dysentery, he arrived in Nanking. He found the town "fascinating", and was pleased with the Minister of Education—"a nice little man who wore national dress: I mistook him for a coolie at first when he came into the room"—who told him that he would receive £700 a year rather than the £800 he had expected, but that he would only have to teach nine to twelve hours a week. The next day he left for Wuhan, a three-day journey up the

Yangtze, on the river steamer *Tunk-mo*. His fellow passengers were two American women, a Yorkshire business man and his sister and an Irish missionary. He particularly approved of the missionary who, it turned out, shared his admiration for Michael Collins. But he was in a euphoric mood, and took a benevolent view of them all: "The business man, amiable. The Americans american, but tolerable. Eddy wouldn't know me now, I've grown so good at tolerating people, and seeing the good in every man." He arrived in Wuhan on Sunday morning, October 5. That afternoon he met the Dean of the School of Letters, Professor Cheng Yuan, and his wife, who were to be his neighbours. From Professor Cheng he learned that he was expected to start teaching—courses in Shakespeare, Modern Literature, and Composition—two days later.

His rejection by the Electors of King's seems to have strengthened him in his desire to teach, but he had never had any practical experience. Until the Sunday, he had not been told what precisely he was to do at Wuhan; accordingly he had not been able to prepare. The prospect was intimidating. There was the further difficulty that his dysentery had worsened, and he was now quite ill, but not ill enough, he felt, to justify taking to his bed and cancelling classes. He had no choice but to improvise lectures at the beginning and he suspected that his students had some difficulty in following his English. Still, "we're getting on," he wrote to his mother. "I'm not frightened—the fortunate part of being ill is that one grows impervious to the world: I could make myself do anything all last week."

As his health began to improve, he entered into the job with great relish. He found the place beautiful, the library "superb", the staff extremely pleasant. Even the large problems of settling down in a strange country did not bother him: he coped with a house that was almost bare of furniture and equipment when he took possession, and with servants (Yang, "a wretched, shifty, rather dishonest creature", and a coolie to help him). His contract with the University called for nine to twelve hours' work a week; having no experience of teaching, he imagined that this would be literally the case and felt that he was being overpaid—"I shall try to do a bit more to salve my conscience." Actually he had very little free time. Lectures and supervisions came to sixteen hours a week; he spent three hours a week studying Chinese; he gave a good deal of time to the preparation of lectures. And, as in most academic communities, social life was conducted in a fairly casual and time-consuming way.

His first reactions to China were warmly appreciative: he delighted in its strangeness, and he delighted in its unexpected familiarity. Shanghai had reminded him of Marseilles; a village on the Yangtze was "pure Provence"; on his first day at the University he described it as a "Mediterranean Cambridge". Professor Cheng was "a friend of Goldie's"; his wife was "sometimes called the Chinese Katherine Mansfield"; he summed them up for John Lehmann as "very much a Chinese Bloomsbury". He found the University people "extraordinarily like Cambridge, very friendly, informal and social: we all live in houses scattered about the hillside, and there is a great deal of dropping in in a casual Cambridge fashion." His own house looked "like a Cambridge don's house, only smaller . . . built of the local grey brick, and set on a steep hillside, near the top. The kitchen and servants' quarters [were] back, set into the hill." He was constantly struck by resemblances in the landscape: "Now in the dusk"—sailing up the Yangtze—"very soft and damp as an English October—we have come to Cambridgeshire and the fens."

There are passages in the letters that read like notations for unwritten poems in *Winter Movement*: ". . . the trees are turning colour—a small poplar with very light round leaves individually flecked with orange-purpled reds. And a red-hot sky, then moon—I walked in the dark, stumbling through deep grass graves, like pest-bogs almost. There was a clouded moon and wild geese flying." Life had its Charlestonian aspects too. A certain 'aesthetic' impracticality in the Chinese was not unreminiscent; and there were episodes in the countryside beyond Wuhan that might have been chronicled in the *New Bulletin*. "A most Charlestonian scene as I walked this evening," he wrote to his mother in November. "A bull water-buffalo gone wild, with half a dozen dogs chasing, and vague people whacking, halloing. Round and about—graves, field, path, crushing a peach orchard and wire fence—how I longed to join in." It was as though he had come half way round the world to find himself reminded at every turn of what he had started from and chosen to leave. He wrote to John Lehmann:

"It's all like ten years or more ago," and to Eddie Playfair: "What a world. The lives one leads. Really so alike."

At first there were moments of "appalling homesickness"; but they occurred at widening intervals. He was really very happy in China, the conditions of his life there were more favourable to his being happy than they had been in the immediate past, and as he feared they would prove to be in the future, in "an England of nervous tension, towns and politics". At Wuhan he could shoot, he could sail, he could roam through the open countryside. He had a boat built for himself in Hankow; it was ready by spring, and thereafter he spent a good deal of time on the river. Most evenings, between five and seven, he would go out with a gun and look for duck or snipe: it was an activity that identified him with the *sahib* rather than the missionary element in Wuhan, which did not displease him; it also marked him off from the confirmed academics: "It's *essential* I should shoot, or I may become a don." These were the simple, familiar outdoor pleasures that counted for a great deal with Julian, indeed were indispensable to his well-being, that he had experienced in the past and whose absence he had lamented in London. But the pleasures (and difficulties) of being a don were new to him; they comprised an important part of his experience in China. He had come out to teach at a provincial Chinese university because he felt he must have the stability it offered him. "The truth of the matter," he wrote to a friend, "is that I want to enjoy life: I'm in a better position for doing so than usual." Even his view of the world crisis lightened: "Can one believe it's even conceivable there'll be a stable *status quo*? Yes, I can, here, teaching literature. But could one in England?" Teaching exhilarated him; he entered into his duties at Wuhan with enthusiasm and dedication. By the end of his first month he was becoming restive. He had never attached much importance to the conventional methods of scholarship; he was much more agile at a discussion, pursuing various fascinating hares of argument—as 'The Good and All That' had demonstrated—than at systematically organizing his material. A course in 'composition', by its very nature, lends itself to improvisation and tricks of personality, and there he did well from the start. But his courses in Modern Literature and Shakespeare were more taxing. "It's fun talking to people," he wrote to Lehmann, "but I haven't yet got very much response. They understand me decently. But God knows I'm really unfit for the job: I have to learn it by doing it." His ambitions were grandiose: not only did he intend to read the books he assigned to his students—"I make up lectures on Macbeth in the process of reading"—but also "endless books on China, on philosophy and criticism, on every manner of subject . . . It's all incomparably odd." To his mother he admitted, "Really, I'm exceedingly ill-trained for anything, and certainly for University teaching work. If I succeed it will be a tribute to my brilliance, charm and determined character rather than anything else."

The solution he arrived at fell short of his ambitions, but was a good deal more realistic. For the Shakespeare course he depended on the 'Arden' edition with its copious footnotes, and his own ingenuity. For the Modern Literature course he chose to deal principally with the writers he knew best. In effect he brought Bloomsbury and the Bloomsbury canon to China. He divided modern writing into two periods, from 1890-1914, and 1914-1936, and began with the earlier, about which he knew less, for practice. Gissing, Henry James and Arnold Bennett were omitted from the syllabus; Samuel Butler, Wilde and Conrad were included. Robert Bridges he found "empty". Rupert Brooke seemed better than he had believed, but he finally decided, "he wasn't a poet—much—but the most remarkable human being I've ever heard of. Of course I feel a certain sympathy with some of his letters from foreign parts, and there is far too much of an analogy—King's, Apostles, etc. I suppose I should have liked immensely to have all his gifts—looks and a fellowship and worldly successes. Not that I've done badly, but it would have been superb to have had that sort of 'brilliant career'." In November, looking forward to the next term when he would be dealing with the writers who mattered to him most, he wrote to his Aunt Virginia that he planned to use one of her novels, but he was not sure which. "I think they must do you, Tom and Yeats." In February, grown secure in his idiosyncratic method, he was venturing afield, trying "to push Proust down their throats", the result, as he put it, of "a recent conversion". Before this, he had not been one of the enthusiasts for the great French novelist—unlike his father, whose *Proust* was one of the first appreciations in English—but he would make annual efforts to read *A La Récherche du Temps Perdu.* Convinced that part of his job was to "try and jog and stir the mind", he also attempted to expound Freud to his students. Here his ambition overcame his judgment, and with characteristic frankness he told Playfair, "it's too difficult for an ignoramus like self to explain." He wanted to familiarize them with the basis of Bloomsbury, the philosophical theories and critical principles, as well as its creative practice. "They'll get 'Cambridge School'—[Clive] Bell to [Frank] Ramsey. Not either principal in detail, though I shall explain Moore to them, I think." And they were to analyse prose passages in the manner of I. A. Richards's *Practical Criticism.* By March, lectures on the "family" were in full cry. He wrote to his aunt, "I get a good deal of quiet fun, too, out of lecturing on all of you: Goldie, Maynard, Bertie [Russell] I've done so far: Clive and Roger for next week." Then would come an occasional foray into the bad-lands, to consider writers like T. E. Hulme and Wyndham Lewis; but soon he would be back in familiar territory: "I am wondering if they can be allowed to read Peter [F. L. Lucas], or will his damned charm corrupt them?" Bloomsbury was the centre from which he operated: minor works in the school of Bloomsbury would receive as much if not more attention than major works outside it. Lawrence and Joyce, two writers whom Bloomsbury could neither comfortably accept nor dismiss, were ignored in his lectures. But of course he had no desire to be *professional* about his job, or to go systematically through a conventional syllabus. He did not consider himself a born teacher or scholar, but rather an expositor, so to speak, of the family business, and a firm believer in the family creed. "Really education is a lot of nonsense; it only happens once in a way as a personal relation—which is why you get it from your contemporaries, family, or friends, or at Cambridge."

Still, he felt that his time teaching had demonstrated he had "some gifts as an educator", and he continued to believe that King's had made a mistake in not giving him a fellowship. Unfortunately, the education at Wuhan did not allow for a closeness between pupil and teacher—without personal relations how much could one teach, or learn? As a consequence, he could never finally settle in his own mind what he thought of the Chinese young. His first reaction was positive. Although he found them perhaps slightly over-romantic and sentimental, he was more impressed by their sensitivity and intelligence: they were educable. Familiarity altered his opinion: he began to feel that the Chinese must be toughened up intellectually: "If I had my way I'd forbid them any English prose that wasn't hard, dry, knobbly, masculine: bring them up on Swift and Defoe, switch them over to Bertie Russell and hard-boiled Americans—somehow get them off this infernal gilt-gingerbread elegance." A month later (again to his mother) he wrote, "They're almost like primitives in the way they can be corrupted by sentimentality, romanticism and nonsense." And he reported to his aunt: "I'm conducting an anti-sentiment and fine writing campaign, which they badly need . . . So much second-rate stuff has been pushed off on them. Stevenson and Lamb and Ruskin and that sort of water intoxicant." He became so impatient with the Chinese that he even felt it necessary to attack their most ardent admirer on the fringe of Bloomsbury, Goldsworthy Lowes Dickinson, whose *Letters from John Chinaman* in 1901 was a forerunner of Bloomsbury's abiding interest in the East. Although Julian felt that "softness" was a particular intellectual vice of the Chinese, more widespread among them than among the English, he was also attacking the quality itself. It was a way to continue his war against romanticism and vague sentimental thinking. These were all the more to be regretted when he detected them in the immediate ancestry of his beloved Bloomsbury. "I can't really see," he wrote to his aunt, "why Goldie was so enthusiastic about them [the Chinese]—except indeed for niceness and charm. And perhaps he didn't mind sentimentality as much as his youngers do." He then went on to deprecate Dickinson in general. He disliked his softness. Perhaps he felt this particularly deeply because he suspected that there might be a streak of softness, of gentility, in Bloomsbury and himself: would they prove hard enough to cope with a threatened world? "He was really, you know, a little soft—that was what made him so much less impressive than Roger. One saw him the whole time wanting to give way to his feelings, but knowing he mustn't. It was charming enough to meet someone so gentle and saintly and generally admirable, and it's charming enough to read him. But I suppose it was something to do with his being repressed and disappointed that made him—'wistful' is almost the word. Whereas old Roger, having had all the women, and so on, he wanted, never seemed to weaken in any way." Against this must be set a passage from a letter to Lehmann, written soon after Julian had arrived at Wuhan, and was still suffering from the debilitating and depressing effects of his illness: "I want to have the untroubled bourgeois holiday again. I suppose I shan't get it for long, ever. You know, I'm not going to be really very good at the new world. I am soft, frightfully—above all when I'm unwell, or rather convalescent. And the detail of life can be a horror, though the essentials are worse. Sometimes I sit miserable in a corner and realise them. I shall one day write down the truth about life—and it will look as sentimental as my poems."

With only one of his students was he able to establish a personal relationship. This was a talented young man in his composition course, C. C. Yeh, who was later to establish himself, in China and abroad, as a writer. Julian found him intelligent and sensitive, full of vitality and courage, and very promising. Eager to help him in his career, he recommended him to John Lehmann, who agreed with Julian's estimate, and later introduced his work in *New Writing*. It was Yeh's case in particular that convinced Julian that education as practised in China was not acceptable. "I'm in a fine rage with the Chinese university system," he wrote to Playfair. "My favourite pupil, a very nice, intelligent youth, a promising writer, and with guts enough to treat me as an equal—such a relief—is on the verge of a nervous breakdown plus insomnia; he has 28 hours lectures a week plus 1 hour's supervision (mine) and about 20 hours of it involves preparing texts." This was a far cry from the *douceur de vivre* of Cambridge, with education as a personal relation, and time for thinking about a subject rather than mere rote-learning. "I suspect the whole country needs a good shakeup," he wrote indignantly. "You see the sahib? But as you know I can get just as cross with the French or the English."[4]

He would always be intolerant of what he considered to be stupidity, and anxious to correct it—"by force if necessary". Faced with an unfamiliar, infinitely complex, and somewhat bewildering culture, he responded in a rather more simplistic way than he might have in the West; but essentially it was the same feeling of intense irritation at other people's stupidities. Soon after his arrival, when he was still living in a state of enforced chastity, which always made him irritable, and which perhaps gave to his fantasies a more sexual colouration than they might ordinarily have had, he decided that the Chinese men were an inferior race but the women were beautiful. What was needed, he felt, was a new and intelligent Tamberlane, who would come along and castrate the men and breed the women to northern European stock.

Writing to his mother a week after his arrival at Wuhan, Julian told her, "I have moments of appalling homesickness, when I want frightfully to be with you again, and in a safe, familiar, friendly world . . . But against these I have moments of exultation, and generally an occupied neutrality that I think would become active pleasure if I stopped being mildly ill. All sorts of details of life are fascinating and curious and sometimes very lovely. And above all there's the real friendliness of the Chengs and the Wangs—and I think I shall find other people whom I can have real and intimate relationships with." Inevitably, this proved to be the case, with only a slight modification—"other people" became "one person". Abroad, as at home, Julian could not keep out of love's way, and he was soon to embark upon what was perhaps the most remarkable, and certainly the most documented, of all his affairs, the closest he was ever to come to a grand passion. It was a quirk of his character, already noticed, that when in love he adored publicity, and nothing made him happier than to dis cuss the progress of his affairs, down to the most intimate details, with his mother and certain of his friends. The older generation of Bloomsbury, in rebellion against the taboos of their Victorian forebears, believed in clear, candid, truthful and rational personal relationships, and accordingly saw no reason to be reticent in matters of sex. But there is a quality in Julian's revelations that is very different from the candour of his elders, and suggests that he was involved not so much in a relationship as in a performance.

In his first weeks in Wuhan he was still too ill to look about energetically for the indispensable mistress; also, presumably, he felt that he must first grow familiar with his new environment. But at no point did he intend that his position, or whatever may have been his commitments in England, should prevent him from living the same sort of life as he had in the past. Everything conspired to make him a libertarian: he saw no reason not to continue to uphold a "Latin-sensual view of *amour*". And as frequently is the case, perhaps more often at a foreign university where the number of women with whom one can talk and make love in one's own language is so few, the possibility of a "real and intimate relationship" appeared in the person of a faculty wife.

In a "casual Cambridge fashion" there was a "great deal of dropping-in", and a great deal of party-giving and party-going among the faculty at Wuhan. This was very much to Julian's taste. He went out often, and gave small dinners of his own, once his cook had proved himself moderately accomplished. "I think we can just manage six," he reported to his mother, "which is enough: perhaps later I shall give a big dinner-party, Chinese style: it's more definite, and consequently easier. But you know how I enjoy entertaining, and now it seems I shall really be able to indulge my favourite vice." Late in November, returning home after a party, he wrote to her: "Your letter answering my first from Wuhan came tonight, and I can't tell you how happy I am. I've fifty things to say to you, and I'm very drunk—alas, solemn, solitary drunk, sobering up on tonic water, only 9 o'clock in the evening. But then, Chinese parties are like that—one has dinner 6.30—heavenly food, and drinking of healths across and around . . . tonight they produced the famous Tiger's Marrow spirit, which is devastating stuff . . . Anyway, I'm wildly happy—I've had two letters of yours in two days. And now I really feel we begin communication again. And life here is the greatest fun—wildly social now—I either entertain or go out five evenings a week: Chinese, missionaries—2 pretty wives, so they're fun . . ."

It was in these circumstances that he met 'K'. She was Chinese, charming, intelligent, sympathetic, civilized, an amusing conversationalist, a talented painter, and, as he was soon to learn, unhappily married. All the omens seemed favourable; the casual social arrangements at Wuhan conspired to bring them together often; he had more or less recovered from his illness, and was ready for an affair. But he was uncertain of the wishes of the lady, and he was uncertain, too, of how deeply he wanted to be involved. Love had become a necessity and a habit, yet at the same time he did not savour it as much as he had in the past: he had grown disillusioned. Some months later, when his affair with 'K' was in full progress, he wrote to a friend, "It's so hard to get a disinterested emotion out of it [love]. I have, sometimes, got something very valuable, but to be quite honest I don't think it's ever been as good as the peculiar pure thrill I can get from nature: it's much more extensive, no doubt, one's affected in more ways, more violently, but I only know two, very momentary, emotions I can get from love which seem to me comparable with the other: one's the pleasure of suddenly realizing your lover's physical beauty—the sort of flash of seeing it which hardly lasts a specious present. The other's the perfect intellectual calm and clarity of satisfied lust, when you've gone beyond the bounds of reason and moderation and even pleasure—rather like sleeping on the rack."

But this is to anticipate. At first he and 'K' were no more than good friends, and he told his mother, "I think we're going to stay that. But it's a ticklish, interesting situation." It remained so a bit longer: "Fortunately she's only reasonably nice-looking, so I'm not yet in love with her." But they continued to see each other, in company, meeting apparently by chance; they went on shopping expeditions across the river in Hankow; there were "emotional conversations". The likelihood of an affair increased. "One changes skies", he wrote to his mother, "not hearts or lives."[5] But for all the sophistication of his attitude—especially as it is made to appear in his letters—he was falling in love. By mid-November he was bothered if he couldn't see 'K' every day. A week later he wrote to his mother, "I've just realised how deeply I'm involved. Oh Nessa dear, you will have to meet her one of these days. She's the most charming creature I've ever met, and the only woman I know who would be a possible daughter-in-law to you (she isn't, being married with a charming child, and 10 years too old) but she is really in our world." In early December there was a "period of storm"—'K' had come upon an unfinished letter of Julian's to his mother, telling of the "affair—it's almost that", and threatened to break off. But things had already gone too far between them for either of them to take the threat seriously. 'K' was in love with Julian, and Julian wrote to his mother that 'K' was "definitely the most serious, important and adult person I've ever been in love with".

The next month he was absorbed in planning the affair. He had already broached to 'K' the possibility of "bed", and she was not unsympathetic, but launching an affair in Wuhan itself seemed fraught with problems. Simply to find a place where one could be alone, and uninterrupted, was difficult. There were always servants hovering about, and the possibility of blackmail was real. He had clear and rational discussions with 'K' about the various obstacles to be overcome, and he continued the discussions in letters to his friends. "It's hard to plan unconventional immorality in this strange town & country," he complained to 'B'. But the problem of a place, at least, was finally settled: they would go to Peking in January—she ostensibly to visit friends—during the long holiday between terms, and there the affair would truly begin.

His mood was jubilant but cautious. He was determined not to let romantic impulsiveness lead him further than the limits set by reason. He wrote to his mother, "Be prepared for a cable saying 'all is discovered', and a demand for money to pay my passage home, or news that I've married her and found some other job in the country. Or that she has committed suicide, as she fairly often threatens. But don't worry about it—the worst would be no more than annoying (I don't really believe in suicide, naturally) it's all a bit unreal. I don't think I shall get permanently involved—of course I've often thought that, and then thought I should, and I've not been to bed with her yet, which always affects my judgment a lot. But after all I never have got involved yet so deeply I couldn't get out. Besides, she really is utterly charming—I don't know anyone I've ever had an affair with I thought you'd like more."[6] In his next letter (a few days later) he brought up a problem to which he had not hitherto given much thought: the husband. "I don't know what his attitude may be, tho' I think he's essentially rational, and won't make a grand fuss. But I don't know if he's to be deceived or told or what." Then there was his fear of scandal—in China—which did not inhibit his wish that all his friends in England should know of the affair. But the major problem was his feeling for 'K': how seriously was he in love with her? That he *was* in love with her he did not doubt, and he was willing to speculate about a future in which she played some part: perhaps they might even marry, or else live together in China, or in England. But an exclusive monogamous passion, such as she would want, was not what he wanted. He could anticipate difficulties. "She's very jealous and I've not really forsworn polygamy." In short, he was in love with her, but in his own fashion; and there was a very simple, powerful force operating behind all these doubts and hesitations—his desire to go to bed with a woman after a long period of enforced chastity. Shortly before setting out for Peking, he wrote to 'B': "I can't think what it will be like to go to bed with a real woman again—I've got so used to fantasy and chastity these months—not even masturbation—only a very rare dream—in the last of these you figured, and, as in life, were charming; and as in dreams—and alas, too often in life—it wasn't very satisfactory."

On January 10, 1936, he boarded the train for Peking. It was a long journey, Wuhan being as far from Peking as Paris is from Milan, and he was *en route* for two days and a night. From the train he wrote exuberantly to Eddie Playfair: "Here I am in a dust storm, in the North Chinese plain, en route for Peking and a 20-days vac with my mistress." And the next day he was there, in "the most fascinating great capital I've ever seen or heard of," much like Paris—as he wrote to his mother, "Could you imagine anything more perfect than coming to Paris [as I have come to Peking] with a mistress who really knows the town, is devoted to one, is perfectly charming, has an impeccable taste in food—it's the dream of a romantic man of the world: the sort of thing Clive ought to do. Also I am meeting Chinese intellectuals, and English, going to the theatre, skating (badly, on bad ice) and making love . . . I suddenly feel very grown up and at ease in the world." The note of enthusiasm is sustained in letter after letter: to Mrs Woolf, "it must be the most remarkable town on earth"; to David Garnett, "the most extraordinary place . . . the right mixture of leisure and sociability and culture with squalor and disreputability"; and to Playfair, "This is undoubtedly the Paradis Terrestre. The sense of amenity of Paris, leisure and antiquity of Cambridge and incredible beauty. Frost and blue sky, and almost too much life in the streets."[7] A greater contrast to Wuhan was hardly to be imagined: the sophistication of a great capital, as against the boring respectability of a provincial university town. He welcomed too the opportunity of meeting the "civilised

English" in Peking, so different from their counterparts in Hankow, all "punch-headed businessmen and dim missionaries". Friends in England had told him to look up Harold Acton, who was then teaching at Peking University, and he found him charming and interesting: "culture up to the hilt" was his verdict, and again, "he really understands Chinese culture". Acton gave a dinner party for Julian, and on a number of occasions served as a most authoritative guide. He took him to the studio of one of the leading Chinese painters, Ch'i Pai-shih, whom Julian described to his mother as "a sage with a long, twisty, thin white beard, skull-cap and spectacles and a charming smile". At length, after much conversation in Chinese between Acton and the painter, they were allowed to see some of his work: "very free, very sensitive water colours," Julian reported, "on long scrolls." The question was broached: " 'Might we buy any?' Yes, we might: they cost six dollars a foot. So we picked." Acton, in his autobiography, recalls Julian in the crowded studio, examining a picture of a carp and attempting to reach a decision. "He examined it questioningly, unable to make up his mind. As he stood there, or drooped, in his shaggy clothes, he reminded me of Roger Fry. He had the same air of puzzled scrupulous refinement. One could see his qualms like porcupine quills. Was there anything in this or nothing? Was it merely a relic of tradition? How spontaneous was it?"[8] Julian was extremely hesitant, but finally, when Acton threatened to buy the painting himself, his decision was precipitated, and he bought it for his mother.

But the greatest pleasure, which indeed had the effect of heightening all the others, was to be there with 'K', who seemed ever more charming and fascinating and pleasing to look at, especially since she did not feel obliged to dress in the style of the University New Life movement, as she did in Wuhan. Although he wrote to his mother that "the mad interlude has put all else out of my head . . . we are very happy and silly," they did behave with a degree of circumspection, she staying at the house of friends, he in a German *pension*. At times they were even more circumspect than Julian would have liked: he reported disapprovingly that "alas in a Chinese restaurant you can't really flaunt a mistress, for you are all partitioned off in little rooms and cubicles". Still, he was there with an enchanting mistress who adored him, and *that*, he now discovered, just that and no more, was what he wanted. Once the affair was truly an affair he found it easy to curb his impetuousness. At the end of their second week in Peking, when he and 'K' were at their happiest together, he wrote to his mother: "Be tranquil, my dear . . . The situation is well in hand and I am quite clear now that marriage would be a disaster. I think even if there is a scandal, it would only mean my returning this autumn instead of next."

The next week—the last of the holiday—he came down with flu, and was confined to his bed in the German *pension*. 'K' was in daily attendance there to nurse him and to distract him. Nonetheless the romantic mood diminished further, and he fell prey to "an unreasonable depression" which he attributed to the aftereffects of flu. Also, he was homesick, and on February 4, he turned twenty-eight. A passionate love affair did not seem to provide the answer to the question that bothered him most: what was he to do with his life? On February 5, he wrote to his mother, "I'm gloomy at being 28 and so little done. And at the fact that when I do come back I shall find myself again with nothing to do, tho' I rather hope I can remedy that at least with a little luck with books . . . The odd thing is having a reputation—in China—as a poet: I feel less like the Chinese idea of a poet than words can express. Well, anyway I've got two years before I'm thirty, and definitely middle-aged, and Stephens are allowed to begin late. Somehow or other I must get my incongruous box of tricks together."

Soon after this they returned to Wuhan, 'K' full of love, Julian full of doubts. Already he had begun to regret all those letters in which he had discussed the possibility of an affair which was now taking place, and so to a close friend he suggested a counter-story which would maintain his reputation as a seducer without seriously endangering his position with those he might have left behind: *they* were to know that he was still free. "As to the Home Front: I've been foolishly indiscreet: one always thinks of correspondents each in a separate cell. The story I suggest is that after a short affair we found it didn't do physically, and was socially too dangerous, and returned to a very pleasant, intimate friendship." It was also to be bruited about that he was getting a singsong girl as soon as he had learned enough Chinese, and he added "Would it were true!"[9]

It was one thing to conduct his correspondence in the manner of *Les Liaisons Dangereuses*; it was another thing to deal with 'K', a "charming and sensitive and intelligent woman" who was passionately in love with him. "I've never seen such intensity of feeling in a human being," he wrote. Unfortunately, he could not respond equally. "It's not true that it's worse to be loved unloving than [to] love unloved, but the passive experience is unnerving." In fact, he had released an emotional holocaust with which he would have to cope the rest of his time in China. This cannot have been entirely unexpected, or even unwanted: it conformed to the pattern of his affairs. In December, before they had gone to Peking, he had already recognized that 'K' was "intense—and possessive . . . also a self-torturer and pessimist asking reassurance. And both jealous and not wanting to lose face." These were ominous signs if his wish was merely for a generous, untroubled "Latin-sensual" partner in bed. Love, desire and the fascination of the chase drove him heedlessly on. There had been an idyll: at the crest of a wave of emotion he had "had the most romantic holiday with her in Peking". A month later, at the bottom of the wave, he was in a mood compounded of weariness, cynicism and regret. "I seriously think it may all end in her suicide . . . It's the awful situation that usually arises when people fall in love with me: I can respond very adequately when I'm with them, but I never really lose my head . . . I am so tired of emotions, my own and other people's. I don't mean I don't have them. But—at any rate until I've shaken off free—I wish I didn't. I've grown too old now for that sort of thing; there are so many things I ought to do or should like to do; I'm really and sincerely convinced now that I think friendship better than love . . . I thought China would be an adventure, but I see it's going to be a period of self-inspection and meditation—perhaps a good thing, but not what I wanted."[10]

He made no attempt to break off from her, however, not only because 'K' had threatened and continued to threaten to kill herself if he did, but because he was still, in his own fashion, in love with her. He resigned himself to the crises and rejoiced in the periods of calm. At the end of February he reassured his mother that 'K' was "returning to Normalcy—i.e., not more than one threat of suicide a week, and I think she's getting on better with her husband. In between these crises—which can be moderately assuaged when I assure her at great length that I love her—she's as charming and amusing, and fascinating as ever." They saw each other almost every morning—at his house—and when they did not, she was unhappy. She resented his seeing other people, particularly other women; she forced him to refuse invitations to parties where she would not be present. As time passed he realized that he had no intimate friends except for 'K' herself, and, as he complained in a letter, "a mistress isn't the same thing by long chalks". The fear of discovery made their love-making less rewarding than it ought to have been: in the mornings, before the arrival of 'K', he would send his servants away from the house, but there was no assurance that they would not unexpectedly return. Beyond this were the dangers of conducting a clandestine affair in an academic community that was "honeycombed with respectability and intrigue". In May he told his mother that his last letter to her had been refused at the post office—"a torn stamp . . . And when they were inquiring who to send it back to, it was opened by one of the professors—an enemy, more or less, of ['K']'s. However, there's not yet been any fatal result but we're nervous." The crisis passed; the affair continued, as cautiously but no less stormily than before. Julian thought of himself as being particularly adept in dealing with women of very strong emotions, but it was always with an air of resignation rather than gusto. Such women seemed to be for him both a necessity and a trial, and the awards and penalties were very evenly balanced. Still, in his affair with 'K' he had one commanding advantage: it was he who loved less. He was quite content to see her only in the mornings; it meant that he could busy himself with all the other things he had to do and wanted to do. He enjoyed having a mistress, but he also enjoyed teaching, and writing letters, and sailing, and shooting, and collecting paintings and bronzes, and wandering through the shops of Hankow, and going to dinner parties. Also, he wanted to see more of China. In May he wrote to his mother about his summer plans: "I shall go up the river to Szechuan and then to Omei Shan, a twelve-thousand foot sacred mountain on the road to Lhasa, about a thousand miles away, by river mostly—then by bus and finally on foot." He would be travelling with Yeh, his "nicest and brightest pupil", and an English geologist; they would leave in mid-June and be gone until the end of August; and afterwards he would have a reunion with 'K' in Peking.

Absorbed in the continuing drama of his love affair, and otherwise occupied in the varied activities of a provincial university town where nothing ever happened, he responded to the politics of the country with diffidence and mild irritation. Not even the recurring possibility of war between China and Japan excited him. He listened dutifully to the gossip, which he reported in letters home as "inside information", but he was part of a community that, as he said, might have inspired Chekhov or Jane Austen, not Malraux: the tiny disturbances of dons and their wives mattered as much as the movement of armies, and the political agitation of undergraduates. "Once again there's a University crisis," he reported to his mother in February, "over exams., and everyone's nerves are jumping. And again there's war talk: I'm scared over the Russian frontier trouble . . . I've inside information that [the Japanese] are preparing a war 'within two months'." Although he did not take this very seriously, he thought it best to reassure her he was in no danger—and in the light of later events, his choice of comparison has its prophetic irony: "However, don't get worried . . . I'm about as far from any possible front as Cambridge is from Madrid." A month later, the possibility of crisis was still to be entertained. He wrote to a friend in the thick of European politics—which seemed 'real' to Julian as nothing in China did—"Life here continues pretty placid—that is, there might be an unholy row or a war with Japan any day, but there's no particular reason to expect either tomorrow. The most noteworthy fact is that I have to go and read a paper to the Hankow Literary Society on Modern Poetry." But while waiting for the crisis to materialize or be dissipated, he had come round to a much stronger and more traditional pacifist position than he had held in London. "I can't think anything worth war . . . Even here, with everyone I know and like wanting war, and with an overwhelming case for it—and knowing too that it's not my own country to get damaged and that I should find it fascinating and wildly exciting to watch—and with intensely sympathetic people, like some of my students, being at once reasonable and patriotic—I find I can't really sympathise . . . It is the last horror, and I can't feel sure enough of any theory to outweigh that certainty. So I'm thankful not to have to make the choice."

That was in February. Throughout the spring there were border incidents, rumours of war and civil war, accounts of Communists fighting government troops in Shensi province. Although Julian was under the impression that the Chinese authorities would not permit travel anywhere at all dangerous, he was privately hopeful that his journey to the north that summer would take him into an area where he might actually see some fighting. In mid-June he cabled to Leonard Woolf to ask if he could help to get him accredited as a foreign correspondent, a notion more romantic than practical, since he was entirely innocent of professional experience. At the same time he wrote to his mother, "We've been having a scare over civil war, but by now it seems calmed down . . . I wondered for a moment whether to send telegrams asking for a job as a correspondent, but decided to wait and see what happened—and now it's probably all over. There may, of course, be another crisis, but it's not unlikely. You're not to bother about it—they fight with paper bullets for the most part, and are terrified of foreigners—or so I've been told." In fact, he had already sent the telegram to his uncle, and when his mother heard of it she was extremely bothered. Whatever reassurance he may have intended by glossing over the truth in his letter, he had only succeeded in convincing her that he was going to put himself deliberately in danger. He apologized once, twice—"I must write again and ask you to forgive me for my telegram to Leonard . . . You see, I really felt that I had to try and do something reasonably adventurous after coming all this way—a kind of self-justification, I think. I know it seems mad to you, and so it does at times to me, but I think I can only get quite sane about adventure and danger and violence if I have some small experience of it. But for the time being there's no question of that."[11] By this time the journey had begun, and he was sailing up-river to Yochow, 100 miles above Hankow. ("There was no sanitation, the food [Chinese] was doubtful, but we got well-boiled Yangtze water to drink . . . The engine throbbed, the boat was pretty crowded, but one could wash in disinfectants. We slept in a line of camp beds on the top deck starboard passage way, forward.") In Yo-chow, government troops swarmed; he saw "snipers with bamboo-sprigged caps practising concealment". And a week later, embarking on a "Min boat" at Ichang at night, "troops flashed lights on us for Red spies or deserters, and were pacified . . . with visiting cards." But encounters of this sort, and there were a few more, hardly constituted the military experience he had anticipated. Still, it was an arduous, uncomfortable, fascinating journey through long stretches of primitive country—by sampan, launch, river steamer, rickshaw, and lorry, and on foot. He wrote long diary-like letters to his mother, from Yo-chow, Chungking, Chengtu, and Fu-Chien-lu in Tibet, the furthest point of the itinerary, where he drank buttered tea, "visited a lamasery and God knows what all." In a letter to a friend, written from Chengtu on July 23, he remarked, "I have violent fluctuations of feeling about the country, which is often charming to look at, sometimes produces a beautiful human being and more often works of art, but is so squalid, diseased and populous it can give one the creeps . . . One effect is to make me at odd moments violently homesick for English country. To be able to sit on the clean grass and smell clean winds, drink unboiled water, bath without disinfectants . . . walk the streets without picking one's way through ordures, and never ride fly-blown sweat stained rickshaws pulled by consumptive children."

In the same letter he remarked, "We hear next to nothing of the outside world, only through the Chinese papers: the Austro-German treaty and now a *coup d'état* in Spain. It sounds pretty gloomy."

The most remarkable, most difficult, and most rewarding stage of the journey out was the last: fifty miles on foot over mountains from Yo-chow to Fu-Chien-lu. Here the sense of being tested was at its strongest, demanding a toughness and resilience Julian was relieved to discover he possessed. There was so much to tell and remember of these final days that he decided to "stop diarying and just impressionize . . . things that stand out most clearly in my mind are . . . my first corpses—just stript corpses lying beside the road, one dead of some intestinal malady—very evident—the other of typhus or opium . . . Then there've been two 10,000 foot passes, both, alas, in rain and mist. It was a fiendish job climbing them . . . There have been bad days—on one I got blistered—and good, as when we got here, a twenty-nine mile stage, by 3.30."

On August 28, he was at the Hotel du Nord in Peking, whence he had flown from Chengtu, and he wrote to his mother to reassure her that he had come through the journey with no worse after-effects than "mere footsoreness—though this of a very superior kind . . . Next time I get grass shoes made to fit me in advance." Then, as though he had paused to listen to her objections, he began a new paragraph: "There certainly will be a next time if it seems at all practicable . . . But who knows what next year may bring?" Then, as though answering the question, he began a new paragraph: "The civil war in Spain makes nasty news to return to."

"After two months' chastity, I naturally feel like a spot of infidelity," he wrote in a letter to 'B' from Chengtu. Then he flew off to Peking and disappointment. 'K' was there, as they had planned, but so too was her husband; and the next week she was to go into the hospital for a minor operation. Earlier, Julian had declared that the two essential conditions for romantic love were proximity and chastity. In Peking, this held true for 'K', but not for himself. "She," he reported to his mother, "is even more in love than before, and I'm terrified, overwhelmed and very much touched. For though I'm extremely fond of her, think her an extraordinary and very valuable human being . . . I can't match that sort of feeling." When they returned to Wuhan in late September, however, they resumed the affair, and nothing—for good or bad—had changed: he found that he was still in a position of doting and irritated dependence upon her. Her jealousy made him "feel extremely guilty and also frightfully tied and hampered". But he made no serious effort to break with her. "Oh these romantics," he burst out, "there's really no contenting them . . . There are moments when I feel all I want is to be back where one can lie about on lawns and talk nonsense."[12] The litany of complaint is constant, but if one sets it against his equally constant affection and admiration for 'K', it becomes clear that his dissatisfaction had less to do with this affair in particular and more to do with the life of the emotions in general. "Like George II," he wrote jokingly to a friend, "I prefer the scandal of a gallantry to the fact," and the notorious kernel of truth can be glimpsed in what he said. "To tell you the honest truth, I feel rather bored with all this love business . . . I should like a fairly prolonged rest from emotions." This, of course, 'K' would not allow him, and his solution was to give way to her, to pretend to emotions which he did not, could not, genuinely feel. "I'm pretty well incapable of romantic love—but am exceedingly attached to her. And remembering what utter hell jealousy is I give way, rather than ride roughshod." But however he might rationalize his feelings, he was still, as he had been since the beginning of the year, committed to a passionate love affair that might at any time be discovered; and when this happened, there would almost certainly be a scandal. The prospect did not put him off. "I always knew 'K' was too desperate a character for me, and I still know I should have to take whatever might be the 'honourable' course." Very likely, this would mean marriage, after a divorce in which he would be named correspondent. The saving thing, he told a friend, "is that divorce in China is easy but terribly face-losing: the husband would look too ridiculous to the students to continue. This is our sheet anchor. I've an idea that quite a lot of people have guessed the essential truth, but aren't going to let themselves realize it because it would be too tiresome. I even suspect race pride will make them loath to admit anyone as remarkable as ['K'] would prefer a foreign devil . . . If I do have to marry [her] to save her face, I can do it under Chinese law—I think—and hence could get an easy divorce later. But it would be hellish tiresome and I shall do all I can to dodge it."[13]

This was his situation in the early autumn of 1936. Passively, but not incuriously, he waited for whatever was to happen.

He wrote hundreds of letters to friends and family—eighty-two were included in the memorial volume *Julian Bell: Essays, Poems and Letters*—and they comprise much the largest and perhaps the best part of his literary production during the sixteenth months that he was in China. For the rest there were one or two poems—

"little cross-correspondences on fairly trivial themes," he told his aunt, "the results being obscure but, to me, rather pleasing". And there were three long essays, cast in the form of open letters, that represent his most ambitious attempt to come to terms with his heritage and with his own times.[14] He himself, in a letter to a friend, referred to the essays, as "my testament to our generation", and in a prefatory Note, written shortly before he went to Spain, he hoped that they would be "relevant and useful". The first, 'On Roger Fry—A Letter to A.', was begun on the voyage out and finished in China, on January 4, 1936. The second, 'The Proletariat and Poetry: An Open Letter to C. Day Lewis', was written in the latter part of the same year. The third, 'War and Peace: A Letter to E. M. Forster', was begun at the very end of his stay in China, in January 1937, and finished on the boat returning to Europe. There is a significant difference between the first two essays and the third—the former are representative of conclusions he had already reached before coming out to China; the latter, however, reflects the dramatic change in his thinking that followed upon the outbreak of the Spanish Civil War.

Roger Fry had died in September 1934. In November his sister, Margery Fry, had approached Mrs Woolf to write his biography. It would be a formidable undertaking, and she needed time to consider. On January 1, 1935, in her diary, she jotted down, "Begin Roger in October . . . Is that possible?" Fry had been a great friend of Julian's, and a great influence upon him. "After you, Nessa dearest," he wrote to his mother, "I think I owe more to him than anyone, even of my contemporaries; perhaps this is hero-worshipping, but I know that my whole way of looking at life, and particularly at the arts and sciences and philosophy is very largely a result of his conversation and example. And my notion of what the arts—and what human relations—can give is very largely communicated by him."[15] He was eager to write something about Fry, and mentioned it to his aunt, who encouraged him, thinking he meant to do a brief memoir, recollections of Roger as he had known him. But in May he wrote to his mother, "As I think of it now it seems to me more a matter of my making a statement of beliefs and feelings and general attitude to life than anything at all like biography. I don't even know how much it will have to do with Roger in the end." He did not actually start writing until September, and when he finished in early January, he was not certain of what he had accomplished. At the end of his stay in Peking, he wrote to Mrs Woolf: "I'm going back [to Wuhan] to try and get my poor students to read you and Tom and all, and see what they make of it. I hope also to find typed my disquisition on Roger: perhaps seeing it all in order I shall be able to make out what it's like. I fear it hasn't really much to do with him." And he added, "I'll try and see if I can rake up any more childhood memories [for the biography of Fry that Mrs Woolf had begun to write]; I can't at the moment, but I know I must have lots." For some reason—perhaps his initial uncertainty—he did not send the "disquisition" to the Woolfs until very late in the spring. By then his doubts had been resolved; he hoped that it would be published as a pamphlet in the series of Hogarth Letters, alongside Mrs Woolf's *Letter to a Young Poet*, Raymond Mortimer's *Letter on the French Pictures*, Rosamond Lehmann's *Letter to a Sister*, and Viscount Cecil's *Letter to an M.P. on Disarmament*. He set great store by this; then, when he returned to Wuhan in September, he discovered that the Woolfs were unenthusiastic about the work and had no wish to publish it.

Julian had given them fair warning; nonetheless, they must have been somewhat taken aback to discover how little his disquisition had to do really with Roger Fry, and how much with Julian himself. Even this need not have counted against it, but the Woolfs, who were in their respective ways dedicated to their work and unrelenting in the demands they made upon themselves, were put off by the evident carelessness of the writing, thinking and organization of the pamphlet. What Julian had sent was *unfinished* work: a first draft. It was another instance of his over-valuation of himself as an amateur.

"The whole publishing business makes me furious," he exploded to his mother. "I do think Virginia is exceedingly tiresome. She wrote me a letter saying she thought my Roger work needed rewriting etc. I really don't believe it. I don't think I could say it any better, anyway not at present. But since they won't have it, there's an end of them."[16] Conceivably he might have profited from his aunt's suggestions, but he was too hurt or too proud to pursue the question further. Indeed, from the time he had been an undergraduate at King's, there was always a degree of ambivalence in his feeling for Mrs Woolf: on the one hand, she was his beloved aunt; on the other, she was the older generation, a writer of great fame and achievements whom he could not help but envy. His way of dealing with the problem was to patronize her a little: "I'm sorry the novel's still on your hands: though it's still a complete mystery to me how you ever produce the things. I often think it would be great fun to sit down and invent stories . . ." She too had mixed feelings on "the damned literary question":

> I was always critical of his writing, partly I suspect from the usual generation jealousy; partly from my own enviousness of anyone who can do in writing what I can't do [presumably she is referring here to Julian's poetry]; and . . . I thought him very careless, "not an artist", too personal in what he wrote, and "all over the place". This is the one thing I regret in our relationship: that I might have encouraged him more as a writer. But again, that's my character: and I'm always forced, in spite of jealousy, to be honest in the end. Still this is my one regret; and I shall always have it; seeing how generous he was to me about what I did—touchingly proud sometimes of my writings . . .[17]

But Mrs Woolf was surely right about the piece itself, which was finally published in the memorial volume, and proved to be very loose and discursive, 'all over the place', or, as E. M. Forster remarked in a comment on the letter Julian had addressed to him, "all over the shop". It is the same complaint that can be made against all his formal efforts in prose, 'The Good and All That', as well as the later essays. He would begin with one idea, appear to develop it, abandon it, launch another, follow it in its course, abandon it, launch another, suddenly return to the first idea: at times one has a sense less of argumentation and exposition than of free association. He himself was conscious that all was not proceeding as logically as it might. "So, after this endless divagation," he begins a paragraph, "I return to my theme." But the next paragraph begins, "I cannot yet get my argument clear", which is not simply a rhetorical device but a statement of fact. He is constantly commenting on his difficulties: "Now I come to the hardest part to write"; "Yet I become conscious that I am again distorting my description"; "But I am going ahead too fast again", and so forth. One can only guess at his method as a writer of prose. The evidence of the essays themselves suggests that he was a writer who thought as he wrote, his thought taking shape and re-shaping itself as he went from sentence to sentence. So that very often the announced intention is not borne out by the end result, which is not to deny that the end result is very often more interesting than the announced intention.

'On Roger Fry' is written as a letter from Julian, "a poet", to A., "a scientist". The aim of the letter, announced in the first paragraph, is "to give an account of one of the few men of genius who have ever made a real synthesis of the attitudes of artist and scientist. I am not trying to write a biography: what is more important is to make explicit an attitude to life; one that combines the sensuousness and sensitiveness of the artist with the clearness and hardness of mind, the resolute intellectualism of an admirable scientist."

He goes on in the next paragraph to admit, "My art lacks means . . . to capture the physical and individual traits which made Roger Fry's company one of the greatest and most vivid pleasures that I have known in human intercourse", and so he will "try to deal with more simply intellectual questions, with an attitude, beliefs, opinions, lines and methods of thought". So much for prologue; we are prepared now for the entrance, so to speak, of Roger Fry. But no—"I shall find it easier to expose his attitude if I first try to define yours and mine . . . it can be summarised by saying that we are Socialists."

Having summarized, he then defines, and there is an interesting elaboration of the point, in Julian's most self-confident manner:

> Like nearly all the intellectuals of this generation, we are fundamentally political in thought and action: this more than anything else marks the difference between us and our elders. Being socialist for us means being rationalist, common-sense, empirical; means a very firm extrovert, practical, commonplace sense of exterior reality. It means turning away from mysticisms, fantasies, escapes into the inner life. We think of the world first and foremost as the place where other people live, as the scene of crisis and poverty, the probable scene of revolution and war: we think more about the practical solution of the real

contradictions of the real world than possible discoveries in some other world.

It might be argued that this is an attitude that has less to do with Socialism than with those eighteenth-century virtues Julian had so long idealized. And so it proves. For after admitting, "I hold the Socialist attitude precariously, against both inner and outer chaos," he continues with a line of thought he had first expounded in letters to John Lehmann in the summer of 1929. "It [the Socialist attitude] has been achieved [by himself] as a result of reflections on the art of poetry, and on the semi-philosophical questions that attract rationalist poets. Conscious like everyone else of the worn-out uselessness of the romantic tradition, I turned back to the classic movement that began in the seventeenth century, and found in Pope and Racine an art that used the rationalist intellect to control without denying the violent chaos of the emotions."

He is now ready to take up his subject, "an exposition of Roger Fry's general attitude", and he declares, "his was a rationalism so subtle and profound that he could cope with, and enjoy, chaos itself: that there was nothing in the universe, apparently, nor in himself, that he could not contemplate with an impartial detachment, ready to accept or reject anything on its merits."

This declaration appears on the fourth page of his forty-seven page essay. Revealing though it might be to do so, we shall not follow him paragraph by paragraph to his final sentence: "The attempt might well baffle genius; it is not for my talents." Our particular interest is in the underlying intention of the essay as it is gradually disclosed: Julian's attempt to import the ideas of Bloomsbury into the 1930s, to prove them as relevant and useful to the age of politics as to the age of art and personal relations that it had succeeded. He felt that Fry summed up in himself the ideas and ideals of Bloomsbury that he, Julian, valued most. Fry's impartiality seemed to him more sensible, for example, than the commitment of Leonard Woolf and E. M. Forster to a humanitarian liberalism ("This silly taste for democracy," as he put it in the 'Letter to Day Lewis.'). Why should one not approach politics, poverty and war, with the same detachment, rationality, scientific curiosity and emotional control as Roger Fry had looked at a painting? This is the central question (or idea) of the essay, and its answer becomes a feat of extrapolation. Having offered a potted summary of "the general position of art in nineteenth century civilisation" and "the 'hard-headed' tradition of Cambridge and scientific philosophy", he arrives at Fry's "disciplined aestheticism . . . I have talked of a 'good taste of the emotions'—it comes to very much the same thing. And the conclusion of the whole matter is to find . . . its value outside the arts, in dealing with 'life'—that is, in systematising and controlling our attitudes in the emotional situations that arise either from our dealings with individuals, or large groups of human beings, or with the brute facts of the world." He is determined to make "the jump from aesthetic to life". And the value of a "disciplined aesthetic" in "life" is that it allows one to control "violent emotions with a view to effective action". Also, it allows one to "to behave rationally". In fact, this was an ideal of conduct Julian had set for himself, as we have seen, as early as 1929; and he seems to have felt, at least while writing the essay, that he had achieved it, however precariously. He had chosen a position on the Left on "impartial grounds: I am a Socialist because I believe that Socialism will tend to maximise human pleasure (and therefore human value) and can give us a stable society free from war in which the not uninteresting possibilities of the human race can be explored." Then, as though to prove his impartiality and detachment, he added, "If I thought Fascism could do as much I should try to get over my traditional instincts and become a Fascist." He was so beguiled with his notion of making Fry a kind of patron saint of the Left that he glided over an admission of some significance: the qualities of the "disciplined aesthetic" that he has singled out "are, in fact, the 'intelligence' and 'common sense' we use in life, since the pure intellect and scientific method can hardly be brought to bear upon most problems; these are presented to us with incomplete knowledge and the need for immediate action." In short, to make a revolution and to look at a painting are two very different kinds of activity; and no practising Communist—John Cornford, for example—would ever deny that there was something to be said for 'common sense' and 'intelligence'.

But there is an air of unreality about the pamphlet that has the effect of dulling its impact: it is very much closet speculation, a recapitulation of favourite themes and notions brought into a new context—a tribute to Roger Fry—but essentially unchanged, and one has no sense of engagement: that these are notions meant to be tested against the realities of politics and war. Something of the same objection must be made to the polemical letter to C. Day Lewis, 'The Proletariat and Poetry'. Julian's intention, as he told a friend, was "to reprove the poets for enthusiasm", and the essay does emerge as a kind of companion piece: he sets the virtues of "disciplined aestheticism", against the vices of "hot Marxism". But for all the cleverness and justification of much of his attack, it remains closet controversy, and it suffers from Julian's having been away from England. One has the sense that he has not really kept up with his rival poets, that he is refighting old wars, the hostilities and jealousies of Taviton Street. Many of the generalizations are in a generalized way true, but the useful attack that is promised—on Thirties Poetry itself, and the effect upon it of a neurotic, emotional, soft-headed attachment to the Left, is never adequately made. Meanwhile his own hard-headedness is leading him down paths of speculation that are not entirely pleasing to contemplate: "The disgraceful part of the German business is not that the Nazis kill and torture their enemies; it is that Socialists and Communists let themselves be made prisoners instead of first killing as many Nazis as they can."

But the course of events of the 1930s was catching up with his essays and speculations. He felt himself under a continuing pressure to move into the role he had been straining towards (and resisting) all his life: the man of action. He had enjoyed his first year at Wuhan, but it had never been intended as a permanent arrangement, nor did he wish it to be. Almost from the time of his arrival in China, he was concerned with the question of what he was to do when he returned to England. And again, as news of European events filtered into the provincial fastness of Wuhan, he was increasingly troubled as to when he should return.

In the spring of 1936, when the League of Nations was attempting to deal with Mussolini's aggression in Abyssinia and there was a possibility that Hitler might move, Julian wrote to Playfair, "I feel if it gets too threatening I shall have to try to get back before it starts: I don't fancy being stranded out here while everything at home pops."[18] This note is sounded again and again in the correspondence. But although he lived with a sense of continuing political crisis, his attitude before the outbreak of the Spanish Civil War was more resigned than determined; rueful, passive, mildly ironic. Very likely nothing would happen, and he would finish his three-year term at Wuhan, and return to England most probably to some sort of political job, perhaps as secretary to someone important in the Labour party. But nothing was definite. "You can't conceive how middle-aged I've grown," he wrote to a friend in April. "I shall return—I suppose in some months' time—thin, bald, liverish, opinionated and passé. Then a last half-hearted fling—I hope Angelica will have plenty of easy-going friends by then. And finally Hitler."

By the spring of 1936 the novelty of being in China, of teaching English literature to Chinese students, of having a fascinating and demanding Chinese mistress, had quite worn off. The visit to Peking in January, where his affair with 'K' was inaugurated, had been a high point. His mood then was exhilarated and self-confident: "I suddenly feel very grown up and at ease in the world." But he was never able to persuade himself for long of the reality of his Chinese present, and thoughts of his European future were only seldom absent from his mind: "I keep thinking about what will happen to me when I return," he wrote to his aunt in February, "How shall I find a steady job, and a wife, and settle down to a contented middle age? How, indeed? However, all sorts of things will have happened by then. Or they may not. Here, in China, where they all expect the end of the world in about three months, I begin to believe it won't end. Perhaps England will just shake about a little, and then Stephens and Stracheys and all will go on as they always have done. Perhaps. But it really isn't likely." That month *Work for the Winter* was being published by the Hogarth Press. He allowed the event to pass by unnoticed in his correspondence, nor did it inspire him, then or later, to a view of himself as a full-time poet. It was part of the oddness, the unreality of things, that he should have a reputation as a poet in China, but none in England, and although there had been one discerning and appreciative review, in the *Times Literary Supplement*,[19] he knew that his second book had not established him, and felt this more keenly than he would admit. To his uncle, who wrote to him about the book in April, and, as his publisher, reported that sales thus far had been small and reviews sparse, he replied, "Many thanks for your letter. I didn't imagine there was much chance of anyone reading verse at the moment. But I was pleased with the *Lit. Sup.* review and one or two minor ones that my press cutters have sent me." And that was all: the rest of the letter was devoted to politics—it was as though he were finally closing a door. Yet if he was not to be a poet, or at least a writer of some sort, what then was he to be when he returned to England? Depressed by his "lack of achievements", he also regretted his "lack of definite specialized abilities". To be splendidly amateur in whatever one did counted for less than he had expected. That he should have written so little poetry while in China—only one minor exercise, 'Post Coitum', can be surely claimed for the period—he himself explains perhaps too simply: he was not miserable enough. One might have expected that the Chinese landscape, or the romantic complications in his own life, would inspire him to poetic statement. Neither did, however. Earlier, as he was setting out for China, he had told 'B' that he must have either misery or stability to work. He seems to have found enough of the latter for prose—the three long essay-letters—but not enough of the former, despite all his agitation with his "Chinese Caroline Lamb", for poetry. In April he complained to Eddie Playfair that "the only person I can talk to intimately is hopelessly in love with me. No one to laugh and crack bawdy jokes with. I'm bored, tired, ill at ease with myself; unless I get some excitement soon I shall get depressed and start writing poetry." But already he was immersed in plans for his journey to the north that summer, with its promise of new excitement, new country to explore, and even the possibility of military adventure.

On July 23, in Chengtu, he learned from a Chinese newspaper of the uprising, five days earlier, of the rebellious generals against the government of Spain. In a letter written on that day he referred to it as a "*coup d'état*", adding "It sounds pretty gloomy," but he had no way of knowing from the brief, rather garbled account that a full-scale civil war had begun. The further he proceeded on the journey to Fu-Chien-lu, the occasions for seeing even a week-old Chinese newspaper grew more infrequent. He was engrossed in the excitements of travel, "the buttered tea and God knows what all!" in the world of the lamas. There was no news from Europe.

In late August, before flying from Chengtu to Peking, he wrote to 'B' that he was waiting to "take up the papers again and face what sounds [like] bloody news of Spain. I suppose it's been filling all your minds the last month?" And from Peking, five days later, after reading the English newspapers, he wrote to his mother: "The civil war in Spain makes nasty news to return to. I can't help wondering who, if any, of my friends are involved. As long as nothing of the kind starts in France."

The questions that had concerned him from the time of his arrival in China—when should he return to England, and what would he do there?—began to take on an air of urgency. From a distance of five thousand miles, he followed events in Spain with the closest attention. But distance made it possible to think a while longer in terms of familiar alternatives. Reassured by his successful year at Wuhan, he wrote, "I'm really rather a good and socratic educator . . . The college [King's] had better give me a fellowship when I return, and let me teach their young men for them." On the other hand: "I think I shall have to see what can be done about going into politics—Labour. Can you see me as a private secretary? I'm incredibly efficient now, you know, after getting porters started at 6.0 every morning." And a month later: "I've more or less made up my mind when I come back to try and find a serious political job—but for choice one where one doesn't make speeches or argue." But in the same letter—September 25, 1936—he preferred "the prospect of being killed in a reasonable sort of war against Fascists rather than just choking out", and concluded, "I mayn't care much about the human race, but I don't like seeing our side beaten in Spain." He was always wary of "enthusiasm"—the charge he had brought against the Thirties Poets in his letter to C. Day Lewis—and he had not yet arrived at, or was not yet ready to announce, a full commitment: that he would fight in Spain, that there was where he meant to risk death against the Fascists. So he appeared to be turning over alternatives for the future in his mind; and in his letters to his mother, whom he knew would be terribly upset if he were to go to Spain, he emphasized his hopes for a political job when he returned. But he had moved the probable date of his return to the next summer—a year earlier than originally planned—and suggested he might even come back in the early spring; he would not hesitate to do so, if there proved to be a Fascist uprising in France, as Claud Cockburn's paper, *The Week* (to which he subscribed) had hinted there might be. Where France was concerned, there was an urgency, an intensity of personal feeling and attachment, that was very different from his feeling for Spain, which was not a country he knew and loved, but a place where "a reasonable sort of war against Fascists" was being fought. Still, for all his determination to proceed reasonably, he must have suspected very early what his commitment would ultimately be. Even to his mother he began—in an indirect way—to advance the possibility that he might go to Spain. On September 20 he wrote to her, "Well, you may be thankful I'm safe in China, for I know in England I should be feeling the only reasonable thing is to go and fight the Fascists in Spain—for even at this range I feel all the talking is silly."

His political beliefs clarified. At the very time when most of his contemporaries on the Left were being caught up in a wave of idealism, he was determined to be as hard-headed and realistic as possible, and thought of himself as a convert to Machiavelli—"much more modern and to the point than Marx." Hence he dismissed the League of Nations, that favourite cause of Goldsworthy Lowes Dickinson's, as hopelessly impotent, incapable either of enforcing the peace, or of putting an end to war. To Playfair, who was in Geneva to attend a session of the League, he wrote, "With luck you may hear the funeral service. An exceedingly good thing if it [the League] could be buried, for then the liberal pacifists would have to jump . . . There just isn't a sound and decent policy visible, everything is going anyway to mean rearmament, and that's bad enough. I only hope we do it efficiently. My motto is going to be vive Machiavel, the only way to make sense out of Marx." He felt that the Labour party should make a show of assenting to the government's policy of non-intervention: "It's silly to think the Tories will give any real help to the Left in Spain—so that all we can do effectively is to insist on neutrality, bring up all shady incidents, be legalistic and tiresome—and give all the underhand help we can . . . The only thing now is to down the Fascists with the minimum of loss and fuss."

Spain had captured his imagination more than he might have wished; the 'Machiavellian' discovered himself emotionally engaged by the struggle. He wrote to a friend in late September, "I fancy being here has kept me from making a fool of myself pretty completely over the business and also salved my conscience; I know I should feel rather ashamed of myself if I'd been in England and not tried to volunteer, which would no doubt have led to some ridiculous fiasco . . . Yet in a way I find it rather more inspiriting to have the prospect of finishing off with a decent fight on one's own side than just going phut in a lethal chamber. As you'll see I'm moving Left in sentiment." To this he added in his next letter, "I don't know which I think sillier, Liberals or Communists —and yet I dislike being a minority of one." In his own way, at various times, he had been a theoretical Marxist and a convinced Socialist and a member of the Labour party, but he had never found a satisfactory political niche for himself in England, nor a cause or movement in which he could whole-heartedly believe. Now he was discovering one—"our side"—that aligned him with much of his generation, but still in his own way.

John Lehmann has written of the outbreak of the Spanish Civil War and its impact upon young English intellectuals of the Left: "Everything, all our fears, our confused hopes and beliefs, our half-formulated theories and imaginings, veered and converged towards its testing and opportunity, like steel filings that slide towards a magnet suddenly put near them. For, as Stephen Spender wrote in the introduction to the anthology of *Poems for Spain* which we produced together two years later, what all felt was that 'the long, crushing and confused process of defeat, which the democratic process had been undergoing, has been challenged in Spain, and this challenge has aroused hope all over the world'. It is almost impossible to convey the strength of this feeling to anyone who was not subjected to the pressures that preceded the summer of 1936, the mixture of relief and apocalyptic hope that flared up as the struggle began . . ."[20] Julian's reaction, as we have seen, was a good deal less affirmative, and perhaps more realistic, than this. Although in a letter to Lehmann in September he burst out enthusiastically, "What a show, GODS what a show," he brought himself up short almost at once with, "And if the Right wins I suppose France next, and then us. What hell." A month later he wrote to Playfair, "Spain is getting badly on my nerves, and now *The Week* are prophesying similar horrors in France . . . I don't see how war [presumably, international] can conceivably be avoided, nor how any kind of decency, democracy, freedom or toleration can survive." At approximately the same time he told his mother, "It really makes me miserable or furious—according to my mood—to read about Spain, and think what it probably means to us." In such moods he was tempted to resign his post and return to England—at least he would be "back in the centre of things where one has a chance to get something done". By contrast, the triviality of teaching "Proust and Sidney in successive hours" was one of the minor horrors of life, "And what a fiddling while Rome burns!" In a new form, confronted by a new alternative of the utmost seriousness—Spain—it was the old problem of what he was to do with his life.

Should he remain in China for another year? Or should he return to England in the spring and make an attempt, through Leonard Woolf, to find some sort of job in the Labour party? Then there was the third alternative. He realized that the greatest obstacle to his going to Spain to fight Fascists would not be the complication of arranging it in London, or resigning from Wuhan and terminating his affair with 'K', but its effect upon his mother. It was really a double problem. Their relationship was extraordinarily close; to endanger it by the possibility of death in battle might seem an act of almost wilful cruelty. And there was the more generalized problem that his mother and many of her friends had been conscientious objectors during the First World War, and were still dedicated pacifists. He knew that she would disagree initially with his feelings about the Spanish Civil War, but he felt it was essential that she understand, was certain that she was capable of doing so—"even when we have perfectly different interests and desire—as mine about wars and excitements—we seem to understand each other"—and it was very important to him that she do so. They were a Bloomsbury mother and son: they would have a clear and rational discussion—understanding would triumph over her feelings of maternal solicitude.

There was tension at all levels of his life in that autumn of 1936. After their difficult meetings in Peking, he and 'K' had returned to Wuhan, and resumed their affair. 'K' was more in love than ever;

Julian was restless and dissatisfied. Devoted though he still was to her, he would not have been averse to a "spot of infidelity". Possible candidates for 'L' and 'M' had appeared at Wuhan, the one Chinese, the other English. About both of them he wrote to his mother that they had not yet "complicated life, tho' they may do so". At the same time, 'K's' marriage, not unexpectedly, was going through a period of storms. Her husband still did not know, apparently, of the nature of the relationship between 'K' and Julian, but he did know that she was spending a lot of time with him, and he resented it. Julian described the situation to his mother: "Scene between ['K'] and her husband followed by nerves and insomnia on her side and on his by a week of almost unbroken silence, followed by his writing in his diary—which is apparently his only means of communicating with her—that the situation had grown unbearable, and then by his telling her that she had to make up her mind what she meant to do. All this about nothing in particular, just her coming to see me, and such like. She seems to have behaved pretty hysterically."[21] The subsequent event—described in this letter, and also in a letter to Playfair, was: "She—oh god how typical of her, of women, of China—started experimenting in a semi-suicidal fashion with her sleeping draught and gave herself a frightful headache."[22]

Then, almost at once, came the always-feared, but never-really-expected-to-happen dénouement: they were caught, in *flagrante delicto*, by the husband. "Well, at last there's been the great row over ['K']," he wrote to his mother:

> Fortunately there's the minimum of damage done. At least, that's what I think; at the moment I feel rather appalled, and I fancy I'm in for a certain amount of misery. Well, for the facts; we were caught—a ridiculous scene reflecting credit on no one; I thought it very comic at the time—so indeed it was—but don't feel like describing it now. Then, an éclaircissement, and a provisional agreement, finally decided this evening—or provisionally finally. Her husband behaved very reasonably considering what an idiotic position he was put in, and that he was pretty much bouleversé, not having got the full truth till the last moment. He offered the obvious alternatives of a divorce by consent—an easy and private affair—a separation without a

divorce or returning to him and breaking completely with me. She has chosen the last. I am going to resign—to ease the tension —on perfectly indifferent grounds; I shall say my family want me to return for undisclosed reasons, presumably disgraceful, and shall tell my friends that I want to return for political reasons, which is true . . . From a purely selfish point of view no doubt I am well out of it, and I am at least happy to think it will relieve you. Possibly she may manage to make some sort of life for herself, though she resisted all my persuasions to separate from her husband and I think it will be very hard indeed for them to get on together . . . I besought her to marry me, foreseeing all the storms that would mean, but reckoning that she would really thrive on them. I think I saw too what a life it would lead me. None the less, she's the only person I know who would be worth it. She rose to the occasion of a crisis, as she always does, and was very superb—it's a pity furious women attract me so much. And so completely charming. It's hard to believe I may never see her again . . . But the temporary solution provides for everyone saving what is left of their faces, which is anyway a good thing.[23]

He sent out the news to his regular correspondents:

To Eddie Playfair—I won't pretend to be heartbroken, but she was the most charming person I ever met, and so much so that I would marry her in cold blood and conscious of all the difficulties of her appalling temperament . . . I shall suffer more than I thought or expected. But Nessa is a sheet anchor for me emotionally, and like previous disasters I have come out of this one harder and older and clearer. ['A'] cleared me of romanticism. ['B'] of timidity and scrupulousness. ['K'] has made me feel that love affairs are really better subordinated to friendship . . . Let me not prophesy rashly–but I will never again if I can help it get myself involved with anyone who demands more than pleasure and conversation . . . I shall probably tell such people as —— and —— and —— and ——.[24]

To Quentin—You've probably heard from Nessa about our catastrophe and my resignation: I expect you'll think it's the best solution; perhaps it is, but it doesn't feel like it at the moment.[25]

> *To 'D'*—She's returning to her husband, and going away for a time, and we've broken communication pretty much. Of course it hasn't gone at all smoothly, since she's also been furiously jealous and utterly miserable, while I've been in one of my states of chronic tearfulness.[26]

But the note of regret is heard most clearly in his next letter to his mother. He had wanted to be free; now that he was, he wished he were not. It was the same duality of feeling he had experienced in each of his love affairs, but more intensely than ever in the past:

> I'm finding out now what I lost, and all the little things. Having seen someone every day for more than a year, and someone so charming, it is very difficult to resign oneself. And then, the alarums and excursions . . . She's such a devil when she cares to be, and yet completely charming. I feel reasonably certain you would have liked her a great deal—tho perhaps not as a daughter in law . . . I try to be sensible, but Nessa, you won't be too cross with me if I do end by marrying her? It's not likely; but I can't see her suffering too much without trying what I can do . . . I write this not to break the ice to you, but to cover a possible disaster.[27]

He had been on the verge of matrimony in the past. It had not come to that then nor did it now. 'K' would not accept his offer to marry her, perhaps because she felt it had been inspired by pity. But although she had promised not to communicate with him, in fact she continued to do so, by letters and even in person, so the crisis was not allowed to abate, and Julian's mood changed from regret to exasperation. "['K'] of course can't accept the situation and writes me secret letters or contrives meetings, etc. . . . I thought I was good at standing emotion, but really I'm jumping disgracefully." Towards the end of November, he found the new turn of events intolerable. 'K' was determined that they must see each other; at the same time she refused to let Julian face it out with her husband, and receive his permission for their meetings. He felt that everything was likely to explode in open scandal, with or without the suicide that 'K' was constantly threatening. Finally, he persuaded her to go to

Peking for a while, and there was calm in Wuhan. "The only pity of it all," he wrote to Playfair, "is that I find I miss her more and more as time goes on, and particularly want to go to bed with her again. But one can't have one's girl and one's peace of mind at the same time." He ran rapidly through a gamut of responses in the wake of the episode: regret, concern for 'K', then an airy cynicism. With the volcano, as he put it, safe in Peking, he could explore the possibilities of 'L': "Now that I've found I can get women to sleep with me by having a reputation as a kind of man women sleep with I no longer bother as much as I used to over my lack of graces."[28]

By the end of November he no longer regretted losing 'K'; he could envision a time, perhaps in England, when he might "persuade her into moderately reasonable behaviour," and if he were able to do that, he told his mother, "I don't know anyone who would be such pleasant company." This was very different from the tone of his letters only three weeks earlier. "I begin to wonder if the tragedy isn't going to turn out comedy after all," he wrote at the end of November, and so it proved. During December and January, his final months at Wuhan, his romantic intrigues—perhaps in reaction to the long and deeply felt passion with 'K'—were in the style of French farce. There was 'L'; there was 'M'; both being managed simultaneously, but neither was to know of the other, especially 'L', who belonged to the long line of "furious women". And 'K' was threatening to return from Peking.

"I seem to get far too involved in love affairs, without being a very emotional person—oh, rather, but not very, nor yet a Don Juan."[29] His women had their revenge upon him, for in reaction to his not caring as deeply for them as they thought he should, they became highly emotional, difficult, furious; he who simply wanted a mistress who would share the pleasures of conversation and bed, found himself with women whom he goaded, unconsciously, into playing the virago. After the disaster of 'K', he summed up a final theory of conduct in a letter to Playfair: "An irregular polygamy and a cynical realism—as long as you realise the reality of the emotions—is about the best that can be done." Putting the theory into practice was not so simple. When he was leaving China he had to balance seeing 'K' in Hongkong, and 'L' on the boat, and he was not at all sure it was worth it. "My only bother now is that I'm getting older, and finding fucking less thrilling but simply inevitable."[30]

In April he had written to his mother, "there'll never be peace until Fascism is destroyed. I'm glad I'm not in England having to make up my mind as to what's the least bad thing to do. As you say, it doesn't really bear thinking about." The news of the Spanish Civil War confirmed him in his view; the last vestiges of pacifism were abandoned. "It's too late too for democracy and reason and persuasion and writing to the *New Statesman* and Virginia signing letters saying it's all a pity. The only real choices are to submit or to fight, and if we're going to fight to do so effectively." This was in a letter to his brother; a few days later he wrote to Playfair, "There's only one thing to be done with Fascists, and that's kill them."

By mid-October he felt certain that Spain would be a destination for him, either before or after his return to England. He did not think of it as an end in itself: the romantic battle for Spanish democracy. It was a preparation, even a laboratory, for the great international war against Fascism he accepted as unavoidable. The earlier question of what he was to do when he returned to England still figured in his correspondence, but almost at a level of fantasy (grandiloquent daydreams of political power), not a real problem that had to be acted upon: the humdrum necessity of job-hunting. But the other question—when was he to leave China—had yet to be resolved. Here the problem was real enough: he did have an obligation to the University, a contract to teach until next June at the earliest. They had behaved very decently to him; if he were to walk out in mid-term, they would be left in an awkward position.

The tragi-comic event of October 28, when 'K's' husband burst into the house and discovered all, precipitated his decision. He seized upon the opportunity to conclude this chapter of his life and begin the next. Persuading himself that he had no choice but to resign, he did so at once, with no sober second thoughts or regrets. But if he had wanted to, he might as easily have stayed, there had been no public scandal, it was to the interest of the deceived husband that there be none, and it was not he but Julian who had proposed the resignation. He had already decided, weeks earlier, that, as he said, he had "had" China; he was contemplating Spain; he knew that at some point in the near future, yet to be decided, he would be leaving Wuhan; it was only necessary to make the decision. Now, in effect, it had been made for him.

He offered his resignation to the University authorities, pleading "family reasons". They were dismayed, regretful, hopeful that he might yet stay; there was some question, under the terms of his contract, of who was to pay his fare back to England, if he resigned. The deceived husband found himself in the equivocal role of having to recommend a position to the University. But by the beginning of December, everything had been worked out; the resignation had been amicably accepted, and he had received his passage home. All that was necessary was to concoct suitable public reasons for his departure, and here Julian was quite in his element, starting various stories on their rounds. In the light of his eagerness for a very bad, or rather, very good reputation as a seducer, he was surprisingly anxious that the true story should not be known. He was almost equally anxious that it not be thought that he was leaving over a row that he had just had with a visiting English dignitary. Officially, he had resigned for "family reasons". Those to whom he felt he owed a more circumstantial explanation, if not the true one, he told that his brother had gone off to Spain, and he was returning to fetch him back. A very few people he told that he was returning in order to fight in Spain himself. This, as he wrote to Playfair, was "in intention true", but he felt constrained to add, "if it's possible and if I can possibly persuade Nessa I must."[31]

In his letter to her, describing the end of the affair and his resignation, he had gone on to speculate about the future. "I am still undecided what I shall do." He raised a number of possibilities—travel, politics, Spain—as though all were to be given equal weight. "I'm going to ask Leonard to find me a job—unpaid, I think—in the Labour party": a notion that would be certain to reassure her. On the other hand he persisted in his belief that, once she understood how he felt, she would overcome her fears and scruples and approve of what he really wanted to do. The letter seesawed back and forth:

> Fortunately the news from Spain is better today; there's no certainty, but if the government holds Madrid I think they may win yet . . . You know that intellectually I agree with you about war, and emotionally too in many ways. But there is one completely irrational side of my mind which can't accept things like Fascist victories even in other countries, but wants to get out and do something. And intellectually and emotionally I have none of your horror of killing human beings as such—only when they are valuable or my friends. Still, all this wouldn't matter much if it weren't my very peculiar mental kink about war as an art—or science—which I share with Quentin. I have never decided whether it is a freakish and slightly neurotic reaction to our pacifist childhood, or whether it is an even more freakish vocation. But I know that the last few days I have begun to feel about Spain not my mere desperation—which I would suppress, except about France, where Charles and Marie [Mauron] are involved, and so much of our own world—but I have been feeling what seems like a professional—no, amateur impatience—about the government defeats. I can't help believing that if I had been in England, and had gone out at the beginning, I might now be in a position to make some difference, and if so, I could have done a good deal. This may very well be a completely false judgment, but if it's a true one then I am clearly not in the position of an ordinary volunteer for a good cause. It needs more careful thought than I feel inclined to give. But perhaps you had better be prepared for my wanting to go, though that's a very different business indeed to going. At all events, much may happen in three or four months; best of all, the Left may be victorious, and there'll be no more nightmare. It's been really hideous this last week here, where I don't think anyone really understands the way it upsets me . . . What a mercy you and I have somehow got outside age limits and can understand each other. I don't know how I should have been able to endure my emotional life and stay sane and rather hard really if it weren't for you.

But Julian was unwilling to recognize a simple and painful truth:

that his mother might very well understand him, and at the same time disapprove and be hurt by what he intended to do. Or perhaps unconsciously he did recognize it: it would account for much of the tension that is so evident in his life during his last three months in China—from the time of the confrontation scene to his eventual belated departure. (Ideally, of course, he ought to have left at once, but the machinery of resignation turned at a stately pace, and he had agreed to remain until the end of the term, so that he was not able to get away until the end of January 1937.) The frenetic, quasi-farcical aspect of his sexual intrigues represents one kind of tension; the fantasies of violence and self-conscious barbarism that erupt in his correspondence represent another. For all his faith in the power of understanding, it was not gaining him his mother's approval, and he could surmise, reading between the lines of her letters, that it was making her miserable. This too added to his guilt and anxiety. "Dearest Nessa," he wrote to her on December 12, "I think we must leave the whole question of Spain till I get back. For one thing, it is very painful, because the only big reason to me for not doing any rather dangerous thing is that it makes you unhappy, however good you are about being reasonable and telling me that I am not to think too much of your feelings and so on. I was horrified at already having given you such a nightmare. So let's leave it all till we can talk together . . . And besides, the war is going so much better, I now hope the republic will have won before I can get back, and then the whole question will be academic."

If he took a cheerful view of the Spanish situation, it was only in part to reassure his mother; towards the end of the year he believed it to be justified by events. Here, paradoxically, was another source of anxiety. Supposing the war in Spain to be over before he could get there—and he was genuinely fearful that he might arrive too late—then he would have to think seriously of some viable alternative for the "three years before facing War" in England: the old problem of finding a suitable niche would reassert itself. Hence the apparent contradictions of his behaviour and thinking: in his own mind he was absolutely clear that he was to go to Spain; at the same time he was conducting a full-scale discussion with family and friends of what he was to do when he returned to England. His mother took heart when she heard that at long last he had actually written to Leonard Woolf for help in getting a political job in the Labour party, and since that was to be non-paying, she began to look about for something additional and lucrative for him. The solution she arrived at had just the air of the improbable that he could relish, without ever taking seriously: he was to become a company director, of a family business importing feathers from China. "It sounds quite wild," he wrote to Playfair. "But apparently it would produce a hundred a year which I should appreciate."

From Leonard Woolf came word that he thought he might be able to arrange something for him through Hugh Dalton. Whereupon Julian embarked in his correspondence upon the game of future politics, and played it as enthusiastically as the war game—indeed, at times he seems to have confused the two—and he gloried in declaring himself at the furthest pole from "idealism, democracy, and liberalism". "Does this horrify you, by the way?" he demanded of Playfair. "It may look pretty bad by the time it gets to England." How seriously did he believe in his rather terrifying daydreams? It was as though, once started, he could not have enough of repudiating the civilized values of his parents: "Let's cultivate the virtues of barbarism," he crowed. Yet he knew very well, in spite of the elaborate plan-spinning in his letters, what the next stage of his life was to be: he was as little likely to settle down as anyone's political private secretary as to become an importer of feathers. With an air of absolute seriousness he was able to write to Quentin of a future *coup d'état* in England, to be led, presumably, by a junta of neo-Machiavellians; but in the same letter, in a single sentence, he brushed fantasy aside: "I don't really think it's much use discussing going out [to Spain] by letter: I have made up my mind to do so if it's in any way possible, and that's that."

The initial impulse to go to Spain—let us say, from mid-September, after the return to Wuhan—was an emotional one: Spain was "the right place to be". But he disapproved of doing things for emotional reasons; thereafter he spent much of his time marshalling intellectual arguments to justify his decision. If he really fancied himself as a military man, then he was obligated to go where the fight he was interested in—against Fascism—was taking place. This was very different, he would have argued, from going as a romantic volunteer in the cause of freedom. Isolated in China, he followed the progress of the war in late-arriving newspapers from England, and grew increasingly impatient when events did not conform to his notions of proper strategy. "I can't help feeling there ought to be a counterstroke," he wrote to Quentin, "above all in the south, where the communications with Africa are exposed—and I should like to hear more of the guerillas. Of course if you can combine guerillas and mobile regulars and a solid defensive you ought to be safe to win—it's the peninsula formula." And a few days later he wrote to Playfair about Kleber's strategy in Madrid: "I can't grasp if [he] is being too clever, or why he hasn't pulled the strings of the bag. I should have thought to bottle Franco and force a surrender wouldn't be hard, and would finish the war." He was being very much the armchair general, shocked that what to him were the obvious steps were not being taken. But the role did not satisfy him; he realized that criticism from a distance of five thousand miles is easy and pointless. He wanted to go to Spain, and he wanted to go to Spain to fight.

He had not been able to unravel the complexities of Chinese politics, nor had he really been interested in doing so. (It seems fair enough then that his Chinese friends should not have understood why he was so exercised about Spain. When 'K' heard that he was going there, she leapt to the conclusion that it was because she had not accepted his offer to marry her; he assured her that this was not the case.) In Spain, by contrast, he felt the issues to be clearly defined—"if only we could beat [the Fascists] off and get breathing space"—and he realized, well before the air raids on civilian populations, that the Germans would use Spain as a testing-ground for new armaments and techniques of warfare. But, as we shall see, the most reasoned statement of his position—the philosophical and political assumptions that justified his progress from pacifism to Spain—is to be found in the long essay 'War and Peace: Letter to E. M. Forster', which he began to write in January and completed on the boat returning home.

Throughout December he had become more and more determined in his attitude, and unshakeable in his insistence to friends and to Quentin that he would be going out to Spain, as though gathering courage for the declaration to his mother, which thus far he had not yet nerved himself to make. "Try to convince Nessa that it'll probably be over before I'm back," he wrote to Quentin, "and that anyway it's not unreasonably dangerous." Three days later, December 27, he wrote to a friend, "My ambition is to join the International Brigade." By now he had come to feel there was an inevitability about his going, and that he must win out against opposition to his doing so, particularly from his mother. His commitment to the Civil War had become a test that he must not fail. "I foresee a fearful hullabaloo about going, and am very bothered about Nessa, who will really mind. But what else can I possibly do? Introspecting, I see that the sentiment of honour is like jealousy; outside reason or good, but ineluctable. Just as, if you're jealous, you must break, there's no cure, so I feel I must go; anything else would be inconceivable. Besides, like all would-be volunteers, I've a profound belief in my own good luck." He told Playfair, "If I don't go I shall feel too bloody to be of use anywhere—certainly none in politics and writing." In another letter, written in mid-January, he announced his plan: "I'm going by sea to Marseilles, and then by hook or crook to Spain. It seems the only rational course." Then, even more insistently: "But what else can I do? It's impossible to let other people go and fight for what one believes in and refuse the risk oneself. All right for lots of people, with real jobs worth doing, or with real dependents, or who don't like killing. But I approve of wars in principle, and no one has any claim on me. And I should never recover from a sense of shame if I didn't go."

Actually, he was all too aware that his mother did have a claim on him—the claim of the extraordinary closeness of their relationship. All through the letters of this period runs the refrain of his concern for his mother and her feelings. As he wrote to Playfair, "I know I shall have a bad time of it dealing with Nessa, for I can't really go until I've got her to agree more or less. The consequence of which is some rather exhausting soul-searching and the winnowing leaves not much behind but maggots. However, my main conclusion is . . . that unless I go I shall be good for nothing."[32]

Vanessa Bell's letters to Julian have not survived, and so we cannot follow their correspondence in detail. Some things can be safely asserted, however. She was emotionally opposed to war, and firmly opposed to her son participating in a war. Her husband and closest friends had resisted the state in its efforts to press them into military service; it is inconceivable that she should not have been disturbed at her son's desire to seek out military experience. These were objections on the level of principle; on the emotional level, given the intensity of their attachment, she would have responded even more strongly to the possibility of his deliberately risking his life. After their first exchange of letters on the subject, pained that he should have made her unhappy, he proposed that they "leave the whole question of Spain" until he got back. Then he changed his tack and wrote to her of the future—"I now realise that I simply must take up politics for a good many years"—not only to reassure her, but also because the question genuinely concerned him. There was a slight confusion of chronology. He meant, although he did not say so, the future *after Spain*; she thought and he allowed her to believe he meant, the future *after China*. But although he was careful to avoid any mention of Spain in his letters, they reveal the state of mind in which he reached his decision to go out there:

> Most of my friends are unutterably squeamish about means; they feel that it would be terrible to use force or fraud against anyone, and that they have souls to save which are the most important part of them. Even most communists seem to me to have only a hysterical and quite unrealistic notion about violent methods . . . I can't imagine anyone of the New Statesman doing anything "unfair" to an opponent. Queer people—but don't you think I'm right? Whereas for my own part—whether from being a Bell or from living with painters or whatever—I can't feel the slightest qualms about the notion of doing anything effective, however ungentlemanly and unchristian, nor about admitting to myself that certain actions would be very unfair indeed . . . Well, anyway, I have written to Leonard, not in quite this style, but asking him definitely if I could find any job in the Labour party. It would also, I think, keep me active and interested, and I can't see anything else that would do

> that. For I doubt if I shall ever be a whole-time writer—at any rate not unless something changes a good deal for me . . .

Then, in a final sentence, quite casually, he repudiated the *summum bonum* of Bloomsbury:

> I don't feel, myself, as if I could ever be satisfied to do nothing but produce works of art, or even really nothing but leading a private life and producing works in the intervals.[33]

Yet it seemed impossible not to touch upon the crucial subject, particularly as he wanted her to meet him in France upon his return, rather than wait for him to arrive in England. (In fact, he was not certain that he would go back to England at all, as it might involve him in difficulties with the Enlistment Act. The simplest solution—this was in December—seemed to be France, then Spain. Spain he was determined on, "by hook or crook". But of course none of this could be mentioned in his letters to his mother.)

> I've been trying hard *not* to write to you about what I want to do, because letters are a bad form of communication when one wants to know what one's doing. It's fiendishly difficult. I was wretched at your having nightmares over me . . . I shan't do anything unless you have seen what I'm after. I think if we talk you'll understand me. You know, I always thought one day we should find ourselves in this position, tho' I didn't expect it so soon. It's very odd indeed; here I'm a sort of Bloomsburyish recluse. In letters, all the old life goes on. And then there's this fantastic world in the newspapers. I simply cannot believe in it— . . . It's quite fantastic to think of you and me in the sort of Corneille situation that seems to be getting set for us. However, it's not going to be genuinely Corneillian if I can help it. I suppose you can remember the same sort of business in '14? I wish it were one of the situations in which you'd feel *exactly* as I do: I think we're pretty much agreed even about this. But I'm a thoroughly unreasonable creature—or so reasonable I recognize my own irrational desires, whichever you like . . . I shall try to take a boat to Marseilles and get there about Feb. 25. Would that suit you? But I'll send you a telegram when I *do* decide. Please don't have nightmares or anxieties—how foolish of me to

> try and stop you when I know I can't. I can only say that when we meet we shall manage somehow to get things tangled out.[34]

Thus, with his own mind made up, but aware that he had yet to convince his mother, Julian left China at the end of January 1937.

'War and Peace: A Letter to E. M. Forster', the third and last of the long essays that he intended as a 'testament' to his generation, is as discursive and disorganized as the Roger Fry letter and the Letter to Day Lewis—Julian is still "all over the place"—but, unlike them, it deals with an actual rather than a theoretical predicament, and one that Julian shared with much of his generation:

> I wish to explain why it is that I, and many more men of military age, have ceased to be pacifists . . . I know that we have to choose war, not peace; I will not pretend this is anything but a choice of evil, not good . . . What reasons can be given for so unnatural a choice? They are reasons of expediency, of necessity, sufficiently familiar to my contemporaries, and sufficiently obvious. Yet it is the appreciation or ignorance of this necessity that more than anything divides the generations. And it is ignorance of them, deliberate ostrich ignorance, that preserves intact the virgin cotton-wool of British public opinion.

This is a very different level of consideration from that of the earlier essays: it is one thing to prescribe a "disciplined aesthetic" for a far distant socialized future, or to reprove one's rivals for too much enthusiasm in their poetry; it is another, to evaluate a *real* predicament from which *real* consequences might ensue, not only for oneself but for much of the world. At his best in the letter to Forster, amidst all the distracting hares that are started and pursued, he is not speculative, but diagnostic: hence, relevant. We know his own solution: that he translated enthusiasm into action and chose to participate in the Spanish Civil War. He prided himself on being hard-headed and Machiavellian, but no true Machiavellian would have felt or written, "It's impossible to let other people go and fight for what one believes in and refuse the risk oneself." In fact, as Forster himself pointed out in the 'Notes for a Reply' which are included along with the essay in the memorial volume, there was a strong strain of idealism in Julian. And he went on affectionately to note, "he is guilty of pretty well everything he condemns except chastity and cowardice".

The letter is written to Forster as the friend and biographer of Lowes Dickinson, whose liberal ideas Julian presumes him to share, and whom he describes as "one of the greatest of the liberals". This proves to be qualified praise:

> When, in his dialogue with Plato, Lowes Dickinson discusses socialism, he does so in terms of justice and right and value. And that is still the ordinary form of discussion of socialism: the socialist is motivated by a sense of pity for human suffering, by a sense of equality or of justice, revolted at the oppressions of civilization. Consequently there is still a good deal of truth in the notion that a socialist is a man with a weak head and a capitalist a man with a bad heart.

The crucial objection to liberalism, then, is that it is "political romanticism: it has no innate sense of human baseness, and can only move between illusion and disillusion". The League of Nations, Lowes Dickinson's "cause", was "made a futility by the liberal inability to think in terms of force . . . it had no backing but reason and goodness, and few men are good or reasonable." And he concludes his indictment of the liberal attitude by pointing out that "nowhere is [it] so strong as it is today in England. Consequently we still think that we can protect ourselves from war and poverty by appealing to sentiment, reason, goodness."

But how is the case against liberalism to be related to the intention of the essay: "why it is that I, and many more men of military age, have ceased to be pacifists"? It is done, after some thirty-three pages of divagations and explorations during which *the* point tends to disappear among a horde of *other* points, by merging liberalism with pacifism. So that, in effect, he is saying: we who were liberals and/or pacifists, believing that men are good and reasonable, and that wars can be averted by appeals to sentiment etc., must now abandon our illusions and accept an "obvious truth":

> Non-resistance means suffering the full power of fascism. And fascism means, not only violence, but slavery, and will not only kill and torture, but will destroy all chance of reasoned, or reasonable or Christian opposition [this in answer to Quaker

> pacifism] and will do its best, with violence and propaganda, to harry out of the world all liberal and humane ideas or men.

And again:

> Non-resistance to war means non-resistance to fascism and a resignation to the disappearance of most, if not all, that we value.

And finally:

> At this moment, to be anti-war means to submit to fascism, to be anti-fascist means to be prepared for war.

This is the central, and most relevant—also the most realistic—point that Julian makes in his essay, but it is only one among a large number of other points, relevant or not, that he felt compelled to make. For example, his acceptance of force as a means to a desired end, what he called "engineering socialism", his odd, aristocratic version of a revolution for the future: all Marxism ("the irresistible intellectual case") and no Marxists ("their lives are mainly evil"). For example, his enthusiastic interpretation of what he called "the military virtues". Here he begins quite calmly: "The soldier's is not perhaps the best of lives for many people: it may not offer a very great number of highly valued states of mind. But it can be a good life . . . it is secular and rational." Soon, however, enthusiasm catches him up, and he is setting forth the virtues that he has always admired—"common sense, an acute intuition of reality . . . practical sagacity and judgment" and so on. He might almost be writing of Roger Fry. "The essential attraction of war and of the military character lies in this submission of the intelligence to facts and of facts to the resources of the intelligence. Such is indeed the procedure of all the admirable human activities: of the engineer, the scientist, the administrator, even, in certain measure, of the artist. The soldier's form of action has certain attractions, of excitement and courage, the others lack—and the consequent evils of death and destruction." He had been attracted by this form of action since early childhood; the political realities of the 1930s—"to be anti-fascist means to be prepared for war"—justified an intellectual commitment that, on an emotional level, unconsciously, had been made a long time before. He might have said, 'I want to go; therefore I must,' but as Forster observed,

"He had a vigorous mind, and had been brought up in Cambridge and places where they argue, so it came natural to him to pop in a bunch of reasons."[35]

When he left China, his decision was made: he was going to Spain to fight in the Civil War on the side of the Republican Government. He hoped it would not be necessary to return to England at all, partly to hasten his arrival in Madrid, partly to avoid being put in a position where he might be dissuaded from doing what he wanted to do. He would arrive in Marseilles in mid-March; he would go to St Rémy to see the Maurons; he would spend time with his mother in Cassis; then Spain—that was the tentative plan as he set sail. He had written a succession of letters, to everyone but his mother, telling what he intended to do, and he had not suggested that she not be told. And surely he underestimated her if he thought that she would not guess, read between the lines, suspect his intentions: the closeness of their relationship made it inevitable. She knew that he was planning to see the Maurons, and was fearful that afterwards he meant to go straight on to Spain. On February 20, when the ship docked at Colombo, there was a letter from her, written in great distress, asking if he had come to a decision, and if he had, to tell her, no matter what.

He cabled immediately, "Undecided." A week later he wrote to her from Djibouti:

> Nessa dearest
>
> I'm very sorry indeed about the muddle—which must have been my fault. I was thinking a great deal about the whole business, and I suppose I must have made up a letter to you in my head and never written it—a thing I often enough do. After which I thought the less I said the better. But I've always been very clear that I should have to convince you before I could do anything, and I thought I'd said so—I certainly did to Charles when I wrote to him asking him to help me—I said that of course it would depend on my persuading you.
>
> Well, it won't really matter much in any event my coming back [to England]—it was really only cowardice on my part; I

> know it will be very much harder to leave again than if I'd never come back. I shall have to see Charles on my way and possibly other people—without committing myself, of course. I'd never had any idea of doing this without talking to you first, you know. But I should like to have a chance to talk to you alone for a day or so, and I don't want much to argue with anyone else—I'm ready enough to talk practicalities and get information, of course, but I don't feel like serious argument with anyone but you, because at root the business is a personal one, not political—I mean that my decision really depends on certain judgments about what is good for me in my own life, since the world at large isn't going to be very much affected. It seems to me to be a matter between me and you. I don't think most of the consequences much matter, but your feelings do.

On March 8 he sent a telegram to her from St Rémy to announce his arrival there. She had decided against meeting him in France as he had suggested, and the Maurons persuaded him that whatever he might ultimately do, he must first return to England: Vanessa must not be hurt. There was a corollary to the argument: if he went to Spain, Vanessa would be very deeply hurt; therefore, ought he to go, had he the right to go? Mauron suggested alternatives for his future; Julian listened, appeared to agree—at least he agreed that he would go first to England. Marie Mauron sent off the good news to a friend in London, who passed it on immediately to Duncan Grant, who telegraphed to Vanessa at Charleston that there was "no question of Spain for Julian. Thank Goodness."

He left St Rémy on March 10, travelling across France by train, and arrived in England on the 12th. He had thought he had made a good and irrevocable decision—to join the International Brigade—but already he was finding that it was easier to come to the decision, than to act upon it. His mother would not join him in France; therefore he went back to England and "the strain of seeing people" whom he knew would attempt to discourage him or question the rightness of his decision. He wanted everything to be simple and clear, and it was not going to be. Even his love life, which he had hoped would subside into a state of quiescence, was proving more complicated than ever. 'M', the second Chinese lady, was in a state of misery; he had spent some time with 'K' in Hongkong and she intended to follow him in the near future to England; 'L', the English girl, had fallen in love with him, he thought, and to his chagrin he appeared to have broken up her forthcoming marriage. His mother was horribly upset about his future plans. Mauron offered him work in France; his uncle had promised to help him find a political job in England, but this was not what he wanted: he wanted to go to Spain as quickly as possible. He wrote to 'B', from the train returning to England, "Life's hell at the moment . . . No one wants me in Spain, and I don't much want myself elsewhere . . . I can just stand the bloodiness of the world if I've something to DO, but everyone is persuaded I'm another political intellectual, and I really think that it's mere *eau de bidet* dishing about ideas and organisations and public opinion. Well, that's that. In a week's time I may have changed my mind. Or Nessa may think I'm right—about myself, I mean—and I may have got myself accepted [by the International Brigade]. I know if, like most of my friends, I didn't care about my parents, I should go unless stopped. Curious, and I suppose an atavism or something, but I really do feel horribly ashamed of myself—shall, rather, if I don't go."

Part Four Spain

1 John Cornford

It is not our purpose here to explore the complexities of Spanish history and politics, or to venture into what Gerald Brenan has called the Spanish labyrinth. One grants the peculiarity of Spanish mysticism, leaves unresolved the enigma of the Spanish character, shies away from an analysis of *casticismo*—Spanishness in all its ramifications. The Civil War began on July 18, 1936, with an uprising on the Right, plotted and led by a cabal of generals, the most notorious among them being Mola and Franco. That was the immediate event. But as Hugh Thomas reminds us, it was "the culmination of one hundred and fifty years of passionate quarrels in Spain. 1808, 1834, 1868, 1909, 1917, 1923, 1931, 1932, 1934 and February 1936; these were the critical dates, becoming more and more frequent, in the inflammation of the Spanish tragedy." In the summer of 1936, "the masters of economic power in the country, led by the Army, and supported by the Church, that embodiment of Spain's past glory" were arrayed against " 'the professors'—many of the enlightened middle class—and almost the entire labour force of the country, maddened by years of insult, misery and neglect".[1] Thus, in the beginning, it was peculiarly and intrinsically a *Spanish* civil war—a struggle between Spaniards—whose origins went deep in the Spanish past; presently another war, of international ideas, ideals, ideologies and ambitions, would be superimposed upon it. For the Western world it became, in Anthony Eden's phrase, the "war of the Spanish Obsession".

The young Englishmen who went to Spain to fight in the International Brigade, or in other ways to help the cause of the Republic, would have been acquainted only with the most recent of the critical dates: 1931, the fall of the monarchy; 1934, the rising of the miners of the Asturias, put down with extreme brutality by the Foreign Legion under General Franco. (John Cornford, as one would expect, was stirred by the events in the Asturias. Victor Kiernan recalled how on one occasion, when he and two others were setting off with John "for an evening's street-chalking—an occupation he enjoyed, as it brought him within powder-smell of the police—he had ready a detailed critique of the rising and the reasons for its failure".) And they would have known—for them it was the crux of the matter—that in the elections of February 1936 a Popular Front of parties of the Left and Centre (from which, however, the Anarchists, the largest working-class party, had abstained) had won a majority of seats in the Cortes; and its leaders were now the legally elected government, rather more to the Centre than the Left, of the Spanish Republic. But even presuming that the young Englishmen knew of the several competing parties and sub-parties of the Left, they would not have been informed enough to distinguish accurately between them or know what policies they favoured: who, for example, were the more inflexibly committed to revolution, the Communists or the Anarchists? Nor would it have been thought necessary to make such distinctions: surely that was the object of the Popular Front, to fuse differences and join forces against a common enemy. Until the summer of 1936, Spain had not made a sizeable claim upon the political consciousness of the young men of the English Left. If they looked to the Continent, it was principally to the Soviet Union, the workers' state, or to Germany, the Fascist state. (It is true that John Cornford, writing in the winter of 1934, had singled out "the Anarchist workers' putsch in Spain" in 1931 as the first in a series of revolutionary episodes that would culminate three years later in the workers' risings in Vienna. But his account of the "putsch" is curiously misinformed, written with more assurance than accuracy. He had not facts enough—and oversimplified those that he had—to support his interpretation of the rioting in

Barcelona.) Accordingly, when the events of July 1936 focused the attention of the young men of the Left in England (and even of a young Englishman in China) upon Spain, it was still a country about whose politics, history, religion, culture and customs they knew very little. Theirs was an outside view, inevitably a simplification, that filtered out the Spanishness from the struggle and made it more manageable, in England at least, than the reality was to prove.

In the early summer of 1936, the problem of John's immediate future appeared to have been resolved when Trinity awarded him the Earl of Derby Research Scholarship. Although he had been exploring (but not very seriously) the possibility of various jobs, he settled for another year at Cambridge without marked reluctance. It meant he could pursue his interest in the Elizabethans, and at the same time continue to play an active role in the student movement he had helped to bring into being. The disadvantage of the arrangement was that he would not be able to see Margot as often as he would like for she would still be teaching school in Birmingham. However, they were counting on a holiday together in August, a week or two in the South of France, and afterwards a few days in Brussels, where they would attend the inaugural conference of the International Peace Campaign. But the news of the Civil War in Spain led them to modify their plan. John's curiosity had been intensely aroused by what he had read and heard: that the Republic, at least in Catalonia, was being transformed into a workers' state at the same time as it was fighting to put down the Fascist uprising. It was something he wanted to see. As he wrote to his father later, "the idea suddenly occurred to me to go to Spain for a few days. I expected at the time the fighting would be over very soon; so in a tremendous hurry I got a letter of introduction from the *News Chronicle* and set out."

In those earliest days of the struggle, the idea of privately organized assistance for the Republic from abroad had not yet taken significant hold, and would not do so until late in the summer. By then the Western powers were arriving at an official policy of non-intervention: to offer no military aid, nor allow the sale of arms, to either side in the Civil War. (In theory impartial, non-intervention proved to work to the disadvantage of the Republic. The rebels, or as they were already designated, the Nationalists, were unaffected by it, since they were early and continuously supplied by Germany and Italy. The Republic, having appealed in vain to France and England, turned for assistance to the Soviet Union, from whom it was forthcoming, but never in sufficiently large quantities to ensure victory.) In England, Spanish Medical Aid was organized by mid-August; its first ambulance and field hospital unit was sent out before the end of the month. Recruiting for the International Brigades got under way in September. But from the beginning there had been individual volunteers from abroad, who crossed the frontier and made their way to Barcelona. The very first to come from England was John Cornford. In fact, although a few Englishmen already on the Continent had arrived in Spain before him, he was to be the first to fight at the front for the Republic. But there is no reason to believe that this was his intention, consciously at least, when he started out from London in early August.

It was all very casually done. He and Margot made the necessary changes in their holiday plan. He would leave London a week or so in advance of her, look round Spain, see what had so engaged his imagination in the past: a war against the Right, and a revolution on the Left. She, meanwhile, would go as they had originally planned to the South of France, and he would join her there as soon as it was convenient.

And so he went—the whole episode so impromptu, so unpremeditated, and so quickly decided upon, that there was neither time nor thought for farewells. Christopher, for example, spent an afternoon with him in late July at the Town Swimming Bath in Cambridge. They parted casually; John went off to London, presumably for the week-end. Then, silence; there were no letters to Conduit Head; and a few weeks later Christopher "heard a rumour" that John was in Spain. Nor had he felt any need to clear his going with the party, or even to let the party know of his intentions: it was not as though he held an official place in the hierarchy with prescribed duties and obligations. He was simply off for a holiday in France, with a detour across the Spanish border, and he meant to be back in England by the end of August. In the rush of departure he paused only long enough to obtain, through the intervention of an acquaintance on its staff, a press card from the *News Chronicle*, establishing his identity as a free-lance journalist. And at the last moment he was joined by a friend from Trinity, Richard Bennett, as curious as himself as to what was really happening in Spain. They arrived in Dieppe on August 6; crossed the frontier at Port Bou on the 7th; on the 8th they were in Barcelona.

Franz Borkenau, an Austrian journalist with whom John would soon become acquainted, had arrived there (by train from Port Bou) three days earlier. Overwhelmed by what he saw, he recorded his first impression in his diary.

> Again a peaceful arrival [he wrote at 11 p.m. on August 5]. No taxi-cabs, but instead old horse-cabs, to carry us into the town. Few people in the Paseo de Colon. And, then, as we turned round the corner of the Ramblas (the chief artery of Barcelona) came a tremendous surprise: before our eyes, in a flash, unfolded itself the revolution. It was overwhelming. It was as if we had been landed on a continent different from anything I had seen before.
>
> The first impression: armed workers, rifles on their shoulders, but wearing their civilian clothes. Perhaps 30 per cent of the males on the Ramblas were carrying rifles, though there were no police, and no regular military in uniforms . . . Very few of these armed proletarians wore the new dark-blue pretty militia uniforms. They sat on the benches or walked the pavement of the Ramblas, their rifles over the right shoulder, and often their girls on the left arm. They started off, in groups, to patrol outlying districts. They stood, as guards, before the entrances of hotels, administrative buildings, and the larger stores [whose owners had fled and which had been requisitioned for organizations and political parties of the working classes] . . . They drove at top speed innumerable fashionable cars, which they had expropriated and covered, in white paint, with the initials of their respective organizations: C.N.T.–F.A.I. [Anarchists], U.G.T. [General Workers' Union], P.S.U.C. (United Socialist-Communist Party of Catalonia), P.O.U.M. (Trotskyists), or with all these initials at once, in order to display their loyalty to

> the movement in general . . . The fact that all these armed men walked about, marched, and drove in their ordinary clothes made the thing only more impressive as a display of the power of the factory workers. The anarchists, recognizable by badges and insignia in red and black, were obviously in overwhelming numbers. And no 'bourgeoisie' whatever![2]

John, too, arriving in the Catalonian capital, was impressed by the evidence of revolution all about him.

> In Barcelona [he wrote to Margot] one can understand physically what the dictatorship of the proletariat means. All the Fascist press has been taken over. The real rule is in the hands of the militia committees. There is a real terror against the Fascists. But that doesn't alter the fact that the place is free—and conscious all the time of its freedom. Everywhere in the streets are armed workers and militiamen, and sitting in the cafés which used to belong to the bourgeoisie. The huge Hotel Colon overlooking the main square is occupied by the United Socialist Party of Catalonia. Further down, in a huge block opposite the Bank of Spain, is the Anarchist headquarters. The palace of a marquis in the Rambla is a C.P. Headquarters. But one does not feel the tension. The mass of the people . . . simply are enjoying their freedom. The streets are crowded all day, and there are big crowds round the radio palaces. But there is nothing at all like tension or hysteria. It's as if in London the armed workers were dominating the streets—it's obvious that they wouldn't tolerate Mosley or people selling *Action* in the streets. And that wouldn't mean that the town wasn't free in the real sense. It is genuinely a dictatorship of the majority, supported by the overwhelming majority.[3]

This was the revolution made visible, but John remained in Barcelona to observe it and, theoretically, to write about it as an accredited free-lance journalist, only a little more than two days. On the afternoon of the third day he was on his way to the front. There, rather surprisingly, and, as we shall see, quite without premeditation, he joined the militia of the P.O.U.M., a small, dissident Marxist party outside the Popular Front.

Each of the various political parties of the Left had its own militia. Together, under the rather weak central control of the Anti-Fascist Militias Committee, they comprised the armies of Catalonia. Their charge was the defence of the Aragon front, a line running through the provinces of Huesca, Saragossa and Teruel, whose capital cities in each case were occupied by the Nationalists. For John, as a dedicated Communist, the logical place would have been with the militia of the P.S.U.C., a recent Popular Front amalgamation, in which the Socialists were much the more numerous, but in which the Communists were becoming increasingly powerful, even before the Russian shipments of arms to the Republic. In 1938, when the party line on the P.O.U.M. was at its most scathing and bent on its destruction, Tom Wintringham, the English Communist military expert, who was one of the originators of the idea of an International Brigade and who rose to high rank within it, undertook to explain why John had not enlisted in the militia of the P.S.U.C. "In Barcelona he found that the militia was being organized by the trade unions and political parties. He had no papers from England: he had not even brought his party membership card with him. So when he applied to the Hotel Colon, then the military headquarters of the party in which Barcelona's Socialists and Communists had joined forces, he was told to wait. Friendly but precise Germans, people taught by Bismarck as well as by exile to carry all necessary documents with them at all times, told him that he could not join the Thaelmann group, or any other unit of foreign volunteers organized by the United Socialist Party, until his standing as a known anti-Fascist was guaranteed by some document or by some person they knew. John was too restless, impatient for this. He flung off to join a rival party's militia, that of the P.O.U.M."[4]

Wintringham, of course, was writing at second—or third or fourth—remove: he was not in Barcelona when John arrived; he may have seen him when he came back there after his release from the hospital in September (Wintringham places this in October), but if so, it would have been at a time when, according to Wintringham, John was "so utterly tired that he could scarcely speak at all". In any event, it is not true that John came from England without his party card, and it is misleading to suggest that "he flung off to join a rival party's militia", as though, having been rebuffed at the Hotel Colon, he dashed in a tantrum down the

Ramblas to the headquarters of the P.O.U.M. at the Hotel Falcon, and there enlisted.

John's leather-bound pocket diary, in which he made very brief and sometimes cryptic entries for each day he was in Spain on his first trip (August 6—September 17) is still in existence. From it we learn that he was at the Hotel Colon on his first day in Barcelona and that he joined the militia at the front six days later. There are no references to the Hotel Falcon or to the P.O.U.M. On the other hand, the reference to the Colon is followed by the notation "P.S.U.C. & my party card", which may or may not have had to do with proving his standing as a "known anti-Fascist". Presumably he had the card with him when he arrived at the Colon and it failed to satisfy the "friendly but precise Germans" there, or he had left it behind in his own hotel room and they were properly suspicious. More to the point, was he, as Wintringham claims, at the Hotel Colon on his first day in Barcelona to enlist—in the recruiting office on the ground floor—or was he simply there, like Borkenau, to gather information at the foreign Press Bureau? An Englishman who spoke no Spanish or German (John did not) might have had some difficulty in making his intentions clear to Spaniards and Germans who spoke no English. It is worth noting that John seems to have toured a number of other political headquarters that first day—flinging himself from one to the next? The diary refers not only to the 'Colon', but also to the 'Marquis'—presumably the palace mentioned in his letter to Margot, which had been requisitioned as a C.P. headquarters—and to 'Hotel National', which was the headquarters of the Anarchists. It is hard to believe that he attempted to enlist and was rebuffed at each.

In September he wrote to his father, "After I had been three days in Barcelona it was clear, first, how serious the position was; second, that a journalist without a word of Spanish was just useless. I decided to join the militia." Actually, he was in Barcelona only two and a half days; by the afternoon of the third day he was already travelling in a party with Borkenau and a French journalist towards the front. In the long diary letter he wrote to Margot Heinemann when he was in the militia (post-August 13), he told her, "I came up to the front and Richard was left behind. Enlisted here on the strength of my party card." We learn from Borkenau that John enlisted at Leciñena, the furthest point at the front that the party was scheduled to visit. If they had continued north to Tardienta, the base of the P.S.U.C. militia, John might as readily have enlisted there. The choice of the P.O.U.M. militia was fortuitous, and it is absurd to read into it a significance it does not deserve. They were there at Lecineña and available to him at the psychological moment, when he wanted to fight Fascists—it was as simple as that.

There can be no doubt, though, that John was restless and impatient in Barcelona after the first exhilarating look round. By the time he left the Hotel National it must have been clear to him that he was fatally handicapped in gathering information—whether for future articles, or for the use of the party—by not knowing Spanish. He had come out from England not only to see the revolution on the Left, but also to see the war against the Right. And he was to join Margot in the South of France not later than the end of the next week. So that when Franz Borkenau, whom he had met on his second day in the city, proposed that he come with him and another journalist on a trip to the front, John leaped at the opportunity. Borkenau's account of the trip begins, "This afternoon [August 11], at 1 p.m., after days of waiting and delays, I finally started for the front in a car of the militia central committee, with an armed driver and one armed guard. We are three in the party, the Barcelona representative of the *Paris Flèche*, Mr John Cornford, a young British communist, and myself."[5]

Borkenau, whose study of the early period of the war, *The Spanish Cockpit*, has proved to be of enduring value, must have been an exciting and challenging man to travel with: a much tougher and more worldly sort of intellectual—of the Middle-European variety—than most John had thus far encountered in his brief life. He was an Austrian, born into the bourgeoisie (his father had been a judge in the time of the Empire) and raised as a Catholic although of Jewish descent. After the war he had joined the German Communist Party, and held a post in the Comintern, but he had broken with the party, objecting to its "lack of realism" and "pedantry".[6] As a journalist, who was also a sociologist and an accomplished linguist, he was well qualified to observe and report and understand what was happening in Spain. Indeed, he seems to have been one of the few foreigners—Gerald Brenan was another—who was aware from the first of the Spanish nature of the struggle, and that such labels as 'Trotskyist' and 'Communist' did not have deep roots in Spain, but were really in large part foreign names for native movements. He understood that the strain of fanaticism in the masses, their capacity for self-sacrifice and spontaneity of action, which had inspired them to rise up against their French conquerors a century earlier, might prove more important in 1936 than any of the international ideologies called into service to provide the terms for the Spanish conflict. John would regret, for Borkenau's sake, that he had broken with the party—for himself, not to be in the party would have been unthinkable—but he was too intelligent, and happily free of sectarian small-mindedness, not to realize that he could learn a great deal from him. And so it proved. Anyone who reads both *The Spanish Cockpit* and John's essay, 'The Situation in Catalonia', will be struck by how attentively the younger man must have listened to the conversation of his Middle-European travelling companion, as they drove towards the front.

They left Barcelona at 1 p.m. Soon they were discovering that the countryside was not as calm as it had appeared to them from the windows of the train, coming down from Port Bou. The revolution was there to be seen, locally, in village after village along the road, but there was little evidence that the need of preserving the Republic on a national scale had yet stirred them. And it was precisely this that John felt ought to be the first consideration. In Barcelona he had heard, as he wrote to Margot, that "the Anarchists appear to be preparing to attack the Government after the fall of Saragossa [which was thought to be in the near future, but in fact never occurred]. That would be disastrous. The only possible tactics for the Party are to place themselves at the head of the [revolutionary] movement [still dominated by the Anarchists], get it under control, force recognition from the Government of the social gains of the revolution, and prevent at all costs an attack on the Government—unless the Government actually began to sabotage the fight against Fascism."

At almost every village they travelled through, the entries were "barricaded and heavily guarded". Borkenau noted that "the guards are picturesque and look as if they were cut out from a Goya painting . . . distinguished from ordinary mortals by red badges with the stamp of their organization, or of the local committee; bandoliers full of cartridges hold their jackets together. Thus they sit on the road, or more often crouch behind a competently constructed sandbag barricade, levelling their shot-guns at the car, or waving them wildly." At each village the procedure was the same. "The guard invariably stops our car and then starts the scrutiny of the documents: the car's 'pass', the passengers' passes, the permits to carry arms, the Press cards of visiting journalists, and sometimes they even claim to see the party cards of the guards and driver. Going through this procedure more than twenty times a day is nerve-racking, but it is done decently, and in most cases without unnecessary delay. The villagers evidently had not tired of performing this duty for many weeks . . ." Yet they appeared to feel the need to do more than this; they had still to grasp "how serious the position was". Borkenau noted that "all the villages and small towns which we passed through, though passionately guarding their own territory, have not sent a single man to the front. The main recruiting for the militia is in Barcelona."[7]

Thus far in the countryside the emphasis had been upon making the revolution, rather than making war. In almost every village Borkenau learned that a political committee, made up of representatives of the various political parties and trade unions, had taken control; priests and the bourgeoisie had fled, or been massacred; without exception churches had been burnt. But "hardly anywhere in this region has there been actual fighting". And there were surprisingly few indications for the travellers that they were approaching the front. "The road is intact and there is less traffic than in peacetime. A few motor lorries with provisions and still fewer with ammunition . . ." By dinner time thay had reached Lerida—the first place John thought worthy of mention in his diary—ninety-eight miles from Barcelona.

They had expected to find much more activity there than in fact they did, for Lerida was a juncture for the roads to Saragossa and Huesca, both of which were major objectives of the fighting on the Aragon front. But there was little happening: "Thirty or forty cars and motor-lorries are parked in the *plaza*," Borkenau noted, "and some of the militia are to be seen in the town; there cannot be more than a few hundred of them altogether." The three correspondents went into the offices of the civil Governor, where a crowd of militia men gathered and talked with Borkenau—John, without Spanish, had to rely on him—of the exploits of Durutti, the Anarchist leader, who was famous as "a sort of avenging angel of the poor. His column is known to be more ruthless than any other in shooting the fascists, the rich, and the priests in the villages, and the glory of its self-sacrificing advance towards Saragossa, is told all through the militia of Catalonia." Details of the advance were not forthcoming, however, and the party adjourned to the plaza in search of dinner. This was not easily found. Food was rationed—for Borkenau, "really the first sign that we are approaching the front". But at length, a group of foreigners sitting in front of a café, eating *tortillas*, invited them to share their meal. "They are very reluctant to disclose their nationality, but as soon as I sit down with them I recognize one of them from newspaper photographs as a Russian Press correspondent." In any event his secretiveness would have served no purpose: "everybody would have recognized him as a Russian from his accent and the few Russian words which he occasionally exchanged with his companions. But he seems to be under the delusion that nobody outside Russia has any knowledge of Russian. For some unknown reason he seems to believe that this secrecy is part of the job of a revolutionary on all occasions. Our conversation again turns on the anarchist problem. We agree that the anarchists are swiftly moving away from their anti-authoritarian dogma towards revolutionary dictatorship. 'But then', he says, 'they must leave their organization and join the Communists.' " Presumably Borkenau translated the remark for John's benefit, for it is very close to his own view that the party must take charge of the revolution. But in his diary John makes no reference to this conversation with the Russian, nor to the earlier conversation about Durutti. After "Lerida", the next entries in the diary are: "Officers. Fraga. Terror. Ferra." And thanks to Borkenau, the significance of these is decipherable.

Fraga was the small town, eighteen miles beyond Lerida and in Aragon itself, where they had spent the night. In the local hotel they met Major Farrar (John's "Ferra"), a regular army officer who had remained loyal to the Government, and who was second-in-command of the Catalan forces. He proved to be very friendly, intervened with the innkeeper to secure them food and lodging, and, surrounded by his officers, talked to them of the war. Admitting that there was a stalemate at the front, he explained it, "But we are in the middle of a social revolution." They were reminded of this yet again when they repaired to the village bar, where the appearance of three foreigners was a "big event" for the peasants. "They immediately start telling us proudly about their feats. Most of them are anarchists. One man with a significant gesture of fingers across the throat tells us that they have killed thirty-eight 'fascists' in their village." (It hardly needs saying that there were comparable executions on the Nationalist side, and John found out about them on this same journey. As a single instance, when he was in Lecineña he was told that "even here, where no working-class organization of any description existed, the Fascists had killed four peasants to 'maintain order' ".)

Fraga was "directly behind the front line". Significantly, the closer they came to the front the more evidence was available to them of military incompetence, indifference or inadequacy. John, with his passion for getting things done efficiently—he was at the opposite remove from the anarchist temperament—must have been reinforced in his conviction of the "seriousness of the position". Thus, on the road between Lerida and Fraga there were only a handful of villages at infrequent intervals. Guards were scrupulously posted at the entry to each village, but between the villages themselves were unguarded miles, the responsibility of no one. It meant that "if an enemy patrol penetrated through the advance guards at the front, it could cut the communications and intercept the traffic without any opposition". In Fraga, Major Farrar and his adjutants were conversing gaily at a table at the inn; there was no question but that Farrar was a man of great courage; but the fact remained that "this whole important section of the Catalan staff had no communication with the front during the whole evening and night, either by telephone or by messenger. Had anything happened, Farrar would probably have remained uninformed for many hours." In the morning, the three journalists were driven north to the aviation camp of the Saragossa front. There were no anti-aircraft guns. When Borkenau asked about this, "some of the pilots agreed that it was surprising that the rebels, for no conceivable reason, had omitted to raid it". That night, he returned to the camp from Fraga and saw "enemy signals given from places not far off, behind the Government lines. In my presence the men discussed how awkward it was that these signals appeared every night, but nobody thought of sending a patrol to investigate."

It was entirely consistent with the prevailing amateur, or anarchist, spirit that the Borkenau party should have come upon the front by accident. "We nearly missed it," he wrote, "it was so tiny." Driving north on the road to Huesca, they had seen one shell bursting in the distance, but did not hear any sound. Then, at the last moment, they were stopped by a guard in the road. They left the car, and climbed a hill to the village of Alcalá de Obispo, which proved, unexpectedly, to be the front itself. An artillery bombardment was in progress, but so ineffectively that they failed to notice it until there was a cry of "Take cover!" Not that there was any real need to do so. From Monte Aragon, one of the chief forts of Huesca, the rebels were shelling what they believed to be the Catalan lines. "Fortunately," Borkenau remarked, "their idea of the position of these lines was entirely erroneous and they were aiming with great exactitude at a spot half a mile from Alcalá, where, as the officers explained, there was nothing but sparrows. A large group of Government soldiers was standing erect on the exposed side of the village, watching for fun." But Government artillery observation, at least at Alcalá, was no more effective. Six light field-guns were at the front of the village and fired from time to time without adequate direction; two howitzers were in place behind the village, but "the observer, most incompetently, stood on the church tower almost in front of the guns". Borkenau concluded wryly, "I do not think that the shelling did much damage to the enemy. In this column there was not one single casualty that day, despite an all-day bombardment."

Even though whenever they heard a shell they would retreat a few steps, the three journalists set about gathering information. In the village there was a column of approximately three hundred men, and a few guards were stationed about a half mile in advance. The greater portion of the column were P.O.U.M. militia, but there were also Army regulars, officers and men, who had remained loyal to the Government. The control of the column was in the hands of a political committee, made up of commissars from the P.O.U.M. and the commanding officer of the regulars. While officers might act as "technical advisers" to the committee, it was the committee that made the final decisions. The Borkenau party discovered the truth of this almost at once. The correspondent for *Flèche* began to take photographs, for which he had applied for permission to one of the officers of the column, but not to the political committee. The committee took offence, abruptly cut short their visit, and ordered them to leave.

In John's diary the only reference to this episode at Alcalá is the word "Artillery". The next entry is "Serineña", a town thirty kilometers further along the road to Huesca, where their car broke down and they were forced to remain until it was repaired. Borkenau's diary entry for August 13 begins, "We have been stuck in Serineña for twenty-four hours, first to my disgust and then to my increasing satisfaction." There had been the usual difficulties in arranging for food and lodging, but finally, after some discussion with the local committee—its head was an anarchist baker—they were invited to eat with the militia, and became acquainted with many of them. Here, finally, they were able to see the more positive accomplishments of the revolution in action. John, in his diary, next noted, "the title deeds", and in his essay 'The Situation in Catalonia' he expanded this to, "I saw a huge bonfire of title-deeds in the Market Square." Borkenau described the event much more vividly. Late in the evening they were taken by their new friend, the anarchist baker, to the plaza, "where a few days ago the church had been burned. There have been executions in Serineña, as everywhere else. Among the total of about a dozen victims was the notary-public, whose house and offices, immediately behind the Plaza, contained all the documents relating to rural property and many other financial matters. Now these documents, together with all others found in his offices, were being burned in a huge bonfire in the middle of the Plaza, so that no valid written evidence of former property rights will survive. The flames rose higher than the roof of the church, and young anarchists went on carrying more material from the notary's house, which they threw on the flames with triumphant gestures. A number of other people silently glared into the flames. It was by no means just a matter-of-fact destruction of some unwanted documents, but an act carrying for its participants a deep significance as a symbol of the destruction of the old economic order."

The next morning there was a realistic corollary to this symbolic event, when they watched a large number of the peasants threshing their wheat collectively. John in his diary refers to "Threshing machines", which had been expropriated from four of the large estates in the vicinity, and were now made available to the peasants of Sérineña by the local committee. In 'The Situation in Catalonia',[8] he wrote, "I saw four of the confiscated threshing-machines being worked. Each peasant brought his grain in turn, and the machines they all worked together." Borkenau had grown sceptical of the talk of agrarian revolution, but what he saw now convinced him of the reality of the improvement. "I picked up the first two anarchist youngsters I met in the streets and asked them to show me the threshing machines. They led me to a group of granaries outside the village. In front of them stood four of the expropriated machines, threshing enormous amounts of wheat. At every one of them a group of about ten peasants was at work . . . together they were threshing the wheat of one of them; they were going to move the machine next day to another granary, to thresh the wheat of the next member of the group. Work was swift, faces were shining, and as far as I could judge the handling of the machines was competent . . . The committee intended to use the machines for threshing the harvest of the expropriated estates, as soon as the peasant collectives had finished their threshing, and to use this harvest as a wheat store for the militia, to be stored in the church."

This was the revolution at its most impressive and valuable—very different from what they had seen and been told at Fraga, where the anarchist nucleus, "under the influence of the Durutti militia column, had helped to kill an enormous number of people in the village, but . . . had achieved nothing else". That it was worth defending was beyond doubt or argument. But the seriousness of the position was this: that the revolution was also vulnerable, *needed* to be defended, and there was a war to be fought: the Fascists were in Huesca, only twenty kilometres away. Given the evidence of Sérineña, the revolution was being waged effectively, intelligently and enthusiastically: could as much be said for the war? And if not, what could one do? What, for example, could John Cornford do?

On the afternoon of August 13 their car was finally repaired, and they drove on to Lecineña, the base of operations for the other, and larger, P.O.U.M. column on the Saragossa front. Their reception was notably more cordial than had been the case at Alcalá, and no restrictions were placed upon them. Both Borkenau and John were impressed by Grossi, the leader of the column. Borkenau described him as "somewhat crude, but *au fond* very appealing, and certainly he possesses the personal allegiance of his column. He is evidently courageous and, being an Asturias miner, is an old hand at revolution, and knows how to handle the masses psychologically." John, in his essay, described him as "an Oviedo miner under sentence of death at the time of the elections, [who] though he may be both reckless and theatrical, is without question a sincere and courageous revolutionary with a mass following". Yet however admirable he might be as a revolutionary, as a leader of militia he was not without defects: "he is deficient as an organizer, and has no conception of the job of warfare. There is obvious rivalry between him and his military adviser. This is a very common state of affairs, which of course results in a considerable amount of disorder." They had evidence of this soon after they arrived, when Grossi arranged for the relief of the advance guards. (They had been on duty for five days—without relief—on the hills about a half mile ahead of the village.) "The whole column, consisting of four *centurias* (hundreds) was summoned to the Plaza, and Grossi addressed them with a short speech from a balcony, saying that things must be put in better order, and that the advance guards should now be relieved. One hour later he himself led the relief and stayed out with them for a whole night." But the ceremony as performed was "more picturesque than military. There was not the slightest sign of military discipline, not even a serious attempt to form orderly ranks . . . What is worse, there is evidently not the slightest attempt to get this incoherent mass organized, disciplined, and trained." And indeed, a degree of chaos and disorganization was a constant of life in the P.O.U.M. militia. What John saw that first day in Lecineña was a fair sample, confirmed by his later experience, and when he was writing an analysis of the situation, he offered as his considered judgment that the P.O.U.M. militia were "disgracefully organized".

Yet the very absence of conventional military discipline led to a kind of gaiety and excitement. In John's diary there occurs the notation, "dances", referring to the time he and Borkenau spent in the tavern. There, among the militia-men, they saw the one militia woman of the column, who had followed her lover to the front. "She was very good-looking," Borkenau wrote, "but no special attention was given her by the militia-men, for all of them knew that she was bound to her lover by a link which is regarded among the revolutionaries as equivalent to marriage. Every single militia-man, however, was visibly proud of her for the courage she seems to have displayed in staying in an advanced position under fire for many hours with only two companions. 'Was it an unpleasant experience?' I asked. 'No, solo me da el enthusiasmo' ('To me it is only inspiring') replied the girl with shining eyes: and from her whole bearing I believed her. There was nothing awkward about her position among the men. One of them who was playing an accordion started *La Cucaracha*, and she immediately began movements of the dance, the others joining in the song. When this interlude was over, she was again just a comrade among them."[9]

The atmosphere must have been charged with excitement for John: to be in the midst of a revolutionary army, an army of comrades, drawn from the working classes, endangered by the Fascist enemy. And to know that if he wanted, he could enlist here, at the front, simply on the strength of his party card—to stay a few days, fire a few shots . . .

Borkenau's entry in his diary for August 14 concluded: "We arrived in Barcelona late at night, with the exception of Mr J. Cornford, who had enlisted in Lecineña."

He had enlisted in the militia of the P.O.U.M. quite impulsively—there is no reference in Borkenau that this had been John's intention, nor in his own diary that he had discussed the matter with Major Farrar at Fraga or been stirred to action when they visited the first P.O.U.M. column at Alcalá de Obispo. At Lecineña he had been at the appropriate pitch of exhilaration and curiosity to act, and that mood sustained him through the remainder of the day and evening after Borkenau and the man from *Flèche* said goodbye to him and started back on the return journey to Barcelona. In the column he met a "little Italian" who could speak a few words of broken English, and they carried on a conversation of a sort—memorable enough for him to make a note of it in his diary, as was the "peasant hospitality" later. But in the morning his mood had changed. Loneliness, isolation and boredom weighed heavily upon him. For the next three days he suffered from a depression blacker and more pervasive than any he had experienced before—even the traditional first days of school—or would ever experience again.

Lecineña had been taken by the column under Grossi in a surprise night attack early in the preceding week. Since then their military activity had been of the most desultory and limited kind. Presumably an offensive was being readied by the Political Committee, the next stage of the P.O.U.M. advance towards Saragossa; supplies were being assembled; and Grossi saw to it that a constant watch was maintained, though the guard roster was erratically ordered, some men being on duty for as long as five nights running before being relieved. John, on his first morning as a soldier, was one of a group assigned to guard duty in the hills a half-mile beyond the town. Beyond these outposts, across the valley and clearly visible, was the village of Perdiguera, held by the enemy.

Unfortunately for John, the "little Italian" was not one of the group, and so there was no one to whom he could talk, except a young Catalan who spoke a few words of broken French; his isolation was now complete. There was nothing to do but watch and wait, watch and wait, under the scorching sun. He had nothing to read, nothing to distract him. "So long as I am doing anything, however purposeless, I feel fine. It's inactivity that just eats at my nerves." This quotation comes from the long letter he started to write to Margot (and that appears in the memorial volume as 'Diary Letter from Aragon') on the afternoon of his third full day in the militia. He had come out to Spain intending to look round, and then to join her—only a few days hence—in the South of France: instead, he had joined the militia. Why? The letter is meant to serve as an explanation—she was the only person now to whom he would feel a need to explain his actions and who he felt certain would understand them—it is also meant to serve as a record of his life in the militia, an amplification of the notes in his diary.

"Darling," he begins, "I'll explain why in a minute, but just at the moment I'm spending whole days at the front with nothing to do, and so I am writing you an immense letter: if it wasn't so hot here I'd try and get my ideas and impressions sorted out, but I can't, so I'm writing everything down just as it comes out."

(This helter-skelter method of putting it all down accounts for much that is vivid in the letter; it also accounts for much that is confusing. For example, the word "yesterday" appears a number of times, but it is not always the same "yesterday" that is being referred to. Comparing the letter and the entries in the diary, one can manage to work out a chronology absent from the letter itself, which was written in instalments of two or three days each, with an interval of a few days between.)

"First of all, a last will and testament. As you know there is a risk of being killed. Statistically not very great, but it exists all the same. First of all, why am I here? You know the political reasons." He felt no need to spell them out, they would have been obvious to them both—that the Spanish working classes were fighting a war against Fascism. But there was another reason. "There's a subjective one as well. From the age of seventeen [he was now twenty] I was in a kind of way tied down, and envied my contemporaries a good deal their freedom to bum about. And it was partly because I felt myself for the first time independent that I came out here."

His father, writing soon after John's death, felt that he had found in Spain an escape from "personal responsibilities".[10] And there can be no doubt, given the circumstances—that he was in Spain alone that August, and on his own really for the first time in years—that the temptation to "bum about" must have indeed been strong. Yet one must be careful to distinguish—as Professor Cornford, writing in haste, did not—between John's two journeys to Spain. The second time he went, he knew very well why he was going and what he was going to do, and it was in no sense "to escape". The first time, however, his enlistment in the militia did have about it an air of recklessness, as though he had seized upon the chance for once to do exactly what *he* wanted, without thought of others. Not that he did not feel some uneasiness where Margot was concerned: he knew that she would not reproach him, that she would understand what he had done, which only made him the more eager to reassure her about their future. "I promise this is the last time I shall leave you unnecessarily. May be that the Party will send me, but after this I will always be with you when I have the chance."

"Well, all that's said," he commented, with a deceptive briskness. Presumably now he was ready to tell her the decisive fact: that he had enlisted in the militia. But, "writing everything down just as it comes out", he could not bring himself to it quite yet. Instead:

> At the moment I am on top of a hill at the front in Aragon. A complete circle of rocky mountains, covered with green scrub, very barren, with a few fields in between. Two kilometres away a village held by the enemy. A grey stone affair with a big church. The enemy are quite invisible. An occasional rifle shot. One burst of machine-gun fire. One or two aeroplanes. The sound of our guns sometimes a long way off. And nothing else but a sun so hot that I am almost ill, can eat very little, and scarcely work at all. Nothing at all to do. We lie around all day. At night two hours on the watch—last night very fine with the lightning flickering behind Saragossa, miles away. Sleeping in the open with a single blanket on the stones—last night it rained, but just not quite enough to get through the blanket. How long we are to be here I don't know.

But what he had been staving off could no longer be unmentioned: "And now comes the catch—I came up to the front and Richard was left behind. Enlisted here on the strength of my party card." And once that painful truth had been blurted out he could go on to write of himself without reserve:

> There was one little Italian comrade with some broken English. Now he's been sent off. So I'm here and the only communication I have is with the very broken French of a young Catalan volunteer. And so I am not only utterly lonely, but also feel a bit useless. However it couldn't have been expected that everything would go perfectly as it did to here. This loneliness, and this nervous anxiety from not knowing when or how to get back, and not yet having been under fire, means that inevitably I am pretty depressed. Even thought of using my press ticket

to get home, but it would be too ridiculous to come out here to fight and go back because I was a bit lonely. So I am here provisionally until the fall of Saragossa whenever that is . . .

In the morning—it was a Sunday—before it was yet hot, the bells of the enemy village of Perdiguera sounded very slow and mournful across the distance. I don't know why, but that depressed me as much as anything ever has. However, I'm settling in now. Last night we began to make ourselves comfortable—dug little trenches to sleep in and filled them with straw. So long as I am doing anything, however purposeless, I feel fine. It's inactivity that just eats at my nerves. But the night before last I had a dream. One of the toughest people when I was small at school was the captain of rugger, an oaf called D—. I was in the same dormitory and terrified of him. I hadn't thought of him for years, but last night I dreamt extremely vividly about having a fight with him, and holding my own, and I think that's a good omen. I don't know how long we stay on this hill, but I'm beginning to settle down to it.

Merely to write "everything down" about what he felt had, as it so often does, the effect of making him more cheerful. Presently, John being John, he was writing "a bit about the political situation", although "that isn't easy to get straight, particularly as I haven't yet heard anyone explain the position of the Party". This was to be a constant complaint, the more vexing the longer he was out of touch. Parenthetically he remarked that "the militia here I am with are P.O.U.M.—left sectarian semi-Trotskyists"—his only mention of an incongruity he did not feel called upon to explain—and went briskly on to the facts of the situation. He drew upon what information he had been able to gather in Barcelona, and, even more, what he had been told by Borkenau. But his interpretation is entirely his own, and consistent with the views set forth in his earlier essays, and indeed on the crucial point he would never waver: that the revolution, to be successful, must be in the control of the party. He accepted that the majority of the workers in Catalonia were Anarchists, and hence, the "most urgent task" for the party was to win them over. Instead of doing this, though, he was afraid that the party might be "a little too mechanical in its application of People's Front tactics. It is still concentrating too much on trying to neutralise the petty bourgeoisie . . . But I don't really know."

The next morning, Monday, the group was relieved and returned to the town. John brought the letter with him, intending to add to it—in any event, it could not be dispatched until someone from the column was going to Barcelona. That day he shaved, and attended a meeting of the Political Committee, although it is unlikely that he could have understood much of its proceedings. The next day he embarked upon German lessons with one of the foreign volunteers in the column, a man named Gerard, and, since there were no dictionaries to be had, with characteristic thoroughness he covered several pages in the diary with lists of vocabulary. There were a number of German and German-speaking comrades in the column, and he was anxious to talk with them, as they were friendly, interesting, and in some respects challenging—one of them, Sebastian, a fat Roumanian, was prepared to hold forth on "the crimes of the popular front", from which the P.O.U.M., as well as the Anarchists, held themselves aloof. But John, even with his German lesson, was hardly in a position to comprehend, let alone contradict, his argument. As it happened, this day, Tuesday, marked a turning point in his feelings. The meeting with the Germans was itself enlivening; and so too was the prospect of military action that began to take shape. The Column was summoned to the Plaza to prepare for an attack. Before they marched out of the town, John in great excitement scribbled a wry message across the top of the last page he had reached in his letter to Margot: "Going into action. Thank God for something to do at last. I shall fight like a Communist if not like a soldier. All my love. Salute."

The next day, resuming the letter, he explained: "We went out to attack, and the prospect of action was terribly exhilarating—hence the message on the top of the page. But in the end we went back without doing anything." He is more succinct in the diary: "the 'attack' that wasn't".

The tone of this second instalment of the letter is markedly different from the first: as he put it himself, "Up till now this letter has been very miserable." Meanwhile he had faced up to the situation: "I came out with the intention of staying a few days, firing a few shots and then coming home. Sounded fine, but you just can't do things like that. You can't play at civil war, or fight with a reservation you don't mean to get killed. It didn't take long to realise that either I was here in earnest or else I'd better clear out. I tried to avoid the dilemma. Then I felt so lonely and bad I tried to get a pass back to Barcelona. But the question was decided for me. Having joined in, I am in whether I like it or not. And I like it."

Together, meeting the German comrades and the prospect of action had worked to restore him to himself:

> I've got a kind of feeling, rather difficult to explain, that my personality, I myself, [is] beginning to assert itself again. For days I've been shoved about from place to place, lost and anxious and frightened, and all that distinguished me personally from a unit in the mass, obliterated—just a unit, alternately worried, homesick, anxious, calm, hungry, sleepy, uncomfortable in turn—and all my own individuality, such strength as I have, such ability to analyse things, submerged. Now that's beginning to be different, I am beginning to adapt. Probably I'll be swept off my feet again when the first action starts. But now I, John Cornford, am beginning to emerge above the surface again and recognize myself and enjoy myself, and it feels good.

Emerging above the surface, he was able to write with detachment of the people's army in which he was serving: "a curious mixture of amateur and professional. There is practically no shouting and saluting. When somebody is told to do something, he gets up to do it all right, but not in a hurry. Officers are elected by acclamation, and obeyed. About half the troops are more or less in uniform, in blue or brown overalls and blue shirts. The rest are more or less nondescript." John himself wore "a pair of heavy, black, corduroy trousers (expropriated from the bourgeoisie), a blue sports shirt, and that alpaca coat, rope-soled sandals, and an infinitely battered old sombrero. Luggage, a blanket, a cartridge case (held together with a string) in which there is room for a spare shirt, a knife, toothbrush, bit of soap and comb. Also a big tin mug stuck in my belt."

Summing up, he looked within himself:

> What is new is the complete feeling of insecurity, new for me, but most workers have it from the day they leave school.

Always in all my work before there has been the background of a secure and well-provided home, and friends that I could fall back upon in an emergency. Now that is no longer here, I stand completely on my own. And I find that rather difficult at first. But I shall manage. Just now, for instance, I have unlimited opportunity to write. And I have plenty of things which for years I've wanted to write. But I can't get them together in my head, things aren't straight enough: all I can put down are my immediate subjective impressions, and I can't think about Birmingham or anywhere else. Oh, for the objectivity of a Nehru. I'll learn: I am learning. But it's going to be something of a testing-time.

At this point, as we can deduce from internal evidence within the letter itself and from the diary, he broke off, and he did not return to the letter until two days later. In the meantime he had had a first taste of action, and an opportunity to see how an army such as he had described would function under fire. It was possible, of course, that officers elected by acclamation might not only be likeable, but prove to have a fair grasp of military strategy, just as it was also possible that a Political Committee might be able to draw up a battle plan. John had attended two meetings of the Political Committee but he had had to cope with the language problem—as he wrote of one such episode, "by now I am getting very used to listening to conversations of which I don't understand a word"—and he was under the impression that a night attack had been planned. At least the objective was clear enough: the village of Perdiguera. On Wednesday night the column gathered in the plaza, and was kept waiting there for an hour or two—it was the familiar army story of 'hurry up and wait'—and John fell asleep twice on the pavement. ("That morning I had decided that so little was happening, and we were getting so much sleep at night, I wouldn't sleep any more during the day.") Finally, they marched off, but soon had halted on the road, and again he fell asleep. Then the march was resumed. "Even then," he wrote, when he continued with the letter later that week, "the indiscipline of our troops struck me. Everyone was whispering, and then everyone would suddenly start shushing and altogether there was quite a noise." But he also noted in the diary that there was "no grumbling". After some distance they left the road, and turned off into the mountains, marching all night "across the little, banked-up strips of field they have in Aragon, through stubble . . . Then gradually it began to get light and I realised that this wasn't a night attack at all. Then far below us on the right we saw the lights of Saragossa. After that we halted for a bit, and a comrade pointed out to me Perdiguera miles below. I had no idea we had climbed so high. Then at last I understood the manœuvre. By a night's march through the mountains we had got completely in the rear of the enemy."

The position was auspicious, but the attack proved a failure. At dawn the advance began. The column was divided into groups, which almost at once began to intermingle: this was only the first confusion.

> Our single column spread out like a fan over the parched earth of the field and we began to move quickly. I threw away the blanket I had carried all night for it was already hot. Then we came over the ridge in sight of the enemy, and at the same time heard an attack open up on the other side of the village. We moved forwards and were soon crouching in the vineyards a few hundred yards from the village, and for the first time heard shot whistling overhead.

John, unlike Julian Bell, was not a student of military strategy, but he had played war games in the dunes on the Norfolk coast, and he was blessed with common sense: he recognized that what ought to be done was not being done. With no one effectively in control, the soldiers were engaged in a fine, anarchic shooting-match:

> It was then our total lack of discipline made itself felt. The houses of the village came quite close on the left, but on the right were hidden by a ridge and only the church tower showed. But it seemed clear to me that we should attack to the right, because there was the enemy machine-gun which was holding up our counter-attack. But no such thing. A group of us crossed the fields in front of the vineyards and crouched with good cover below an olive field, the last stretch before reaching the village. Another group dashed off to attack the houses on the left and managed to get right up to them. All this time I hadn't

the faintest idea who was winning or losing. Then I began to understand the planless nature of the attack. The group I was with was recalled back to the vines. There I began to collect the completely unripe grapes in my hands and suck the juice out of them. It didn't do much to relieve thirst, but it left a clean acid taste in the mouth. Then I saw the group which had taken the houses on the left come pouring back and take shelter. All this time I had not felt the least nervousness, but that may be because so far no one had been hit. I was surprised that the kick of my mauser was so slight—I hadn't had a chance of using it before—but all the same I couldn't get it under control . . . I couldn't see any of the enemy, and so confined myself to shooting at doors and windows. Then quite suddenly we heard the noise of enemy planes. We crouched quite still among the vines: I was together with a long Italian, Milano, a member of my group, and did what he did. Apparently the planes didn't notice us. They confined themselves to bombing the other side of Perdiguera, where we were attacking. But after the bombardment our forces were completely dispersed—not out of cowardice, no one was in the least frightened, but simply through lack of leadership, no one had said where to go and all had taken cover in different directions. So Milano decided to retreat, and I followed him. A group of about fourteen collected, and we marched back. Presently we came to a well—a big, open, stone affair about six yards across. On top was floating a dead rat. We stopped for a drink, though Milano said we might be captured because of it. Then, as we were going back, we saw a group of men in the vines and marched back to them. But they weren't many there. I went to sleep for a few minutes in the vines, but was soon woken up and told we should retreat. We retreated to a big stone barn on a slope above the well [where] a discussion was held. At last one comrade, a strong and intelligent-looking worker in overalls, took the initiative and introduced some kind of order. I couldn't understand the discussion, but I made out that a committee of three was being elected to take a decision on what to do. And in the end it was decided to retreat.

The retreat itself—getting back to Lecineña—had its moment of danger at the beginning; thereafter, it was merely exhausting, a test of endurance. John's entries in his diary for his fourteenth day in Spain (August 21) conclude: "The retreat. The well under fire. Milano's footsteps in the hills. The Bombardment. The march back. Water. Pine, cypress, marble." The next day, safely back, he could elaborate upon these notes in his letter to Margot:

> I borrowed a mug off a comrade to go down to the well for a drink. I had a drink and several others followed. (We had been about twenty-five in all in the barn). Then suddenly bullets began to whistle very close—zip-zip-zip. We crouched under the shadow of the stone rim of the well. Then eventually we sprinted up the fields in short bouts, bent double with the bullets all around us. After that we could retreat in peace. We marched back across the fields to the hills. My throat was utterly dry, so thirsty I could not swallow, and hungry and very weary. It was only by a desperate physical effort of the guts that I was able to move one foot after the other. The climb up the mountains was a serious affair because the heat of the sun was colossal. I placed myself behind Milano, who was a mountaineer, and followed as closely as I could the deliberate economy of his footsteps. We reached the top, and in spite of the fiasco I was beginning to feel better. At least, I felt equal to the others, when, before, I had felt rather like a sham soldier . . . Nearing the top the breeze was a real relief, and we came into a pine-wood, the first proper vegetation for days. Then as we came out of the wood we saw some sheds below on the right. We went down to look for water. There was a well and a lame old man sitting by it. We hoisted the water in a leaky bucket. Just to show how thirsty I was, though the bucket was leaking rapidly I was able to fill and empty the cup (⅔ pint) five times before the bucket was empty . . . Then we went off to the barn and slept for three hours. Afterwards the old man put us on to a road, we moved slowly down, at his cripple's pace, through cypress woods, past those barren strips of climbing fields, past great slabs of marble sticking out of the hills, stopping at every well to drink. The worst was over. The rest was down hill. When we reached the first outpost we learned that five men had been killed in the frontal attack that day. Then home, past the big amphitheatre round the stagnant village pond with its

green reeds, past the bare strip of earth which was a football ground, and back into Lecineña.

The attack on Perdiguera had been a fiasco, but John had gained a great deal from this first experience of battle: he no longer felt himself a sham soldier, and, as he wrote to Margot, "After having seen all the mistakes in organisation, all the inefficiency, and yet the revolution is winning, I think I shall have far more confidence in my own organising ability in such a situation." To which he added optimistically, "There are a whole lot of things I think I could do if I understood the language." But since he did not understand it, there was little he could do but meditate, make notes in his diary, continue his letter to Margot, and otherwise fall into the routine of a soldier who has time to kill. "How to pass the day—I wash my shirt." The next entry reads, "the grammar", which would suggest another German lesson—perhaps from Sebastian, the fat Roumanian. In any event he did have a discussion with Sebastian about "organisation".

That night he was one of a group that was moved by lorry to an abandoned monastery a few miles further along the road to Huesca. Presumably a new attack in a new direction was being prepared, but John was preoccupied with the earlier failure at Perdiguera. In the diary he entered an unsparing "Note on military position", based upon what he had experienced and observed in this column of P.O.U.M. militia. Even if the "revolution" appeared to be winning, there remained a question of the "duration of war". How could it be fought to a successful conclusion when the militia was hamstrung by "incompetence" and "lack of technicians, of discipline, of training, of intermediate officers"? From these bleak general observations he went on to consider specifically "How the attack should have been made." His points, set against the full account he gave in the letter, are clear enough, even in this compressed form:

(1) Exploration the road
(2) Water & machine guns
(3) Cut the road
(4) definite groups, objectives, commands.

And he concluded with a reference to "the machine gun on the right" which no one had attempted to put out of action. The very fact that John was not a military expert, but was simply exercising his common sense and powers of observation, makes his indictment the more devastating. The attack had not failed on abstruse points of generalship, or on an inequality of men and arms, but on the most rudimentary considerations of tactics and preparation.

The next day John wrote to Harry Pollitt, the head of the party in London, perhaps only to acquaint him with his whereabouts, but perhaps also to inform him of the realities of the military situation, about which Pollitt would have learned little from the propaganda being issued in Barcelona.[11] Each political party had its own newspaper in which were reported the continuing victories of its own militia. As John remarked caustically to Margot, "Today I found with interest but not surprise the distortions in the P.O.U.M. press. The fiasco of the attack on Perdiguera is presented as a punitive expedition which was a success."

It was John's good fortune—what he called "the luckiest accident of the whole war"—that among the group stationed at the monastery were five "German comrades", some of whom could speak English, and so he could talk with them, have the kind of political discussion upon which he thrived. It made a considerable difference. On August 23, his sixteenth day in Spain, he noted with clinical interest: "Loneliness partly over," and on the 25th, "Return of enthusiasm." Looking back, it seemed to him that "the days spent in the village alone were the hardest I have yet spent in my whole life. It was the same loneliness and isolation as the first term in a new school, without the language and without any kind of distraction of something to do . . . But the Germans are a splendid lot—and incidentally have treated me with a quite extraordinary personal kindness; and at last I can live in the present, get outside of my own mind, and carry on until it is time to go back. I was never more glad of anything in my life than the accident which threw me together with them."

There was a curious fact about the German comrades to be reported, which perhaps explained their being in the militia of the P.O.U.M. "Four of them are ex-members of the party; one still a member. They left because they genuinely believe the C.I. has deserted the revolution. Partly, perhaps, it is the uprootedness of emigrants. I do not know enough of the Spanish position to argue with them successfully." Nor had he solved the "language difficulty". In the diary he noted: "Political discussion in three languages." One wonders, though, how much he got from it, or how closely he followed the arguments of "The Stalinist (Emile) & the P.O.U.M. members." In any event, the equivocal status of the German comrades—revolutionaries *outside* the party, and hence adrift, of doubtful use to the revolution—only served to strengthen him in his own allegiance: "I am beginning to find out how much the Party and the International have become flesh and blood of me. Even when I can put forward no rational argument, I feel that to cut adrift from the Party is the beginning of political suicide." The pity of it was that the Germans were "the finest people in some ways I've ever met. In a way they have lost everything, have been through enough to break most people, and remain strong and cheerful and humorous. If anything is revolutionary it is these comrades." Or, as he put it in the diary, "I recognize the revolution in individuals." Paradoxically, it was they, ex-members of the party, who had made him feel like a revolutionary again. "Before, I was too lost to feel anything but lost," he told Margot. "Now I'll fight like hell and I think I'll enjoy it."

The opportunity to fight seemed at hand the next day. "Again into action for the attack on Huesca," he wrote expectantly. It was time to bring the letter to a close—suppose he should not survive this new, more ambitious attack? Rounding off his account, he was at pains to reassure her that all was well with him: "So far there has been no fighting in this advance, and [I have been] only under an inaccurate rifle fire for a few minutes. And I am now rested and fed, and feeling happy and content. All I want is some English cigarettes, some English tea, strong (insular, but can't be helped)."

Characteristically, the attack did not actually get under way until two days later (August 27) and then it was aimed not at Huesca, but at Perdiguera again. The time between had passed agreeably; the diary entries for August 25 and 26 record a succession of conversations, and a growing intimacy with the German comrades:

> (August 25)—We explore the building. L'affaire Fosco. Time begins to move. Return of enthusiasm. Herbert on the capture of Lecineña. Karl's story.

(August 26)—A german lesson. The peoples front in Germany. The discussion on art. Herbert's escape . . .

Then on the 27th came the shelling of Perdiguera. Contrary to John's expectations, the detachment took no part in the attack, but remained on duty at the monastery to guard against a surprise infiltration by the enemy, coming down the road from Huesca itself. There was the sound of the bombardment in the middle distance; apart from this, the day was uneventful: another German lesson; a discussion of the death penalty. The next day, however, he was violently ill. He had been on guard duty in the morning; afterwards, all at once, he was suffering from "fever, stomach, diarrhoea". He spent the rest of the day stretched out in a dark, empty cell in the monastery, trying to sleep. That night, sick though he was, he went out on guard again. He was paired with Karl, one of the German comrades, with whom he had a "two hours" talk, not of politics but of his wife and daughters, and of much else on that *gemütlich* order, which at least had the virtue of distracting him from his discomfort. In the diary he noted proudly, "I begin to understand German." He also noted the kindness of Karl, who kept pressing wine upon him, so that the pain was gradually blunted, and when his guard turn was finished, he was able to sleep. In the morning he sufficiently recovered for a visit to the near-by village, but it was a tedious day: "Rien que les heures."

The next day came the "order to move". The detachment piled into an expropriated bus and drove all night towards Huesca: "Gasoline. The lights. Discomfort in sleeping." At dawn they arrived at Monte Aragon, a height some five miles from the town; the attack was to be launched there.

Wintringham and other military experts have written disparagingly of the tactics of the P.O.U.M. militia.[12] On the second attempt they had taken Perdiguera, and so were brought closer to Saragossa, their announced objective. Then, quixotically, they called a halt to their successful advance. Quixotically, they turned their attention to Huesca, the other main objective on the Aragon front, about fifty miles from Saragossa, and, like it, never to be taken by the Government. Perdiguera, a village of considerable strategic importance, since it controlled the only road over the rocky Sierra of Alcubierre, was simply abandoned by the P.O.U.M. militia once it was theirs. Defence of the village was left in the hands of the local peasants, and the column roared off to Monte Aragon. (A few weeks later it was re-taken by the Fascists, and its inhabitants were massacred.) There is no doubt that Huesca appeared to be a more vulnerable target than Saragossa, and that the newspapers in Barcelona were calling for victories: this may well account for the change in tactics, as Wintringham suggests. That Grossi and his column would do whatever he wished, without pausing to consult other militias in the area, is not unlikely. Despite the Central Militias committee in Barcelona, and the command in the field of Colonel Villalba, who was stationed in Barbastro, thirty-five miles from Huesca on the road to Lerida, liaison was more a fiction than a reality of the front. The P.S.U.C. had a column operating in this area; so too did the Anarchists, the famous column of Durutti; and there were the two P.O.U.M. columns. Add to them some regular soldiers, keep in mind that no group was eager to co-operate with any other, and one can imagine the prevailing confusion—or worse. (Hugh Thomas tells of a P.S.U.C. lorry that was carrying loot from the front to Barcelona. It was stopped on the road by soldiers of the P.O.U.M., who shot the guards as robbers and sent them back in coffins to the headquarters of the P.S.U.C. at Tardienta.[13])

John had been twelve days on the Saragossa Front, and he was to spend approximately as long a period on this new front—what he called "the last mile to Huesca"—but the record of what happened to him there is necessarily less detailed than before: he did not have enough opportunities to resume the diary-letter to Margot, and we must depend for immediate documentation upon the jottings in his diary. These make it evident that there was much more military action on the Huesca front than he had previously experienced: not a single attack and withdrawal such as he had participated in at Perdiguera, but a prolonged, hard-fought, and ultimately indecisive campaign. At the beginning it must have seemed as if Huesca was closer to surrender than Saragossa had ever been, for the P.O.U.M. column, starting out in the morning from Monte Aragon, by nightfall was virtually at its doorstep. In 'The Situation in Catalonia', John described their entering the tiny stone village of Tierz, the last before Huesca, a distance of only five kilometres from it. "One of the things I remember most vividly is how, when we marched into Tierz . . . in spite of the fact that they had been deluged with stories of rape and atrocity by the retreating Fascists, the villagers came out of the Market Square to welcome us, and took us off to their houses where they had ready prepared meals and beds in the straw."

The diary entry for the first day at the Huesca front, August 31, begins at dawn with the "arrival" at Monte Aragon. They left their blankets and other gear in the bus, and moved out into early morning light. (The "energy candy", issued to them the night before, was eaten up almost at once—before it was really needed, and hence, "wasted".) Advancing like "guerillas over the ploughland" —which was alternately "wet & dry"—they entered the woods and continued forward, still undetected. So far there had been no sign of the enemy. Then: "Firing. Aircraft. The shrapnel cloudlets . . . Advance & halt. The machine guns on donkeys . . . Heavy bombardment." They continued to advance, climbing up hill, and coming into open country again. "Under fire over the ploughland. The first view of Huesca. Descent amongst the ripe grapes. Down the stream. A halt. The road winds across Huesca." And while they halted, he considered the vegetation: "Beetroot? weeds, greener." Soon it was time to be on the move again: all day they pressed steadily forward. At nightfall they marched into Tierz. "Rice, water, cooked meat. Sleep in the rich hay." Later that night while he was on guard duty there was a "false alarm"; in the darkness he heard "machine gun echoes".

So ended the first day. The next day, September 1, the enemy was in retreat, withdrawing into the town; there, however, they held firm, and they were not to be dislodged. In the diary John noted: "Breakfast. Two prisoners. A man killed. The grapes. The duck. Sleep." Later in the day the attack was resumed. "The enemy bombardment. Guns on the hill. First sight of troops in retreat. Firing from behind the wall." Then a period of quiet: "the mosquito-ridden night". In the silence he listened to the sound of "trains behind Huesca", coming into the town, and he wondered, "Has the attack been bungled?"

Thereafter it was a stalemate, with the P.O.U.M. column in Tierz, and the Fascists in Huesca, and the fighting continuing but without achieving a change in position. The diary alternates between periods of calm and violence. On September 2, "a dull morning"; then, "the village bombardment". September 3: "A dull day." He might have been in the abandoned monastery again. There were German songs to be learnt and sung, and the political discussions and speculations were resumed. The night before, on guard, he had asked himself, "Will they attack?" That night, on guard again, the enemy was "Mosquito!" But at dawn there was a surprise attack which cut the road. And the next day there was another bombardment of the village. There were bursting fragments of steel in the air. The house where John and the German comrades had discussed "the psychology of fear" and "the advantage of the limited view" was hit by shells. At once he posed a mock topic for discussion: "Is it a gigantic experiment to show organic connection between positive content of bourgeois democracy & the Soviet Revolution?" So much for ideological considerations when one was being shelled! No one in the house had been hurt, though, and in spite of the bombardment, the position had not been materially altered for either side. John's note continues: "The road occupied . . . We talk to the prisoners. A good meal with coffee. No Tobacco all day."

For the next few days the stalemate continued; Huesca had not been taken, and no new attack was launched. The principal military activity of the column was to guard their prisoners, whose numbers grew each day as more and more deserters kept coming over from the Fascist lines. But the heat of summer was suddenly at an end, and the conditions of life became more arduous. John recorded: "The first cold night. Insects on the floor." Having no duties but an occasional turn on guard, he over-ate, meditated on "Food and bureaucracy" (the next day he noted "Two hours wait for the meat"), read *La Batalla*, the P.O.U.M. newspaper, discussed the military position with Herbert, one of the German comrades, and made notes in his diary for what was to become 'The Situation in Catalonia'. After the last of these notes he drew a line, then wrote: "English Self Importance diminishes to froth—you can't play at revolution."

On the night of September 7 there were ominous signs that all was not well with him: "Asleep! by the shit house. Beginning of sickness." Yet he refused to give in to it, and went out to stand guard as usual. The next day, however, September 8, was a day of horror. He came down with the same acute stomach disorder as before, and a high fever. His gun was stolen. He was so ill that it became evident he would have to be hospitalized. The diary entry for that day reads: "Gun stolen. Sick. Lie all day indoors. No guard." The next morning he was in great pain. Waiting to be moved, he lay stretched out on a mattress. The German comrades came to say goodbye: "Walter consoles. Herbert's vino." He was carried out to the truck, and "the worst bit" was the ride back to Serineña, where a hospital had been improvised for the militia and put in the charge of a local doctor. The precise nature of John's illness has never been established; at the least it was disabling, and he suffered a few truly difficult days. On September 10, he began to "feel better". He was given a bath; Richard came out to visit him from Barcelona—"I talk all day." At last he could have "news of the C.P.". And he even insisted upon doing "some stretcher bearing"—characteristically, for he would not let illness stop him doing what he could to be useful. In a burst of high spirits, he concluded: "Vive la revolution. I can eat & shit." But in fact he was still quite ill, and his diary entry for the next day reads simply: "The deadly day at Serineña." On September 12 he was well enough to be moved to Lerida; and on the next day, his thirty-seventh day in Spain, he was back in Barcelona, still a part of the P.O.U.M. column, still ill. Wintringham found him "ill with fever and exhausted", and about to be sent back to England.[14] His first journey to Spain was at an end.

The most enduring result of John's journey to Spain was the poetry it inspired: three poems, the first after a long silence, and, so far as we have been able to determine, the last he was ever to write, belong to this time, September 1936. Two of the poems were written while he was at the Huesca front; the third after his discharge from the hospital, very likely in Barcelona, but possibly a little later, upon his return to London. Published for the first time after his death—in *Left Review* and in *New Writing*—and anthologized and referred to with some frequency since—they are counted justly among the memorable poems of the Spanish Civil

War. They are also of unusual autobiographical interest: a kind of summing-up and intensification of the 'raw material' recorded in the diary and elaborated in his letter to Margot.

In the diary for September 2, after "The village bombardment" he noted "A poem", and then "On guard at the Fascist house". That day too he turned almost to the end of the diary, many months beyond the consecutive daily notations, and proceeded to fill five pages with poetry. At the top of the first of these pages he wrote "2 Sept Tierz". Then, in pencil and leaving no space between lines, he began:

> Here in the barren hills of Aragon
> This month our testing is begun.
> Here what VII Congress said
> If true, if false, is live or dead,
> Speaks in the Oviedo mauser's tone.

This, with revisions also indicated in the diary ("*All round* the barren hills of Aragon/*Announce* our testing has begun") was to become the second stanza of Part 2 of 'Full Moon at Tierz: Before the Storming of Huesca'. (The title is a later addition; in the diary the poem is untitled.) Comparing the first draft (the diary version) with the published poem, one discovers remarkably few textual changes: so few that one can safely assume that John's method of composition was to write the stanzas in his mind, as it were, before setting them down on paper. Line by line, stanza by stanza, he knew what he wanted to say; but of the organization of the poem as a whole he was much less certain. The order of stanzas as they appear in the diary is very different from their order in the poem in its final state.* John himself was responsible for the final arrangement—he attached numbers to the stanzas in the diary—and his task was somehow to yoke together the seemingly disparate ideas (and voices) of the first draft into a logical and significant progression. It might be said that the problem of technique that confronted him as he set to work to give coherent emphasis to what he had written found a symbolic parallel in the

* Thus, the first stanza in the published version is the ninth stanza in the diary; the second stanza, the eighth; and the third, the tenth. Or, taking the poem as it was originally written, the first stanza in the diary became the fifth in the published version; the second, the seventh; and the third, the eighth.

theme of the poem itself: the fusion of "I" with "We", the two voices in which it is written.

'Full Moon at Tierz' is a meditation on the eve of battle by a young Communist who has become a soldier in Spain. He knows that he will be tested in the battle, and that it will be a test, too, for the party in which he fervently believes. Communism was John's spiritual country; not surprisingly, it proves to be an essential element of the poem, determining its thought and inspiring its positive emotions, much as patriotic fervour of a different but analogous kind inspired Rupert Brooke to write '1914'. Three months earlier John had dealt impatiently with a book of verse by an acquaintance: "The poems are too much: Look, I'm a Marxist, but even so I think flowers are beautiful and I can fall in love, etc., without being in any way false. But that seems really to me like for Cézanne to say: 'Look, I'm an impressionist but I'll paint half my pictures pre-Raphaelite just to show you I can.' What I mean is, to be revolutionary means to approach the whole reality there is, which is different and wider than other people's, in a different way. Not just to demonstrate that you are human, although that may be, as it were, a necessary foundation stage." These hasty sentences might serve as a preface for, and even a criticism of 'Full Moon at Tierz', for the whole reality is often lost sight of in abstractions, and the necessary foundation stage is shown to us only belatedly.

The poem begins portentously, in a tone of deliberate impersonality, as though spoken by a seer:

> The past, a glacier, gripped the mountain wall,
> And time was inches, dark was all.
> But here it scales the end of the range,
> The dialectic's point of change,
> Crashes in light and minutes to its fall.

The abstractions and metaphors proliferate, taking us still further from reality and deeper into the visionary world of the seer:

> Time present is a cataract whose force
> Breaks down the banks even at its source
> And history forming in our hand's
> Not plasticine but roaring sands,
> Yet we must swing it to its final course.

And if we ask who we are, we are told, in the final line of this first section, "We are the future. The last fight let us face." But the tone is rigorously impersonal: we have heard only another portentous generalization.

Then, immediately, as the second section begins, a new voice is heard, and the poem comes alive, comes down from "history" to a time and place that John himself knows, not the cataract of "Time present", but Spain, September 2, 1936:

> Where, in the fields of Huesca, the full moon
> Throws shadows clear as daylight's, soon
> The innocence of this quiet plain
> Will fade in sweat and blood, in pain,
> As our decisive hold is lost or won.

When he speaks of "our decisive hold", it is plain statement of military fact; the "we" to be understood here are his comrades and himself, a military unit; although presently the "we" enlarges to include his party:

> All round the barren hills of Aragon
> Announce our testing has begun.
> Here what the Seventh Congress said,
> If true, if false, is live or dead,
> Speaks in the Oviedo mauser's tone . . .
>
> We studied well how to begin this fight,
> Our Maurice Thorez held the light.
> But now . . .

(Abruptly here the "we" is circumscribed; again it will become himself and his comrades at the front.)

> But now by Monte Aragon
> We plunge into the dark alone.
> Earth's newest planet wheeling through the night.

It was the night of September 2, 1936. He was on guard duty. He wondered, "Would they attack?" Stanza after stanza formed in his mind and were written down in the diary. In what became section 3 of the poem, he spoke out directly in his own voice—"the foundation stage"—paraphrasing what he had written earlier in his letter to Margot, and making more evident what he meant when he told her, "the party and the International have become flesh and blood of me".

> Though Communism was my waking time,
> Always before the lights of home
> Shone clear and steady and full in view—
> Here, if you fall, there's help for you—
> Now, with my Party, I stand quite alone.
>
> Then let my private battle with my nerves,
> The fear of pain whose pain survives,
> The love that tears me by the roots,
> The loneliness that claws my guts,
> Fuse in the welded front our fight preserves.

In the final stanzas of the poem, which occupy the same position in the diary version, there is again a change of voice. The fusion he has prayed for has occurred: the "I" has truly become "We":

> Now the same night falls over Germany
> And the impartial beauty of the stars
> Lights from the unfeeling sky
> Oranienburg and freedom's crooked scars.
> We can do nothing to ease that pain
> But prove the agony was not in vain.
>
> England is silent under the same moon,
> From Clydeside to the gutted pits of Wales,
> The innocent mask conceals that soon
> Here, too, our freedom's swaying in the scales.
> O understand before too late
> Freedom was never held without a fight.

One might wish that the poem had ended with these stanzas in which a dignity of language and a beauty of phrasing combine to show John at his most impressive as a poet. But there was a crucial political point to be made, and in order to make it he chose deliberately to sacrifice individuality and subtlety of language to slogans, quotations, and snatches of song—his final lines are from the

Italian '*Bandiera Rossa*'—whatever would emphasize the point boldly, simply and memorably. In effect, it was a rallying cry, based upon what he had already learned in his three weeks at the front, and it would determine his actions when he returned to England in September:

> Freedom is an easily spoken word
> But facts are stubborn things. Here, too, in Spain
> Our fight's not won till the workers of all the world
> Stand by our guard on Huesca's plain
> Swear that our dead fought not in vain,
> Raise the red flag triumphantly
> For Communism and for liberty.

He finished 'Full Moon at Tierz' on the night of September 2, drew a line beneath it, and wrote another poem. Or he may have written this second poem—in its own lyrical fashion as much a final statement or testament as the first—the next morning, before the anticipated attack on Huesca was to get under way. As it happened, September 3 proved to be "a dull day"; the attack did not take place; between German songs and political discussions he may have used the free time to revise the two very different poems he had written under the shadow of the approaching battle. The second of the two, much briefer than 'Full Moon at Tierz' and untitled in the diary, was originally published as 'Poem' in *New Writing*, and then, in the memorial volume, as 'To Margot Heinemann'. It is John's most famous poem:

> Heart of the heartless world,
> Dear heart, the thought of you
> Is the pain at my side,
> The shadow that chills my view.
>
> The wind rises in the evening,
> Reminds that autumn is near.
> I am afraid to lose you,
> I am afraid of my fear.
>
> On the last mile to Huesca,
> The last fence for our pride,

Think so kindly, dear, that I
Sense you at my side.

And if bad luck should lay my strength
Into the shallow grave,
Remember all the good you can;
Don't forget my love.

A legend has grown up over the years that this very simple and beautiful lyric is John Cornford's "last poem". That the legend happens not to be true in no way detracts from the poignancy and sincerity of John's feelings, or the felicity of their expression. Nor does it serve much purpose to emphasize the absence of political content in this poem addressed directly to the woman he loved. Especially since the third of the poems that he wrote in September 1936—and therefore, to the best of our knowledge, his last—'A Letter from Aragon', is as political and committed as the first, 'Full Moon at Tierz'. But it was written (one would guess) less impulsively, less at fever-haste (upon the eve of battle) than its predecessors; and with an irony and preciseness of observation that set it apart.

Since 'A Letter from Aragon' does not appear in the diary, it cannot be as closely dated as 'Full Moon at Tierz' or 'To Margot Heinemann'. But it is explicitly autobiographical, and, taking into account the events it describes, it would seem that, at the very earliest, it might have been written on September 13, the day after his release from the hospital at Sérineña. But this is most unlikely. Given his numbed state in Barcelona, as described by Wintringham, and given the fact that the poem is not in the diary (which does include late notes on strategy and recruiting), and given the nature of the poem itself, a recollection of happenings that have been considered and deliberated on, it seems far more likely that 'A Letter from Aragon' was written when John was on the point of departure, not from the front, but from Spain itself.

The poem, written in free verse, begins with the statement, "This is a quiet sector of a quiet front", which will be repeated at intervals thereafter as an ironic refrain or chorus. Meanwhile we are shown four vignettes of life on the "quiet sector". Two are based upon John's experiences in Tierz; two upon his experiences in the hospital in Serineña. He was too ill to record the latter when they occurred; but the former are to be found, briefly noted, in the diary for September 2, that extraordinary day when John was not writing poems but living them. Here now is the entire entry for that day:

> Night. A dull morning. The excursion before lunch. Shells. Women in panic. The funeral in the rubbish dump. Walter's photo. The village bombarded. A poem. On guard at the Fascist house. Will they attack? The meal & arguments.

From these details, two are selected for the poem.

First, "The funeral in the rubbish dump". This becomes:

> We buried Ruiz in a new pine coffin,
> But the shroud was too small and his washed feet
> stuck out.
> The stink of his corpse came through the clean pine
> boards
> And some of the bearers wrapped handkerchiefs
> round their faces.
> Death was not dignified.
> We hacked a ragged grave in the unfriendly earth
> And fired a ragged volley over the grave.

Second, "Shells. Women in panic", which becomes:

> But when they shelled the other end of the village
> And the streets were choked with dust
> Women came screaming out of the crumbling houses,
> Clutched under one arm the naked rump of an infant.
> I thought: how ugly fear is.

For a third time the refrain is sounded: "This is a quiet sector of a quiet front." The irony deepens: "Our nerves are steady; we all sleep soundly." And without transition:

> In the clean hospital bed my eyes were so heavy
> Sleep easily blotted out one ugly picture,
> A wounded militiaman moaning on a stretcher,
> Now out of danger, but still crying for water,
> Strong against death, but unprepared for such pain.

Then the refrain once more, but shortened: simply—

This on a quiet front.

Death is undignified; fear is ugly; pain, intolerable. Yet it is not the whole reality of this war:

> But when I shook hands to leave, an Anarchist worker
> Said: "Tell the workers of England
> This was a war not of our own making,
> We did not seek it . . ."

There is a dramatic appropriateness in this conclusion, very different from the exhortations of 'Full Moon at Tierz'. A Spanish worker speaking to a young Englishman who has come to take part in the struggle is allowed to be grandiloquent. The splendid sentiments (or slogans) in their rising and falling cadences have the power to move us still:

> . . . "Tell the workers of England
> This was a war not of our own making,
> We did not seek it.
> But if ever the Fascists again rule Barcelona
> It will be as a heap of ruins with us workers beneath it."

On September 12, John was thought to have recovered sufficiently to be released from the hospital. But he was still very weak, exhausted and feverish, and in no condition to be returned to duty as a rifleman at the front. Accordingly, he was sent from Serineña to Barcelona, to the headquarters of the Anti-Fascist Militias, where his immediate future would be determined. There seems to have been no thought given there to terminating his enlistment, nor did he request it. He was still in the militia, and as much committed to the cause as he had ever been. Yet it was out of the question for him to rejoin the column under Grossi at Tierz. Finally it was decided that he should return to England for a three weeks' leave—not, however, the traditional convalescent leave one would expect in the circumstances, but what he himself called "a special propaganda mission".

There is no diary entry at all—the preceding day's had been simply "Barcelona"—for his thirty-eighth and last day in Spain, September 14. No doubt he had too much else to do, arranging for his departure later that day, which proved to be uneventful. Equipped with the right papers, he had as little difficulty in leaving the country as he had had in entering it five weeks before. The next morning he was in France. There, at 5 a.m. in the railway station in Toulouse, he wrote to his father. (After his death, Professor Cornford labelled this "John's last letter to me Sept 15 or 16, 1936".)

> Dear Dadda—I've written to you several times from Spain, but I'm rather afraid because I've had no replies, that nothing has been getting through. So I'm afraid you may have been anxious about where I am. After I left you in Cambridge the idea suddenly occurred to me to go to Spain for a few days. I expected at that time that the fighting would be over very soon: so in a tremendous hurry I got a letter of introduction from the *News Chronicle* and set out. After I had been three days in Barcelona it was clear, first, how serious the position was: second, that a journalist without a word of Spanish was just useless. I decided to join the militia: and wrote you at once, but I'm terribly afraid that owing to censorship troubles nothing in English or German from the front has got through. I haven't yet been discharged from the militia, but have been sent back for a period of 3 weeks on a special propaganda mission: but I'll be able to talk over the whole position with you as soon as I am back. Had a fairly quiet month on the Saragossa and Huesca fronts, actively did only a little skirmishing; passively, was bombarded a bit, but only with fairly light artillery and air bombs. On that sector it is more an endurance test than anything else.
>
> I hope you haven't been too much worried about me. Give my love to Hugh and Clare, if they aren't yet back at school. I hope it's been a good holiday.
>
> Yours very affectionately
> John

The "special propaganda mission"—which almost certainly John proposed to his superiors in the militia, rather than they to him—was that he should recruit a group of volunteers in England

and return with them to Spain to fight for the Republic. The idea did not spring suddenly into being on that last day in Barcelona; it had been taking shape in his mind ever since the botched attack on Perdiguera, on August 20. His subsequent experience had only strengthened him in his conviction that the fighting columns in Aragon, loosely organized in principle and chaotically disorganized in practice, needed, more than anything else, an example of small, disciplined formations under proper command. To his superiors in Barcelona he would have spoken of this in tactful generalities; it would hardly have done to point out to them that as military strategists, disciplinarians and organizers he thought them deplorable. At headquarters the appeal must have been phrased rather like the concluding lines of 'Full Moon at Tierz'—he would bring back his English comrades to fight "for Communism and for liberty". But when he was on leave in England he explained his idea in all its ramifications to his friend Andrew Knight,* whom he had known at Cambridge, and Knight was so impressed by it that he immediately volunteered for the group that John was taking to Spain. As Knight has recently recalled, part of John's idea was "simply that this group, by among other things, shaving every morning, and of course more importantly acting as a disciplined formation, would give some kind of example to the extremely irregular levies that were then fighting the war". This was the special propaganda mission that brought John home to England.

He arrived on September 16, and during the next three weeks he was only seldom at rest. He saw, fleetingly, a large number of people, each of whom seems to have taken a different impression of him. Hence the apparent contradictions: that he was elated, that he was depressed, that he was enthusiastic, that he was resigned, and much else besides. Since he was not an automaton or a poster hero, he might well have been all these things without inconsistency. It was a time when he was living under extraordinary pressure; he had had a hard month of battle and illness, from which he was not entirely recovered; he knew that he was returning to danger and the possibility of being killed. Under the circumstances, an unremitting cheerfulness might seem a kind of idiocy: at the least, mere callousness. Of course, impressions of

* A pseudonym.

what afterwards proves to have been a last meeting are bound to be highly subjective. As one might expect, the impressions formed by those whom John was leaving behind in England, to whom in effect he was paying a series of farewell visits, are more likely to strike a note of melancholy and fatality than do those of the young men who were going out with him to Spain. Andrew Knight, for example, emphasizes John's "great enthusiasm" and "great optimism", and so too does the novelist John Sommerfield, another of the group, both in his contemporary account, *Volunteer in Spain*, which was dedicated to John's memory, and in recollections some twenty-eight years later.

The pace of these three weeks in England was hectic—inevitably so, since there was so much to be done and the time so limited. Still, he was able to enjoy some tranquil days with Margot—the first week-end he spent with her in Birmingham; and she came to Conduit Head and to London as often as she could to be with him. These were the happiest memories he took back to Spain. In November he would write to her from Madrid: "I'm glad as I could be that the last few days I had with you were as good as they could be." There was a quiet week-end, too, at Dartington with Michael Straight, and peaceful conversations with his father at Conduit Head. But the major part of his time was used up in recruiting the group he would take to Spain, and his personal life, so to speak, was made subordinate to it. Meetings with family or friends tended to be brief, unexpected, and arranged at a moment's notice, fitted in to an overcrowded schedule. Even Christopher, then an art student living in Chelsea, only saw him once, and his account of the occasion is as vivid a glimpse of John at this period as we have:

> . . . one evening in September, the telephone rang and I heard his voice at the other end. He was back on leave, and I saw him for one evening in London: he was dressed in old flannels and the rope-sole shoes of the Spanish worker; his face was yellow with the effects of jaundice and a long journey. He was at a high pitch of nervous excitement and wanted to talk, he said, in order to get calm. Unable to speak fast enough to keep pace with his ideas, he recounted his experiences, analysed the situation in Catalonia, speculated on the future of the struggle

('I have no doubt whatever who's going to win this war'). We walked together as often before, down the King's Road, he talking and I listening. People in the street watched us curiously. Then we parted, John still too excited to sleep; and that was the last time I ever saw him.

Michael Straight saw him in a more subdued aspect. As soon as he had heard that John was back in England, he wrote to him to suggest that he come down to Dartington with Margot for as long as he liked. John replied by postcard on September 21:

> Dear Mike
>
> I can't come till Thursday, but will then, if that's O.K. by you. I'll send you a wire saying what train I'm coming by as soon as I know where I'm coming from.
>
> Salute, John
>
> M. is working and can't make [it] anyhow until weekend; & it's a bit of a way to come, but we'll work out something to do about that anyway.[15]

As it turned out, Margot was obliged to remain in Birmingham, and John came alone to Dartington for what Straight remembers as a rather melancholy visit, very different in mood from the exuberant good times there the preceding April, when John, happily drunk, had flung out his legs in a Russian dance with the Michael Chekhov theatre company. Now he was quiet, even sombre, abstracted, reluctant to talk about what had happened to him in Spain. It was clear, though, that he was under no illusions about the nature of war itself; that his experiences in the front lines had been enough to teach him that it was very different from the smiling triumphs celebrated by the propagandists of both sides—as he wrote later to Margot, "No wars are nice, and even a revolutionary war is ugly enough." He did tell Straight that the military position of the Republic was less favourable than the Government was yet willing to admit, and he was concerned about the Nationalist advance towards Madrid, which was taking place these very days when he was at Dartington. But the fact that he had to face returning to what appeared to be a worsening situation in no way altered his determination to return. That he was going back was a settled thing, and it became evident in numerous ways during the week-end. He was preoccupied with what he would need at the front, since he had learned from experience that one did well to equip oneself before starting out, and he drove into a neighbouring town with Straight in an unsuccessful attempt to buy a revolver and a helmet. Once, in conversation, when Straight spoke of his need to excel, John replied that he felt this too, but a thousand times more strongly. Certainly he was conscious of his responsibility in leading a group of friends and comrades back to the war—it was essential that he lead them well, just as it had been essential earlier, on the Aragon front, that whatever physical timidity he may have felt, must be overcome. Something of this determination, which was a crucial part of his character, illuminates the snapshot of John that Straight took on this week-end and that has come to represent him in his most famous aspect, as a fighter for Spain.

The problem of finding a revolver was solved at Conduit Head. John had written to his father that he wanted to talk over "the whole position", and when he was in Cambridge again he did his best to explain the course of action to which he was committed. Professor Cornford, on principle, would not interfere with him; and whatever reservations he may have felt, he did not express openly, or only very mildly. We know that he saw the whole position as being more complex than John admitted it to be. Like most liberal intellectuals in England then, he was a sympathizer with the cause of the Spanish Republic, and in October (after John's departure) he was an official sponsor of a meeting in Cambridge to raise money for British Medical Aid to Spain. But he felt there was a personal element in the position John had taken, motives for action quite apart from political ideas or principles, which he summed up as "an escape from the hot entanglement of personal responsibilities". However, he seems to have been unwilling to confront John with these directly, and Mrs Cornford, who might have done so, was ill and away at the time, and so the hard questions were not asked. John, in any case, would have argued that abstract ideals counted for more than personal allegiances in the struggle for Communism and for liberty. Professor Cornford granted this: "The reward of giving at last *all* he had to a cause that promised, at least, to be the cause of liberty, was a brief but exalted happiness, not to be bought at a lower cost."

Yet we can glimpse the misgivings he must have felt, saying goodbye to his brilliant son, in the final paragraph he wrote (and then cancelled) for his memorial essay: "I see a boat slipping out of harbour & breasting the first waves beyond the bar. The youth at the helm is so confident that he has made the sheet fast; and while one hand is firm on the tiller, the other holds a book, from which he glances up only now & then to set his course closer to the wind that is driving him into the heart of the storm."

It seems fair to conclude from all this that the father regretted his son's going to Spain, but that it would have been contrary to his convictions, as it would also have been ineffective, to try to stop him; instead, in a splendidly practical and symbolic gesture, he gave him the revolver that he had carried in World War I.

The idea of a group of volunteer fighters was John's own, which occurred to him in Spain, and which he began to put into practice as soon as he returned to England on September 16. Unbeknownst to him, others in the party were thinking along similar lines. Six days later, on September 22, Maurice Thorez, the French Communist leader, went to Moscow and proposed to the Comintern the formation of International Brigades, to be led by Communists but in which non-Communists would be welcomed, that would fight in Spain on the side of the Republic. The proposal, which according to Hugh Thomas had been raised earlier at a Comintern meeting on July 26, was now favourably received, and activity got under way immediately. "The formation of the International Brigades now became the main work of the Comintern. Each Communist party was instructed to raise a given number of volunteers. In many cases, the prescribed figure was higher than local parties could possibly attain. Most of the ablest leaders of the Comintern, not already involved, like Togliatti, in Spain, were employed in this way. The future Marshal Tito, Joseph Broz, at first was at Paris organising from a small Left Bank hotel, the flow of recruits through his so-called 'secret railway', which provided passports and funds for the East European volunteers."[16] Curiously, though, word of all this appears to have been slow in reaching the party in England. Andrew Knight has pointed out that John "had no idea, of course, any more than we had, that the International Brigades were in formation". And it seems reasonable to assume that Harry Pollitt did not learn of the activity in Paris before October 5 at the earliest—that is, after John's departure—for if he had known of it, he would certainly have had no reason to keep it secret from John, nor would he have encouraged him to continue recruiting what was virtually an independent unit of his own. In fact, if John had come back to England a month later than he did, his line of action would have been different and simpler: he would have volunteered for the International Brigade, and he would have gone out to Spain with a group recruited not by himself but by the party. As it was, he acted with a fair degree of independence, although he went to see Harry Pollitt immediately, and secured his approval and promise of assistance—that the party would pay for the transportation of the group.

Even before arriving in England, John had considered, and jotted down in the diary, some of the questions and details involved in gathering together a group of volunteers:

1. Secrecy.
2. For what wanted—discipline.
3. Who is wanted?
4. When to go? Fare.
5. What to take.
    1) Money
    2) Shirts, sweater, pants
    3) Towel, soap, razor, toothbrush
    4) Books. Cards. Chess
    5) Knife
    6) *Light* knapsack
    7) Passport
    8) Shoes—overcoat?

Teeth & typhoid

The question "Who is wanted?" can best be answered by consulting the list of prospective recruits that he drew up when he was in London, and after consultation with Pollitt. There are thirteen names in all. After one, he noted, "Speaks Spanish. Rifle shot"; after another, "7 yrs. in cadet corps"; after another, "Machine gunner, Territorial"; after another, "New Zealand army training, Machine gun"; after another, "Cadet Corps"; after another, a refugee from Nazi Germany, "Reichswehr". Eventually the group he chose was fined down to six—five Englishmen and a German—and it is evident from his choices that John was profiting by the lesson of his own inexperience in Catalonia. He wanted men who not only were dedicated to the cause but also were qualified in one way or another to fight for it effectively. Quite apart from its exemplary function, he believed that this group of volunteers (and others like it) could contribute to the ultimate military victory. He told Andrew Knight that "he was convinced that the weakness of the Franco side was manpower, and that within a short time the total mobilization of the Republic forces would produce an army capable of winning the war". He made the same point to Harry Pollitt when he went to see him at party headquarters in King Street. On that occasion, or on another soon afterwards, there was a young man in Pollitt's office, Sam Russell, with whom John had been slightly acquainted in the student movement. Russell had received his degree from University College, London, earlier in the summer; he was only recently back from a period of duty with an Officer Training Corps; and he had planned to go out to Egypt the next month to take part in an archaeological dig. Assuming that the Republic would need arms not men from abroad, he also assumed, like many others in the days before the non-intervention policy, that the legal government would have no difficulty in buying arms enough to put down the Fascist rebellion. Now, hearing John put the case for foreign volunteers with the utmost conviction, speaking so excitedly that it was difficult always to follow his ideas, Russell was profoundly impressed. The time no longer seemed right for him to be going to the Nile Valley to dig for artifacts. Instead, he joined the next group of English volunteers, that followed John's about a week later, and caught up with them in Paris.[17]

The group had been recruited; the three weeks' leave was almost at an end; it was time to start back to Spain. On October 4, the day before he was to leave England, John wrote to J. R. M. Butler, his tutor at Trinity:

> I am writing this letter to resign my scholarships, as by the time this reaches you I shall already be on the way to rejoin the

unit of the Anti-Fascist Militia with which I have been fighting this summer. I am sorry I did not have time to discuss it personally.

I should like to take this opportunity of thanking you, and through you other Fellows of the College I have not had time to write to, for the tremendous personal kindness and interest you have always shown me, even though you must have looked with disfavour on many of my activities.

Yours sincerely,
John Cornford[18]

The next day he went round to the Spanish People's Front London Information Bureau at 3 Victoria Street to obtain a 'safe conduct' letter which apparently he thought would facilitate things for himself and the group when they arrived at the Spanish Frontier. The letter, which was addressed to the "Company Jaime Miravitlles, Conselleria de Defensa Barcelona", described John as a member of the Communist party and of the Anti-Fascist Militia of Catalonia. It stated that he was returning to Barcelona, having completed his mission in England, and that he was bringing with him, "to serve Anti-Fascist Spain", five British volunteers and one German. Each of the men was identified by name, along with a descriptive phrase—thus, for a single example, "the good shot John Sommerfield".

The letter to his college tutor and the 'safe-conduct' letter together lead us to a consideration of the peculiarity of John's military status at this time. Technically, he was still a member of the P.O.U.M. and, ostensibly, he was going back to Spain "to rejoin" the unit he had been fighting with in the summer. But was this truly the case? He is sharply critical of the P.O.U.M. in his essay, 'The Situation in Catalonia', which he wrote while in London: ". . . the dominant policy is provocative and utterly dangerous. It is a parody of the Bolshevik tactics of 1917: without taking into account that whilst Kerensky was carrying on an Imperialist war, Companys and Casanovas [Republican leaders] are fighting an anti-Fascist war . . . Their militia is the worst organised on the Aragon front; even brave and intelligent leaders like Grossi are incapable of giving their troops proper political, military, or organisational training . . . They have little left beyond their sectarian political leaders: a well-produced newspaper, *La Batalla*; and two to three thousand of the worst-organised militia; brave enough, but incapable of a real sustained offensive through sheer inefficiency." It is hard to believe that John would voluntarily affiliate himself again with an organization he held in contempt, even though its troops would profit from the example of a small, disciplined formation. Very likely he intended making a new arrangement for himself and the group, once they had arrived in Barcelona. As it happened, however, the possibility never arose: their future was settled for them in Paris.

That last day in England, October 5, he found time, or made it, amidst the preparations for departure, to telephone Margot in Birmingham to say goodbye, and Reg Snell, with whom he had not been able to arrange a meeting, and Ray in London, who came to the station to see him off. He clearly had a more final sense of leaving than had been the case before: not that he expected to be killed, but he knew that this time he was going out to fight, presumably for as long as the war lasted, not simply (as he had thought in August) for a few days' observation. Yet he was cheerful enough, saying goodbye to Ray, and his spirits were high when he boarded the night train for Paris with the others of the group.

They were wearing the new heavy boots that John had recommended, and in their light knapsacks were khaki overalls and the other items he had listed as essential. Books especially he insisted upon. Last time, in the haste of departure, he had taken none with him, and desperately missed them in Aragon. As he had written then to Margot, "By far the greatest need is for something to read." And he warned the group, "The worst thing about this war is not discomfort, nor even danger, but boredom." To avert it he brought with him now in his light knapsack the first volume of *Capital* and the *Tragedies* of Shakespeare.

Their passports were stamped in Dieppe on the morning of October 6, and they went on to Paris, where they reported to, were taken in hand, and taken over, by the Comité d'Entr'aide au Peuple Espagnol, who sent them to a hotel in the Belleville district and told them to wait there for orders. It was then, Knight recalls, that "John's scheme for a small but well-disciplined (and well-shaven) English unit attached to a militia column was lost and forgotten in the welter of languages and nationalities that we found in the little hotel that we were sent to. There were German exiles, many with the mark of the concentration-camp on them, Polish miners and peasants, Italians, Frenchmen, Hungarians, Greeks, all of them kicking their heels in the café, waiting for the word that would send them south." Whatever the functions of the Comité had been a few days earlier, it was now evidently the Paris organizing centre for the International Brigade, into which it proceeded, automatically as it were, to co-opt John and his group. The question of their future in Spain had been settled: like all but a very small minority of foreign volunteers thereafter, they would fight in the International Brigade.

In fact, the Cornford group was the nucleus of what was to become, on December 27, 1936, the British Battalion. But in Paris, in early October, they were only seven, although later that week they were joined in the polyglot hotel in Belleville by a second and larger group of English volunteers, among them Sam Russell, which brought their total strength to twenty-one. (Eventually there would be 2,762 Englishmen who would fight in the International Brigade before it was disbanded in November 1938. Approximately eighty per cent of the volunteers came from the working class; sixty per cent were Communists when they joined the Brigade, twenty per cent more became Communists while serving within it. The casualty rate was very high: of the 2,762 volunteers, 543 were killed, and 1,763 were wounded.)[19]

John used the time in Paris while waiting for orders to see to it that the members of his group were properly equipped. At his urging they all bought revolvers, which, together with Professor Cornford's, for several days were the only weapons in the International Brigade. Armed, they were impatient to be under way; and presently, towards the end of the week, the order came. They went by night train to Marseilles, arriving at dawn; then were hidden all day in the outskirts of the city; and at dusk driven through the teeming streets to the docks, where they embarked for Spain.

The ship was sailing under the Anarchist flag. When they

reached the harbour of Alicante on the morning of the third day, they were reassured to see that the Communist flag and the flag of the Republic were being flown alongside the Anarchist flag above the Custom House. Those who were alarmed by the apparent power of the Anarchists got no support from John: "I think the Fascists are more dangerous."

They disembarked, made what has been recalled as a triumphal march through the town, ate their way through a loaf of bread and a tin of sardines per man, and entrained that evening for Albacete, the capital of the province of La Mancha. About one hundred miles from Alicante and one hundred and fifty miles from Madrid, it had been selected as a training centre for the International Brigade. The mood of the journey was exhilarating, for all along the way, at every station, they were welcomed by enthusiastic demonstrators, who waved the red flag of the Communist party, and plied them with grapes and wine. It was not until late at night that they arrived at Albacete.

They were not the first. They had been preceded a few days earlier by a group of about five hundred, mostly French, with a smattering of Poles and Germans. And they would be followed in the months ahead by increasing numbers of volunteers from abroad and other foreigners who had been fighting elsewhere in Spain who poured in to Albacete to become members of the International Brigades. The intention was to form national battalions—predominantly French, Italian, German, and so on—and within a few months there would be a sufficient number of volunteers from Britain for a battalion of their own—where at last the natives would speak English and the tea be properly brewed—but in October in Albacete John and his group and the other English who had joined forces with them were hardly enough to form a platoon. One of them recalled that "in the immense sifting process which went on during the next few days it was only natural that so small a group as ours should be overlooked. We appointed John political delegate to urge our demands and to keep up the morale of the group—which was no light matter. We were impatient to get to the front, to get arms, to be trained, and all that happened was that we were at last officially attached to the French battalion which regarded us quite frankly as a nuisance, because of the difficulty of having every order translated on the spot." Still, now that they had an official identity, as a machine-gun section in the Compagnie Mitrailleuse of the 'Commune de Paris' Battalion (also known as the 'Dumont', for its commander), they were officially ready to be trained.

The commander of the base was the fearsome, and fearful André Marty, a top French Communist who had led a mutiny in the French Black Sea fleet in 1919, and subsequently had become known as an anti-militarist. Addressing the troops in his charge, Marty vented his spleen on those "who are impatient, who wish to rush off to the front at once. These are criminals." Then he modulated upward to a vein of high-minded good sense: "When the first International Brigade goes into action, they will be properly trained men, with good rifles."[20] But these splendid and optimistic assurances had little to do with the realities of training, at least as they were experienced by the English machine-gun section in the 'Dumont' battalion, whose equipment "at one point consisted of a Lewis-gun (British), a Saint-Etienne (French), a Colt (American) and a Bergmann (German). Each of these guns needed a different type of ammunition."[21] But even if the equipment had been first-class and ample, there would not have been sufficient time to master it, for training was to be abruptly cut short.

The conditions of life in the overcrowded base were primitive in the extreme—indeed, the overcrowding grew so intolerable that the training of the 'Dumont' was interrupted, and they were moved from Albacete to nearby La Roda, where conditions were not noticeably better. Most of the group suffered from bouts of diarrhoea; the lavatories were painfully few, and filthy—until finally, in desperation, John and Sommerfield faced up to the ordeal of cleaning them. The promised uniform amounted to no more than a black beret. The promised arms, when they were issued, proved to be 1914 American Remingtons. Then there was the language problem of a unit of Englishmen working and living with Frenchmen—all comrades together, of course, but there were continual haggles. What newspapers should be ordered? Why must the French use so much garlic in their cooking? And why didn't they serve tea?

Life was pleasanter, as it usually is in the army, during off-duty hours:

In the evenings [Sommerfield recalled] we strolled about the town and sat in cafés. Everything was very cheap and there were pleasant drinks and interesting sweet cakes. Marcel, who had attached himself to B. and liked to be seen going around with the English, usually came with us ... He suggested that we should go and sing outside the brothels; it didn't seem to be a particularly interesting way of spending the time.

"Well," he said. "We could go inside afterwards."

"You ever heard of the pox?" I said.

He had.

"Well, it's not considered a disease in Spain, it's just a habit."

He said, "*Merde alors* . . ." and sulked. He got us to a scruffy little bordel one night, though, and it was pretty awful. We didn't wait for him.

There was an odd atmosphere of excitement and slightly hysterical gaiety in the town at night. The streets were crowded with militiamen in overalls and rope-soled shoes, wearing funny little cadets' hats, mostly with Anarchist or Communist badges stuck in them. Overalls were becoming a national dress. Obvious middle-class gentlemen strolled about in beautifully tailored boiler suits. For the first time in history, John pointed out, the middle-class was beginning to take its fashions in dress from the workers.

It was significant, I said.

"Yes," said John. "Significant."

Everybody said it was significant and John roared with laughter. When he laughed he bellowed. He was a grand chap, he was one of the best people I had ever met in my life. We used to laugh together for hours.[22]

And there was the memorable day when they were excused from training so that they could help the peasants harvest their saffron. Carrying large burlap sacks, they went into the fields alongside the Spanish women, whose good looks and admiration for the "Internationals" added to the pleasure of the occasion, and they filled their sacks with the valued yellow flowers. And later in the day, when the crop had been gathered, they returned to the barns and emptied their sacks on the hard earth floor, and sat down among the thousands of blossoms, and picked out the stamens.

It was an occasion when the significance of the war, *why they were there*, made itself felt more poignantly and more powerfully than when they were going through the routines of their inadequate training or being harangued in French by André Marty.

When the group had arrived in Albacete, they had chosen John to be their "political delegate", and it was taken for granted that he was their leader. But once they were attached to the 'Dumont' he thought it better to quit both positions "officially", proposing that the task of delegate be taken over by Andrew Knight, who spoke better French than he, and that the group elect Fred Jones, an ex-Guardsman with experience of war and a working knowledge of French, as their leader. Privately, John told Knight, "I think I could handle our little lot, but I don't fancy ordering old soldiers about." But with or without official title, John remained the leader of the group—he could not help but be so. "Tempers were still frayed. Most of us could not speak anything but English", Knight recalled. "Worst grievance of all: we had been here for weeks and not seen a rifle . . . It was on [John] that fell the responsibility for maintaining discipline and harmony in the group." Which he did most effectively. There was a succession of minor daily irritations, and through them all John persevered, never losing his enthusiasm, or his fierce nervous intensity. He gave the impression of always being on the move, with his odd, loping gait and his head bobbing, solving problems as they arose, settling grievances, and generally keeping the morale of the group high by his own determined example. Outwardly he was all confidence; inwardly he seethed. We can glimpse something of what he felt during the time spent training in a letter to Margot written in November:

> We English did badly, we were a national minority very hard to assimilate, mucked about between one station and another, starting work on one kind of gun and then having it taken away from us, taking part in manœuvres which those that didn't speak French couldn't understand. When we at last got down to work with the machine gunners our training was interrupted almost before we started, and we were switched through to the front.

The training of the International Brigade at Albacete was cut short, or, more precisely, was broken off for better or worse, by the beginning of what has been called "the central epic of the Spanish conflict": the battle for Madrid. The phrase is Robert Garland Colodny's, and he justifies it in these terms:

> It was this struggle, beginning with the collapse of Republican arms at Toledo in September 1936, and ending with the victory of the Madrid armies at Guadalajara in March 1937, that determined the duration and characteristics of the rest of the conflict. Hence, it was the central episode of the Spanish War, its focal point for six months. The crucible in which was formed the Ejercito Popular, the People's Army, was the front of Madrid. Here were created the myths which plague the historian. Here, due to international intervention, the Spanish struggle lost its purely national character and became at once a civil war of a profoundly Spanish type, a war of independence waged by a section of the Spanish people against German, Italian and Moroccan armies, and a clash of supra-national ideologies that aroused the deepest passions of peoples far removed from the immediate Spanish interests at stake.[23]

The battle began on November 7: a small, effectively armed Nationalist force, made up principally of Moroccans and legionaries, against the people of Madrid. Both sides were supported by foreign tanks and aircraft—German and Italian bombers for the Nationalists, Russian fighter planes for the Loyalists. The Government had left for Valencia, but a comparatively young military group was organizing the defence of the city, and in it the Communists were destined to play an important role. Hugh Thomas has concluded that "it was impossible to know how much of the spirit of resistance, emanated from the cellar headquarters of the Ministry of War, derived from Miaja [the Loyalist commander] and how much from the Russian General Berzin whose office was a few doors away. Certainly the resistance owed much to the propaganda and administration of the Communists, Spanish as well as Russian."

However it was inspired, there was resistance of a passionate and immediate kind. At dawn the Nationalists launched their attack on the west of the city with a heavy artillery bombardment. It was then that *¡no pasaran!*, that slogan that so stirred the liberal imagination of the 1930s, came vividly into being, in word and deed. All that morning Madrid Radio was broadcasting "orders to build barricades. Masses of workers left for the front lines, many without arms, ready to take up the rifles of those killed. La Pasionaria's voice was heard incessantly on the loud-speakers in the streets, exhorting women to prepare to pour boiling oil on those who came to attack their homes . . . A women's battalion even fought before the Segovia bridge. Children also helped with building barricades."[24] But this extraordinary outpouring of civilian resistance only served to point up the gravity of the situation: the city might yet fall. There was a need not only for a horde of courageous Madrileños to man the barricades, but also for trained fighting men, equipped with rifles, bayonets, grenades and machine-guns, and skilful in their use. It was under these circumstances that the International Brigade came to Madrid.

Late in the morning of the 5th, training activities had been abruptly suspended at Albacete. The men of the various units that made up the first International Brigade (the XIth) were confined to barracks and told to pack their gear and be ready for departure at a moment's notice. It was understood that they would be going to Madrid, where, as they had read in the news-papers, a Fascist army was moving into position to launch its attack. That afternoon at the base there was a belated distribution of equipment. "Some got extraordinary dark-blue short coats," Sommerfield recalled, "some ammunition belts, some socks, some caps, some vests, some boots, some bayonet frogs, some scarves, some gloves. Everybody got *something* and no one everything. We marched off looking like a lot of scarecrows, and in filthy tempers because of the rush and of not getting things we needed."

They marched for about a half mile to a field, and then, after an hour's wait in which nothing happened, they turned round and marched back again, past the barracks and on to the station, where they halted in the road outside. By now it was late in the day. "The sun was setting, an enormous bloody sunset over the quiet fields. Lorry-loads of ammunition were unpacked in the road (to deceive the enemy, John and [Sommerfield] said). The packing cases were British, Mark VII, 1917 [and] looked as if they had been around a bit. They were labelled for Bologna and re-addressed in Italian . . . Each man was issued two flimsy cloth slings holding fifty rounds apiece."

In the dark, waiting interminably for the train, they were in high, excited spirits—"a wild joy". They sang 'The Old Grey Mare' and 'She was Poor but She was Honest'. Then, at last, the order came to get aboard, and they "jammed together in the corridors, getting into a tangle of packs and rifles and blankets and water-bottles, stumbling over each other and shoving to get into the compartments and falling into seats".

In the course of his four weeks on the Aragon front, and in his three weeks at Albacete, John had mastered two techniques for coping with the exasperations and difficulties of military life: a deliberate retreat into a massive apathy, a determination to *feel* as little as possible; and, in contrast, a heightened sense of comedy: "This is a peculiar kind of a war, and there's more unnecessary discomfort caused by carelessness and disorganisation than a man can bear, if he takes it seriously. The only thing to do is to laugh at it. If you look at it long enough it seems funny." The 150-mile journey to Madrid, which did not properly conclude until the morning of November 8, offered John almost continuous opportunities to put one or other of these techniques into practice. Several hours after leaving Albacete the train crawled to a stop in Alcazar, half-way to Madrid, where they were ordered to transfer into waiting lorries—it was said that the line ahead was under fire. The journey, which to this point had been merely stupefying, in the fug of an overheated, overcrowded, unventilated train, now assumed the proportions of a nightmare. It was the middle of the night, and bitterly cold. Forty men of the machine-gun company of the 'Dumont', including all the English, with their packs and rifles and blanket rolls, were crammed into the last of the open, ordinary-sized two-ton lorries waiting outside the station. The driver, a dare-devil Spaniard with a fine disregard for the niceties of the road, set off in pursuit of the convoy ahead, but lost it almost immediately. Sommerfield, writing a few months later, recalled that "the road was terrible, the roads were terrible all the way, little country lanes with bumps and curves and we went fast and it was cold, wind blew and our eyes watered, noses ran, and we were jammed together too tightly to reach for handkerchiefs or lift arms to wipe away the drops. It was the worst ride you could imagine and it went on and on all through the night for hours and hours, getting colder all the time, the discomfort becoming agony, and no relief to look forward to because no one knew where we were or to what place we were going." Knight, writing twenty-eight years later, recalled, "on the curves in the dark the swaying movement of the packed mass of men holding onto each other, because there was nothing else to hold onto, was extremely terrifying, and there was a great deal of vomiting. Altogether, it was a most unpleasant trip."

Daylight revealed an empty landscape; there was no trace of the rest of the convoy. Finally they arrived at Alcalá de Henares. "The lorry stopped, opposite the Town Hall, by a splendid burnt-out church. It was a quarter past nine. We had been in the lorry for nearly eleven hours. We got out, hardly able to walk, numbed, bruised to the bone, exhausted, stiff, hungry and thirsty." The section leader and the lorry-driver went into the Town Hall to confer with the local People's Front Committee, who would telephone headquarters in Madrid perhaps, to find out where they were to go. "So lost as to be officially non-existent", the others went into a near-by café where they drank scalding coffee and began to feel "like human beings again . . . John took off his great overcoat. (How we had laughed at him in the hot days as he had trailed about in that monstrous coat, green and aged, that reached down almost to his heels. With that, an ammunition belt strapped around him, rifle slung on one shoulder and blanket across the other, his high cheekbones, sculptured almost Mongol face, he looked like something in a bad picture of the retreat from Moscow. But now he had the laugh on us. No one else had an overcoat. We hadn't known about the cold in Spain.)"[25]

When they came out of the café they were recognized by the townspeople standing about as Russian soldiers who had come to fight for the Republic. "*Viva Rusia!*" It made an appropriate beginning to a day of absurdity, as they drove about, in and out and around Madrid, in search of the XIth Brigade, and in particular their comrades of the 'Dumont' Battalion, whom they found at last, toward nightfall, in Vallecas, a drab village on the outskirts of the city which was being used as a kind of staging-area or assembly point for the International Brigade. It was there, the next afternoon—the nineteenth anniversary of the Russian Revolution, an event the Brigade took cognizance of, and the first day of the battle for Madrid—that the Compagnie Mitrailleuse received their machine-guns. When they were uncrated, they were found to be elderly Saint-Etiennes, a French gun which had proved unwieldly and inefficient in World War I, and which had the further disadvantage of being unfamiliar to the company, who had been trained for the Lewis-gun. Eventually, the commander of the Brigade, Kleber, would see to it that they got the Lewises they wanted (although not as many as they would have liked); meanwhile, though, they had to put up with the exceptionally heavy Saint-Etiennes, how heavy they were not to discover until the next day.

In the early morning hours of November 8 they entrained again, but this time for a short ride into Madrid: they were there in twenty minutes. It had been cold and drizzling through the night; when they came out of the station, the pavement was filmed with ice, and the French would shout, "*Attention ça glisse.*" Burdened with heavy equipment, they waited until all the troops had come in from Vallecas—some estimate the total as low as 1,900, others as high as 3,500—and then they stepped out smartly, marching in disciplined formations along the Gran Via towards the front, which proved to be the University City. The arrival of the International Brigade in Madrid is one of the most celebrated events of the war, and has given rise to some of those 'myths that plague the historian'—was it, for example, the triumphant entry it is sometimes called? The men of the Brigade, weighed down with cumbersome equipment (Sommerfield was staggering under a Saint-Etienne, as well as pack, blanket and full field paraphernalia) and exhausted after three nights of very little sleep, were inclined to hold a somewhat jaundiced view of the event. "Ours was no triumphant entry," Sommerfield wrote, "we were a last, desperate hope, and as, tired out, ill-equipped, and hungry, we marched through the windswept streets, past the shuttered shops and the food queues, I thought that the hurrying people on the pavements looked at us as if we were too late and had come only in time to die." Yet there is ample testimony that their arrival immensely heartened the people of Madrid. The historian Juan Marichal, for example, who was then a schoolboy in Madrid, still speaks of the thrill of excitement, pride and reassurance that he felt as he watched the soldiers who had come from abroad to fight for the Republic march past. If, like all military parades, this was propaganda, it was propaganda of a peculiarly valuable kind: at a time when the city was in grave danger, these troops and the weapons they carried on their back were visible evidence of the determination to defend it.

The long march across Madrid ended in the Western outskirts, towards which the Fascists were advancing, in the new, unfinished campus of University City. The 'Dumont' Battalion bivouacked overnight in the building of the Faculty of Philosophy and Letters; John and his section were assigned to a lecture-room on the top floor; and in the comparative luxury it afforded them, their spirits rose: "the delights of sleep . . . the pleasures of a bath." Sommerfield greeted the University with a cry of rapture. He had an intelligent appreciation of taking advantage of, and indeed of taking, whatever comforts might be unexpectedly available. John would describe him to Margot as "a good soldier, and a good scrounger which is very important in a badly equipped army". Sommerfield himself wrote rhapsodically of "wash-rooms and lavatories, whose shining taps, white tiles, wooden seats, shower-baths, and crystal globes filled with green, translucent liquid soap, inspired us with the most profound emotion; weeks of brief and uncomfortable washing in yards under taps or with buckets of water drawn from wells, and our present accumulated dirt, gave the white, glistening aloofness of those rooms a paradisiacal aspect; and the cloistered calm of the rows of lavatories whose doors all stood invitingly open, revealing an austere geometry of patterned tiles gave promise of a luxury that we had been long denied." His rapture is understandable, given the fact that at Albacete there had been four primitive toilets for eight hundred men.

There was no sense of immediate danger, although gunfire could be heard in the distance. In the morning they were having coffee in the road outside the building, before starting off for the front, when a large aeroplane flew over, and "there was a heated discussion about its nationality—some claiming it was Russian, others that it was Spanish. The discussion was cut short by the sound of falling bombs and the airplane was then positively identified as a three-engined Italian Caproni." The leader of the group, Fred Jones, had already gone up ahead to the front with one of the English gun crews, and was "so confident that all was quiet"—John wrote to Margot—"that he hadn't appointed a successor." Now, as the bombs fell, inflicting no casualties but occasioning considerable panic, John took charge, and presently he got his men into formation again. Then, before they could get under way, they were heavily shelled by what John recognized as '75s. For the others, it was their "baptism of fire":

> We heard a sound which most of us [Knight recalls] knew only from the movies as the sound of arriving shell fire. The aim was good and the explosions took place among our ranks. The ground did not offer any cover and most of us simply scrambled forward over the edge of a bank which took us down into a sort of valley and at least got us out of sight, if not out of range, of the enemy artillery. Down on the lower ground we sorted ourselves out, and most of us realized ruefully that we had left our weapons behind. John and a small section with him were the only exception—they had brought their machine-gun down.

Again, John took charge, saw to it that the abandoned weapons were recovered, ordered the machine-guns of the unit (there were four in all!) be set up for action, and they waited for the rest of the day for an attack that did not take place. The group had come through its "baptism of fire" unscathed. But the four Lewis-gunners who had gone up ahead to the front with Fred Jones had not fared so well. They had taken part in the attack that Kleber had launched on the night of November 9, and that had cleaned the Nationalists out of most of the Casa de Campo—a large wooded area, just outside the city, on the further side of the Manzanares. But the cost in lives had been high. Of the four, one, MacLaurin, was dead; another, Steve Yates, was missing and presumed dead; and a third severely wounded. MacLaurin had been at Cambridge with John, and he wrote of him to Margot: "He did really well. Continuously cheerful, however uncomfortable, and here that matters a hell of a lot. Well, it's useless to say how sorry we are; nothing can bring him back now. But if you meet any of his pals, tell them (and I wouldn't say it if it weren't true) he did well here, and died bloody well." And writing of the four in another letter, he concluded: "It's always the best seem to get the worst."

There had been the night in "Philosophy and Letters", and then there were three weeks in the open, in the Casa de Campo, and the countryside beyond—the front—and then "Philosophy and Letters" again; meanwhile Madrid had not fallen, nor would it fall. Being English, they looked at the landscape and discovered resemblances, as Julian Bell had done in China. For John, the Casa de Campo was "rather Sussexy to look at: but behind to the right a range of the Guadarama, a real good range with snow against a very blue sky". And Sommerfield wrote of "a certain quiet day when we rested by a stream whose clear current bore away the last fallen leaves, and the firing had died down into an intermittent shooting in the woods above that were like an English scene in the late autumn countryside, when the guns crack and pheasants tumble out of the air while the echoes of the shots are fading amongst the hills".

They were one of the many units of the XIth and XIIth Brigades that participated in a great flanking attack on Aravaca, a village held by Franco's Moors, five miles along the road to El Escorial. Fighting was fierce but inconclusive. John felt the operation was mishandled: "We advanced into position at exactly the wrong time, at sunset, taking over some abandoned trenches. The Fascists had the range exact and shelled us accurately. Seven were killed in a few minutes." But the Moors exposed themselves recklessly, and were killed in the hundreds. Later there were too many of them to bury: their bodies were heaped up in a great mound and burned, and "the smell of roasting flesh haunted the night". After a harrowing day and night in their target trench where they were continuously exposed to shelling, John and his group were ordered back to a rest area behind the lines: there the main problem, he told Margot, "was the intense cold; and we were sleeping out without blankets, which we had left behind in order to carry more machine-gun ammunition". Meanwhile the fighting was still going on as fiercely as ever, and John grew restless: he went back up to the front as a volunteer stretcher-bearer to help bring in "the badly mangled Poles who were attacking over half a mile of completely open country under accurate shrapnel fire".

For the Brigades, Aravaca was "a costly failure". For John and his group the most tragic loss was Fred Jones, their leader. John wrote of him: "He was a tough; bourgeois family; expelled from Dulwich. . . Has been three years in the Guards, a hell of a good soldier, unemployed organizer, etc. Did magnificently here. Kept his head in a tough time after our Captain got killed, and was promoted to section leader. Then we had to make a night march back. There was a lorry load of wounded behind us. The lorry driver signalled, but wasn't noticed and got no answer. The four lines were so indeterminate that he thought we were a Fascist column and accelerated past us. Someone put up a wire to stop the car. The wire was swept aside, caught Fred Jones by the neck, hauled him over the parapet and killed him. We didn't see what happened: and to give some idea of the way we felt about him, after his death none dared to tell the English section for several hours. Well, we shall have to get along somehow. But that's a hell of a way to have your best man killed."

In spite of the failure of the attack on Aravaca, and in spite of the tragic losses within the group, in spite of hardships, exasperations and regrets, he held firmly to two convictions: that Madrid would not fall, and that one day he would return to Margot. On November 21, just two weeks since his arrival in Madrid, and in the same letter in which he reported the deaths of MacLaurin, Yates and Jones, he wrote to her, "Our International Brigade has done well. Continuous fighting, heavy losses, many of them simply due to inexperience, but we've been on the whole successful . . . I don't know what the press is saying over in England: but Madrid won't fall: if we get time to organise and to learn our guns, we shall do very well." But he was not prepared to deceive her: "There's a tough time ahead, and those that get through will be a hell of a lot older. But by Christ they'll learn a lot." And he concluded:

> The losses here are heavy, but there's still a big chance of getting back alive, a big majority chance. And if I didn't, we can't help that. Be happy, darling. Things here aren't easy, but I never expected them to be. And we'll get through them somehow, and I'll see you again, bless you, darling.
>
> John

I felt very depressed when I wrote this. Now I've eaten and am for the moment in a building. I feel fine. Warm. I'll get back to you, love, don't worry. God bless you.

In mid-November Durutti had arrived in Madrid with a column of 3,000 Anarchists to participate in the defence of the city, and "demanded an independent sector of the front so that his men could show their prowess". Miaja, the commander of the Madrid garrison, put him in charge of the Casa de Campo. On November 15 he was to launch an attack against the Nationalists, with Republican artillery and air support. Accustomed to the weaker troops on the Aragon front, the Anarchists could not cope with the machine-guns of the Moors, and the Nationalists broke through, across the river and into the city. They were beaten back, but they were still in occupation of most of the buildings in the University, after violent fighting in each one, sometimes floor by floor, and this battle continued until November 23, at which point it was immobilized in a deadlock. The four square miles of the University City now became the tragic microcosm of the battle of Madrid. "What Kleber had lost, he was determined to take back. Mola [the commander of Franco's forces], cheated of Madrid, resolved to have, at least, all of University City."[26]

The Fascists could advance no further, having failed to hold the strategically placed Philosophy and Letters Building. It had been taken from them by the French of the XIth Brigade in "a really good bayonet attack". John and his group had been "in reserve for all this"; now they were sent to Philosophy and Letters, and thus began what could be considered the idyll—if war is allowed its idylls—of their time in Spain. The group had been hardened in battle; they had suffered some heart-rending losses, but they had proved they could endure hardships; they had come as volunteers to fight for a cause in which they believed, and now, in these last days in Madrid, they saw that Fascism, for the first time, had truly been stopped. John and his friends were there on the front line, within shouting distance of the Spaniards, Germans, Italians and Moroccans in the next building, who were fighting to win Spain for Fascism and had been stopped.

"This was our best front line period," John wrote. "Comfortable, above all warm, and supplies regular. A great gutted building, with broken glass all over, and the fighting consisted of firing from behind barricades of philosophy books at the Fascists in the village below and in the Casa Velasques opposite."

They decorated their quarters, two lecture rooms—which were also the front line—tacking up travel posters which they had found in the building. One showed the Alhambra, and the slogan beneath was 'The sun is waiting for you in Spain'. Another showed a bullock cart and happy peasants, and its slogan was, 'Spain—the charm of the East! the comfort of the West!' In this curious setting, their warfare had a touch of the eighteenth century. Sommerfield described it: "We built barricades with volumes of Indian metaphysics and early nineteenth-century German philosophy; they were quite bullet-proof. On the floor of our room we spread carpets; we found a clock and a barometer and hung them on the wall; some tourist "Come to sunny Spain" posters were found, and . . . put up as a mockery to the climate. Life here was quiet, orderly. On clear mornings, about eleven o'clock, we were bombed. A few shells came over late in the afternoon; the rest of the time we sniped, read, talked, studied Spanish, or dug trenches." And he and John played a great deal of chess at this time. Another of Sommerfield's memories is of reading *Jane Eyre* in "the large bare room with November wind and rain blowing through the shattered windows that were barricaded with books, behind which our machine-guns stood . . . There I was rolled up in a piece of old carpet reading away like mad, the war noises, intermittent gunfire, thin wail of bullets, distant crunching of bursting shells . . . remote . . . I lived in that extraordinary, passionate, *stable* world of the book." Reading was a crucial occupation, and John's copies of *Capital* and the *Tragedies* of Shakespeare were in demand.

As one reads the descriptions of this period written by various members of the group, one glimpses something of the eternal fascination of war, the sense of comradeship and companionship it engenders, no matter how intensely the participants believe that wars should be fought only in the last resort. Andrew Knight: "We were as happy as I think men can possibly be in the front line of a modern war. We were under cover from the deadly cold that so far had been our worst enemy. We had leisure to talk and smoke in physical comfort, and, greatest pleasure of all, it was safe to take off our boots at night. The only drawbacks to this battle paradise were the fact that we were a perfect target for artillery, and the realisation that we might be completely cut off at any moment. Here we discussed art and literature, life and death and Marxism during the long day, and as the evening drew on, we sang. Nothing delighted John more than the sort of crude community singing that is common to undergraduate parties and public bars alike . . . With John Sommerfield we formed a famous trio, and our version of 'She was Poor but She was Honest' was a thing to bring solicitous political delegations down many dark corridors to find out what was the matter."

The chanciness and danger of their position was emphasized one day in the course of a reading period. They had just discovered part of the library in the basement of the building, and had brought upstairs stacks of Everyman's classics. John had begun to read *The Cloister and the Hearth*; Sommerfield was in the midst of De Quincey's reminiscences of the Lake Poets. John looked up to remark that Charles Reade was an excellent historian, but the conversation was never continued. There was a huge explosion, and the room was black with smoke. A shell had come through the wall, destroying a 'Sunny Spain' poster in its wake, and exploded in the room. It proved to be one of their own anti-aircraft shells, wildly off-course in an attempt to bring down one of the increasing number of planes that were bombing Madrid at an ever-quickening tempo. When the smoke cleared, three men were seen to be wounded, one of them John, who was bleeding profusely from a head wound. He himself dismissed it afterwards as "a small cut". But the wounds were sufficiently serious for the call to go out for stretcher bearers, and when dusk made movement safer they were taken off to the hospital.

John spent one night in the "very nice Secours Rouge Hospital", where he found the service more eager than efficient: "the amateur nurses wash your wounds like scrubbing the floor". They also gave him a huge bandage around his head which struck his companions when he returned the next day as both romantic and somewhat comical—he was an epitome of the wounded hero. The bandage was so huge that he could not put on his helmet, and now, with his dark face, he looked even more like a Moor.

Characteristically, John had come back from the hospital too soon. He spent the next two days doing heavy work digging trenches in frozen clay and taking part in defensive action in University City. "The afternoon of the second day I think I killed a Fascist," he wrote to Margot. "Fifteen or sixteen of them were running from a bombardment. I and two Frenchmen were firing from our barricades with sights at 900. We got one, and both said it was I that hit him, though I couldn't be sure." Then he added, as always regarding himself with dispassionate candour, "If it is true, it's a fluke, and I'm not likely to do as good a shot as that again."

Later that day the English group was withdrawn from University City and placed on reserve status again in the Casa de Campo: here they reorganized. They were now down to twelve members from the original twenty-one, the others having been lost through death and injury. The man who had replaced Fred Jones as leader of the group knew no French, which had mattered not at all in University City, but in the Casa de Campo liaison would again be necessary. John, whose French had improved considerably since Albacete, was formally elected leader. There was another among the twelve, an old soldier, a veteran of the Argyll and Sutherland Highlanders, and a Communist since 1922, who John felt had a greater claim to the leadership than himself; but since he knew no French, his appointment would have had no practical value. John, however, after his election, made it a point to say that he was sure Jock Cunningham would go far once there was a British Battalion, and indeed, little more than a month later Cunningham would be returning to Madrid in command of the British No. 1 Company.

There had been two days of strenuous activity; now John concluded them by going for a long walk with a friend in the direction of the Guadarrama. When they returned, his wound had begun to hurt again. The next morning, suffering from "a kind of retarded shock, I think", it was necessary for him to go back into the hospital. On December 8, he wrote in a second letter to Margot, "Excuse incoherence, because I'm in hospital with a slight wound and very weak." But after a few days, although not yet recovered, he grew restless. Humphrey Slater, who would become a Commissar in the British Brigade, went to visit him in his sick-bed, and happened to mention that "there were two or three of us arranging to spend the evening together in the Miami Bar. John was not going to miss anything and refused to stay behind. He walked slowly up the dark Gran Via, a bit shaky with a touch of concussion. The screaming crashes of enemy shells inside and round the skyscraper telephone building opposite the bar we were going to, made us rather less interested in seeing the sights of the town than we had been when we started. But Cornford insisted upon pushing one towards the explosions and whining splinters, slowly, unsteadily."

John had had one very hard month in Aragon, and now he had had another hard month, as (comparatively) a veteran at Albacete and in a position of responsibility in Madrid, when he was not yet twenty-one. He had been a leader at Cambridge, but he was dealing now with men's lives. Strong as he was, intensely as he felt, passionate as was his dedication to the cause, the strain of day after day of battle told. A great sustaining force for him was his love for Margot, and he testified to it in the few letters he had a chance to send back from Spain. He wrote in his letter to her of November 21: "For five weeks I scarcely missed you, everything was so new and different, and I couldn't write but formal letters. Now I'm beginning to wake up a bit, and I'm glad as I could be that the last few days I had with you were as good as they could be. I re-read your letter to me yesterday, and I was proud as hell. And as you say there, the worst won't be too hard to stand now. I don't know what's going to happen, but I do know we're in for a tough time. And I'm glad that you are behind me, glad and proud."

His second long letter, which recapitulated much of the news in the first—"There is an English comrade going back, and this is my first chance of an uncensored letter"—was written from the hospital on December 8, and it reflects the stoicism and realism and passion of which John was capable. He did not delude himself that wars could be romanticized, despite those good days in University City; he knew that fighting and being wounded, and seeing or hearing of one's friends dying were not pleasant things. "No wars are nice," he concluded, "and even a revolutionary war is ugly enough. But I'm becoming a good soldier, longish endurance and a capacity for living in the present and enjoying all that can be enjoyed. There's a tough time ahead but I've plenty of strength left for it. Well, one day the war will end—I'd give it till June or July, and then if I'm alive I'm coming back to you. I think about you often, but there's nothing I can do but say again, be happy, darling. And I'll see you again one day. Bless you, John."

Perhaps the most memorable statement of his love for Margot comes in the long diary letter he wrote when he was at the front in Aragon. In the published version of this letter in the memorial volume, one paragraph ends: "But I promise this is the last time I shall leave you unnecessarily. Maybe that the party will send me, but after this I will always be with you when I have the chance . . . ." And the next paragraph begins: "Well, all that's said. At the moment I am on top of a hill at the front in Aragon." Between them, however, as represented by the four dots, he had written:

> I love you with all my strength and all my will and my whole body. Loving you has been the most perfect experience, and in a way, the biggest achievement of my life.
>
> The party was my only other love. Until I see you again, bless you my love, my strength. Be happy. I worked for the party with all my strength, and loved you as much as I was capable of. If I am killed, my life won't be wasted. But, I'll be back.

On December 14, Franco's forces, launching a new attack towards the road to El Escorial, an important supply route, took the village of Boadilla del Monte, about twelve miles from Madrid. The International Brigades were called in to meet the attack. John, only a few days from the hospital, and his head still wrapped in a bandage, along with the rest of his group went into battle once again. It was during this battle that the two English groups in the Brigades met at last. The other, which had come out somewhat later, had trained with the Thaelmann Battalion (XIIth Brigade) at Albacete. Their original number of eighteen had been reduced to ten by the time of the battle of Boadilla, and in this battle another eight were killed. Of the two remaining, one was killed at Brunete the next July, and the only one to survive the war in Spain was Esmond Romilly. Romilly had met Cornford in England—he too, it will be recalled, had been a familiar of the Parton Street bookshop, whither he had fled from Wellington—but they had not yet met in Spain. (Romilly, in his book *Boadilla*, reports a meeting in Madrid, with one of John's group who told him they envied his group's being with the Germans, since they were convinced they must be easier to get along with than the French, and that they had asked, or were considering asking, for a transfer. Romilly refrained from pointing out that *his* group was as firmly convinced that the French must be much easier to get along with than the Germans.) But the two acquaintances from London were to meet on this battlefield: "For me," Romilly wrote, "the most important incident was when someone called my name, and I saw John Cornford with his head bandaged." And he added that John "fitted into my category of Real Communists".[27]

The counter-attack by the two International Brigades, supported by Russian tanks, was successful, and on the night of December 15, John's group had a peaceful sleep in what remained of the Church of Boadilla. The next day was spent in defending the town. John led out his men in the morning rain to a barn in a near-by field, where they set up their Lewis and Maxim machine-guns, and watched the infantry counter-attack up the hills, only to be driven down in the afternoon "under a withering fire". Watching them come back, Jock Cunningham predicted, accurately, that there would be a Fascist attack the next morning at dawn. As one of the group recalled:

> The storm burst as John was taking us up to relieve a Spanish machine-gun post. We found ourselves under fire from the heights where we were meant to relieve, and a few minutes later, as we squeezed and strained ourselves into the earth, the remains of our front line came crawling back, pointing up and shouting excitedly, 'Los Fascistas, los Fascistas'. As if we didn't know. There was nothing for it but to go back and hold a line in front of the village. So back we went . . . dragging the guns over the ploughed land that crumbled as the bullets hit it.
>
> For the rest of the morning we held the road to the village, firing at close range into lines of attackers that were crossing our line of fire to outflank us. The most disturbing feature of

the situation was the withdrawal of the infantry companies on our right and left flanks. Jock Cunningham, commanding Number Two gun, came down to join us and reported two men killed. John ordered the rest of the crew down from its exposed position on the crest of the road, and so we were all together again. Things looked pretty desperate. So far as I could see, our two English machine-guns (one of them badly jammed) were the only thing between Boadilla and the Fascists. But it was obviously our job to cover the retreat and not a man murmured when John announced that we were to hold on. Meanwhile the aeroplanes came over and added to the confusion. We were getting at last to the stage where we could cease worrying and laugh. We sighted four Fascist tanks coming up the road towards us, and just at that moment big shells began to fall on the village just behind us. The sight of this concentrated destruction being hurled on twelve men and one Lewis-gun was too much for me. I turned to John and we burst out laughing.

It was clear that the time had come to retreat, and in fact, the entire battalion was preparing to withdraw from the village. Boadilla, in its ravaged state, fell to the Fascists, who that day also took the village of Villanueva de la Canada, eight kilometres to the north, then paused. The battle did not resume until January 3 and continued thereafter for another twelve days. Its ultimate results were ten kilometres of road for the Nationalists—but the Loyalists still had an alternative route open through the mountains—and heavy casualties on both sides.

By the end of the first part of the battle of Boadilla—or the battle of the Madrid-Corunna road, as Thomas calls it—that is, by December 17, of the original twenty-one English attached to the 'Dumont' only John and four others were left to continue fighting. All the others had either been killed or wounded. And of the four, none was a member of the group that John had recruited in London. In August he had written from Aragon that the risk of being killed was "statistically not very great". On November 21 he had written to Margot that "there's still a big chance of getting back alive, a big majority chance." After Boadilla, did he continue to believe this?

In Albacete by this time about 150 further English, Scottish and Irish volunteers had arrived, enough to form an all English-speaking company—the No. 1 Company—and the five surviving English veterans of the 'Dumont' Battalion were recalled to join them, presumably to assist in their training and to serve as officers. Before setting out, John went round to the hospital in Madrid to visit Andrew Knight, who had been badly wounded at Boadilla. He did his best to raise his friend's low spirits. He joked with him, and pretended they would be going into action together again, and spoke spiritedly of a long report he had handed in to headquarters, "with recommendations for future engagements". In fact, he had not yet entirely recovered from the effects of his head wound, and however cheerful he might have been at pains to appear, the recollection of comrades lost, killed or wounded, must have been with him constantly. "We can do nothing to ease that pain/But prove the agony was not in vain."

The British were forming a section in the Marseillaise Battalion of the new XIVth Brigade, and they were fortunate in their commanding officers. The military commander of No. 1 Company was the elegant and brave George Nathan, a former officer in the British army, and the political commissar was a well-known Communist intellectual, the novelist Ralph Fox. John joined them in training at Madrigueras, about twenty miles from Albacete. But he had hardly arrived there when the company (and the battalion) was ordered to the Cordoba front, where a new campaign was about to get under way. John, his head still bandaged, was looking so haggard, and was so obviously in need of rest, that it was proposed that he remain in Madrigueras rather than go to the front, and help in training the English volunteers who were expected to be arriving at the rate of fifty to a hundred a week in the near future. He rejected the proposal. He found being at the base boring and lonely after the front, and he was unwilling to be left behind. Perhaps, somewhat like Siegfried Sassoon in World War I, he had come to feel that the only bearable reality of war was one's experience of it at the front.

On Christmas Eve, 1936, the 145 Englishmen of No. 1 Company, 12th Battalion, XIVth Brigade, left Madrigueras by train for Andujar. Among them were John Cornford and the four survivors, Jock Cunningham, Joe Hinks, Jock Clarke and Sam

Russell, each of whom had been appointed leader of a machine-gun unit. Thus, effectively divided and in separate positions along the front, the last members of the original group of twenty-one were to be finally dispersed.

The new campaign was intended to relieve the pressure on Madrid by a diversionary attack on Fascist territory in the South. There the Government held the province of Jaen, and the Fascists the adjoining province of Cordoba. And Cordoba, the capital city, was only eighty-two miles from the most important city in rebel hands: Seville. The objective of the Loyalist forces was to head down the valley of the Guadalquivir towards these two cities. About fifteen miles beyond Andujar, where they detrained, off the main road, was the village of Lopera, the rebels' principal outpost. Up to there the Brigade had advanced without undue difficulty, although they had been strafed by planes, and one of the Englishmen, Nat Segal, was killed, the first dead in the new draft. But now they were bogged down, so badly that at one point headquarters issued a communiqué saying: "During the day the advance continued without the loss of any territory."[28] The Brigade took up positions in the olive groves around Lopera, and around another walled village, Villa del Rio, a little further along the road to Cordoba.

The commander of the 12th Battalion was a French officer, Major Lasalle, who appears to have been a coward, a fool and a rigid disciplinarian. Later he was to be shot as a Fascist spy, which he may or may not have been—there is some doubt on the charge. Lasalle was operating a good distance in the rear, and he ordered No. 1 Company, with whom he had had a number of quarrels during the training period, to take Lopera, promising to send up full support. In fact, he never did. Nathan, however, took him at his word, and organized several attacks on the village, none successful. On Christmas night, or after midnight on the 26th, the company got to the crest of a hill above Lopera, where they spent a miserable night in the cold. In the morning they were driven back by strafing planes that had no trouble in spotting them, since the olive groves afforded little protection or camouflage. Again and again during the next three days advances were attempted and beaten back. Nathan finally ordered his men to spread out in a long thin line along the crest. His theory, a valid one, was that if they went over the ridge, at the top of which they would make splendid targets, all at once, they would have a better chance of survival than if they went over in small groups, a few at a time. He waited now for the support to arrive that had been promised him; he sent out scouts to watch for it. None was forthcoming; there were only repeated orders from Lasalle's messengers to attack. At last Nathan led his men with his gold-tipped swagger stick over the crest. Then they were stopped by a blaze of machine-gun fire. Hastily they began to dig in, and since they were without entrenching tools they attempted to use their tin plates as shovels. Lacking support, or effective machine-guns of their own, there was nothing more they could do. There were sections armed with modern Colt machine-guns in the battalion, but they had received no orders to participate in the attack, and were at too great a distance to be summoned. The machine-guns of No. 1 Company were twenty-year-old Chauchats, most of which jammed on their first shot; most of the rifles were older Austrian Steyrs which, lacking their special ammunition clip, had to be used as single shots. On the 27th the Fascists counter-attacked heavily. Nathan was left with no choice but to withdraw and join the rest of the battalion. They spent another night of cold and discomfort; neither their packs nor blankets had been sent up to them; food had to be searched for. The number of dead and wounded was already ominously large. Retreating, they had had to leave the dead where they fell, and the wounded to the mercy of the Fascists. Yet the next day, December 28, No. 1 Company attacked again, and in three advances got almost to the walls of the town. This time they were supported by French machine-gun fire, but the operation was badly co-ordinated: at one point they were under fire from their own guns. The battle went on for four hours. Lasalle was in the rear; there was no one to order the two other companies, which were available, into the assault. Aeroplanes swooped down; the Fascist artillery and machine-gun fire mounted in intensity; the company was being decimated. Finally Nathan had to order a retreat, and leave for the last time what had come to be known as the "English crest". Among the dead left behind was John Cornford.

It is perhaps appropriate that the exact circumstances and even the date of the death of one who left life to become myth should be shrouded in uncertainty. The various accounts that exist have come almost without exception from men who were not there at the battle for Lopera. Sam Russell, who was there, last saw John when they detrained at Andujar; thereafter he was with his own machine-gun unit, as John was with his. Humphrey Slater wrote in the *Daily Worker* that John was killed while "leading a brilliantly successful counter-attack near Lopera". The obituary notice in the *Cambridge Daily News* stated that he had been killed while reconnoitring in advance of the lines. Peter Kerrigan, months later, in the *Volunteer for Liberty*, the English-language newspaper of the Brigade, wrote that he was killed when endeavouring to reach a wounded comrade; William Rust in his history of the Brigades, *Britons in Spain*, repeats this version. Andrew Knight heard that he had been killed by machine-gun fire. Michael Straight, who wrote the anonymous obituary for *The Cambridge Review*, stated there that he had been killed while leading his men. But Straight had also heard that he was shot in error by his own men, and indeed, almost anything might have been possible when new recruits, unaccustomed to battle, were facing their first engagement under the worst possible conditions.

On December 28, 1936, the Commander of the Marseillaise Battalion was shot—but not in battle. André Marty himself had come furiously to the headquarters of General Walter, the Commander of the XIVth Brigade, and there Major Lasalle was charged and tried as a spy, found guilty and shot. Wintringham did not think he was a spy, or if he was, he was a fool, as he would have been better advised to have sought a staff position than to command a battalion. "A staff officer has plenty of opportunities for a little quiet sabotage, something effectively not done at a vital moment. Whereas all that Commandant L. did, and did not do, amounted to the botching of a minor offensive—nasty, but not vital."[29]

Yet it had cost the lives of many brave men, among them Ralph Fox, at the age of thirty-six, and John Cornford, who had turned twenty-one on December 27, 1936. On that day, or on the next, he was killed in action. His body was never recovered.

2 Julian Bell

He returned to England on Friday, March 12, 1937. In the evening there was family reunion at Charleston for which the Woolfs came down from London. That morning Mrs Woolf had noted in her diary, "Julian back today". He greeted them in Chinese dress, a long silk robe, lilac-coloured, buttoned up to his chin. He was affectionate but cool, at times almost severe, although he laughed a great deal. His elders felt at once that he had been changed by his experience in China, was much more sure of himself than he had ever been in the past. But that evening there was a determination on everyone's part to maintain the gaiety of the occasion, and a careful avoidance of the question uppermost in their thoughts: what he intended to do. He had brought back gifts for them all, and these were opened now in their bright paper wrappings: earrings and small jewels for Vanessa and Angelica; and for Mrs Woolf a glass fish. Julian explained, "I saw it in the market and I said that's my dear Aunt." It took them back to his early childhood, when Aunt Virginia would bring him toys to float in the bath, enjoying them as much as he did himself. But all that was long in the past; now they were struck by the change in him. He wore his Chinese robe like an armour, protecting himself against their love and solicitude.

The next afternoon he went over to Monk's House for tea with the Woolfs. Their first impressions were confirmed. Julian had always been a fascinating mixture of childishness and a very real seriousness; now it was the latter that dominated. Mrs Woolf did not consider the change altogether a happy one so far as the immediate future was concerned. While she admired the evident signs of a new maturity and strength, she also recognized a certain stubbornness and obstinacy which was bound to be intensified, or perhaps had even been called into existence, by his determination to go to Spain in opposition to his mother—with whom, doubtless, her sister agreed. Spain was not mentioned that afternoon, however, although there was talk of politics with Leonard Woolf. But his aunt felt that his very avoidance of the subject proved that his mind was already made up; he knew she would be critical of his going, if only because it would cause so much unhappiness to Vanessa, and therefore he chose not to discuss it with her. So again, the occasion was all cheerfulness and affection on the surface, and sadness and disquiet beneath.[1]

Julian was in England until early June, a young man with a purpose. There was no doubt in his own mind that Spain was his objective, and his friends and relatives recognized this almost immediately—that was the change in him: his unwonted determination—although they continued, the older generation at least, to attempt to dissuade him from it, and in one particular were successful. Meanwhile, as he waited for the machinery to turn, he carried on in a very 'Julian' fashion his multi-levelled existence: art, love and politics. He was not at all a fatalist; he did not mean to 'sacrifice' himself in Spain; he intended to survive, and afterwards, when he came back, to enter upon a political career of some sort, either in party politics, or as a polemicist. He conferred with Hugh Dalton, and in April he was canvassing for the Labour party in Birmingham. It was "a queer business, not awfully inspiriting," he wrote to his mother. "The proletariat just lumpish and dull. The real politics a fair lot of work, and plenty of tiresome driving. I canvass and exploit my smile and Cambridge manner, not too badly." Birmingham itself he summed up as "filthy and unholy and stinking, but with compensations".[2] But the result itself was discouraging. Two months later, on June 5, the day before he left for Spain, he wrote to Marie Mauron, "*les véritables prolétariens votent solidement pour les conservateurs, comme toujours*".

He had not abandoned his literary activities. He had seen to it that the stories of his favourite pupil, C. C. Yeh, were translated and sent on to John Lehmann, who chose one of them for the first number of *New Writing*. He revised and arranged into a book the polemical essay-letters he had written in China. He wrote a hostile review (for the *New Statesman*) of *Towards Armageddon*, by General Fuller, then on the extreme Right, in which Julian advanced his theory that the military establishment would be better ordered under Socialism than, as the General suggested, under Fascism.[3] He assembled a set of informative, albeit very compressed, notes for a memoir—prompted to this by a reading of Gibbon's *Autobiography*. But he wrote no poems. He had come to view his writing, as he viewed his life, as dedicated to a purpose. He had absolutely no interest (for himself) in Bloomsbury's belief in the sanctity of the work of art. In May he wrote to his brother that his essays were "meant to cause pain to intellectuals, thought if possible, but pain anyway. It's no use persuading woollies and softies and c.p. hysterics into being honourable and common sense soldiers. But it is just worth publishing my reflections for those who are capable, but want a lead. You see, it's a matter of changing attitudes, not immediate policies. Consequently it's far more important to me to get attention than assent."[4]

His writings became polemical, and were intended to serve his purpose; so too were certain occasions. He revisited Cambridge, to see old friends and favourite haunts, but also to speak to a gathering of Apostles—the Society had been recently revived—on the military virtues. Michael Straight, John Cornford's friend, who was among the company, describes Julian, "wearing a strange cloak and a hat of black lamb's wool" brought back from China, and tells how "he spoke of the soldier as his new-found ideal; beneath the outward argument lay his inward affirmation, that henceforth he would carry out the obligation of his generation as he saw it, but with the soldier's detachment, the soldier's disinterested devotion to duty. No one present, as I remember, understood all that he was saying; no one certainly grasped his point: that in a world in which no cause was above reproach, one had still to choose, and at the same time, to maintain one's own integrity."[5]

This talk was of a piece with his conviction of what writing must be: useful work, intended to convince people of a certain point of view, or at least to make them aware of it, to call into question what they thought they believed. "My own proposals," he wrote to Lehmann on the day he left for Spain, "comprise one small book, polemical and likely to cause annoyance if only I can get it read." Impatient and full of ideas and 'all over the place', he would not follow the example of his elders who made writing a work of art, no matter what their subject. His aunt complained of this. Her objection centred on the seeming carelessness of his attitude towards writing, not on what he chose to write about. Polemics were not unknown in Bloomsbury. There were her own *Three Guineas* and *A Room of One's Own*. Works by Leonard Woolf and Keynes. The response to Clive Bell's political pamphlets had been precisely of the sort that Julian would have welcomed. Most of the copies of his anti-war tract of 1915, *Peace at Once*, were seized and burnt by the order of the Lord Mayor: a tribute to his power to annoy. Julian was never as secure in this power: he slashed out too haphazardly. In March he wrote to his mother, "I finished the thing I was writing [the Letter to E. M. Forster] and think it bad, but can't face doing it again." He was perhaps too severe in his final judgment, but he was as conscious of his defects as any of his critics: "The worst of it is that I've said all I had to say about as clearly as I can say it. But it won't come alive, it's just one thing after another, and prose is such wretched stuff to correct in bulk because one can't see the bits of it simultaneously. I mean I can keep a whole poem in my head and make changes accordingly. But it's all I can do to remember my argument, and I know lots of the transitions are the most frightfully abrupt jerks and don't make very good sense. Altogether it's a bad business." Conceivably, at some point in the future he might have bettered the work, but, as he wrote in the prefatory note he provided for the essays on his last day in England, he lacked "the time and opportunity for a really minute and scrupulous revision"; nor, one suspects, did he feel very urgently a need to revise. He had not come back from China to further his literary career; nor to participate in a round of social activities and amorous intrigues—"*une vie personelle quelque peu compliquée*"; nor to lay the groundwork for a future career in politics. He had come back, primarily, to convince his mother of the rightness of his decision to participate in the Spanish Civil War.

Bloomsbury's objections to his going to Spain had to do, as one might expect, with questions of personal relations—Vanessa must not be hurt—and with questions of rationality: was it a sensible course of action that he proposed for himself? They were brought up short by his determination to go, his conviction that he must do this thing which he felt, whether rightly or wrongly, was necessary to do, and which transcended even his great love for his mother. It was not only, then, a conflict of ideas between the older and the younger generation of Bloomsbury, but also between reason and romanticism. For there can be no question, no matter how Julian attempted to rationalize his decision, that he was spurred on, at the deepest level of feeling, by a romantic ideal of Honour and the Test that must not be failed, against which Bloomsbury's clear-headed appeals to reason could not hope to succeed.

David Garnett tells how he went down to Charleston "to try to persuade him that he would be far better employed in helping to prepare for inevitable war against Hitler than in risking his life in Spain where he could take no effective or important part". But Julian was "immovably set upon going", and Garnett was so impressed by his seriousness that he only "roughly advanced" his prepared arguments. They were standing in the walled garden, "by a little marble bust of his grandmother Julia, as a young girl". Julian listened carefully, but his mind was made up "Even if he could do nothing much in Spain, he argued that his experience might be valuable and what he saw might teach him a good deal about modern methods of warfare." Garnett did not feel he could deny this, and their discussion ended. "A few moments later we were standing by the Charleston pond, and looking at him as he eagerly watched the sticklebacks darting in and out of the weeds, I could not tell whether he was happier when he was a man or when he went back to being a child."[6]

Garnett's was the argument of reason; similarly, Mrs Woolf was persuaded that he might do more for the cause in which he believed if he remained in England and worked for it there—presumably by writing propaganda, helping to raise money, signing petitions, expending his powers, as Auden put it, "on the flat ephemeral pamphlet and the boring meeting". Action of that sort, no matter how sensible or useful, would hardly be likely to appeal to Julian. (Going to Spain, as he perhaps realized, would set him apart from most of his literary contemporaries: the majority of volunteers for the International Brigade came from the working classes, not the 'Oxbridge' intelligentsia.) Mrs Woolf, increasingly concerned for Vanessa, meanwhile cast about for spokesmen for her own position. She arranged for him to meet with Kingsley Martin and Stephen Spender, both of whom had been in Spain, apparently hoping that they would convince Julian he could be as useful to the cause of the Republic in London as in Barcelona. But his mind was already made up: he told Spender he was "joining for the duration of the quarrel".

Conviction—a belief in the rightness of his decision—made it simple to disregard appeals to reason. Appeals to sentiment, based on his lifelong and unshakeable attachment to his mother, were far more formidable and difficult to cope with, especially when it was she herself who made them. We will never know the nature or contents of their talks. It seems fair to assume, though, that his mother told him of her abhorrence of war, and of her disapproval of his going to participate, on every possible ground, ranging from personal concern (her fear for his safety) to points of principle. She and Clive Bell had never wavered in their convictions as pacifists. They would have agreed with the sentiments Julian had expressed in the letter to a friend from which we have already quoted, which he had written just one year earlier, in March 1936: "I can't think anything worth war—not even saving Russia or smashing Musso . . . It is the last horror, and I can't feel sure enough of any theory to outweigh that certainty." In August 1938, a year after Julian's death, Clive Bell in his pamphlet *War Mongers* (published by the Peace Pledge Union) declared himself "an out-and-out pacifist" in opposition to those who "hate Fascism and Nazism more than they love peace . . . A Nazi Europe would be, to my mind, heaven on earth compared with Europe at war . . . the worst tyranny is better than the best war . . . War is the worst of all evils."[7] But with the outbreak of the Spanish Civil War, which he saw as a first battle in the coming international war against Fascism, Julian had ceased to be a pacifist and had written his 'Letter to E. M. Forster' to explain why; appeals to him on that level would leave him unmoved. But on the level of personal feeling he could not help but be affected by his mother's concern. Their private conversations—which they shared with no one, keeping no diaries, writing no letters—continued unresolved until almost the end of April. Hints of tension between them were glimpsed rarely. On the afternoon when Julian and Bunny Garnett had talked in the garden at Charleston, they had afterwards gone over to Rodmell to visit the Woolfs. When it was time to leave, Julian remarked ironically, "If I'm late, my mother will think I'm killed." The remark, trivial in itself, suggested that the strain was beginning to tell: usually she was "Vanessa"; she would be "my mother" only jokingly, or as now, when her anxiety made it so painfully difficult for him to do what he wanted. Those closest to them both knew that had it not been for Vanessa, he would have gone directly to the International Brigade and not returned to England at all.

He would not yield in his determination to go out to Spain, but at length, having recognized the intensity of her feeling, and indeed of his own where she was concerned, he agreed to compromise: he would go, not as a soldier in the International Brigade, but as an ambulance driver for Spanish Medical Aid. This was a concession not only to her principles—to drive an ambulance was an approved activity in war-time: Garnett had done so in World War I—but a concession also to her fears for his safety. The casualty rate among drivers for Spanish Medical Aid—at least as reported—was remarkably low: only one man lightly wounded, Julian told Marie Mauron in the letter in which he announced his departure for Spain, "*avec la Croix Rouge, conduire un ambulance. C'est un compromis . . .*"

Here perhaps one must take note of a curious detail: that Mrs Woolf was told by Vanessa that the crucial factor in bringing Julian round to a compromise had been some letters he was shown describing the plight of a young English Communist in the International Brigade. The young man in question, who had gone out impulsively to Spain, was appalled by the horrors of the battlefield, and disillusioned by the strict military discipline that was imposed by the Communist leadership of the Brigade. It seems highly unlikely that Julian was influenced in any significant degree by this correspondence, no matter what his mother chose to believe. His own decision to go out to Spain was in no sense unpremeditated; he took a hard-headed view of death and suffering as the necessary evils of war; as an admirer of the "military virtues", and as a serious student of military affairs, he would entertain no idealistic notion of a peoples' army free of rank and discipline. One can only conclude that, as a kindness to his mother, he allowed her to think that he was making this compromise not simply as a concession to her fears for his safety, but for other reasons as well.

Why had the discussions with his mother, to whom he would listen with more respect and love than to any other person, led only to this compromise which fell far short of satisfying her wishes? (True, he was not to bear arms, but he was still going to Spain, he would be on the battlefields, he would be exposed to danger.) Chiefly, it would appear, because he had made a commitment to himself to go, which he refused to break. It was his obligation and test, he felt, to prove himself to himself, as a significant member of his generation who could make a contribution of example, experience and knowledge, rather than languish in a backwater, whether in London or China, as a mere second-generation and second-rate Bloomsburian. His determination seemed to Mrs Woolf evidence of how he had changed, but determination was not really a new aspect of Julian's character. It was simply that now, for the first time, with absolute seriousness, he had fixed on something to be determined about. As he had written to 'B' some years before, in a very different context, "I see everything in terms of struggle and victory and defeat, and get an obstinate 'no surrender' feeling. But there it is—I'm like that, and now it's too late for me to change."

Clearly, his going to Spain represented a break away from the domination of his elders and of Bloomsbury. It was the difference of the generations again, Art (the 1920s) versus Politics (the 1930s), Detachment versus Commitment, the swing-round, albeit unconsciously, to the principles and scruples of the Sir Leslies. And so, not surprisingly, his elders could never arrive at an entirely satisfactory explanation of Julian's going. Mrs Woolf made the point eloquently:

I go on asking myself, without finding an answer, what did he feel about Spain? What made him feel it necessary, knowing as he did how it must torture Nessa, to go? He knew her feeling . . . and yet deliberately inflicted this fearful anxiety on her. What made him do it? I suppose it's a fever in the blood of the younger generation which we can't possibly understand. I have never known anyone of my generation have that feeling about a war. We were all C.O.s in the last war. And though I understand that this is a 'cause', can be called the cause of liberty and so on, still my natural reaction is to fight intellectually: if I were any use, I should write against it: I should evolve some plan for fighting English tyranny. The moment force is used, it becomes meaningless and unreal to me. And I daresay he would soon have lived through the active stage and have found some other, administrative, work. But that does not explain his determination. Perhaps it was restlessness, curiosity, some gift that had never been used in private life, and a conviction, part emotional, about Spain. Anyhow Q. said during one of our walks . . . "If he hadn't gone he'd have been absolutely miserable" and said it with such conviction that I believed it. My own feeling then about his going wavers: I'm sometimes angry with him; yet feel it was fine, as all very strong feelings are fine; yet they are also wrong somehow; one must control feeling with reason.

In late April, after "so many arguments", he agreed to compromise. He got in touch with George Jeger, the Organizing Secretary of Spanish Medical Aid, and made arrangements through him to go out to Spain as an ambulance driver.

Spanish Medical Aid had come into existence in early August 1936, a few weeks after the outbreak of the war. By the end of that month it had already sent a unit out, under the leadership of Kenneth Sinclair-Loutit, a contemporary of John Cornford's at Cambridge, which set up a field hospital on the Aragon front.

In the months since August 1936 S.M.A. had sent out further units to various parts of Republican Spain, where they established hospitals on the Madrid front, the Cordoba front, at Cuenca, Murcia and Albacete. Spanish Medical Aid requirements were simple, and Julian easily fulfilled them. His only difficulty was in learning to drive a lorry, which he found very different from a small car, but which he mastered in his own fashion and thereafter drove with the same high-spirited disregard for the rules of the road as had terrified his friends in the past. Also there were lessons in mechanics—if one's lorry broke down, one had to be able to repair it—lessons in Spanish; lessons in First Aid—how to know if someone is dead, he wrote gaily to Marie Mauron. All this demanded a good deal of his time. So too did his "slightly complicated" personal life. 'K' had arrived in London; and there were other young women, her predecessors and successors, who were also eager to see him. He had been leading, as he wrote to Marie Mauron, "*une vie de crises, travaux, leçons, etc*". But finally the date was set for his departure: he was to leave England on the seventh of June.

Two nights before, on a Sunday—a warm summer-like evening—there was an impromptu family dinner in London. The Woolfs called in, it was all very casual, and deliberately so: in fact, it was the last time that they were to see Julian. Lottie, the maid, was out, and Vanessa and Virginia cooked dinner; Julian, in shirt-sleeves, hovered around them, talking, joking, seeing that the toast did not burn . . . After dinner, the conversation turned to politics: a three-sided conversation with only the men taking part. Mrs Woolf, proud of her nephew as she always was, noticed how well Julian held his own with Clive and Leonard: he was no longer a boy to be indulged. But politics was never a subject to engross the Stephen sisters, especially Vanessa, and they went out into the Square with Angelica and gossiped in the warm summer night. Presently the men joined them. At one point Mrs Woolf remarked lightly to Julian that she would leave Roger Fry's papers to him in her will. At once he replied, "Better leave them to the British Museum." They both knew what he was thinking—that he might be killed in Spain—and both quickly turned the conversation elsewhere. Later, when it was time to go, they walked across the Square, Julian and his aunt to the front. Mrs Woolf asked if he might not have time to write something in Spain and send it to them. In effect, she was making amends for the way in which she had dismissed his paper on Roger Fry. "Yes," he said, "I'll write something about Spain. And send it if you like."

Then he and Vanessa drove off in her car. The others stood at the door, watching. Julian leaned out and waved, and called, "Goodbye until this time next year."

When he was still in China and had only the vaguest notions of how one became a volunteer, he had thought he would have to cross into Spain illegally, on foot, alone, in the guise of a hiker, eluding the guards at the frontier. Hence he had written to Quentin to get him a Swedish knapsack and maps of the Pyrenees—the request which had so distressed his mother. As it turned out, it was all a good deal less romantic and more conventional than he had imagined it would be. Spanish Medical Aid was an accredited, non-combatant organization: it was only necessary to sign an undertaking that one would not participate in any belligerent activity, and to pass a driving test for an ambulance—thereafter one travelled perfectly legally with a passport into Spain.

Julian went out with a convoy of ambulance trucks, driving across France. On the third day, June 10, they reached Perpignan. "It's been a stiffish drive, but not bad fun," he wrote to his mother. "We celebrated the sight of the Pyrenees with a smash, the man in front of me in the convoy coming off a corner and turning clear over. By miracle, he wasn't hurt at all . . . I've spent my afternoon delivering French rhetoric to hurry camions [through the town]. In general I'm the only one of the convoy who talks fluent French—none of us talks decent Spanish! It's really rather fun—very like last year's journey to Fa-Tsien-lu. Some of the country looks lovely, and we [that is, he and his mother] must see it again in peace. In general I'm enjoying life a lot . . . and all's boyscoutish in the highest."

Crossing the frontier without event, the convoy proceeded down the Costa Brava—"still, to appearances, a charming, peaceful country: posters and troops a bit, but masses of leisurely civilians"—to Valencia, since the previous November the seat of the Government of Republican Spain, and where were located the headquarters of the British section of Spanish Medical Aid. Sir Richard Rees, when he had arrived on the same errand as Julian three months earlier, had found this command post in charge of "an English peer who might have come straight from Pall Mall, and an

Anglo-Italian peeress who might have come straight from the Lido".[8] One would expect Julian to report details of this kind to his mother, and no doubt he would have done so if he had had time and quiet enough—as it was, there were "too many minor events and really I'm too stupid to write good letters". And again—in the same letter from Valencia, on June 13—"I'll try to write longer and better letters." And in the concluding paragraph: "I'll try to write more . . . But it's an unpropitious atmosphere." Which no doubt it was, for letter-writing, but he was immensely enjoying himself, his spirits were high, and he reassured her that, "So far war has meant nothing worse than hard driving." Nor did he regret coming out, then or later. "I'm extremely content . . ." he wrote. And this, without qualification, was to be his attitude throughout his short happy life in Spain: ". . . it's the sort of life that suits me."

Once he had reported to headquarters—to the peer and the peeress?—he had little to do in Valencia for the next few days but hang about "waiting for orders—just like war—and China". He had been given one quasi-official task: to drive up into the mountains to buy eggs for the unit. On the return: "I broke a passenger's nose on the windscreen, thanks to my infernally fierce brakes." But on the whole the tone in these first days was of a "Mediterranean holiday", and there was time enough for a picnic and bathing at a seaside villa, to attend a "goodish" bullfight, and to listen to gossip of the war which was "plentiful and contradictory, and not really worth repeating". In his exhilarated mood—"it's a very good life to live"—he could even persuade himself that his "military and political education" had begun, that he was "seeing a number of things at first hand one had only read about before"—which, of course, was an important reason for his coming to Spain. But thus far nothing of any real military significance had offered itself: he speaks only of driving through Valencia "in almost pitch darkness". And to have understood so early the politics of the Republic, even merely to have sorted out the various factions struggling for power within the Government and outside it, would have required him to be an observer of superhuman acuteness and political sophistication.

At the time of his arrival, June 13, the most extensive military activity was in the north, in the Basque provinces, the hard-fought campaign that would end with the fall of Bilbao to Franco's forces on the 19th. Politically, the chief concern of the moment was the liquidation of the P.O.U.M., a sequel to the internecine rioting in Barcelona in May. The fighting in the north, with the Catholic Basques firmly on the side of the Republic, and the ideological war within the war in Barcelona, were complicated aspects of a struggle that was far more complex than most of the foreign volunteers who came to participate in it suspected. Julian, newly arrived in Valencia, would have been familiar only with the gossip of the cafés or the simplifications of the press, to neither of which he paid much attention. After all, he had not come to Spain to unravel the complexities of Spanish politics, but to gain military experience. He was waiting impatiently in Valencia for the end of "this preposterous holiday", and for the beginning of his official duties as an ambulance driver. There were a number of destinations to which he might be sent, and judging from the career of Richard Rees in Spain, it is evident that members of the Medical Aid service were moved about widely and frequently. Rees, an Etonian, a Socialist, a great friend of George Orwell and Middleton Murry, and former editor of the *Adelphi*, had come out to Spain in April. In the two months since then, he had been stationed in Valencia, at Cuenca, about fifty miles from Madrid on the Madrid-Valencia road, and also on the Cordoba front. Julian thought it likely he would be based at the convalescent hospital at Cuenca, "at first, anyway", which would have been a comparatively quiet assignment. But in fact he was sent up to Madrid—as was Rees, from the Sierra Morena—for the new offensive the government forces were about to launch, rumours of which had been bruited about in the cafés for the past two months.

It was a notable instance of how political considerations had their effect upon military decisions. As Hugh Thomas tells us in his history of the war, several Republican officers of the high command proposed an attack on Estremadura in the south-west. Largo Caballero, the Socialist Prime Minister, supported the idea; the Communists opposed it, and endorsed a proposal of the new Russian chief adviser, General Kulik, to mount a campaign at Madrid, "striking down from the Republican positions along the Corunna road towards the little town of Brunete, cutting off the Nationalists in the Casa de Campo and the University City".

"This military quarrel," Thomas points out, "merged into the larger Communist feud with Largo Caballero." In mid-May, after the rioting in Barcelona, there was a cabinet crisis. Largo Caballero resigned, and was replaced as Prime Minister by Juan Negrin. Negrin, a moderate Socialist, "was ready to make any political sacrifice to win the war. This of course led him, as it had led Largo Caballero and Prieto, into close relations with Russia, since, as before, Russia remained the only source of arms. Furthermore their political moderation and ruthless realism in face of the war made the Spanish Communist party, throughout Negrin's ministry, the most useful political party in Spain."[9] What this meant, so far as the proposed offensive was concerned, was that the Estremadura scheme was abandoned and the Communist plan prevailed: an attempt was to be made to cut off the besiegers of Madrid from the west. Whatever the military value of the plan, its political propaganda value was undeniable. In the eyes of the world, Madrid was Spain; it was the heart of the Republic; the effort to break the long siege would be certain to attract a maximum of sympathetic attention. This was the background, with which he had no way of being acquainted, of the battle of Brunete, in which Julian was soon to be involved.

By June 22 he had been sent up to Madrid. Undoubtedly he had heard rumours of the coming offensive, but "not much news now that's much use," he wrote to his mother, "you must have far more in London. What we do hear doesn't sound nice." But he was not prepared to write her a detailed account of what he was doing, for he knew that that would only alarm her, and as usual there was "really no time at all for writing". This, his next to last letter to her, was written late at night while he and his fellow drivers waited for the telephone calls that would summon them again to their ambulances, driving back and forth to wherever there was fighting on the outskirts of the besieged city, and in the countryside beyond, bringing back the wounded, and then away again. It was arduous work. "Fortunately I've partnered myself, more or less, with Rees, who's nice and competent." Between them they had "a very hard two-days' driving, about 500 miles", in a constant shuttle to and from the front. Yet his spirits were wonderfully high: "the people are often charming and almost always amusing . . . The country is lovely—as you'll remember—and singularly unmilitarized: true, one is stopped fairly often by guards, but they're all extremely friendly. Madrid is utterly fantastic in the way it keeps the war on one edge and a fairly ordinary civil life going on—you can take the metro to the front, etc. . . . It's utterly impossible to give the full fantastic effect of it all. But I find it perpetually entertaining and very satisfactory." He had only one complaint—that he had not been close enough to the actual fighting. "Tell Q. that so far I've only hearsay about technique. I'll see what I can tell him later." And so to the final paragraph: "My Spanish improves, but still has awful fade-outs into Chinese. Good-night—I'm very sleepy, and goodness knows what will happen tomorrow. But it's a better life than most I've led." This was not simply a declaration intended to reassure his mother and lessen her anxieties; it was what he truly felt, what he truly believed.

A week later, on July 1, he wrote what proved to be his last letter to his mother from Spain. (Or he may have written other letters in the next three weeks which she did not receive.) It begins: "There is a sudden crisis here—at last—and rumours of an attack." In fact, the Republican army was now almost ready to launch its "long-discussed offensive". The build-up had been in progress since mid-June. There was a massive assemblage of troops and equipment in and about the town of El Escorial. Within the enormous San Lorenzo del Escorial palace itself, two hospitals were set up to receive casualties; one of the courtyards was designated a motor pool for the ambulances of the Medical Aid service. The Republican army, which included the XIth, XIIth, and XVth International Brigades, "numbered 50,000 in all. It was supported by 150 aircraft, 128 tanks and 136 pieces of artillery."[10] Clearly, Julian was going to take part in one of the largest, and, as it proved, one of the most costly offensives of the war.

"So far"—he was writing to her five days before the battle began—"it's all an uneventful life of minor events." There had been a "furious struggle", in the best army tradition, to keep the house where the Medical Aid drivers were billeted from being taken over by a transport corps—and here his fluent French again proved useful. "It's all the oddest out-of-the-world business you can imagine." But it was not without its grim aspect also: he mentioned that Richard Rees had "had his dose of horrors, evacuating badly wounded patients to a rear hospital about a hundred miles off. It was a grim story—not possible to write." What he chose not to let her know was that this was one of the occasions when he had shared the driving with Rees. And even in the course of writing to her, he had had to break off for a "new crisis". When he resumed the letter the next day he explained that he had spent the interval in a twelve-hours' drive, midnight to midday, "evacuating lightly wounded some fifty miles over very bad roads. I've discovered that I can fall asleep with my eyes open—or pretty near."

He was growing impatient; his military instincts were being "badly shocked, both on a large and a small scale"; he was getting "very angry over organization"; he had "the worst forebodings for anything so public as our present operation". Against this was the prospective satisfaction of seeing "something at first hand . . . it does mean, personally, excitement and events".

> One thing [he concluded]—I do think I'm being of real use as a driver, in that I'm careful and responsible and work on my car—a Chevrolet ambulance, small lorry size. Most of our drivers are wreckers, neglect all sorts of precautions like oiling and greasing, over speed etc. Any really good and careful drivers out here would be really valuable.
>
> The other odd element is the Charlestonian one of improvising materials—a bit of carpet to mend a stretcher, e.g.—in which I find myself at home.
>
> I don't know what will happen to this—I expect continue in a few days, after another false alarm.
>
> No, all clear and morning.

At dawn on July 6 the offensive was begun. Republican troops moved south from El Escorial towards Brunete, some fifteen miles distant, on the road leading into Madrid from the west. If the town could be taken and held, control of the road would fall to the Government, and the Nationalist forces who had been fighting on the outskirts of Madrid since the previous autumn would be cut off from supplies and reinforcements. All went with remarkable ease at first. The Nationalists apparently were surprised by the offensive—which seems odd, considering the publicity that had surrounded it and that had given rise to Julian's forebodings—and Brunete was in the hands of the Republicans by noon.

Two days earlier, an International Writers Congress, attended by some eighty writers from twenty-seven countries, all of them dedicated supporters of the Republic, had got under way in Valencia. On July 6 the Congress was moved to Madrid—a strategic change of scene which gave the visiting writers a more vivid sense of being in the midst of the struggle; indeed, in the quieter intervals between speechmaking and applause, the sound of gunfire could be heard in the distance. During the afternoon session there was a dramatic interruption when a group of soldiers, fresh from the front, "rushed up to the platform carrying two Fascist banners taken at Brunete and the uniform of a captured Fascist colonel, and a whole handful of women's gold lockets which this same colonel had appropriated in the course of a raid on the civilian population. The soldiers announced that an advance of sixteen kilometres had been made since daybreak. Their offensive . . . was succeeding beyond expectations."

The news from the front grew progressively worse in succeeding days, but by then the delegates were caught up in a battle of their own: whether or not to vote a motion of censure against André Gide, who had written an unfavourable account of his travels in Russia in *Retour de l'U.S.S.R.*, and as Malcolm Cowley remarked, "Sometimes the struggle was drowned out by the sound of guns." Between sessions they were driven out in limousines, like minor royalty, to raise the morale of near-by peasant villages; and in Madrid itself "the waiters' trade union and the town council made it a point of honour to make such arrangements as to prevent their foreign guests from noticing any difference in the standard of living between Paris and Madrid".[11]

Julian himself was a poet and intellectual; he might as logically have attended a Congress of Writers in Madrid as driven an ambulance on the Brunete front. Yet one feels quite safe in saying that if he had, he would have detested it. When he heard of it—originally, in letters from London—he dismissed it in a few satirical phrases to Rees. Like John Cornford, he had chosen to be a man of action, and there is every reason to believe he was happy in his choice. The rhetoric of the Congress, cast in the mould of heroic clichés—however sincerely it may in some cases have been intended—would have convinced him that he had chosen well.

On July 7, the British Battalion of the XVth International Brigade captured the village of Villanueva de la Canada on the Brunete–El Escorial Road. But the advance, as Hugh Thomas points out, was slowed by an extraordinary confusion:

> Brigade upon brigade were sent through a small breach in the Nationalist lines, and became mixed up with each other. The known political background to the attack caused Republican officers and non-Communists in general to grumble about the direction of the battle . . . By midnight on the first day of the attack, Varela [the Nationalist commander] reported to Franco that a front had been re-established. Twenty-four hours later, 31 battalions and 9 batteries had arrived in reinforcement of the Nationalist position. The battle, fought on the parched Castillian plain at the height of summer, assumed a most bloody character.[12]

Julian was now as much in the thick of things as he could have hoped: at last he was having his experience of war. Admittedly he was a non-combatant, but in the Brunete campaign the ambulance driver was as exposed to danger as the soldier; the job to be done demanded strength, endurance, resourcefulness and courage. If Julian was denied the satisfaction of bearing arms, he was granted the satisfaction, denied to the ordinary soldier, of knowing that what he was doing was actually useful. The amateurishness, confusion and contentiousness that seem to have marked much of the military action throughout the war were not unknown in the Medical Aid service, but proved of less moment there once an action had begun. Unlike the ordinary soldier who waits for the orders of his superior officers, who wait for the orders of *theirs*, and so upward, as in the instance of the Brunete campaign, to the very highest political and military levels, the ambulance driver has a clear-cut idea of what he must do, and his is the responsibility for getting it done. It is an aspect of war where initiative and a talent for improvisation particularly count. In the circumstances, Julian thrived.

The medical unit established a kind of sub-headquarters for ambulances among the olive trees outside Villanueva de la Canada. When rebel planes flew over, strafing or dropping bombs, the drivers took shelter in the trenches that the Fascist troops had dug and abandoned on the second day of the battle. It was there too that they would try to sleep at such odd, infrequent off-duty moments as came their way. They were continually on the move, driving out to the various first-aid stations along the front to collect the wounded, and returning with them to the hospitals at the Escorial, while day after day, night after night, the battle continued. By day, "villages, towns and fields were sprayed with steel from planes, guns and machine guns. At night whole square kilometres of earth would go up in flame." Ambulance drivers were only seldom able to take advantage of the "illusory safety of trenches and dug outs", and casualties among them were heavy: by the end of the three weeks' Brunete campaign, one half of the British Medical Unit had been killed.

Much of the driving was done at night. "It was a second or third class road," Rees has recalled, "filled with shell holes and usually thronged with military traffic; and lights were forbidden. Since I got no regular sleep during the whole three weeks I was sometimes obliged to pull up and go to sleep in order to avoid dozing off at the wheel; and I did this with complete callousness, giving no thought at all for the state of the wounded men in the ambulance. If an aeroplane flew over, the more conscious among them would begin shouting to me: 'Hombre! We shall be bombed! Drive on! Do you want to kill us all?' But I was at a point of fatigue where I believe I wouldn't have stirred if I had been sitting on a bonfire which I knew someone was setting light to."[13] This callousness, as Rees calls it, had to be adopted if one was to do one's job efficiently—after all, it would have been a doubtful service to the wounded to fall asleep at the wheel while driving—and it was entirely in accord with the attitude of hard-headed realism, the refusal to give way to sentimentality, piety or squeamishness, that Julian had advocated in his 'Letter to E. M. Forster'.

There he had written, "I have always been grateful for being made, as a child, to look at a stag having its throat cut, and that I have reached the stage of contemplating a corpse in the road without a Baudelairian extravaganza of horror. This seems to me the common human experience, and I have never perceived in myself any evil consequences. It is this making a moral principle of a physical squeamishness that is the greatest weakness of all religion, and most of all pacifism. To hate war because it is wasteful of good lives and useful objects is rational; to hate war because killing is wicked is defensible; but to hate war only because a battlefield of carrion makes you sick is hardly adequate: one hates a channel crossing on the same grounds, yet is, none the less, ready to go to France." Forster, in his 'Notes for a Reply', singled this passage out: "The analysis of squeamishness helps me. By next year [1939] it is probable that some of us will be killed and all of us have to see dead people lying about. Our own deaths we must meet with equipment of longer standing, in fact, with all our civilisation, whatever that may be. But Julian's tips may come in useful over corpses."[14] Detachment (or callousness) is the recommended attitude for the battlefield; pity is a civilian luxury. One feels certain that Julian would have approved Rees's statement that his "most disagreeable experience of war so far had been its disgustingness rather than its terror. The chloroform-like odour of decaying corpses all through the hot breathless nights and the peculiarly loathesome sickly sour smell of the dust in the trenches . . . And the sight of dead bodies lying slumped grotesquely beside the road, like life-size wax dolls, was disgusting and sinister rather than pitiful."[15]

On July 9, the Republicans captured the village of Quijorna; on the 11th, they took two further villages. But Boadilla, beyond Brunete on the road to Madrid, although repeatedly attacked, would not yield. By July 13 offensive action was at an end. "Henceforward the Republicans would be attempting to defend the positions which they had won. On July 15, after further fierce fighting around Boadilla, orders were given for trenches to be dug. The Republic had gained a pocket of land about twelve kilometres deep by fifteen wide."[16]

When Julian had arrived at the Escorial, he had been delighted to discover that one of the doctors assigned to the hospital there was an old friend from King's, Archie Cochrane. Neither had known the other was in Spain; they had a brief, exultant reunion, and brief but enlivening encounters thereafter. The battle raged about them day after day—there was hardly time for more than a cigarette together when Julian would drive his ambulance into the motor court. Cochrane himself had been with the medical unit since the previous September; he had seen so much of the suffering and cruelty of war that he had come to live on a kind of "grey plateau" of feeling. Julian, with his exuberance and vitality and unflagging spirit, brightened his life immeasurably.

Rees, of course, saw him much more often, and he was similarly impressed. It seemed to him that Julian was having the most wonderful time of his life. He was extremely serious about his work—down to the smallest details—determined to do whatever had to be done with a maximum of efficiency and a minimum of fuss. At the same time he was enjoying it all, observing, making suggestions, explaining to Rees his idea of 'Socialism from above' as they drove across the battlefields, being unmistakably 'upper class' in his manner—but Julian never tried to be anything other than what he was, and he felt no need or desire to pretend to be a member of the proletariat. He had come to Spain, hoping to be in the midst of a major battle, and it turned out that he was in a better position as an ambulance driver to see what was going on than if he had been a soldier in the British Battalion. He wanted to learn about modern warfare; quite logically, in the sense that the totalitarians, Hitler, Mussolini and Stalin, were using Spain as a laboratory, he was there to observe their experiments. Political subtleties and allegiances did not overly concern him. He had never thought of Spain as the incarnation of an ideal, nor had he been swept up in a rush of ideological enthusiasm—hence he did not run the risk of being disillusioned: only of being killed.

Early in the morning of July 15, his ambulance was smashed by a bomb—he himself was unhurt. Since there was no other car available for him to drive, he volunteered to go up to the front as a stretcher-bearer. It was the morning of the last fierce fighting around Boadilla. Julian was put in charge of a squad of thirty stretcher-bearers, and went out to work in that very dangerous sector. Towards nightfall there was a lull in the battle. The Republican forces fell back. For the next three days, there was comparative calm at the front, and the stretcher-bearers took advantage of it to bring in the dead. On the morning of the 18th, the Medical Aid unit received a new lorry: this was to be Julian's. As the lull in the battle still continued, he proposed driving out to fill in the shell-holes in the road, which would make the evacuation of the wounded quicker and less painful. It was a practical, concerned, and enterprising thing to have done; it showed that Julian was thinking about the situation, and working to improve the efficiency of his unit. But he would not have the time to complete the job. Suddenly on that day, July 18, 1937, the first anniversary of the outbreak of the Civil War, the battle of Brunete was renewed, with a violent counter-attack by the Nationalists. Their planes roared overhead, dropping bombs indiscriminately. Julian was driving his ambulance along the road outside Villanueva de la Canada. This time his luck was at an end.

Later in the day, a wounded ambulance driver, so covered with dirt as to be unrecognizable, was brought into the Escorial hospital on a stretcher. Cochrane was in charge of the receiving room; he ordered the man to be cleaned. It was only after this was done that he recognized him as Julian. As soon as he examined him, he realized that he had been mortally wounded: a shell fragment had penetrated deep in his chest. All that could be done now was to make him as comfortable as possible.

Julian was still conscious, still cheerful. He murmured to Cochrane, "Well, I always wanted a mistress and a chance to go to the war, and now I've had both." Then he lapsed into French, reciting indistinctly lines of what Cochrane thought might be Baudelaire. Soon after he fell into a coma from which he never awakened.[17]

He was one of the 35,000 men—25,000 on the side of the Republic, 10,000 on the side of the Nationalists—whose lives were lost in the battle of Brunete. The battle itself continued for another six days and ended in a stalemate. It is supposed to have provided interesting material for military theorists on the use of the tank. The Nationalists regained much of the territory taken by the Republican forces, including the town of Brunete; the attempt to gain control of the road into Madrid from the west, which had been the principal object of the offensive, had failed. The Republic had won a strip of territory, five kilometres deep along fifteen kilometres of front. And together with a few other villages it continued to hold the ruins of Villanueva de la Canada.

Julian was taken to the mortuary of the hospital in the Escorial, and there Richard Rees saw him, covered except for his head and shoulders. There was no sign of any wound. He looked "very pale and clean, almost marble-like. Very calm and peaceful, almost as if he had fallen asleep when very cold."

Notes and Sources

This book has been based on relevant published material, on interviews, and on manuscripts, most of them in the possession of the Bell or Cornford families. *Bell*, in the notes, refers to *Julian Bell: Essays Poems and Letters* edited by Quentin Bell with contributions by J. M. Keynes, David Garnett, Charles Mauron, C. Day Lewis and E. M. Forster (London, 1938). *Cornford* refers to *John Cornford: A Memoir* edited by Pat Sloan (London, 1938). Letters and other documents are not noted when their date has not survived, or when the closest known approximation to the date is given in the text, or whenever material which might have been supplied in a note appears already in the text, or, in many cases, when such documents have been published in the memoir volumes. When a name has been omitted, it has been done so deliberately. One number may refer to a series of quotations from the same source.

Part One: *Julian Bell*

I 'A Bloomsbury Childhood'

1 Clive Bell, *Old Friends* (London, 1956), p. 126.
2 Virginia Woolf and Lytton Strachey, *Letters* (London, 1956), pp. 9–14.

3 R. F. Harrod, *The Life of John Maynard Keynes* (London, 1951), pp. 116–17.
4 Bell, op. cit., p. 28.
5 E. M. Forster, *Goldsworthy Lowes Dickinson* (London, 1947), p. 110.
6 J. M. Keynes, *Two Memoirs* (London, 1949), p. 82.
7 G. E. Moore, *Principia Ethica* (Cambridge, 1903), pp. vii, 188–9.
8 Keynes, op. cit., pp. 82–3
9 E. M. Forster, *Howards End* (London, 1910), p. 124.
10 Desmond MacCarthy, *Memories* (London, 1953), pp. 174–5.
11 Harrod, op. cit., p. 114.
12 *Bell*, pp. 10–12.
13 *Bell*, p. 3.
14 David Garnett, *The Flowers of the Forest* (London, 1955), p. 1.
15 Ibid., p. 112.
16 *Bell*, pp. 11–13.
17 Garnett, op. cit., p. 124.
18 Ibid., p. 161.
19 Ibid., p. 176.
20 *Bell*, p. 13.
21 G. F. Jones to authors, October 9, 1963.
22 *Bell*, pp. 13–14.
23 Ibid., p. 15.
24 J. Duncan Wood to authors, November 18, 1963.
25 S. W. Brown, *Leighton Park* (Reading, 1952), p. 182.
26 T. C. Elliott to authors, October 13, 1963.
27 John Lehmann, *The Whispering Gallery* (London, 1955), p. 141.
28 Virginia Woolf, *A Writer's Diary* (London, 1953), p. 63.
29 *Bell*, pp. 18–19.
30 Lehmann, op. cit., p. 142.
31 *Bell*, p. 8.

II 'A Young Apostle'

1 *Bell*, pp. 19–20.
2 *The Cambridge Review*, issues of November 4, 1927; January 20, May 18, November 2, November 16, 1928; April 30, 1929.
3 *Bell*, pp. 20–1.
4 Lehmann, op. cit., pp. 146–7.
5 *The Venture*, June 1930.
6 Lehmann, op. cit., p. 144.
7 To Quentin Bell, October 18, ?1927.
8 *Bell*, p. 5.
9 Lehmann, op. cit., p. 143.

10 Lehmann to Bell, July 3, 1929.
11 *The Cambridge Review*, November 7, 1930, p. 98.
12 Ibid., March 1, 1929, pp. 317–18.
13 To Lehmann, September 15, 1930, part quoted Lehmann, op. cit., p. 146. All letters now in Berg Collection, N.Y. Public Library.
14 To Lehmann, October 21, 1930.
15 To Lehmann, ?Autumn 1930.
16 Lehmann to Bell, November 4, 1930.
17 To Lehmann, November 5, 1930.
18 To Lehmann, July 6, 1929.
19 Lehmann, op. cit., p. 165.
20 Lehmann to Bell, December 30, 1930.
21 Lehmann, op. cit., pp. 172–7.
22 Lehmann to Bell, December 14, 1931.
23 Lehmann, op. cit., p. 174.
24 Lehmann to Bell, December 24, 1931.
25 Lehmann, op. cit., p. 182.
26 Michael Roberts, *New Signatures* (London, 1932), pp. 7–15.
27 Stephen Spender, *World Within World* (New York, 1951), p. 126.
28 Roberts, op. cit., p. 17.
29 Forster, *Goldsworthy Lowes Dickinson*, pp. 207–8.
30 V. Woolf, op. cit., p. 261.
31 To Lehmann, ?Spring 1932.

III 'Searching'

1 Charles Mauron in conversation, August 11, 1962.
2 Lehmann to Bell, July 11, 1930.
3 *New Statesman & Nation*, December 8, 1934, p. 870.
4 To Lehmann, August 9, 1930.
5 *Bell*, p. 7.
6 To Lehmann, October 6, 1931.
7 *New Statesman & Nation*, December 8, 1934, p. 872.
8 Lehmann to Bell, March 21, 1932.
9 ?July 11, 1932.
10 To Lehmann, April 8, 1930.
11 See Frederick Grubb, 'In but not of: A Study of Julian Bell', *Critical Quarterly*, Summer 1960, pp. 120–6. Also his *A Vision of Reality* (London, 1965).
12 *New Statesman & Nation*, March 24, 1934, p. 458.
13 To Lehmann, September 15, 1930.
14 To Playfair, December 23, 1930.
15 To Vanessa Bell, ?May 2, 1931.

16 ?January 10, 1934.
17 Harrod, op. cit., pp. 450–1.
18 *New Statesman & Nation*, December 9, 1933, pp. 731–2.
19 Lehmann, op. cit., pp. 276–7.
20 Quoted as relevant to Julian Bell in Noel Annan, *Leslie Stephen* (London, 1951), p. 40.
21 Julian Bell, *We Did Not Fight* (London, 1935), pp. vi–xix.
22 *New Statesman & Nation*, February 16, 1935, p.224
23 To Lehmann, Spring 1934, part quoted Lehmann, op. cit., p. 277.
24 'Visualization of Marxism' was finally published in the small anthology Lehmann did do in the October 17, 1934, issue of *The New Republic*. 'Redshanks' had been published on its own in the September 26, 1934, issue.
25 Lehmann to Bell, October 21, 1934.

PART TWO: *John Cornford*

I 'Rupert John Cornford'

1 *The Collected Poems of Rupert Brooke*, edited by Edward Marsh (London, 1918), pp. cxxxviii–cxxxix.
2 Ibid., p. clvii.
3 Gwen Raverat, *Period Piece* (London, 1952), pp. 188–91.
4 To William Rothenstein, December 12, 1938, Rothenstein Papers, Houghton Library, Harvard. Quoted in William Rothenstein, *Since Fifty* (New York, 1940), p. 293.
5 Raverat, op. cit., pp. 219–21.
6 *Rupert Brooke*, pp. xli–lxviii.
7 Raverat, op. cit., pp. 280–1.

II 'Stowe'

1 For Roxburgh and Stowe see Noel Annan, *Roxburgh of Stowe* (London, 1965). We are most grateful to Lord Annan for allowing us to see his book in manuscript.
2 Quoted by Sidney Schiff in a letter to Pat Sloan, March 23, 1937.
3 W. H. Auden to Cornford, May 4, 1932.
4 J. F. Roxburgh to J. R. M. Butler, September 19, 1932.

III 'London'

1 Frances and Francis Cornford to J. F. Roxburgh, January 29, 1933.
2 Philip Toynbee, *Friends Apart* (London, 1954), p. 18.

3 George Barker in *Coming to London* (London, 1957), p. 55.
4 *The Listener*, April 25, 1934, p. 714.

IV 'Cambridge'

1 A Group of Contemporaries, 'Cambridge Socialism 1933–1936', *Cornford*, pp. 97–115. For David Guest, see *David Guest* edited by C. Haden Guest (London, 1939).
2 G. de Freitas in *Recollections of the Cambridge Union*, edited by Percy Cradock (Cambridge, 1953), p. 137.
3 Victor Kiernan, 'Recollections', *Cornford*, p. 116. Unless otherwise indicated, quotes about John in Cambridge come from Kiernan, 'Recollections', *Cornford*, pp. 116–24 or A Group of Contemporaries, 'Cambridge Socialism 1933–1936', *Cornford*, pp. 97–115.
4 Mrs Cornford to Reg Snell, n.d.
5 *Student Vanguard*, May, 1933, p. 23.
6 Keith Briant, *Oxford Limited* (New York, 1938), p. 241.
7 Neal Wood, *Communism and British Intellectuals* (London, 1959), p. 52.
8 *The Cambridge Review*, February 8 and 22, 1935, pp. 226, 267.
9 *Cornford*, pp. 125–33.
10 Spender, op. cit., p. 225.
11 Monroe K. Spears, *The Poetry of W. H. Auden* (New York, 1963), p. 154.
12 *The Cambridge Review*, November 2, 1934, p. 61.
13 Ibid., February 22, 1935, p. 268.
14 Ibid., February 8, 1935, p. 221.
15 *Cornford*, pp. 134–50.
16 *The Cambridge Review*, February 8, 1935, p. 232.
17 *Ibid.*, March 1, 1935, p. 283.
18 Ibid., February 8, 1935, p. 225.
19 'For R.J.C.' *New Writing*, Autumn 1937, p. 59.
20 In *Christianity and the Social Revolution* (London, 1935), pp. 237–61. Quoted from pp. 242, 255, 260.
21 *Cornford*, pp. 159–69.
22 Toynbee, op. cit., p. 108.
23 'Notes on the Teaching of History at Cambridge', *Cornford*, pp. 151–8.
24 Straight to authors, January 10, 1963.
25 *The Cambridge Review*, November 8, 1935, p. 95.
26 See Peter Kemp, *Mine Were of Trouble* (London, 1957).
27 *The Cambridge Review*, November 29, 1935, p. 95.
28 Straight to authors, January 10, 1963.

29 Wood, op. cit., p. 52.
30 Previously unpublished.

PART THREE: *Julian Bell in China*

1 June 22, ?1934.
2 All letters written by Bell from China are in chronological order in *Bell*, pp. 28–187, unless otherwise indicated.
3 September 2, 1935.
4 To Playfair, March 20, 1936.
5 To Vanessa, October 31, 1935.
6 Ibid., December 17, 1935.
7 To Playfair, January 22, 1936.
8 Harold Acton, *Memoirs of an Aesthete* (London, 1948), p. 378.
9 To Playfair, February 3, 1936.
10 February 12, 1936.
11 To Vanessa, June 27, 1936.
12 To Vanessa, September 16, 1936.
13 To Playfair, September 4, 25, October 4, 1936.
14 'On Roger Fry', *Bell*, pp. 258–305; 'The Proletariat and Poetry', pp. 306–27; 'War and Peace', pp. 335–90.
15 To Vanessa, September 24, 1935.
16 Ibid., September 20, 1936.
17 Virginia Woolf, 'Reminiscences of Julian' (unpublished), p. 4.
18 To Playfair, April 13, 1936.
19 *Times Literary Supplement*, February 29, 1936.
20 Lehmann, op. cit., pp. 273–4.
21 To Vanessa, October 20, 1936.
22 To Playfair, October 21, 1936.
23 To Vanessa, October 31, 1936.
24 To Playfair, November 1, 1936.
25 To Quentin, November 1, 1936.
26 November 7, 1936.
27 To Vanessa, November 8, 1936.
28 To Playfair, November 12, 21, 1936.
29 To Vanessa, November 29, 1936.
30 To Playfair, December 5, 1936, January 30, 1937.
31 Ibid., November 12, 1936.
32 Ibid., December 26, 1936, January 4, 1937.
33 To Vanessa, November 29, 1936.
34 Ibid., December 24, 1936.
35 Forster, *Bell*, pp. 391–2.

Part Four: *Spain*

I 'John Cornford'

1 Hugh Thomas, *The Spanish Civil War* (London, 1961), p. 110.
2 Franz Borkenau, *The Spanish Cockpit* (Ann Arbor, 1963) (first published, 1937), pp. 69–70.
3 *Cornford*, pp. 197–211.
4 Tom Wintringham, *English Captain* (London, 1939), p. 45.
5 Borkenau, op. cit., p. 93.
6 Gerald Brenan, 'Foreword', Borkenau, op. cit., p. viii.
7 Borkenau, op. cit., pp. 93, *passim.*
8 *Cornford*, pp. 212–35.
9 Borkenau, op. cit., pp. 105–6.
10 Unpublished paragraph of Professor Cornford's memoir.
11 Letter mentioned in diary, 16th day.
12 Wintringham, op. cit., pp. 48–9.
13 Thomas, op. cit., p. 237.
14 Wintringham, op. cit., p. 50.
15 Straight to authors, September 18, 1964.
16 Thomas, op. cit., p. 298.
17 Interview with Sam Russell, July 12, 1963.
18 *Cornford*, pp. 181–2.
19 Percentages from Thomas, op. cit., p. 298. Figures from Wood, op. cit., p. 56. Thomas (p. 637) queries the exactness of these figures. See William Rust, *Britons in Spain* (London, 1939), p. 210.
20 Thomas, op. cit., p. 302.
21 Wintringham, op. cit., p. 50.
22 John Sommerfield, *Volunteer in Spain* (New York, 1937), pp. 24 *passim*. (This book is extremely useful on John's second trip to Spain.)
23 Robert Garland Colodny, *The Struggle for Madrid* (New York, 1958), p. 9.
24 Thomas, op. cit., pp. 322–3.
25 Sommerfield, op. cit., pp. 52–3.
26 Colodny, op. cit., p. 79.
27 Esmond Romilly, *Boadilla* (London, 1937), pp. 265–7.
28 Thomas, op. cit., p. 347.
29 Wintringham, op. cit., pp. 83–4. For the battle see Wintringham, op. cit., pp. 85 *passim*, and Thomas, op. cit., p. 348. On John's death see Humphrey Slater in *Ralph Fox*, edited by John Lehmann, T. A. Jackson and C. Day Lewis (London, 1937), p. 13; Peter Kerrigan, *Volunteer for Liberty*, August 13, 1938; Rust, op. cit.,

p. 26; Walter Greenhalgh, 'When We Fought Franco', *Reynolds News*, July 2, 1961, p. 5, July 9, 1961, p. 5; and *Cornford*, pp. 196, 251.

II 'Julian Bell'

1 V. Woolf, 'Reminiscences of Julian'.
2 To Vanessa, April 23, 27, 1937. Quotes from letters, unless otherwise indicated, are in *Bell*, pp. 187–98.
3 *New Statesman & Nation*, June 5, 1937, pp. 934–5.
4 To Quentin, May 3, 1937.
5 Straight to authors, December 3, 1962.
6 David Garnett, *The Familiar Faces* (London, 1962), p. 166; *Bell*, p. 8.
7 Clive Bell, *War Mongers* (London, 1938), pp. 2–12.
8 Richard Rees, *A Theory of My Time* (London, 1963), p. 95.
9 Thomas, op. cit., pp. 430–4.
10 Ibid., p. 460.
11 Malcolm Cowley, 'To Madrid III', *The New Republic*, September 15, 1937, p. 154; Jef Last, *The Spanish Tragedy* (London, 1939), p. 199.
12 Thomas, op. cit., p. 462.
13 Rees, op. cit., p. 100.
14 *Bell*, p. 392.
15 Rees, op. cit., p. 101.
16 Thomas, op. cit., p. 462.
17 The account of Julian's death is based on Keynes, *Bell*, pp. v–vi; Leonard Crome, 'Letter', *New Statesman & Nation*, August 28, 1937, p. 308; conversations with Professor A. C. Cochrane and Dr. Philip D'Arcy Hart; Rees, op. cit., as well as conversation with and a letter from him, from which the final quotation has been taken.

Index